Manor
Kedleston Hall
DERBY
bury
Calke Abbey

Belton House
Grantham House
Woolsthorpe Manor
LINCOLN

LEICESTER

Peckover ...
Priest's House
Easton-on-the-Hill

Oxburgh Hall

Lyveden New Bield
CAMBRIDGE

wood House
WARWICK
Baddesley Clinton
ughton Court
Charlecote Park
borough Hall
n House
Fleece Inn
NORTHANTS
Canons Ashby House
NOTTS

Anglesey Abbey
Wimpole Hall

Angel Corner
Ickworth
SUFFOLK
Melford Hall

Bridge Cottage

Claydon House
vshill Manor
Ascott
Waddesdon Manor
worth
an Villa
HERTS
Shaw's Corner
The King's Head
Aylesbury
ESSEX
Paycocke's

OXFORD
Princes Risborough Manor House
Buscot Park
West Wycombe Park
Cliveden
Hughenden Manor
Fenton House
Sutton House
Eastbury House

Ashdown House
Greys Court
Basildon Park
Osterley Park
LONDON
Carlyle's House
Ham House
Rainham Hall
Owletts
Tudor Yeoman's House

BERKS
SURREY
Quebec House
The Vyne
Hatchlands Park
West Green House
Clandon Park
Polesden Lacey
Oakhurst Cot.
Standen
Chartwell
Knole
Ightham Mote
Old Soar Manor
Stoneacre
KENT

HANTS
pps House
Hinton Ampner
Uppark
WEST
Petworth House
SUSSEX
Bramber Castle
Sissinghurst Castle
Smallhythe Place

mpesson
House
Mottisfont Abbey
Bateman's
EAST
SUSSEX
Monk's House
Bodiam Castle
Lamb House

Alfriston Clergy House

ton Lacy

Miles
0   10   20   30   40   50

THE NATIONAL TRUST:
HISTORIC HOUSES
OF BRITAIN

THE NATIONAL TRUST: HISTORIC HOUSES OF BRITAIN

Adrian Tinniswood

FOREWORD BY
Gervase Jackson-Stops

Harry N. Abrams, Inc., Publishers, New York

For Helen

First published in Great Britain in 1991 by
National Trust Enterprises Limited, London

Library of Congress Catalog Card Number: 91–73754
ISBN 0-8109-3411-6

Published in 1992 by Harry N. Abrams, Incorporated, New York
A Times Mirror Company

Picture research by Samantha Wyndham

Designed by Newton Engert Partnership

Maps drawn by N. S. Hyslop

Production by Bob Towell

Printed and bound in Italy by Grafedit S.p.A., Bergamo

HALF-TITLE:
Detail of one of William Burges's carved capitals at
Knightshayes Court, Devon. (*NTPL/John Bethell*)

FRONTISPIECE:
The staircase at Castle Drogo in Devon. (*NTPL*)

PAGE SEVEN:
The Duke of Somerset's arms and supporters – the bull
and the unicorn – over the chimneypiece in the marble hall
at Petworth, West Sussex. (*NTPL/James Pipkin*)

CONTENTS

ACKNOWLEDGEMENTS

Many people have helped in the writing of this book. Margaret Willes, the Trust's Publisher, initiated the project, and she and Gervase Jackson-Stops were kind enough to read the whole manuscript, correcting numerous mistakes and making unfailingly helpful suggestions. Needless to say, the errors which remain are all my own work.

A number of colleagues and friends have also commented on individual parts of the text and given me the benefit of their specialised knowledge. I would particularly like to thank Martin Drury, Historic Buildings Secretary of the National Trust and all his regional representatives: James Lees-Milne, for sharing his memories of the early years of the Country Houses Scheme; David Thackray, the Trust's Chief Archaeological Adviser; Cherry Ann Knott for her considerable help with the section on Sudbury Hall; and John Hodgson for his good ideas. Thanks also to Caroline Henley for keeping her head when all around were losing theirs.

I am grateful to Samantha Wyndham for her diligent and inspired research on the pictures for the book. A large proportion of these come from the National Trust's Photo Library at Queen Anne's Gate, and are marked NTPL together with the name of the photographer. Those credited to the National Trust are either from regional photo libraries or from the Trust's historic archives.

Lastly, I would like to pay tribute to all those past and present staff members of the National Trust without whose research this book could not have been written, and without whose care and foresight many of the the houses described in it might not be here at all.

Adrian Tinniswood
April 1991

The long gallery at Sudbury Hall, Derbyshire. This was restored by the National Trust in 1969–70, with advice from John Fowler. (*The National Trust/John Roberts*)

Foreword

The public perception of the National Trust is now so bound up with the great houses in its ownership that few people realise how little they counted to its original founders. In fact the Trust has only seriously been concerned with country houses and their collections for a mere forty out of almost a hundred years of existence. And, even then, they seemed to come more by accident than design: as a way of avoiding the disastrous effects of capital taxation, rather than part of a deliberate policy of preservation.

However unplanned this development – in the manner of so many other British institutions – it has gathered its own momentum, and it is fascinating to look back on the shifts of emphasis that have occurred in that time, the very different reasons for acquiring houses then and now, and the changing priorities which the Trust faces in conserving and maintaining them.

Before the start of the Country Houses Scheme, described in the first chapter of this book, a few buildings were taken on by the Trust, usually to save them from imminent destruction, and usually because of their picturesque 'Old English' qualities. None of them dated from after 1600, and none of them contained significant contents, or even particularly significant interiors. Whether modest domestic dwellings like the Clergy House at Alfriston, more substantial manor houses like Barrington Court, or castles like Bodiam and Tattershall, these could be considered works of 'natural beauty' almost as much as of 'historic interest'.

It was perhaps only the advance of knowledge about seventeenth- and eighteenth-century architecture, promoted by writers like Sacheverell Sitwell and Christopher Hussey, and by the newly founded Georgian Group, that finally aroused an interest in houses and their contents as a single entity. The appalling loss of pictures, sculpture and furniture through the auction rooms, threatening the existence of these 'corporate works of art', came to be recognised, and, somewhat reluctantly at first, the Trust began to realise it must act, if this great national asset was not to be wholly squandered.

Even with the advent of the Country Houses Scheme, purely architectural standards tended to predominate, however. It was no accident that early houses continued to be most appreciated, from Knole, Blickling and Hardwick to more modest squires' houses like Lytes Cary and Great Chalfield. Petworth was accepted for its internationally famous art collections, but many others – like Montacute, Clandon, Beningbrough and Shugborough – were taken after the dispersal of contents, and the idea of introducing pictures and furniture from other sources to give a lived-in look was still considered perfectly acceptable.

Of course, the Trust could only take what houses it was offered, and only when there was a sufficient endowment to maintain them, so its area of choice was always limited. But despite this, the acquisitions of the 1960s and 70s, including Standen, Knightshayes, Cragside and Castle Drogo, showed an increasing respect for Victorian and Edwardian architecture. At the same time there was a greater awareness of the many different aspects of a country house estate: its archaeological remains (like the medieval old hall at Tatton, and the priory buildings at Mottisfont), its industrial monuments (like the wharf at Cotehele, or the mill at Dunham Massey), its domestic offices (most notable at Erddig and Lanhydrock), its home farm (like those at Wimpole and Shugborough).

Nevertheless, a particular worry at this period was the widening gap between the endowment which the Trust needed, and the capital sum which a donor could be expected to raise. It was not until the founding of the National Heritage Memorial Fund in 1979 that another source of funding became available, and the Trust's role in saving houses could become more positive. Significantly, Canons Ashby, the first to be acquired with the Fund's help, and A La Ronde, the most recent, had both been accepted on merit in the earliest days of the Country Houses Scheme, but had consistently fallen down on financial grounds. Nor would Calke and Kedleston have been remotely possible without the assistance of the NHMF: the former of particular importance as a document of social history rather than for its architecture or the quality of its collections.

In recent years, private trusts set up by owners of historic houses have enjoyed almost as much tax relief as the National Trust, and acceptable alternative uses have been found for many houses which remain well protected by the listing system. That has left the Trust more as an ultimate safety net than as a place of first resort for owners in difficulty. Indeed, the adaptation of Cliveden as a luxury hotel has shown that, in the right circumstances, its houses too can profit from an alliance with private enterprise.

Apart from the gradual furnishing of houses which came virtually empty in the early days of the Country Houses Scheme, the Trust has also found partners who could enliven them in other ways. The National Portrait Gallery's displays of Elizabethan and Jacobean, Civil War, and baroque portraits, at Montacute, Gawthorpe and Beningbrough respectively, could hardly represent a more appropriate use, and the same could be said of exhibitions of costume at Killerton, musical instruments at Hatchlands, and the history of photography at Lacock.

On the whole, the Trust has always been conservative in its attitude to the display of historic interiors, preferring to keep the layer-on-layer of different generations, than to return to one particular period. At Ham and Osterley, where these later contributions had been largely removed, it was prepared to support the more purist approach of the Victoria and Albert Museum, which owned the remaining contents and which, from 1949 to 1990, administered both properties on the Trust's behalf.

The few full-scale redecoration schemes the Trust has undertaken itself were an attempt to revive empty or underfurnished houses in the late 1960s and early 70s, with bolder colour schemes and upholstery by John Fowler at Shugborough, Clandon and Sudbury, and by David Mlinaric at Beningbrough. These did not pretend to be archaeologically precise, but were free interpretations based on the paint 'scrapes' then available, and on knowledge of other houses of the same period. But in general the Trust has tried to avoid controversial reconstructions and to let the houses speak for themselves, through the different generations of previous owners, whose portraits gaze down from panelled or damask-covered walls.

Wherever possible, too, the Trust has encouraged these families to retain their links with the properties they gave. It adds immeasurably to visitors' experience of a house to find it still inhabited as a family home, with all the small impedimenta of everyday life – flowers, books, photographs and contemporary works of art – rather than presented as a dead museum.

That also explains the Trust's attitude to 'interpretation': the fashion for spoon-feeding visitors with information, rather than allowing them to discover the history of a place for themselves. As a general policy, free flow has always been preferred to guided tours, and exhibitions, which tend to overshadow or even replace the actual experience of a house, have been kept to a minimum. Stables are obviously more satisfactory full of horses than converted into exhibitions about hunting or racing, and the same applies to brewhouses, bakeries, laundries and all the other buildings supporting a great house. A very important part of this approach has been the provision of informative guidebooks and general literature about the Trust's possessions, making the latest historical research freely available: a service to which it is hoped this book will itself contribute.

The real revolution has not therefore come in the way the Trust's houses are displayed or presented but in the way they are conserved. For a long time, the national museums were pre-eminent in this field, with the Trust seeking their advice and practical help with particular problems. Over the last twenty years, however, a formidable team of conservators has been built up within the organisation. Many eighteenth- and nineteenth-century methods of good housekeeping have been revived, blinds (and ultra-violet filters) have cut down the damaging effects of daylight, case covers have protected precious original upholstery, tapestries have been painstakingly repaired, and the effects of wear and tear carefully monitored. The Trust is also proud to have contributed to the revival of many traditional crafts and materials, from hand-loom weaving and block-printing down to the production of lead paint and limewash.

In its original charter, the National Trust was charged to hold its possessions 'in perpetuity'. The course of natural decay may make that something of a pious hope, but we are now better equipped to make the attempt than at any previous time in our history. Even after the tragedy of the Uppark fire, we can look forward with optimism to its rebirth, confident that its haunting beauty will be recaptured.

This book, devoted to the Trust's country houses, is not just a catalogue recalling past achievements, but a celebration of a living tradition that has never enjoyed greater popularity or greater support.

Gervase Jackson-Stops
Architectural Adviser to the National Trust

Chapter One

Changing Hands

THE NATIONAL TRUST AND
COUNTRY HOUSES

*Alas! how curious it is that these works of art only
begin to obtain a wide appreciation when they are
on the verge of being destroyed. What country
houses of any size, one wonders, can hope to survive
the next fifty years?*

Osbert Sitwell, 1935

In 1928 the architect Clough Williams-Ellis announced the death of the country
house. 'It is a fact, patent to all and deplored by some, that the large-scale private
paradise is already obsolescent.' The obituary notice, which appeared in his *England
and the Octopus*, an angry piece of conservationist polemic, gave a number of reasons
for the country house's demise: changes in the social order, which led many owners
to 'abdicate from a position that they find uncongenial and slightly ridiculous';
crippling taxation; poor estate management; and 'expensive tastes incompatible
with the low returns from landowning'.

But if the country house as an institution was dead, Williams-Ellis wasn't about to
let it lie down. It was inconceivable that this unique synthesis of architecture,
contents, setting and historical associations should be allowed to disappear simply
because shifts in the structure of post-war society were eroding the power of the class
that had created it. Yet the inconceivable was happening, and something must be
done to stop it, not because of any sense of loyalty to that class, but because the
country house belonged, in a sense, to everybody. It was part of our common
inheritance, part of what the 1920s called 'the national treasure'.

Williams-Ellis's solution was simple. A commission should be set up to list those

Philip Kerr, 11th Marquess of Lothian: 'If a body like the National Trust were willing to equip itself
to become a landlord on an ampler scale, it would gradually draw within its orbit quite a large
number of historic furnished houses.' (*The National Trust*)

country houses which really deserved protection 'as national monuments and as characteristic and precious parts of England'. The buildings on that list would be scheduled, and their owners would be exempted from rates and certain taxes; in return, they would open their doors to the public, under carefully framed conditions, and agree to refer any alterations to a statutory body set up for the purpose.

In the years that followed, others took up the challenge. In January 1930, a *Country Life* editorial headed 'Our National Inheritance' called on the government to 'do something practical to prevent the constant breaking up of beautiful properties into ugly building estates and the dispersal abroad of well-nigh priceless collections':

> The state has already exempted from death duties works of art of public interest. Why should it not extend this principle to parks and woods and open spaces such as those of Goodwood, which, though privately owned, are always open for public enjoyment, and to houses such as Knole, which are in reality national treasure houses of beautiful things?

That the country house was in crisis, that the 'breaking up of beautiful properties' was reaching epidemic proportions, was not in doubt. Throughout the twenties, great estate after great estate was falling prey to developers and speculators. Income tax, land tax and rates were taking more than 30 per cent of estate rentals; in 1919 death duties, first introduced in 1894, were increased to 40 per cent on estates worth more than £2 million; and during the slump in land values that followed the end of the war some six million acres had come under new ownership. 'England is changing hands,' lamented *The Times* in May 1920, as collections which had taken centuries to assemble were dispersed at auction. Staircases, chimneypieces, ceilings, whole rooms were stripped out and sold off;[1] and hundreds of country houses were pulled down, their walls reduced to rubble. But individual calls for the government to do something to alleviate the crisis had about as much effect as individual calls on the government usually have. What was needed was some organisation to coordinate the campaign, to act as an umbrella under which the disparate band of conservative noblemen and crusading radicals could gather.

In many ways, the National Trust was a natural candidate for the job. Formed in 1895 as a private charity dedicated to acquiring and protecting 'Places of Historic Interest or Natural Beauty', it was already just such an unlikely alliance of landowners and radicals. Moreover, it had practical experience of the problems involved in maintaining country houses. The buildings in its care included the sixteenth-century Barrington Court in Somerset, which had been bought in 1907, largely with the help of a £10,000 donation from a Miss J. L. Woodward, and which

---

1 And sometimes whole houses. A rather mysterious entrepreneur named George Ferdinando bought Basildon Park in Berkshire in the 1920s and offered to dismantle it and re-erect it anywhere in America for one million dollars. There were no takers, although some of the plasterwork found its way to the Waldorf Astoria in New York, which still boasts a Basildon Room.

Barrington Court, Somerset: the National Trust's first country house, acquired in 1907.
(*NTPL/Neil Campbell-Sharp*)

had nevertheless proved to be an enormous burden until 1920, when in return for a long lease Colonel A. A. Lyle agreed to restore it. The Trust's other major country house, the late-Elizabethan Montacute, also in Somerset, which had failed to find a buyer when it came on to the market in 1929 and two years later was being offered at a scrap-value of £5,882, had been bought by the Society for the Protection of Ancient Buildings in 1931. It was handed over to the Trust in the following year – an act of generosity made possible only by a further act of generosity, a cheque for £30,000 for its purchase and upkeep, given by the philanthropist Ernest Cook.

At a National Trust dinner in 1933 the Director of the Courtauld Institute, Professor W. G. Constable, said that the organisation must act, and act quickly, to preserve the country house – by which he meant that it should launch in earnest the campaign that Clough Williams-Ellis, *Country Life* and others had called for. And then in July 1934, Philip Kerr, 11th Marquess of Lothian, gave a speech at the

Trust's annual meeting at Inner Temple Hall. He asked whether the Trust might not extend its protection – which, in spite of Barrington and Montacute, had until then been largely confined to areas of coast and countryside, and smaller vernacular buildings – to 'another part of our national treasure . . . the historic dwelling houses of this country'.

In fact the main target of Lothian's speech was not the Trust, but the Treasury. He had been hard-hit by death duties on succeeding in 1930 to his cousin's title and estates, which included Blickling in Norfolk, and the experience had left scars. When Lloyd George wrote to congratulate him on his inheritance, he had replied: 'I shall have to pay to our exhausted Exchequer almost forty per cent of the capital value of a mainly agricultural estate. In my capacity as an ordinary citizen I think highly of these arrangements but as an inheritor of a title and estates thereto they will prove somewhat embarrassing.' In his speech to the Trust four years later, he said that most country houses were under sentence of death, 'and the axe which was destroying them was taxation, and especially that form of taxation known as death duties'. (The audience cheered.) The Trust should draw up a list of mansions of national importance, and lobby the government to make certain concessions. Scheduled houses should be exempt from death duties unless they were sold, or even if they were sold, provided that they were preserved as a whole; their owners should be allowed to set against tax any money spent on upkeep or restoration; and if these measures failed, a property should be de-rated.

Like most campaigners of the time, Lothian's chief concern was to find a way whereby an owner could continue to live in his ancestral home. Hence his emphasis on changes in fiscal policy. 'Nothing is more melancholy than to visit these ancient houses after they have been turned into public museums,' he said. 'If they are to be preserved, they must be maintained, save for a few great palaces, for the uses for which they were designed.' But he closed his speech with one last suggestion, one that was eventually to have tremendous implications for both the National Trust and the country house – so tremendous that his words, reported in *The Times*, deserve to be quoted at length:

> Why should not the National Trust equip itself to hold properties bequeathed, or given to it, or acquired by it, on terms not unlike those which governed Lord Lee's munificent gift of Chequers? He believed that if a body like the National Trust were willing to equip itself to become a landlord on an ampler scale, it would gradually draw within its orbit quite a large number of historic furnished houses. The essence of the case was that the houses should be both furnished and sufficiently modernised in their domestic arrangements to be easily let, and, if possible, should have enough land or endowment to cover the cost of maintaining the structure. The Trust could then seek suitable tenants, using the rents it received either for improvements or to balance expenses on houses it could not let.

As things stood in 1934, Lothian's suggestion that the charity should itself 'become a landlord on an ampler scale' must have seemed far too daunting a prospect, especially in view of the Trust's experience in trying to maintain Barrington Court.

In any case, an Act of Parliament would have been necessary to enable the Trust to take on a house, its contents and estate, together with an endowment in the form of land or investments to pay for maintenance.

But Lothian's speech did mark the beginning of a concerted campaign to save the country house. It was followed three months later by another speech, this time by W. Harding Thompson, who told the national conference of the Council for the Preservation of Rural England that a survey should immediately be carried out to establish which houses were worth saving, and that an owners' association should be set up to lobby the Treasury for the 'remission of duties in approved cases in exchange for regulated public access at specified times'. This was the line which the National Trust itself took. In February 1936 its Secretary, Macleod Matheson, arranged a reception to launch a new federation of owners. Its aims, said the Trust's chairman, Lord Zetland, would be to compile a list of the most important houses, which would be approved by the Office of Works; to offer access and information to the public; and – last, but certainly not least – to 'endeavour to obtain, in the interest of the preservation of a national heritage of great historical and artistic value, some relief from the burden of taxation'.

The idea met with a deafening silence. Country house owners, reluctant to give up their independence, gave it little encouragement. And the government was understandably rather wary about the political consequences of awarding tax concessions to a group that was still perceived by the majority of voters to be the wealthiest class in society, even if such concessions were to be given in return for guaranteed public access.

Faced with such a stalemate, the Trust launched its own initiative. Lord Zetland and Macleod Matheson decided that if Parliament could be persuaded to pass the legislation necessary to overcome a daunting array of obstacles, such as the difficulty of breaking entails, and the likely infringement of the laws of property involved in an owner's giving a house and estate to a charity and then continuing to live in it, the Trust would indeed become a 'landlord on an ampler scale'. It would accept country houses and their contents and estates, with the proviso that an endowment in the form of land or money should also be given to enable the property to be maintained. The newly appointed secretary of the Trust's Historic Country Houses Committee, James Lees-Milne, drew up the list of important houses that everyone had been demanding for so long; and the owners of those houses – some 250 in all – were canvassed for their opinions. The attractions of the scheme, both to the owner of a country house and to the general public, were outlined in a *Times* leader in October 1936:

> The advantage to the owner combines freedom from responsibility with the assurance that the connection of his family with the family seat shall not be sharply and completely broken. The advantage to the public combines freedom of access to treasures of natural and artistic beauty with the preservation of the character and occupation which makes the difference between a dwelling and a museum, a country place and a public playground.

Parliament did pass the required new legislation, in the form of the two National

Trust Acts of 1937 and 1939; the Country Houses Scheme, as it was called, was launched; and the National Trust, by default rather than by design, embarked on a path which would turn it into the largest holder of country houses in Britain.

There is a certain irony in the fact that the first country house to come to the National Trust in the late 1930s was no venerable mansion of antiquity, but a building only eight years older than the Trust itself. In 1936 Sir Geoffrey Mander, the owner of the late-Victorian Wightwick Manor near Wolverhampton in the West Midlands, heard from his friend Sir Charles Trevelyan that he was negotiating to leave his eighteenth-century home at Wallington in Northumberland to the Trust. (In fact Trevelyan made it over during his lifetime, stating in a press release in November 1941 that he 'had a double motive for his action. He is a Socialist and believes it would be better if the community owned such houses and great estates. He was also influenced by Lord Lothian with whom he discussed the whole question some years ago.') Trevelyan's idea appealed to Mander. Fortunately – and quite remarkably, considering the low regard for all things Victorian between the wars – it appealed to the National Trust as well, and in 1937 Wightwick became the first of the new wave of Trust acquisitions.

However, in the beginning that wave seemed more like a ripple. By the end of 1941 the Trust had acquired Wightwick, Wallington and Blickling (left by Lord Lothian, who had died in December 1940). Hatchlands in Surrey had been offered by the architectural historian H. S. Goodhart-Rendel, and accepted; Stourhead in Wiltshire had been promised; and Old Devonshire House in Bloomsbury, London, had been given and then destroyed by German bombs. Seven other negotiations had foundered for one reason or another, including Canons Ashby in Northampton-shire, where the owner had died and his successor held different ideas about the future of the house.

In February 1942 Lord Esher, chairman of the Trust's Country Houses Committee, was expressing concern about the slow progress of the scheme: 'I am disturbed by the failure of the Trust to obtain any considerable number of country houses, and by the apparent difficulty of reaching agreement between the Trust and those owners who have shown an inclination to take advantage of our services.' A major sticking point was the question of an endowment. Then, as now, the Trust required enough land or capital to maintain the house, and many owners were understandably rather cautious about the idea of making over most or all of their ancestral estates to a small private charity.

But still houses did continue to come, thanks largely to the untiring efforts of James Lees-Milne, who resumed his duties as secretary to the Country Houses Committee after being invalided out of the army in 1940, and spent the rest of the war travelling the country, negotiating with prospective donors. By 1945, the National Trust's fiftieth anniversary, the charity held seventeen country houses, ranging from the black-and-white splendours of Little Moreton Hall in Cheshire and Speke Hall, Merseyside, to West Wycombe Park in Buckinghamshire, with Nicholas Revett's Greek Revival portico, and the Victorian Italianate of Charles Barry's Cliveden, also in Buckinghamshire.

In the same year, the election of Attlee's Labour government sent a frisson of fear through the country house-owning classes. A series of *Country Life* articles on 'The Future of Great Country Houses' which appeared in the November, four months after the general election, was defensive, almost paranoid, in its efforts to justify private ownership – as if the writers, all owners of country houses, were afraid that Attlee and his Chancellor of the Exchequer, Hugh Dalton, were set to storm the Winter Palace. Privilege means public service, declared Burghley's Marchioness of Exeter, and all the privileged ask 'is that they may be permitted to continue to serve and that the scales shall not be too unfairly weighted against them.' Meanwhile Christopher Hussey, architectural editor of *Country Life* and donor (in 1970) of Scotney Castle and Garden in Kent, was anxious 'for the electorate to disabuse itself of the common confusion between a great historic house and housing': 'It has not been seriously suggested that these buildings could materially contribute to the housing shortage, hopelessly situated and designed as they are to that purpose, yet the feeling is probably at the back of the minds of some people who regard the great house as somehow inimical to their just aspirations.'

But in the context of the country house at least, the most revolutionary measure enacted by Attlee and Dalton was to set aside £50 million for the creation of a National Land Fund, which was to be used to acquire property for preservation as a memorial to those who had died in the war. Such property would be passed on to an approved organisation. Dalton also revived a little-used provision in the 1910 Finance Act which had allowed property to be given to the Inland Revenue in lieu of tax, and proposed that in future 'much more use should be made of this power to accept land in payment of death duties'.

There were some who saw these measures as the first steps towards the compulsory nationalisation of historic houses. But their immediate effect was to make it much easier for owners to leave their houses to the National Trust, which was one of the organisations recognised by the Treasury as a suitable recipient for property given in lieu of estate duty. In 1947, on the death of the 5th Earl of Mount Edgcumbe, Cotehele House in Cornwall – described by James Lees-Milne at the time as a West Country Knole – was the first country house to be transferred to the Trust through National Land Fund procedures. Far from storming the Winter Palace, the Attlee administration had done more than any previous government to ensure that the country house would be preserved for all time, and that, if they chose to do so, those who lived in it might continue to enjoy their occupancy.

As the number of country houses held by the National Trust continued to grow, and as the public demand to see and enjoy them grew with it, it became apparent that the pre-war ideal – that once transferred to the Trust, a house should simply continue as it always had, without any change save that of legal ownership – would have to be modified. The more extravagant private schemes to turn 'stately homes' into profitable tourist enterprises, complete with safari parks and other attractions, were scorned by the Trust. (In 1966 Lord Antrim, then chairman, announced to the annual general meeting that the organisation's job was 'not to involve itself in the entertainment industry. We take over these places to keep them in their natural state, and not to provide more holiday camps.') But it was clear that the Trust must adopt a more positive role in presenting its historic houses to the visitor; clear, too,

that public access – which when the Country Houses Scheme was first mooted in the 1930s had been seen as of secondary importance – was coming to be a vital factor, something which, while never eclipsing the Trust's primary duty to conserve for posterity a building, its contents and its setting, could no longer be left to chance.

The situation was complicated (as indeed it still is) by the different circumstances in which country houses came to the Trust. Some, like Uppark in West Sussex (acquired in 1954), Dyrham in Avon (1961) and Felbrigg in Norfolk (1969), were intact, fully furnished, and quite perfect as they were. For these, change was unthinkable – the Trust's job was simply to preserve them. Others were already in decline, or for one reason or another were empty of all furniture; and on these houses the Trust was forced to impose its own taste in furnishings and interior decoration. Clandon Park, Surrey (1956); Beningbrough Hall, Yorkshire (1958); and Sudbury Hall, Derbyshire (1967), all fall into that category. At Sudbury, for example, a house with state rooms that were sparsely furnished, but that contained the most exquisite Caroline plasterwork and carvings, John Fowler – who acted as the Trust's adviser on interior decoration during the 1960s and 1970s – chose not to fill those rooms with furniture and textiles that had no connection with the house, but instead to emphasise the existing decorative features. In a move that aroused considerable controversy at the time, the balustrade of the staircase, which was covered in layers of graining and varnish, was stripped and painted white; the plaster ceiling above it was painted in two tones to throw its decoration into high relief; and the walls were given a coat of strong yellow ochre. The overall effect may not have any precedent in the Caroline period – but it works, and Fowler's interiors have themselves become part of Sudbury's history.

All the same, ideas have changed and scholarship has advanced in the decades since the redecoration of Sudbury Hall. Today the National Trust cares for some two hundred historic houses and castles in England, Wales and Northern Ireland, from the fourteenth-century Bodiam (Sussex), that most romantic of all medieval ruins, to Castle Drogo (Devon), the Lutyens fantasy equipped with all modern conveniences, which was only completed in 1930 – two years after Clough Williams-Ellis announced the death of the country house. And in the fifty years or more which have passed since the inception of the Country Houses Scheme, the Trust's response to the conservation and interpretation of those buildings – and in many cases, their surrounding estates – has inevitably changed to take account of an ever more complex range of issues and expectations.

When, for example, Erddig in Clwyd was acquired in 1973, the unusually rich evidence of life below stairs led to a departure from the traditional practice of bringing visitors into the house through the front door. Instead, they are steered through the estate yard, with its smithy, joiner's shop and bakery, and in through the servants' entrance. The social structures at Erddig are every bit as interesting as the art-objects and the interiors, and the presentation of the house reflects this. And

Clandon Park, Surrey: the morning room, redecorated in the 1960s by John Fowler. (*NTPL/Erik Pelham*)

21

Calke Abbey, Derbyshire:
even a time-capsule needs
a sound roof. Fundamental
conservation work was
necessary following the
National Trust's acquisition
of the house in 1985.
(*NTPL/Rob Matheson*)

at Calke Abbey in Derbyshire, taken over in 1985, the decision was made to preserve the peculiar 'time-capsule' quality of the house – where virtually nothing has been thrown away since the mid-nineteenth century – by deliberately limiting the extent of the restoration. Paintings were left with their layers of darkened varnish. Dilapidated furniture was made sound, but was not over-polished. Interiors were repaired as necessary, but (with a couple of exceptions) were not redecorated.

A completely different approach has been adopted at Uppark in West Sussex, which was devastated by fire in August 1989. Here the Trust was faced with some difficult choices. Should it complete the fire's work and demolish what remained; or make the ruins safe and leave them as a memorial to a once-great house? Or should it embark on a major rebuilding programme to restore Uppark to its former glory? It chose this last course, a decision which reflects Uppark's enormous architectural importance, but which has left the organisation facing perhaps the greatest challenge in its long history.

The National Trust's policy towards each building is to respond to its uniqueness, to provide different solutions for different problems of restoration, interpretation and presentation. The problems change with the years. And so must the solutions, since the fact that a country house changes hands, the fact that its ownership shifts from the individual to the collective, need not, and must not, mean that it loses those qualities that made us all value it in the first place.

But what *are* those qualities? As we walk through the great halls and long galleries, we think – a little guiltily, perhaps – about what fun it must have been to live in them (always the master or mistress, never the servant). Depending on our political stance, we wallow in nostalgia for a vanished age, or rejoice in the downfall of the class that built them. But only the most hardened philistine can fail to be moved by their most potent appeal – their sheer beauty, the creative vision of the artists and craftsmen who made them.

And in the end, the Trust's historic houses must speak for themselves: it is the personal experience of that beauty, that creative vision, which justifies all the time

Uppark, Sussex: its restoration after a major fire in 1989 is one of the greatest challenges the National Trust has ever faced. In the first phase of restoration the whole house was enclosed in a weatherproof skin. (*NTPL/Will Webster*)

and money involved in their preservation. Of the thirty houses described in detail in the following pages, some would probably have survived intact if the Trust had not existed; some would perhaps have adapted to changing circumstances, becoming schools, or hotels, or business centres. But others might have disappeared – and their loss would have impoverished us all. It would be facile to suggest that the National Trust has single-handedly saved the country house from extinction – government grants, tax concessions, rising land values and a buoyant market for works of art have all played their part. But there is no doubt that because, nearly sixty years ago, a small private charity, with few members and even fewer resources, was forced to put itself forward as a guardian of our architectural heritage, reports of the death of the country house have been greatly exaggerated.

Chapter Two

Moats and Manor Houses

1250-1550

*First the usher must see that the hall be trimmed in
every point, and that the cloth of estate be hanged
in the hall ... and that the high table be set, with
all other boards, cupboards, stools and chairs
requisite within the hall, and that a good fire be
made.*

Early sixteenth-century household regulations

Great Chalfield Manor in Wiltshire has a lurid early history. Originally owned by
the Percy family, the estate was the subject of a series of ownership disputes following
the death in 1356 of Sir Harry Percy, the last male member of the Wiltshire branch
of the family. Sir Harry had had the misfortune to marry as his second wife
Constance, described in a late-medieval cartulary as the 'bedfellow and cousin to
Master Robert Wayville, bishop of Salisbury'. After persuading her husband to give
her a plausible title to Chalfield, Constance resumed her 'naughty life' with the
bishop, causing the hapless Harry to set off on a pilgrimage to Jerusalem – whether
in expiation for his wife's sins or exasperation at his own folly is not recorded.

Sir Harry died on the way at Cologne, and for the next fifty years the manor was
the subject of claims and counter-claims by Constance's family and the heirs of
Sir Harry's daughter by his first marriage, until in 1467 a 'perilous covetous man'
named Thomas Tropnell resolved the issue by buying out both sides. He built
himself a new house on the site, and after his death in about 1488 the family

Bodiam Castle, Sussex; built in the 1380s by Sir Edward Dalyngrigge. An aerial view of the castle
from the south-east. (*NTPL/Unichrome*)

25

An early nineteenth-century watercolour by J. C. Buckler of Great Chalfield Manor in Wiltshire. (*NTPL/John Freeman*)

continued to hold the estate, until the middle of the sixteenth century when the male line ended abruptly and rather gruesomely with the death of Giles Tropnell:

> As hunting putting one end of a pair of dog couples [leads] over his head running after his sport and leaping over a hedge, the end of the dog couple which hung at his back took hold of a bough, [and] kept him from touching the ground until he was strangled.

But Great Chalfield has more to offer us than an errant wife and an accidental hanging. In spite of later alterations and a massive Edwardian restoration,[1] the house that Thomas Tropnell created is a case-study in fifteenth-century domestic architecture, which builds on early medieval traditions while looking forward to the more sophisticated mansions of the later Tudors.

Great Chalfield's position behind a protective moat (probably the legacy of an earlier Percy building) immediately links the house to the past, and to the 5,000 or more moated sites which sprang up all over the country during the thirteenth and fourteenth centuries, ranging from grand castles like Bodiam in Sussex, through gentry houses such as Ightham Mote in Kent, down to the smallest farmsteads. Defence is the obvious reason for encircling a dwelling with a water-filled ditch, but the need for drainage, the desire for an accessible supply of fish and waterfowl, and the simple wish to emulate more aristocratic fashions, all played a part.

---

1   1905–12, by Sir Harold Brakspear, who also restored the cloistral buildings at nearby Lacock Abbey.

The movable screen in the hall at Rufford Old Hall in Lancashire. (*NTPL/Mike Williams*)

Nor is it just the moat that proclaims Great Chalfield's debt to previous centuries. Tropnell's mansion consisted, like all substantial houses of the period, of a complex of chambers and service rooms ranged round a series of courts – lodgings for family and servants, kitchens, other domestic offices and storage areas. And at the heart of that complex is the great hall, its timbers painted with his somewhat obscure motto, *Le jong tyra belement* ('The yoke draws well'), and his badge of a double ox-yoke.

In its most common surviving form, the early medieval hall was raised up over a ground-floor storage area – the eleventh-century Bayeux tapestry shows Harold's hall at Bosham as a raised chamber over a vaulted basement – although there were plenty of ground-floor exceptions. It would usually have a partition at one end, in some cases perhaps no more than a leather curtain, to divide off the lord's sleeping area. The prevalence of raised halls seems to have been due primarily to considerations of defence, and as the thirteenth century enjoyed increasing security, the hall tended to come downstairs (although first-floor halls were still appearing in the later fourteenth century). But whether on the first or the ground floor, the hall was the focal point of the first medieval country houses. Not only was it the room in which the lord ate in state, but it was also here that the whole household gathered, and, in its earliest days, that they lived and slept.

As at Great Chalfield, the typical ground-floor medieval hall was entered at one end, via a cross-passage at right angles to its length; the passage was partitioned off from the main body of the hall by a screen, at first movable but later incorporated into the structure of the building. (Rufford Old Hall in Lancashire still contains a fine example of a movable screen.) There would often be three doorways in the opposite wall, as at South Wingfield Manor in Derbyshire, Clevedon Court in Avon and Penshurst Place in Kent: these usually led to the kitchens and other food preparation areas.

On a dais at the end of the hall farthest from the screen, the lord presided over the rest of his household, who would be seated, probably on benches, at trestle tables ranged down its length. As the hub around which other elements of the household revolved, the hall was the setting for daily quasi-public gatherings – and the medieval emphasis on hospitality to all-comers, as both a social duty and a means of displaying one's power, meant that such gatherings in the hall were public in a very real sense. The hall's importance in this respect was indicated in the early Middle Ages by the fact that, with the chapel, it was often the only stone structure on the site, all other accommodation and domestic offices being built of timber.

The decoration and furnishing of such halls was relatively sparse, a reflection of the transient nature of the early medieval household, which might move on once or twice every month, as the lord divided his time amongst his often widely spread estates, taking with him his servants, bedding, furniture and kitchen equipment. Even in the early sixteenth century, when progresses between estates were much less frequent, the Earl of Northumberland required a baggage train of some twenty-seven wagons when he moved between houses, taking with him a vast array of household goods, including:

> The stuff in the chamber where my Lord and Lady lyeth, the stuff in the chamber where my Lord dineth ... the hangings of the three altars in the chapel, the surplices, the altar clothes ... the kitchen stuff as pots, pans, trivets, racks and pastry-stuff ... with the two beds for the three cooks to lie in ... the smith's tools, the joiner's tools, and the painter's ... a bed for the smith, a bed for the joiner, a bed for the painter, a bed for the two minstrels and a bed for the two hunts[men] and all their apparel ...

To begin with, walls were whitewashed – interior stonework was rarely left bare – and perhaps painted with red lines to simulate masonry blockwork. (External stonework might also be whitewashed: in 1240 the keepers of works at the White Tower of London were ordered to ensure that lead drain-pipes were properly installed, so that 'the wall of the said Tower, which has been newly whitewashed, may be in no wise injured by the dropping of rain-water'. And four years later the great tower at Corfe Castle in Dorset was whitewashed externally.) Woollen cloths – as opposed to tapestry, which was not in general use in country houses until the fourteenth century – were hung about the dais end of the hall. Originally introduced to keep draughts off the lord, they became steadily more elaborate, until it became the norm for the lord's place to be distinguished by intricately painted or woven cloths and canopies of state.

But as the Middle Ages wore on, first the king, and then his courtiers, and finally even untitled landowners outside the court circle, men like Thomas Tropnell, took to eating in state in their own sleeping lodgings, the solar, rather than in the hall. As a result, the solar gained a ceremonial importance which was reflected in its decoration. (At Great Chalfield that importance is expressed externally by a beautiful semicircular oriel window of six transomed lights rising from traceried panels.) Perhaps more importantly, that withdrawal from the hall marked the beginning of a quest for privacy that would progressively break down the community of the country house, culminating in the upstairs-downstairs, green baize door system of social apartheid of the nineteenth and early twentieth centuries.

In the solar, which became known as the 'great chamber' in recognition of its new status, the lord's servants would set up his board before his 'bed of estate' and load his cupboard with cups and plate, wine and beer. It was to this great chamber – usually on the first floor beyond the dais end of the hall – that a procession of servants carrying food would wind their way from the kitchens, down the length of the hall, where the rest of the household were assembled in readiness for their own meal. The procession would be met by the marshal of the hall with his rod of office, calling, 'By your leave, my masters', and at his cry, everyone would stand and remove their hats in homage to the lord's food as it passed by. There in the great chamber the lord would eat beneath his canopy of state, served on bended knee by household officers who took 'sayes' (samples) of each dish to ensure that it was fit to eat, who washed his hands, and offered him his cup while holding a smaller cup under his chin to catch the drips.

There were, of course, variations in social behaviour from one household to another, variations which depended on rank, on geographical proximity to the court – which tended to determine changes in fashion – and on personal predilection. A great nobleman like John of Gaunt, who in the 1380s ran a household of about two hundred, would have expected and received much more deferential and ritualised treatment from his servants than minor gentry like Tropnell – although, since we know that the latter served for a time in the 1420s as steward to the powerful Hungerford family, it is tempting to assume that his first-hand knowledge of the way in which a great household functioned might have led him to emulate it at Great Chalfield. But in spite of variations, the general principle, that day-to-day behaviour-patterns in the medieval country house constantly and consistently underlined the lord's position at the head of a hierarchy, tended to operate to a greater or lesser degree in all gentle and noble households.

After the hall and the great chamber, the third component of the medieval country house was the chapel. Every house of any substance possessed one, together with a chaplain who perhaps doubled as a secretary,[2] and – in larger households – a full compliment of choir and clergy. Mass would be celebrated every day, although the lord himself would occasionally hear it privately in his lodgings, or through a squint which looked down into the chapel. The chapel was usually placed either close to those lodgings on the first floor, or at ground level beyond the parlour,

---

2   Chaplains served in various capacities: at Dunster in Somerset, the Luttrells' chaplain in the early fifteenth century, John Bacwell, was also steward and treasurer to the household. And in 1417–20 John de Lyghley, chaplain to William Cromwell of Tydd in Lincolnshire, bought in foodstuffs and other goods, audited estate accounts, escorted Cromwell's wife when she travelled, and acted as a courier, moving money to and from France.

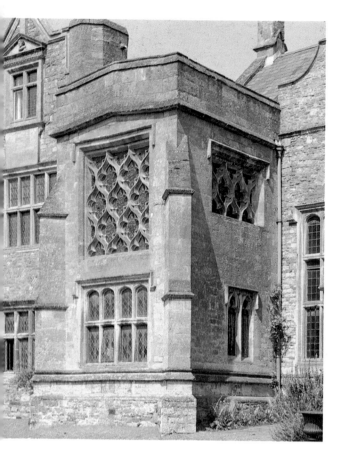

ABOVE: Thomas Tropnell of Great Chalfield: a 'perilous covetous man'. The five-fingered hand can be seen on the left-hand side of the mural. (*NTPL/John Bethell*)

LEFT: The early fourteenth-century first-floor chapel with elaborate tracery, at Clevedon Court, Avon. (*NTPL/Jeremy Whitaker*)

which usually opened off the dais end of the hall. A number still survive, including those at National Trust properties like Clevedon Court (*c.*1320); Lytes Cary, Somerset (early fourteenth century); Ightham Mote (mid-fourteenth century); Bodiam Castle (1380s); Bradley Manor, Devon (dedicated 1428); and Cotehele, Cornwall (1480s). The fact that some smaller manor houses – Great Chalfield, for instance, and its Wiltshire neighbour Westwood Manor, which dates largely from the 1490s – seem not to have possessed chapels of their own may be due less to their size and more to the close proximity of the parish church, which in both cases is less than fifteen yards from the house.

These three elements – hall, great chamber and chapel – constituted the public face of the later medieval country house. The best decoration, in the form of tapestries, plasterwork and fine furnishings, was lavished on them; ritual, both secular and religious, was concentrated in them; and the lord consistently used them as a prominent architectural expression of his wealth and power. But that public face could only exist with the support of a large and complex substructure, consisting of both buildings and people. Of the two, the buildings are perhaps the easiest to itemise, although their utilitarian character has inevitably meant that they were more prone to alteration and modernisation than the public areas. For while later generations may have been ready and willing to respect the attractions of a medieval great hall without too much difficulty, medieval kitchens, bakehouses and slaughterhouses held no such charms.

The most important service rooms in the house were the kitchen and its attendant offices – not surprisingly, since by the later Middle Ages food and drink was accounting for between 55 per cent (in larger households) and 85 per cent (in smaller ones) of all expenditure. Besides the kitchen, most houses of any size contained a buttery, where ale and wine were kept under the aegis of a yeoman of the buttery, or butler; a pantry, where bread, and perhaps serving dishes and linen, were laid out by the yeoman of the pantry or pantler, ready to be taken into the hall at mealtimes; a pastry-house and a bakehouse; a brewery; a slaughterhouse; and a range of storage cellars, sculleries and larders.

Accommodation was the other basic need which governed the structure of the medieval country house. As the public and ceremonial role of the great chamber developed towards the end of the Middle Ages, it became rarer for the lord actually to sleep there. By the later fifteenth century he and his wife and children would be more likely to have lodgings either opening off the chamber, or perhaps – as the increasing desire for privacy made families reluctant to eat in state regularly, and as architectural fashions changed – at first-floor level at the opposite, lower, end of the hall. This arrangement had two advantages. It enabled an owner to have relatively self-contained lodgings away from the great chamber, reserving that room (and any lodgings attached to it) for special occasions or for important visitors. And it allowed him to achieve a certain symmetry in the architecture of his house, with balancing sets of principal lodgings placed at either end of the hall. One can see the idea in practice at Great Chalfield, where the great chamber at the east end of the hall has its counterpart in Tropnell's own private lodgings at the west. Here the main room is a ground-floor parlour, complete with a curious mural of a man with five fingers and a thumb on each hand – possibly a portrait of Tropnell himself, although it isn't known whether the five fingers were the result of a congenital deformity or simply an artist who couldn't count. And above the parlour is a bedchamber and closet. The exterior gable of these lodgings carries Tropnell's arms, to advertise their function.

In some cases the idea that the lord's lodgings should be given some form of separate architectural expression went a step further, and led to the development of the residential tower, self-contained but sited within the complex. Its progenitor, the Norman keep within a stockade, was essentially a communal space where a household or garrison could gather together, although it usually did contain a relatively private chamber for the lord. But as the keep lost ground to the turreted curtain wall, which could guard a large complex of buildings within its boundaries and so provide more spacious and comfortable quarters, a number of fortified houses were built or adapted to take as their focal point tower-lodgings for their most important occupant. In the early twelfth century at Sherborne in Dorset, for example, Bishop Roger of Salisbury built a great tower next to his communal hall. And at the beginning of the fourteenth, Robert Thorpe added a square tower (with elaborately painted interior walls), clearly intended as the chief lodgings of state, to an earlier hall at Longthorpe in Northamptonshire.

However, if one excepts the pele-towers of northern England and Scotland, which evolved in response to the need for sudden defence, it was in the fifteenth century that the residential tower really came into its own. At Raglan, Gwent, in South Wales, Sir William ap Thomas built a self-contained tower block between 1430 and 1445, isolated within its own moat and only accessible via a drawbridge. At Caister in Norfolk, Sir John Fastolf, a veteran campaigner in the Hundred Years' War, built himself a striking set of lodgings in a slender five-storey tower, circular without and hexagonal within, between 1432 and 1446. And at Ashby-de-la-Zouch in Leicestershire, William, Lord Hastings added a 90-foot tower to the castle which had been granted to him by Edward IV in 1464. Consisting of a storage area, a kitchen, a hall and a solar, all placed above one another and capped with a machicolated parapet, it had a portcullised entrance on the ground floor and an underground passage connected to the cellar of the main kitchens thirty yards away; and it was provided with its own independent water supply in the basement.

The tower as an architectural statement also forms part of the rationale behind the late-medieval vogue for the gatehouse tower. This first came to prominence in the castles of the thirteenth century, when the keep was replaced by the curtain wall as the main line of defence, and as a result the weakest part of that wall – the entrance – needed to be heavily fortified. But it was soon appreciated that such fortified gatehouses were not simply functional: they also served as introductions to the building itself, and over the next two hundred years they became focal points for the conspicuous display of wealth. The massive late fifteenth-century brick tower at Oxburgh in Norfolk is one of the most impressive examples of this type of dual-purpose structure. And while nowhere near as grand as Oxburgh, the gatehouse tower at Ightham Mote belongs to the same tradition: it is at once a defence and deterrent against unwelcome intruders (although hardly against a serious assault), and a statement of its owner's prestige.

While we can usually see evidence of the lord's own accommodation, it is much harder to say where the rest of the household slept. Personal servants probably slept on straw pallets either inside or outside the lord's lodgings. The early fifteenth-century *Book of Courtesy* recommends that such pallets should be at least 9ft by 7ft, suggesting that they were shared – a common enough practice, to judge from the passage from the Northumberland household regulations quoted above, which refers to 'two beds for the three cooks to lie in', a bed for the two minstrels and a bed for the two huntsmen. Such beds would have stood either in barracks-like dormitories, or, in the case of the cooks, perhaps even in the kitchens themselves. At the upper end of the scale, senior servants – the steward, the treasurer, the chaplain and the master of horse – often had private lodgings of their own, with their own personal attendants sleeping on pallets at the door.

These somewhat haphazard domestic arrangements, and the lack of precise evidence about them, are brought sharply into focus when one looks at the main resource on which the lord's prestige rested – people. By the end of the Middle Ages a great man might run a household of 300–500. In the early sixteenth century the 13th Earl of Oxford had about 300 in his service; around the same time, the Duke of Buckingham had between 400 and 500; and the Earl of Northumberland and

Cardinal Wolsey both employed 500.[3] These were exceptional, of course: gentry households of the period averaged about seventy, and even those of the nobility were usually no larger than 150–160. But even these figures demonstrate that it was not so much the buildings, the fine furnishings, the trappings of wealth, that provided and maintained the medieval lord's powerbase: it was his army of household officers and servants – the waiters and grooms, minstrels and falconers, cooks and scullions and arras-menders and armourers.

This army, and the sense of community and belonging which bonded its members to their lord and to each other, were what enabled the medieval country house to survive as a social unit. Twice a day, in the late morning and late evening, when the lord or his steward presided at the high table over communal meals in the great hall, everyone – the whole 'family', as the lord would have called all those in his employ – were expected to attend. Regulations and ordinances for households of the period make it clear that being absent from hall at mealtimes was a serious offence. Also, great pains were taken to ensure that everybody, from the senior officers down to the kitchen boys, attended chapel – or almost everybody, since the lord would often make use of his squint in the relative privacy of his chamber. Penalties for non-attendance ranged from fines to the imposition of a bread-and-water diet. Like some modern-day sociologists, medieval lords were convinced that the family that prays – and eats – together, stays together.

To judge from accounts of the period, this family was carefully organised into separate departments with their own clearly defined functions, rather like the staff of a Victorian country house. However, such accounts often mask a much more flexible arrangement, with kitchen boys and grooms waiting at table as the need arose, and waiters getting involved in the preparation of meals. There were also other fundamental differences between the medieval household and its Victorian descendant. The first, and most obvious, was that apart from washerwomen and attendants on the lady of the house, her daughters and any young children there may have been, the medieval household staff was male – a legacy of its origins in the military garrison. Many of the lower servants may well have been recruited for the duration of the lord's stay, returning to their families when the wagons began to roll on to the next destination.

The second difference was that, in contrast to the Victorian domestic set-up, the medieval household tended to be a microcosm of the world outside its walls. Its members were drawn from all ranks of society. In a great lord's house there were knights, providing the necessary military know-how; the elder sons of gentle and aristocratic landowners, for whom, in Ben Jonson's words, the household was 'the noblest way/Of breeding up our youths in letters, arms/Fair mien, discourses, civil exercise,/And all the blazon of a gentleman'; younger sons, for whom service was a career (hence Thomas Tropnell's position in the Hungerford household); yeomen

---

3 By comparison, in Edwardian times the enormous Penrhyn Castle in Gwynedd, North Wales, employed thirty-six indoor staff, ten in the stables, nineteen in the gardens and seven laundrywomen – seventy-two in all.

officers; and menials and boys – the cooking and cleaning staff who no doubt did most of the physical work. (And, in an early harbinger of mid twentieth-century practice, some households in the thirteenth century brought in outside staff to do the house-cleaning.)

It was this collection of men and boys that defined and upheld the lord's power. Great castles like Bodiam or Chirk (Clwyd, North Wales), fortified mansions like Tattershall or Oxburgh, and smaller manor houses such as Great Chalfield and Westwood – however status-conscious their builders may have been – were all primarily functional units rather than the pyrotechnic architectural displays of wealth that the country house was to become in the later sixteenth century. It was the household that sustained that cloak of mystique and ritual which constantly reminded the world of the great lord's position, and it did so much more effectively than grand buildings or lavish decoration, his timbered hall or his canopy of state. It was the household that sustained the core of physical strength necessary to maintain that position in a world where force mattered more than law. And, most importantly of all, it sustained itself, as the most tangible public proof of the lord's ability to command respect and loyalty.

Bodiam Castle

EAST SUSSEX

Bodiam Castle, 3 miles south of Hawkhurst on the border between Kent and Sussex, was built in the 1380s by a soldier of fortune, Sir Edward Dalyngrigge.

Looking down on the castle was like looking into another world, I can find no words to describe the beauty. It was a heavenly summer morning, and I felt, as I looked at this divinely inspired picture, that I dared not take my eyes off it, for fear that when I looked again it would have disappeared in a mist or a cloud – it could only be a fairy castle.

There is something magical about Bodiam. The spell that the 'fairy castle' cast over Grace Duggan, shown over the site one summer day in 1916 by her husband-to-be George Curzon, still has power today. It confounds one's critical faculties, so that at the sight of its high round towers rising from the clear waters of the moat, dry architectural and historical judgements are suspended, giving place to an attractively vague synthesis of Malory and Walter Scott. Bodiam is the romantic ruin *par excellence*, conjuring up a hazy vision of a Merry England of colourful tournaments and desperate sieges in which noble lords did noble deeds, and knights-in-armour really did rescue damsels in distress.

The truth, of course, is rather different. There was little either merry or noble about the castle's builder, Sir Edward Dalyngrigge. He was a mercenary and a freebooter, much of whose wealth was derived from a campaign of terror against the civilian population of France during the 1370s and 1380s. And his motives in

Bodiam Castle from the north-east. (*NTPL/Alasdair Ogilvie*)

fortifying Bodiam may well have been rooted not only in a desire to protect his country against imminent French invasion – the ostensible reason for his receiving a royal licence to crenellate in October 1385 – but also in the need to protect himself from the local peasantry.

Bodiam's origins are closely bound up with the Hundred Years' War. Dalyngrigge's wealth, which enabled him to build the castle; the threat of invasion, which made it necessary; and even the shape of the building itself – all have their roots in the series of conflicts which began in 1339 as the young Edward III pursued his claim to the French Crown.

One by-product of the hostilities was the formation of 'free companies', bands of battle-hardened veterans who remained in France, nominally answerable to their monarch but in reality selling their services to the highest bidder and, in Froissart's words, making war 'upon every one that was worth robbing'. One of the most notorious of these free companies was led by the English knight Sir Robert Knollys, who from his stronghold at Derval in Picardy terrorised the surrounding neighbourhood, ignoring treaties and truces and often subordinating military objectives to his own financial gain. To quote Froissart again, Knollys would march his company at a leisurely pace 'until he came to a very rich part of the country', when he would approach the most important town in the area and ask its governors, 'How much ready money they would give, if he would not pillage it.' His company's reputation was such – Loire peasants were said to throw themselves into the river at the mere mention of his name – that the money, sometimes as much as 100,000 francs, was usually forthcoming.

Knollys himself grew immensely rich as a result of the looting and extortion that he carried out in the King's name, as did a number of his lieutenants. One of these was Dalyngrigge, a member of an established Sussex family from Dalling Ridge near East Grinstead, who had crossed to France in 1367 with Lionel, Duke of Clarence, the third son of Edward III. By the time he came back to England in 1377, having fought in Knollys' company for some years, Dalyngrigge too had accumulated a large fortune. And by the following year that fortune had been supplemented by estates at Bodiam, which he obtained through his marriage to Elizabeth Wardeux, an heiress whose family had held the manor since the early fourteenth century.

During the years following Dalyngrigge's return from the wars, England was swept by a series of invasion scares. At the beginning of July 1377, just ten days after the death of Edward III at Sheen in Surrey, a French fleet attacked the Isle of Wight and burned Rye and Winchelsea in Sussex. As a result, defences across the country – and particularly along the south coast – were re-evaluated and strengthened. The old castle of Southampton was modernised; Rochester in Kent was refortified; Carisbrooke on the Isle of Wight was updated; and the King's master mason, Henry Yevele, designed new fortifications for Canterbury. Even as far away as Cornwall, the Duchy was ordered to modernise the decrepit castles of Tintagel and Trematon, in case the French should 'take and hold some fortress in our realm of England, and in particular on the sea coast, from which they can make war and ravage our said kingdom'. As an experienced veteran, Dalyngrigge himself was called on for advice. His military expertise led to his being appointed to survey and improve Winchelsea's defences in 1380, and he was a member of a commission called to fortify Rye in 1384–5.

The general air of insecurity which pervaded southern England was intensified by the insurrection of 1381, in which peasants from Kent, Sussex, Essex and Bedfordshire marched on London to demand the repeal of Richard II's poll-tax. The Archbishop of Canterbury and the Lord Treasurer were killed, as was the peasants' leader, Wat Tyler (another veteran of the French wars). And the brutality with which reprisals were taken by the boy-King's men, with a flagrant disregard for undertakings which the King had given personally to the peasants in London, left a legacy of anger and resentment, not only towards the Crown, but also towards the men responsible for putting down the insurrection. Those men included Robert Knollys and Edward Dalyngrigge.

Faced with popular unrest at home and the threat of invasion from abroad, Dalyngrigge's decision to replace his wife's moated manor house at Bodiam with a more secure residence is perhaps not surprising. It was, in any case, state policy to encourage private landowners to play their part in strengthening southern defences. With the Crown pouring money into maintaining the defences of Calais, funds were short, and a number of private castles were put up at this time. These included

Scotney in Kent, which was fortified by Roger Ashburnham after the French raids of 1377, and Cooling, where John de Cobham, another of Knollys's lieutenants, was licensed to fortify his house on the north Kent marshes in 1381. Bodiam itself was of rather more strategic importance than it seems today: until the seventeenth century the River Rother, which passes a few hundred yards to the south, was navigable all the way from the Channel port of Rye.

In October 1385, a few months after the south coast had been alerted to another possible invasion (a French fleet of 1200 ships had massed at Sluis in the Low Countries, ready to set sail for England), Dalyngrigge received a licence from Richard II:

> that he may strengthen with a wall of stone and lime, and crenellate and may construct and make into a castle his manor house of Bodiam, near the sea, in the county of Sussex, for the defence of the adjacent county, and the resistance to our enemies, and may hold his aforesaid house so strengthened and crenellated and made into a castle for himself and his heirs for ever.

He decided, though, that rather than convert the timber-framed moated manor house of the Wardeux family, he would start afresh on a new site. Building work probably started early in the following spring, while Dalyngrigge was away in France, serving as Captain of the Breton port of Brest – although it was by no means unknown for builders to jump the gun and begin work before their licence to crenellate had been issued. It is possible that the King's master-mason Henry Yevele, who worked on the fortifications at Cooling as well as at Canterbury, had a hand in the design. Both have gunports resembling those in the gatehouse at Bodiam. On the other hand, Bodiam's similarity to French military architecture suggests that the castle may have been the work of an engineer with experience in the French wars. Perhaps Dalyngrigge himself contributed to the design.

Externally, at least, that design was dictated by purely military considerations. The aesthetically pleasing forms of the drum towers at each corner of the rectangular building had a practical function, providing a wide angle of fire without blind spots, and eliminating corners which would be vulnerable to bombardment; while the beautiful expanse of moat made a surprise attack on the castle difficult, and effectively prevented the mining of the walls – a skill at which French engineers were particularly adept.

The approach to the main gatehouse was originally via a long timber bridge at right angles to the main north-south axis of the castle, which would have exposed the right flank of any attackers preparing to storm the entrance. This led from the west bank of the moat, over a drawbridge, to an octagonal island outwork. A second bridge (probably also a drawbridge) connected the octagon to the next line of defence, a two-storey barbican, with gates at either end and a portcullis. From here, a third drawbridge formed the approach to the main gatehouse of the castle. It was defended by gun-loops in its walls and machicolation slots above, and contained three doors, three portcullises and a complex of *meurtrieres* (or murder-holes) incorporated in the vaulting of its ceiling, through which slaked lime, stones and boiling tar or water could be poured on the hapless intruders. Dalyngrigge was

clearly determined that no one, whether French invader or revolting peasant, was going to gain unauthorised access to Bodiam.

However, Dalyngrigge's new building had to fulfil two quite separate roles: side by side with its military function went that of manorial residence of one of the most important men in the east of the county, and within its rather forbidding walls it contained all of the accommodation that would be expected of a house belonging to someone of Dalyngrigge's standing. Ranged along the south wall of the castle, across the courtyard from the gatehouse, were the domestic offices, the buttery, pantry and main kitchen; and the great hall, reached via a screens passage which also gave access to a secondary entrance – the heavily fortified postern tower in the centre of the south wall, decorated with the arms of Robert Knollys as a tribute to Dalyngrigge's former leader. To the east of the hall lay lodgings for Dalyngrigge's family and important visitors: a large ground-floor chamber, perhaps a day parlour; a great chamber above; and another large room with a private pew leading off it, overlooking a ground-floor chapel. This range also gave access to lodgings in both the south-east drum tower and the rectangular projecting tower in the centre of the east wall. Most of these lodgings were provided with privies, as, indeed, were many of the other chambers in the castle. Bodiam contained more than thirty, all of which discharged directly into the moat.

The south-west tower contained a dovecote and a well, important sources of food and water should a siege ever take place, and the west range of rooms was largely given over to lodgings and service rooms for Dalyngrigge's household. The military nature of that household is emphasised by the provision of a secondary kitchen and another hall, suggesting a clear distinction between the garrison personnel and Dalyngrigge's own servants, who presumably ate in the great hall.

Looking at the ruins of Bodiam's interior today, one finds it hard to imagine the castle as it was in the 1390s, as Dalyngrigge ate in state on a dais either in his great chamber or, on important occasions, in the hall; or as he sat in his private pew, hearing mass celebrated by the castle chaplain in the chapel below. It is hard to picture the colourful interiors, wainscoted or hung with tapestries, or plastered and covered with bright paintings and stencilling; or to imagine the frantic preparations for the arrival of an important visitor, as chambers were made ready, beds and tables set up, and hangings brought out of storage, while the members of the garrison lounged around in the courtyard playing dice or cards. It is hard, too, to imagine the squalor, the stench, the coarseness and casual violence and brutality of day-to-day life.

The French invasion, the prospect of which had provided the stimulus for the building of Bodiam, never came, and by the time the castle was finished in the early 1390s the threat of war had receded. Edward Dalyngrigge continued to play his part in national and international affairs. In 1390 he was involved in negotiating a truce with the King of France, and two years later Richard appointed him Keeper of the Tower of London and Governor of the City, following a dispute between the King and the Lord Mayor. How much time he actually spent at his new castle at Bodiam is a matter for conjecture: it cannot have been long, since by 1395 he was dead, and had been succeeded by his son John.

In 1469 Bodiam passed from the Dalyngrigges to the Lewknor family, and from them to a succession of owners. There is no evidence that it ever saw the military action that Sir Edward had anticipated – and that one suspects he would have relished – although it was taken, apparently without a struggle, by Richard III's supporters in 1483. Its ruinous state probably dates from the time of the Commonwealth, when, like so many castles, it was partially dismantled and some of its outworks pulled down in order to make it undefendable.

By the end of the eighteenth century Bodiam had begun to assume the role of romantic ruin, a memorial to the England of olden times. Topographical artists such as S. H. Grimm and Samuel and Nathaniel Buck came to draw it. Tourists made excursions to see 'the noble remains of the square castle of Bodiham'. And the first tentative attempts were made to preserve it: initially by John Fuller, who bought the castle in 1829, apparently in order to save it from being demolished for its building materials; then by George Cubitt, who purchased it from Fuller's grandson in 1864, and did a great deal to repair the crumbling exterior walls; and, from 1919 onwards, by George Nathaniel Curzon, the famous Viceroy of India and owner of Kedleston Hall in Derbyshire.

The first time Curzon set eyes on Bodiam he fell 'an immediate victim to its charm', and determined that 'so rare a treasure should neither be lost to our country nor desecrated by irreverent hands'. Enchanted with a building which 'transports us at a bound to the days when the third Edward was fighting his foreign wars or the hunchback Richard was casting his nefarious die for the throne', he tried to buy it from Cubitt (who had been created Lord Ashcombe in 1892). Ashcombe refused to part with Bodiam, but Curzon persisted, and in 1917, the year after he had brought Grace Duggan down to see the 'fairy castle', Lord Ashcombe's son agreed to the sale.

In 1919 Curzon began a comprehensive and scholarly programme of restoration, aided by William Weir of the Society for the Protection of Ancient Buildings. The moat and basement areas were excavated, ground levels were established, rubble, trees and ivy were cleared away and the stonework was repaired with new stone. On Curzon's death in 1925, Bodiam (along with Tattershall in Lincolnshire, another castle that he had saved and restored) was left to the National Trust. His will read:

> Convinced that ancient buildings which recall the life and customs of the past are not only an historical document of supreme value, but are a part of the spiritual and aesthetic heritage of the nation, imbuing it with reverence and educating its taste, I bequeath for the benefit of the nation certain properties which I have acquired for the express purpose of preserving the historic buildings upon them.

Curzon's will admirably defines the twofold appeal of Bodiam today. On the one hand its proud towers and ancient walls are the stuff that dreams are made of, evoking a spiritual and aesthetic response in all but the hardest academic hearts. At the same time it is indeed 'an historical document of supreme value', reminding us not only of the architectural achievements of our medieval ancestors but also of the barbaric and brutal nature of the world in which they lived. The romance of Bodiam is undeniable – but there is a corner in each of us, perhaps, which sympathises with the Georgian aesthetician Uvedale Price's analysis of the appeal of ancient castles: 'The ruins of these once magnificent edifices, are the pride and boast of this island; we may well be proud of them, not merely in a picturesque point of view; we may glory that the abodes of tyranny and superstition are in ruin.'

LORD CURZON IN UNEMPLOYMENT.

This cartoon of Lord Curzon by Sir Mark Sykes was drawn in the membership book of a London dinner club dating from about 1914.

Tattershall Castle

LINCOLNSHIRE

The great tower at Tattershall Castle, $3\frac{1}{2}$ miles south-east of Woodhall Spa in Lincolnshire, was built in the 1430s and 1440s for Henry VI's Treasurer, Ralph, Lord Cromwell.

The reason usually given for the wave of great tower-lodgings which appeared in the late Middle Ages is an obvious one – a need for protection. Many factors combined to produce a general feeling of insecurity, a fear of attack from both without and within. First of these was the anarchy that prevailed during the mid-fifteenth century as a result of weak and disorganised central government. Add to this the hiring of mercenaries, perhaps already veterans hardened in the battles of the Hundred Years' War, to serve as the military wing of a great lord's household – a practice which increased significantly as the old feudal ties faded. And then there was the lawless behaviour of power-hungry local warlords, such as the Duke of Suffolk who was accused by Parliament in 1448 of having in his household 'manslaughterers, murderers and common, openly noised misdoers' and of committing 'great outrageous extortions and murders ... to the full heavy discomfort of the true subjects of this your realm'.

The self-contained tower-lodging was, so the argument goes, a response to this insecurity, a last line of defence against attack from outside and a safe zone in which the lord and his immediate household need not fear the sort of treatment from his hired killers that he was so happy to see them mete out to others.

In fact the truth is more complicated. While there is no doubt that some towers were primarily defensive – as demonstrated, for example, in the unusually thick walls (8ft 7in on the ground floor) and lack of ground-floor windows to the Hastings Tower at Ashby-de-la-Zouch – the tower-lodging was more than just a bolthole. It was also, as noted in the introduction to this chapter, a public architectural expression of its owner's power and a response to the changing nature of the medieval household. It signalled a growing reluctance on the part of the lord to share the communal life that was such a feature of earlier households – a retreat that William Langland had already lamented in the 1300s:

> Wretched is the hall ... each day in the week
> There the lord and lady liketh not to sit.
> Now have the rich a rule to eat by themselves
> In a privy parlour ...

Both of these factors – the desire to express status and the wish for privacy – are exemplified in what is probably the most famous of all fifteenth-century tower-lodgings, Tattershall Castle.

The man responsible for Tattershall was Ralph, 3rd Lord Cromwell (1394–1456). He was the grandson of an established Nottinghamshire landowner who, through his marriage to an heiress, Maud Bernack, had added considerably to the

family's estates in Nottinghamshire and Lincolnshire. Ralph Cromwell served in France, where he saw action at Agincourt in 1415, before inheriting in 1419 and embarking on an active political career which included the offices of Constable of Nottingham Castle, Warden of Sherwood Forest, and, from 1433 to 1443, Lord High Treasurer of England to Henry VI.

Cromwell's construction work at Tattershall, which he began around the time of his appointment to the Treasurership, involved adapting an earlier castle already standing on the site. Robert de Tateshale had received a licence to crenellate in 1231, and although little evidence remains from his time it seems that his building was enclosed within a moat and an irregular-shaped curtain wall, with seven or eight round towers at the angles. Cromwell retained this arrangement, but added a second, outer moat which completely encircled the first (rather than running into it, as it does today), to create a complicated and well defended approach not unlike that at Bodiam. Welcome and unwelcome visitors alike had to negotiate a bridge over the outer moat which led to a gatehouse, then turn left and over a cross-moat with a second gatehouse, before finally arriving at a third bridge and gatehouse which commanded the entrance to the inner ward itself.

Cromwell also retained the buildings that stood in that inner ward. An engraving of 1726 by Samuel Buck suggests that these included a north-south great hall close to the western curtain wall, with kitchens at its lower, south, end reached via a screens passage (missing in Buck's view). The engraving also shows the remains of what must have been a chapel against the south wall, with a fifteenth-century chantry chapel attached. There was presumably a solar or great chamber to the north of the hall, although by Buck's time this had been replaced by what looks to be an early seventeenth-century cross-range.

OPPOSITE: Ralph Cromwell's tower lodging at Tattershall, Lincolnshire. (*NTPL/John Bethell*)

BELOW: Samuel Buck's view of the east front in 1726. (*NTPL/Mike Williams*)

It was in order to improve this accommodation – together with the other offices and lodgings which must also have been ranged around the inner courtyard, but which had vanished without trace by the early eighteenth century – that Cromwell squeezed his building in between two of the old round towers on the western curtain wall and behind the old hall, with a two-tier covered passage running between that hall and the new tower. The joist holes for this passage can still be seen on the east front of the tower. His inspiration, and perhaps even his choice of brick as the building material, may have come from Europe, where during his soldiering he must have seen examples of the tower keep, which was still fashionable in the fifteenth century. Several of the craftsmen he employed, notably his master brickmaker Baldwyn Docheman (Dutchman?), certainly came from abroad.

Projecting out into the inner moat, the brick tower had five main chambers placed one on top of another, with further rooms built into the thickness of the walls and in three of the corner turrets (the south-east turret held a staircase). The basement level, which contained a well, may have been used for storage; while the main ground-floor chamber, which like the basement is completely self-contained and offers no access to the upper floors, was probably a parlour, either for communal use or for Cromwell's steward and other senior servants.

The three floors above were the Treasurer's lodgings of state. One can only conjecture as to their precise use, which in any case probably varied according to circumstances, but they may have functioned as (in ascending order), a hall, a great chamber or audience chamber, and a withdrawing chamber containing Cromwell's bed. The spiral stair in the south-east tower continues up to a projecting gallery equipped with missile holes, and ends with a walkway at the top, carried on the roof of the gallery.

The little surviving evidence suggests that all three rooms of state were splendidly and comfortably fitted out. Each of the main chambers has corbels high up on one

Cromwell's withdrawing chamber on the third floor. The overmantel shows his arms and a rebus on the Treasurer's name.
(*NTPL/John Bethell*)

wall, and it has been suggested that these corbels supported the rich canopies that hung over Cromwell as he presided over his high table, sat in his chair of state or lay in his bed. Drainage shafts built into the thickness of the walls and ultimately discharging into the moat show that there were privies on each floor. And all the main chambers except the basement were heated by fireplaces which have decorated chimneypieces carved with the symbol of the Treasurer's purse. (The one in the withdrawing chamber on the third floor shows a punning rebus incorporating the Gromwell weed, *Lithospermum*.) Each of the main chambers would also have been plastered, wainscoted or hung with tapestries. Wooden blocks high up on one wall of the hall suggest a rail for hangings, or for fixing wainscot.

The motive behind the building of Ralph Cromwell's great new lodgings was not primarily security. Unlike the Hastings Tower at Ashby, the tower at Tattershall is not completely self-contained, and was meant from the first to be linked both to the old great hall and to a new kitchen range which was built to the south at the same time as the tower. Its position, breaking through the original curtain wall out into the inner moat, and its fenestration – there are large windows on all four storeys of the exposed west front – show that Cromwell was more concerned with display than with defence. Even the machicolation gallery, which is corbelled out over his withdrawing chamber, may well have been intended as much as a prestigious architectural feature (like the machicolations which Archbishop Bourchier installed over his gatehouse at Knole a few years later) as a serious device for inflicting death and destruction on besieging troops by hurling lethal substances on them.

Cromwell made other alterations to the old castle at Tattershall, including several new ranges – probably stables and additional lodgings – in the area between the outer and inner moats. He also founded almshouses for thirteen elderly couples, and rebuilt the nearby parish church, where he created a college of priests to pray for his soul in an attempt to ensure as much comfort in the next life as his tower-lodgings provided in this. Neither the church nor the buildings in the outer ward were completed by the time of his death in 1456.

Tattershall had fallen into decay by 1726, as Buck's engraving shows. The moats had been filled in, and the stones from the older parts of the castle had been taken away and re-used elsewhere: by chance, Cromwell's choice of brick as a building material probably saved the tower from being similarly recycled.

No one, except for the occasional antiquarian tourist – and A. W. N. Pugin, who used several of the Tattershall chimneypieces in his designs for the Houses of Parliament – seems to have cared overmuch about the castle's decline, until 1910, when the news broke that Albert Ball, a former mayor of Nottingham who had bought the site the previous year, was to sell it on to be dismantled. Writing thirty-six years later, but still brimming with righteous, and splendid, indignation, Clough Williams-Ellis describes what happened next:

Along comes a junk man, who rightly guesses that there must be good money in the wonderfully sculpted heraldic stone fireplaces. Having acquired the legal right so to do, he yanks them out and trundles them off to market – their ultimate destination presumably America.

45

But it is the twentieth century now, so there is a hue and cry, not, of course, of 'Stop Thief!' (because of the indubitable if astonishing legality of the enterprise), but of 'Hi! Is it really possible that our most lovely and historic architectural treasures can be thus made away with by private individuals and is there no law to prevent it?' The shaming answer, of course, being 'It is and there isn't'.

An appeal is made to the National Trust. The response is inadequate. The monumental mantelpieces have almost booked their passages, the battle is regarded as lost, when Lord Curzon steps down as *deus ex machina*, waves his golden wand – and the captive stones are released, to be brought home in triumph by their liberator.

So Tattershall was saved at the eleventh hour (and its chimneypieces rescued from a German dealer) by George Curzon, who was to play knight in shining armour a few years later to another neglected medieval ruin, Bodiam Castle. With the help of William Weir, the architect from the Society for the Protection of Ancient Buildings who would help with the restoration of Bodiam, he reinstated the chimneypieces, excavated the moats, and replaced floors, roof and windows. Curzon left Tattershall to the National Trust on his death in 1925. Today, the buildings which once surrounded it long gone, Cromwell's great tower stands in glorious isolation – no longer the sumptuous lodging that it was in the fifteenth century, perhaps, but just as proud, just as impressive, just as stately.

Ightham Mote

KENT

Ightham Mote stands 6 miles east of Sevenoaks. The core of the house dates from the 1340s; significant additions were made in the late fifteenth, sixteenth and seventeenth centuries.

Detail of the gallery ceiling at Ightham Mote, showing the Tudor colours and symbols of the English and Spanish royal families. The boards may originally have come from a pavilion set up for some great court occasion.
(*NTPL/ Rob Matheson*)

The south and west fronts. (*NTPL/Rob Matheson*)

The older a building is, the more likely we are to be faced with perplexing blanks in its history, questions which can never satisfactorily be answered. Why was it built, and why was it built here? Who were the masons and carpenters, the craftsmen whose work has survived for centuries but whose names have long since been forgotten? Why was this range added, or that set of lodgings replaced? What was it like to live in?

The deeper we dig, the scarcer the sources of information become, until we are left with nothing but a name, the name of the man or woman who centuries ago, and for some unknown reason, chose to build themselves a country house.

At Ightham Mote, we don't even have that.

The first recorded owner of Ightham, a Staffordshire knight and veteran of the French wars named Sir Thomas Cawne, took up residence in about 1360, around the time of his marriage to Lora Morant from nearby Chevening. His effigy, in full armour, still lies in the parish church. Until recently it was assumed that Cawne and his wife were responsible for the mid fourteenth-century buildings which form the earliest parts of the complex. But modern research has shown that these buildings were put up in the 1330s or 1340s – before Cawne's time – and the name of their originator remains a mystery.

But while we may not know *who* built Ightham, we do have a good idea of *what* he or she built, in spite of a complicated series of alterations and additions made by the generations that followed. When Sir Thomas Cawne moved into Ightham, the house consisted of a group of buildings, probably enclosed within a four-sided moat. Ightham was known as 'La Mote' in Cawne's day, and common sense suggests that the 'Mote' in the present name derives from its moat, although a rather more fanciful explanation has it that the word is really a corruption of the Anglo-Saxon 'moot', or assembly.

Within the moat, the main buildings – which are all that survives from this period – were ranged along the eastern side of the enclosure. They included a two-bay hall, two storeys high, of roughly coursed ragstone, sparsely lit and ventilated with a roof-top louvre; a high, narrow chapel above a vaulted crypt, also of ragstone, which lay to the north-east of the hall; and lodgings for the owner and his family – a solar on the first floor of a largely or wholly timber-framed building, set against the north end of the hall. A second solar was added not long after, and a stair of some sort gave access to the upper floor. There was almost certainly a kitchen range, including a buttery and pantry, opening off the southern end of the hall opposite the solar block. And no doubt there were other buildings on the site, probably of timber. The whole area within the moat may well have been enclosed by walls or wooden palisading, with lean-to lodgings and dormitories, a brewhouse, a bakehouse, store rooms and stabling ranged around this primitive stockade. But, as with other houses of the period, the lord's solar and, even more importantly, the communal rooms – the hall and the chapel – were the focus of the house. They were its heart.

Perhaps the easiest way to imagine living conditions at Ightham for Sir Thomas Cawne and his extended family is to look at the rather whimsical half-timbered dog-kennel which stands in the courtyard. Like Dido, the St Bernard for whom the kennel was built in 1891, the fourteenth-century occupants of Ightham must have endured uncomfortable, dark and draughty living conditions, too hot in summer and too cold in winter. Like Dido, they undoubtedly accepted those conditions without complaint. And like Dido, they probably had fleas.

By modern standards, life must have been intolerably harsh: there was virtually no privacy, and, as noted in the introduction to this chapter, most members of the household would have slept on straw pallets in the hall or the kitchen, or in the dormitories in one of the lean-to buildings in the courtyard. Only the Cawnes themselves – and conceivably their steward, and one or two of the other senior officers – possessed beds, and even in the family's own lodgings in the solar block their personal servants would have been on hand day and night. There would have been only one chair in the house – Cawne's own, on which he sat in state at mealtimes. Everyone else made do with low benches, stools, or the various chests and coffers that were the only forms of storage space. The tables in the hall were probably simple boards laid on trestle frames; only the lord's board, or high table – and perhaps a cupboard, set up in the hall at mealtimes to hold the display of plate – would have been covered with a cloth.

Between 1300 and 1380 the regular monthly or twice-monthly movement from one estate to another, which had been common in the early Middle Ages, gave way to more prolonged stays of four to six months in a single dwelling. But in spite of this general tendency for households to give up the nomadic existence of their

The courtyard, complete with Dido's late-Victorian Gothic Revival dog kennel.
(*National Monuments Record*)

forefathers, the household at Ightham would still have been geared to travel, and the scarcity of large fixed furnishings must have reflected this.

Sir Thomas Cawne died in 1374, leaving 'La Mote' to his son Robert. By the 1440s the house had passed, through the marriage of Robert's daughter Alice, to the Haut family. And it was with the Hauts – Richard, who died in 1487, and his son Edward, who inherited when he was still a child and who sold Ightham in 1521 – that the process of bringing the house into line with rising standards of comfort and convenience began. Either Richard or Edward built a new west range across the courtyard from the hall and solars. Although this has been substantially altered, it probably contained an additional set of grand lodgings – for either the Hauts or important guests – above an entrance linked by a bridge or causeway to the area beyond the moat. They also replaced any temporary buildings that may have stood on the south side of the courtyard with a more permanent block, and, some years after the west range was completed, inserted a three-storey gatehouse tower over its entrance, complete with a late medieval 'letterbox'. (This was an L-shaped slit in the stonework which enabled visitors both to pass messages and shout an identification through to the porter, who was responsible for granting admission.)

But if the Hauts began the tower, it was probably their successor, Richard Clement, who completed or remodelled it. The archway on the moat side is medieval, while that facing the courtyard is Tudor, and several panels of glass in the first-floor windows show Clement's arms.

Richard Clement's barrel-vaulted long gallery, later converted into a chapel.
(*NTPL/Rob Matheson*)

Richard Clement was an ambitious if rather minor courtier who had begun his career in the service of Henry VII, becoming a page of the King's Privy Chamber and remaining at court after Henry VIII's accession to the throne in 1509. The following year he married an heiress, Anne Whittlebury, and in 1521 he bought Ightham Mote and began a substantial building programme which involved not only the completion of the gatehouse tower but also the creation of a fourth range to the north. The ground floor of this north wing was largely taken up with an open loggia linking the gatehouse range with the original solar block, while above it Clement installed a spectacular gallery, now known as the Tudor chapel. The idea of a gallery probably originated in France in the mid-fifteenth century, and by the early 1500s the Ightham-type arrangement of open cloister with closed gallery above was becoming increasingly fashionable. In 1509 the London house of Henry VII's hated 'fiscal judge', Edmund Dudley, was similarly ordered; so was The Vyne in Hampshire (1520). Such rooms had various functions: they were part access corridors, part exercise rooms – Tudor physicians constantly stressed the importance to one's health of regular walking – and part withdrawing chambers to the main solar or state lodging.

The most remarkable feature of Clement's gallery is its barrel-vaulted ceiling of boards painted with royal emblems: the roses of York, Lancaster and Tudor; the fleur-de-lis; the portcullis of Beaufort; the Castile castle; and the Aragon pomegranate and quiver. Alternate boards show lozenges of white and green with roses and fleurs-de-lis at the intersections, and the ribs have chevrons and the Tudor colours of green and white. It has been suggested that these boards originally formed part of a temporary pavilion set up for some great court occasion, perhaps even for the joustings and pageantry which took place in the summer of 1520 when Henry VIII met Francis I of France at the Field of the Cloth of Gold. But wherever the ceiling came from, its message is clear: it is a proclamation of Richard Clement's loyalty to his king, and an announcement of his importance as a member of the royal court.

Clement died in 1538, and Ightham Mote passed eventually to Sir William Selby, whose family remained at Ightham for three centuries. During that time successive generations of Selbys responded to each new fashion as it came along. A Jacobean staircase and chimneypieces were installed; Palladian and Gothick windows were inserted; the walls were hung with hand-painted eighteenth-century Chinese wallpaper or covered (by Richard Norman Shaw) with Old English panelling.

In 1889 the Selby family sold the house to Sir Thomas Colyer-Fergusson, on whose death in 1951 it was bought by a consortium of local businessmen in an attempt to preserve it. Finding the cost beyond them, they in turn sold it to Charles Henry Robinson, an American industrialist.

Robinson's story is a romantic one. He first fell in love with Ightham Mote as a young man, when he saw a picture of it in a London art-dealer's shop. Then, a few years later, he came on the house by chance during a cycling tour of southern England, and saw that it lived up to his expectations. After building up a fortune in the paper-making industry, he saw it once again, this time in a sale advertisement in *Country Life*, and rushed over to England to make an offer. It was accepted, but travelling back to the United States on the *Queen Mary*, Robinson had second thoughts and wrote a letter withdrawing that offer. Fortunately for Ightham Mote, he didn't post the letter, and over the next three decades he made much-needed repairs and installed his collection of seventeenth-century English furniture.

Soon after his purchase of Ightham Mote, Robinson let it be known that he intended to bequeath it to the National Trust. He died in 1985 – his ashes are interred in the crypt – and in the same year the Trust took possession.

Today Ightham has something of the air of an architectural style manual, although – miraculously – the alterations and additions seem to have complemented rather than marred its original medieval character. Walking round the house in the 1990s, one can still strip away the centuries of change and return, in one's mind's eye, to the days of Richard Clement, the Haut family, Sir Thomas Cawne, and the anonymous character who, more than 650 years ago, presided over his or her long-forgotten household and heard Mass in the chapel. We may never know who built Ightham Mote – but we can be grateful.

Cotehele

CORNWALL

Cotehele, on the west bank of the River Tamar 8 miles south-west of Tavistock, was built between the late fifteenth century and 1627, incorporating parts of an earlier medieval house.

[Cotehele] consists of a large hall full of old armour and swords and old carved chairs of the times, a drawing room hung with old tapestry, the skirting-board of which is straw, the chair seats made of the priest's vestments. A chapel which is still in good repair. The window painted glass but damaged and defaced. A small bed chamber, two closets and a dressing-room all hung with old tapestry. Above stairs there is a drawing-room, the chairs black ebony carved, and a cabinet the same, and four bedchambers all hung the same. At breakfast we ate off the old family pewter, and used silver knives, forks and spoons which have been time immemorial in the family and have always been kept in this place.

The description is Queen Charlotte's, set down after her visit to Cotehele with George III in 1789. By that time the brown and grey slate-stone house, hidden away in the woods above the Calstock reach of the Tamar, was already widely known in antiquarian circles as a remarkable survival – like the knives and forks – from 'time immemorial'; even, if one were to believe Horace Walpole's characteristically ironic overstatement, from before the Flood: 'I never did see Cotehele, and am sorry. Is not the old wardrobe there still? There is one from the time of Cain, but Adam's breeches and Eve's under-petticoat were eaten by a goat in the ark.'

In fact Cotehele's origins, while not exactly antediluvian, do date back to the end of the thirteenth century. The buildings on the site today may well incorporate parts of the house put up by the de Cotehele family, who held the estate until the death of William de Cotehele sometime before 1336. But it is to the Edgcumbes, who acquired Cotehele in 1353 through the marriage of William's daughter Hilaria to William Edgcumbe, and who held it for the next 600 years, that the house owes its present appearance – and in particular to Richard Edgcumbe (d.1489) and his son Piers (1468/9–1539).

Time has lent a certain romance to Richard Edgcumbe's eventful career as an outlaw, soldier and courtier – a career which nearly killed him on several occasions. He is first heard of being ambushed on his way to Cotehele by a gang of thirty-four armed men led by his neighbour, Robert Willoughby of Bere Ferrers, with whom he was engaged in a violent feud. He escaped, although Willoughby's men later attacked the house and tried to burn it, beating one of Richard's servants 'to the hurt and damage of . . . twenty pounds and more'.

Richard's next brush with death came in 1483, when he allied himself with the Duke of Buckingham's forces against Richard III. After Buckingham's defeat and execution Edgcumbe was outlawed, and went into hiding at Cotehele, where he was tracked down by the King's agent, Sir Henry Trenowth of Bodrugan. Trenowth,

A painting, now hanging in the chapel at Cotehele, Cornwall, of Sir Richard Edgcumbe's tomb at Morlaix in Brittany, which was destroyed in the French Revolution. (*Country Life*)

whose reputation for 'robberies, despoileries of merchants [and] strangers, murders, as well by water as by land, entries by force and wrongful imprisonments' had already led the local Cornish gentry to petition the Crown for his removal, threw a cordon round the house and posted a watch at the gate. But Edgcumbe slipped out, cut the sentry's throat, and made off down to the river with Trenowth's men hard on his heels. With considerable presence of mind he took off his cap and threw it into the waters, and then hid in the undergrowth. His pursuers, 'looking down after the noise, and seeing his cap swimming thereon, supposed that he had desperately drowned himself, and gave over further hunting'.

Once the coast was clear, Richard escaped to Brittany, joining Henry Tudor and returning to fight at Bosworth in 1485. Henry rewarded him with a knighthood, the post of Comptroller in the King's Household – and Henry Trenowth's estates.[4] Richard Edgcumbe's last years were spent on various royal missions, including embassies to Calais, Scotland and Ireland; he died at Morlaix in 1489, while fighting in the service of Anne, Duchess of Brittany.

---

4   The story goes that Edgcumbe finally had his revenge on Henry Trenowth of Bodrugan, chasing him into the sea at the headland south of Mevagissey which became known as Bodrugan's Leap.

When he wasn't being chased or cutting throats, Richard embarked on a major rebuilding programme at Cotehele, a programme that was continued after his death by his son, Piers. The layout of the house, a series of ranges one room deep grouped around an entrance court and two secondary service courts, may owe something to the original Cotehele, although the extent of the Tudor remodelling and the subsequent patching-up of the stonework by later generations make it extremely difficult to establish exactly what form this earlier house took. It is also hard to distinguish the contributions of father and son. It seems, though, that Richard – who is unlikely to have made any significant alterations to the house until the more settled but rather short period between 1485 and his death in 1489 – was responsible for the embattled gatehouse to the south which guards the entrance into the main courtyard, and the barrel-vaulted chapel in the north-west corner of that courtyard, which replaced one built by his great-uncle Peter Edgcumbe and licensed by the Bishop of Exeter in 1411. Richard's chapel still contains the clock that he installed in the late 1480s – the earliest domestic clock in England still unaltered and in its original position.

The body of the house lies to the north of the main courtyard, its entrance aligned with the Gothic arch of Richard Edgcumbe's gatehouse. This north range, which contained all of the elements one might expect to find in a domestic building of this date – a hall rising up the full height of the house, with a ground-floor parlour and first-floor great chamber at its upper end, and kitchens at its lower end – is part of Piers' contribution to Cotehele, made at just that point in English architectural history when the functional nature of the medieval country house was beginning to give way to a more self-conscious desire for both comfort and display. The arrangement and treatment of the rooms in the north range reflect this transitional phase in a number of ways.

Piers Edgcumbe may still have presided in state over his household in the hall on high days and holy days, but by the end of the fifteenth century it had become essentially a room where the servants ate, and the absence of a screen to conceal the service end from view reflects this. And yet the hall was also the first room to be seen by any visitor. It was an introduction to the house, and as such it was essential that it should create an immediate impact, proclaiming its owner's standing.

At Cotehele, several devices combine to create such an impression. Apart from its size – at 42ft by 22ft it is far and away the largest room in the house – there is the massive moulded granite fireplace, and the panels of heraldic glass in the windows, each emblazoned with the arms of important Edgcumbe connections and relations – the Hollands, the Tremaynes, the Durnfords, the Cotterells, the Raleighs, the Trevanions, the Carews, the St Maurs, the Courtenays and the Fitzwalters. But most impressive of all is the open roof, with its seven bays of arch-braced trusses. Each bay is filled with four tiers of richly moulded wind-braces, a Gothic lattice-work which is both functional – giving the necessary rigidity to the whole structure – and superbly decorative, a breathtaking opening to Cotehele's splendours.

That Piers Edgcumbe's great chamber should also be thought worthy of an elaborate arch-braced roof, again with moulded wind-braces, is an indication of the shift in emphasis from the communal hall to the owner's own lodgings as the focal

The north side of the entrance courtyard, showing the great hall. (*The National Trust/George Wright*)

point of the house. (Unfortunately the great chamber roof has been concealed behind a later ceiling, and is no longer open to view.) Piers' lodgings are, in fact, accorded the same importance as the hall: they too are of ashlar, with wide mullioned and transomed windows; they too have large fireplaces. And the great chamber itself (now partitioned off into the Red Room and the South Room) contains squints into both the chapel and the hall. The retreat from communal living entailed fewer opportunities for personal supervision, and these squints enabled the Edgcumbes not only to maintain a metaphorical presence at communal activities but also, on a more practical level, to keep an eye on the behaviour of the household – a possibility that would of itself have had a salutary effect on their servants.

In spite of Cotehele's reputation in the eighteenth and nineteenth centuries as a Tudor time-capsule – 'all the rooms retain their ancient furniture,' wrote one visitor in 1840, 'and the latest not more modern than the reign of Elizabeth' – there are no furnishings left from Piers' remodelling. Indeed, there is nothing from the Tudor period at all, except perhaps for a late Elizabethan armchair in the hall, and a French cabinet dating from about 1570. But Piers was unwittingly responsible for the fact that relatively few changes have been made to the structure since the sixteenth century. His first wife was a heiress, Joan Durnford, and the marriage in 1493 not only enabled him to continue his father's building works at Cotehele, but also brought with it substantial estates on both sides of the Tamar. In 1553 Piers' son Richard built himself a new house on what had been Durnford land at the mouth of the river. And from that time on, Mount Edgcumbe, as it was known, became the family's principal seat, allowing Cotehele to escape the vicissitudes of fashion.

Some changes were made to the house, nevertheless. In the 1620s Sir Richard Edgcumbe (c.1570–1638) – or, according to one story, his father-in-law, a Flemish merchant named Thomas Coteel – added a castellated tower to the north of Piers' great chamber and parlour, containing an additional set of lodgings which could be used either as a self-contained guest wing or as a more private group of chambers for the family. And in the 1650s the Royalist Colonel Piers Edgcumbe (c.1610–67), who had moved his household from Mount Edgcumbe to Cotehele during the Civil War to avoid the attentions of the Parliamentarian stronghold at Plymouth, made a further attempt to bring the accommodation up to date, altering some of the chambers in the Tudor north range and replacing the old winding newel stair with a more convenient and fashionable set of straight flights. Most unusually for the period, the Colonel re-used several of the late fifteenth- or sixteenth-century windows in the new work – perhaps a very early instance of an antiquarian respect for the past, or perhaps simply evidence of thrift.

The family returned to Mount Edgcumbe after the Colonel's death, but they continued to use Cotehele as a secondary residence, as the rather bizarre story of Lady Anne Edgcumbe demonstrates.

In about 1675 Lady Anne, the wife of another Sir Richard (1640–88), died after a mysterious illness, while the family were staying at the house. One night, shortly after her body had been placed in the family vault, the local sexton crept down, lantern in hand, and attempted to remove a gold ring from her finger: 'Not succeeding, [he] pressed and pinched the finger – when the body very sensibly moved in the coffin. The man ran off in terror, leaving his lantern behind him. Her Ladyship arose, and taking the lantern, proceeded to the mansion house.' History doesn't record Sir Richard's reaction to the sight of his dead wife, lantern in hand, standing at the door like one of Arthur Rackham's illustrations to *Tales of Mystery and Imagination*. But Lady Anne obviously made a full recovery from her nightmarish ordeal, since five years later she gave birth to a son, another Richard.

It has recently been suggested that this Richard (1680–1758) and his son George (1720/1–95) – who entertained George III and Queen Charlotte during their visit in 1789 and was created Earl of Mount Edgcumbe on that occasion – were responsible for refining and emphasising Cotehele's self-consciously antiquarian atmosphere, by introducing the remarkable collections of tapestries and furnishings commented on by Queen Charlotte. The majority of the hangings, which contribute more than any other items in the house to that air of antiquity, date from the second half of the seventeenth century. They may perhaps have been transferred from

A watercolour by Nicholas Condy of the great hall c.1840.
(*Plymouth City Museum and Art Gallery, Mount Edgcumbe House Collection*)

Mount Edgcumbe – many have been drastically cut to fit their present positions – or, more intriguingly, perhaps they were bought second-hand in the eighteenth century in a deliberate attempt to create interiors that evoked the past.

Such a move would have been in line with the growing taste for the architecture and artefacts of the past, a taste which blended archaeological scholarship with the Romantic penchant for melancholy and melodrama described by Thomas Warton in his *Pleasure of Melancholy* (1745):

> O lead me, Queen Sublime, to solemn glooms
> Congenial with my soul; to cheerless shades,
> To ruin'd seats, to twilight cells and bowers.

It would, moreover, have been a taste that the family were well placed to satisfy without inconvenience: they could live in comfort at Mount Edgcumbe, reserving Cotehele as a refuge to be visited and enjoyed as the desire for 'solemn glooms' took them. (Richard Edgcumbe seems to have had a natural affinity with Warton and the Graveyard School. When his favourite dog died, he had the skeleton mounted in his garden house at Mount Edgcumbe, where he used to go and talk to it.)

By the first half of the nineteenth century, Cotehele had become famous among antiquarians and tourists who, fed on a diet of Scott and Byron, came to see its Tudor architecture and supposedly Tudor contents, and, of course, to revel in its Romantic links with Merry England. The Edgcumbes, however, rarely visited the house, and according to the 4th Earl's *Records of the Edgcumbe Family*, it was left in the care of a local farmer, 'under whose regime the arms in the hall are said to have received a coat of brown paint every seven years, and the pictures a wash of gin and water every spring and fall'. It wasn't until 1861, when the 3rd Earl's widow decided to make her home there, that the house began to enjoy something of a revival in its fortunes. The east range, which had contained a large butler's pantry, with cellars below and servants' accommodation above, was remodelled to form comfortable modern living quarters for the dowager Countess, although – as always with Cotehele – the alterations were made with remarkable tact and sympathy for the existing structure.

In fact, tact and sympathy are the keynotes of Cotehele's long history. The response of generations of Edgcumbes to their ancient home has been to respect its character; to work with, rather than against, the spirit of the place. Thus, in contrast to so many medieval country houses, where self-conscious eighteenth- and nineteenth-century attempts to create a Romantic antiquarianism have all but eclipsed that spirit, Tudor Cotehele has taken whatever fortune brought – the tapestries and furnishings, the various structural changes – and made them part of itself. Cotehele may not be quite the remarkable survival from olden times that Queen Charlotte and Horace Walpole thought it to be, but it is something more. It is a house that has survived five centuries of changing taste with its integrity intact.

In 1947, after the death of the 5th Earl of Mount Edgcumbe, Cotehele was accepted by the Treasury in lieu of death duties and transferred to the National Trust, the first historic house to come to the Trust through the National Land Fund. The principal contents were transferred through the same procedure in 1974, after the death of the 6th Earl.

Baddesley Clinton

WARWICKSHIRE

Baddesley Clinton, in the Warwickshire countryside 13 miles south-east of central Birmingham, was built or remodelled by the Brome family in the fifteenth century, on the site of a thirteenth-century moated farmstead. It was adapted over the next 400 years by members of the Ferrers family.

Baddesley Clinton can lay claim to a unique honour in the history of the English country house. On 8 January 1897 an illustrated article on the house appeared in the first issue of a new magazine (opposite a piece on 'H.R.H. The Princess of Wales's Pet Dogs'). After setting the scene with a colourful description of Warwickshire country houses in general – 'mailed knights have dwelt within their walls, fugitives

Baddesley Clinton. This photograph appeared in the first issue of *Country Life* in January 1897. (*Country Life*)

in troublous times have fled to their secret chambers, cavaliers have knocked at their oaken doors' – the author, John Leyland, finally came to Baddesley itself:

> About seven miles from Warwick ... all amid the silent woods, its grey walls and timber gables reflected in a lake-like moat, stands the old Hall of Baddesley Clinton. Its aspect carries you back hundreds of years. You will readily, if so disposed, conjure up an old-world history when you look at it, and if you have any antiquarian interest – and who has not at least a tinge of it? – you can easily forget for the time that you are living in the Nineteenth Century.

Not a particularly startling piece of prose, but its significance lies in the fact that the new magazine was Edward Hudson's *Country Life*; and the article marked the beginning of that journal's long-running series on country homes that has done so much to mould twentieth-century perceptions of the historic house.

'Badde's Ley', Badde's wood or clearing, dates back to before the Conquest. In 1066 its Saxon holder, Leuvinus, was unceremoniously replaced by the Norman knight Geoffrey de Wirce, who was granted the manor by William the Conqueror. Two hundred years later it was owned by Walter de Bisege, whose granddaughter married Sir Thomas de Clinton in 1290 – hence Baddesley Clinton. At the end of the thirteenth century the Forest of Arden was being settled, and a number of defensive ditches were dug in the area to protect the new farmsteads; it may be that the moat at Baddesley dates from this time, and that Sir Thomas was the first to construct a house on the site of the present building.

Certainly there was already a manor house there by the middle of the fifteenth century, when John Brome, who bought Baddesley in 1438, made a number of repairs. Estate accounts show that in the 1440s workmen were paid for tiling a new building at the end of the hall, for 'the nogging of the privy house', and for transporting a quantity of ashlar to the site from the quarry that Brome had opened up on the estate (primarily as a commercial operation supplying hearthstones and burial stones, rather than for his own purposes).

John Brome was a successful lawyer and entrepreneur. Besides his quarry, he also owned a tile kiln which he rented out to a tenant at half the value of the tiles produced. But the law was not held in particularly high regard in the middle of the fifteenth century, as Brome was to find out to his cost. The weakness of central government and the casual way in which great noblemen took the law into their own hands (already noted in connection with the crop of tower-houses built during the period (page 41)) affected all levels of society, and gave rise to a wave of violent resolutions to property disputes. In 1448, for example, Margaret Paston clearly anticipated an extrajudicial outcome to her husband's disagreement with Lord Moleyns over the ownership of the manor of Gresham outside Cromer in Norfolk: 'Right worshipful husband, I recommend me to you, and pray you to get some crossbows, and windlasses to bend them with ... and also I would you should get two or three short poleaxes to keep with doors.' She was right. The next year Moleyns' men dragged her from her chamber at Gresham and threw her out of the house.

A similar experience befell the Bromes. One Saturday night in June 1450 a gang of armed men broke into Bromes Place, their house in Warwick, 'and took away money, deeds and evidences' – which suggests another quarrel over ownership. They then went off to Baddesley:

> Where the wife of the same John Brome then lay in, and there laid the place about for to have broken in at the opening of the doors, and then went to the house of John Underwood, a tenant of the said John Brome, and the same John Underwood there beat and left as for dead.

The fact that the gang lay in ambush suggests that Baddesley was already fortified in some way by this time, although the present gatehouse is rather later.

John Brome seems to have emerged from this incident relatively unscathed. But he was less fortunate eighteen years later, when, on 9 November 1468, he was killed in the porch of the Whitefriars' Church in London by John Herthill, Steward to Warwick the Kingmaker, again in an argument over property. In 1471, and true to the spirit of his age, Brome's second son Nicholas killed his father's murderer at Longbridge, just south of Warwick.

Avenging his father's death was one thing, but murder seems to have been Nicholas's natural response to events which displeased him. Shortly after he inherited Baddesley Clinton on the death of his mother in 1483, he walked into the parlour there and found the parish priest chucking his wife under the chin. He killed him. Those with a vivid imagination can still see the bloodstain on the floor of the solar in the east range.

It is perhaps easier to understand Nicholas Brome's quick temper than it is to understand the building in which the bloody deed was committed. So much has been altered, dismantled and rebuilt over the centuries; the function, shape and often the decoration of almost every room has been modified by succeeding generations. To take just a few examples: the great hall chimneypiece, which, with its strapwork panels and heraldic shields, is one of the most important Elizabethan features in the house, was only moved there in 1742, perhaps from an earlier hall, perhaps from the great parlour. At about the same time, what is now the drawing room was fitted with earlier panelling, old armorial glass and a Jacobean chimneypiece, all moved from elsewhere in the house. A tower in the south-west angle is part fifteenth-century, part Georgian; the gatehouse was only crenellated in the early nineteenth century; and so on. In short, Baddesley's building history is more complicated than most, and parts of that history are still being unravelled – as the rather circumspect account that follows makes obvious.

On Nicholas Brome's death in 1517 the house passed to the Ferrers family, as a result of his daughter Constance's marriage to Sir Edward Ferrers. By this time, or soon after, the house consisted of three ranges grouped around a small courtyard and themselves encircled by the moat. The gatehouse range to the east and the west range opposite, both of which survive from Nicholas's time (although much altered), would have contained domestic offices and family lodgings, respectively. They were linked by a two-storey great hall which then stood where the opening in the courtyard now is, along the north side of the moat.

This arrangement was considerably modified by succeeding members of the Ferrers family, and in particular by Henry Ferrers (1549–1633). Henry altered the

The great hall. (*The National Trust*)

gatehouse range, constructing a spectacular room – perhaps a new great chamber, perhaps a withdrawing chamber or gallery to the solar next door – over the entrance itself. He also built a fourth range of rooms to the south, thus completely enclosing the courtyard. This included the room traditionally known as the great hall (a function that it must have assumed when the original hall to the north was dismantled). On the floor above there was another important lodging, now named after Henry Ferrers but once a chamber of state, and in the nineteenth century called the state bedroom. The bed itself is actually a nineteenth-century composite piece using largely seventeenth-century materials.

Henry Ferrers kept a close personal watch on the details of the work, as his diary shows – an entry for 2 March 1629 records the installation of the great carved heraldic chimneypiece in the new lodging:

> I went to the Radclifs [the joiners whom he employed] being at work in the great chamber who have finished and set up the chimneypiece ... which I like well but the unicorn is not set up for the crest, and is as I think made too big and the horn too big, and too upright, and the eyes ill set and sidelong.

Henry's keen eye for a well turned unicorn's horn stemmed, like the armorial glass in several of the windows at Baddesley and the shields on the hall chimneypiece, from his enthusiastic interest in history and genealogy. Known in the family as 'the Antiquary', he spent much of his life in historical research, relating to both national events – he planned, but never completed, a history of the kings and queens of England – and local affairs. William Dugdale of Blythe Hall in Warwickshire drew heavily on Ferrers' research for his famous work on the *Antiquities* of that county, published in 1656.

Like the rest of the Ferrers family, Henry was a devout Catholic, at a time when a series of repressive laws had culminated, in 1593, in an Act that barred Catholics from moving more than five miles from their home, and threatened with exile those who would not or could not pay heavy recusancy fines. Henry was circumspect enough to avoid serious persecution: like many Catholics at the time, he simply kept his head down and went about his normal business. But Baddesley Clinton itself was the scene of a great deal of clandestine activity. During the 1590s it was let to Anne Vaux and her sister Eleanor Brooksby, recusants who turned it into something of a meeting place for priests. Evidence of their operations remains in the form of three 'secret places', the most famous of which, a drain at the base of a converted privy shaft in the western range, sheltered nine or ten Jesuits, secular priests and laymen for four hours in October 1591, when the house was unexpectedly searched. Three of the men who survived that day – Father Garnet, Father Southwell and Father Oldcorne – were later martyred for their faith.

Over the years that followed, and in spite of the occasional good marriage – which precipitated frantic bouts of building and renovation – the Ferrers' Catholicism ensured that they rarely rose above the status of lesser, and often seriously impoverished, gentry. Even if they had the inclination to replace their ancient moated manor house with a more modern and convenient building, they simply didn't have the resources to make any sweeping changes. By the nineteenth century

A painting by Rebecca Dulcibella Orpen of the great hall in the 1870s, showing Marmion Ferrers, Lady Chatterton and Edward Heneage Dering. (*The National Trust*)

Baddesley had more or less assumed the shape that it has today. The medieval north range had been demolished, leaving the courtyard enclosed on three sides only; an old farmyard in front of the house had been cleared away and the present outbuildings put up; much of the external timber-framing had been replaced by brick; and most of the Elizabethan and Jacobean fittings had found their final resting places.

In the late 1860s the house was occupied by a charming, if somewhat earnest, group of artistic friends: Marmion Ferrers, who was the last Ferrers in the direct male line to live at the house; his wife Rebecca Dulcibella Orpen, an accomplished painter, whose work provides us with an evocative and romantic picture of Victorian Baddesley; Lady Chatterton, a romantic novelist; and her husband Edward Heneage Dering, who wrote rather dreadful didactic three-deckers on the moral supremacy of Catholicism. The complexities of their relationship were of Bloomsbury proportions. Lady Chatterton was Rebecca's aunt; Dering was an old friend of Marmion. And, if a 1923 article in *The Times* is to be believed, Dering was really in love with Rebecca but had married Lady Chatterton by accident, having asked her permission to court her niece and been so misunderstood that she had accepted his proposal herself. He was apparently too chivalrous to disillusion her. True or not, the year after Marmion's death in 1884 Rebecca and Dering were married, Lady Chatterton having died in 1876.

Baddesley Clinton's fame as what the *Country Life* article called 'a truly quaint and beautiful domestic survival of the English country life of the olden time' dates largely from the period after Dering's death in 1892, when Rebecca presided over the old house alone and visitors came to pay homage at a shrine to a long-lost culture. Given the time, and given the house, that is not so surprising. The time was just that point at the end of the nineteenth century when the country house was coming to represent that stability and continuity which many felt to be lacking in modern urban life. And the house possessed, and still possesses, all the qualities that could possibly be required of such a symbol. First, a tranquil moat on which, as John Leyland carefully pointed out, 'swans glide gracefully'. Second, an extraordinarily attractive blend of building materials – stone, brick and timber – which gives it that aura of a house that has adapted with ease, over a period of centuries, to changing needs. Add to this a comfortable, intimate scale – no wealthy, powerful courtier ever felt the need to turn it into an architectural expression of that wealth and power – and a lurid and romantic history in an age when even violence, murder and religious persecution became 'quaint' when viewed from a safe enough distance. As it slowly gives up its secrets, Baddesley still has much to tell us, both about life under the Bromes and the Ferrers and about changing attitudes towards the past.

After Rebecca Dering's death in 1923 Baddesley Clinton passed to her first husband's great-nephew. During the 1930s some of the contents were bought by Baron Ash of Packwood House (also in Warwickshire and also a property of the National Trust). Then in 1940 the house was sold to Thomas Walker, a relation of the Ferrers family. In 1980 his son, Thomas Ferrers-Walker, transferred it to the National Trust through National Land Fund procedures.

Chapter Three

Proud, Ambitious Heaps

1550-1630

Now, Penshurst, they that will proportion thee
With other edifices, when they see
Those proud, ambitious heaps, and nothing else,
May say, their lords have built, but thy lord dwells.

Ben Jonson, 'To Penshurst', 1616

A mistrust of modern architecture isn't confined to our own times. Ben Jonson's poem 'To Penshurst' praises the centuries-old home of the Sidney family, and places it in opposition to those 'proud, ambitious heaps' which were springing up all over Britain, symbols of a more ostentatious age.

In criticising the new architecture, Jonson was voicing concern over one of the most significant features of the period from 1550 to 1630: an acceleration into the shift away from the medieval emphasis on behaviour, in the form of hospitality and the keeping of state, towards the *trappings* of wealth as a manifestation of degree and social superiority. As the sixteenth century wore on, the country house continued to divest itself of its more obviously functional features. The characteristic defensive structure of the Middle Ages, with its inward-looking ranges of lodgings grouped around a courtyard, its communal lifestyle, and its emphasis on the role of the owner as father to an extended 'family', was gradually giving way to the architectural showplace.

The desire to advertise one's wealth and prestige has, of course, played its part in the creation of many a country house: the Elizabethans and Jacobeans weren't alone

Wollaton Hall, Nottinghamshire (1580–8), from a painting by Jan Siberechts.
(*Yale Center for British Art, Paul Mellon Collection*)

Buckland Abbey, Devon: one of a number of church properties that were converted to domestic use after the dissolution of the monasteries. Sir Richard Grenville's conversion of the abbey's crossing tower and transepts can clearly be seen in this view of the south front. (*NTPL/Martin Dohrn*)

John Chapman's stone table in the muniment room at Lacock Abbey, Wiltshire: one of the most sophisticated home-grown products of the Renaissance in sixteenth-century England. (*NTPL/Nick Carter*)

in erecting proud, ambitious heaps. But at few other points in English history was this motive such a major consideration in the design and furnishing of the aristocrat's home, as writers of the time made clear. In the 1586 edition of his *Description of England*, William Harrison noted that the houses of the nobility were 'so magnificent and stately [that] the basest house of a baron doth often match in our days with some honours of princes in old time'. And his observations on contemporary Continental building practice were just as relevant to his native country: 'Each one desireth to set his house aloft on the hill, to be seen afar off, and cast forth his beams of stately and curious workmanship into every quarter of the country.'

Like a child with a new toy, the Elizabethan and Jacobean country house builder delighted in 'stately and curious workmanship,' in the creation and interplay of new forms, new motifs, new plans. Building was a political act, and the corrupt courtier in Spenser's *Mother Hubberds Tale* (1590), who lined his own pockets from the public purse and 'lifted up his lofty towers thereby,/That they began to threat the neighbour sky', was not merely enjoying his ill-gotten gains: he was putting them to good use, employing them to confirm his new-found position in society.

Most of the main protagonists in this movement away from traditional values belonged to a new generation of career politicians who made their names – and their fortunes – at the Tudor court. For them, as for so many Tudor noblemen, Thomas Cromwell's drive to convert monastic lands into hard cash for the Crown in the 1530s presented a perfect opportunity to expand their estates, and to build. Large numbers of country houses whose names are still familiar to us today had their genesis in the dissolution of the monasteries. Sir John Cope acquired the priory lands at Canons Ashby in Northamptonshire in 1538; Newstead Abbey in Nottingham-shire – actually an Augustinian priory – was granted to Sir John Byron, ancestor of the poet, in 1539; the Carthusian monastery at Longleat in Wiltshire which Sir John Horsey bought from the Crown in 1539 was sold the next year to Sir John Thynne; Nostell Priory in Yorkshire was suppressed in 1540 and its lands and buildings given to one of Cromwell's henchmen, Thomas Leigh; Sir Richard Grenville bought the Cistercian Buckland Abbey in Devon in 1541; and William Herbert, later 1st Earl of Pembroke, was granted the Benedictine nunnery at Wilton in Wiltshire in 1544.

Some of those who bought Church estates from the Crown during the 1540s were minor gentry, and content to remain so. Others were something more – talented, unscrupulous, seeing in the dissolution a means of acquiring land (and its necessary adjunct, a country house) to further their ambitions, not always with total honesty. One such was William Sharington, who paid £783 for the convent and estate at Lacock in Wiltshire in 1539.

Sharington was a crook. He was made Vice-Treasurer of the Bristol Mint in 1546, and took advantage of his position to clip the coins and debase the coinage, in order to lend money to his friend, Lord Thomas Seymour, who was plotting against Edward VI and the Protector Somerset. However, the bonds of friendship loosened somewhat in 1549 when both Sharington and Seymour were arrested and accused of treason. Sharington promptly confessed his crimes, and put the blame firmly on Seymour, who was beheaded. The shady financier was pardoned; his confiscated estates were returned to him, on payment of an £8000 fine; and he was allowed to return to Lacock, dying in 1553.

What is interesting about William Sharington – apart from his colourful, though far from uncommon, approach to public affairs – is his handling of the conventual buildings at Lacock. With a curious blend of conservatism and modernity, he demolished the abbey church, retained most of the ground floor rooms in the adjoining cloisters more or less intact, and converted the upper levels into a series of galleries and chambers. Aside from the preservation of the medieval work, this sort of piecemeal conversion is not in itself particularly remarkable. Sir John Byron was doing much the same at Newstead (although he didn't bother to demolish the church), as was Sir John Thynne at Longleat. No doubt the arrangement seemed natural to builders who had grown up with the medieval disposition of lodgings and offices around a central courtyard.

But some of the ornament at Lacock, the work of a mason in the King's Works called John Chapman, shows that a new sophistication was creeping into English country house design. In particular, the delicately carved chimneypiece in the Stone Gallery (converted from the nuns' dormitory), and the octagonal tower which Sharington added to the south-east corner of the sacristy to serve as muniment room and belvedere, both display a knowledge of classical Renaissance ideas which was rare at that time. John Chapman's beautiful stone table in the centre of the muniment room, its octagonal marble top supported by four satyrs holding bunches of fruit above their heads, ranks as one of the most sophisticated home-grown products of the Renaissance in sixteenth-century England.

During the following decades Renaissance motifs continued to filter into the mainstream of country house architecture, usually via France and Flanders. Native craftsmen tended at first to use them more clumsily than Chapman had done at Lacock, often simply applying scrolls, pilasters and other decorative details to what were still basically Gothic forms.

However, a number of houses built during the 1560s and 1570s show an increasingly confident knowledge of classicism. The Strand façade of Somerset House in London, built for the Protector Somerset between 1547 and 1552, was one of the first attempts at a uniformly classical treatment, and influenced several members of the group of Protestant courtiers in his circle, including William Cecil and John Thynne. Sir Thomas Lucy's Charlecote Park in Warwickshire has an imposing two-storeyed porch with pairs of Ionic pilasters and coupled Corinthian columns, which dates from about 1572. And at Longleat, Thynne – a good friend of Sharington's – finally wearied of living in a converted church, and between 1572 and 1580 created one of the most spectacular Renaissance houses in England. By 1586, William Harrison could report: 'if ever curious building did flourish in England, it is in these our years wherein our workmen excel and are in manner comparable with old Vitruvius, Leo Baptista [Alberti], and Serlio'.

It is with Longleat that the distinctive features of the Elizabethan country house begin to emerge, as the courtyard house of the Middle Ages gives way to a more secure, extrovert type of architecture, tall, compact, heavily fenestrated, and above all balanced and symmetrical. With its regular façades, pilasters and antique busts, it remains (externally at least – not a single Elizabethan interior outlived Jeffry Wyatville's remodelling in 1806–13) one of the most perfect examples of sixteenth-century Renaissance building to survive in England.

But this flowering of Renaissance ideals proved to be something of a false start. Already by the time of Longleat's completion in 1580, the pioneers of Elizabethan architecture were moving on to a peculiarly English synthesis of Italian, Flemish and Gothic styles. Robert Smythson, Thynne's master-mason at Longleat, led the way in his designs for Wollaton Hall in Nottinghamshire, providing his patron Sir Francis Willoughby with a flamboyant *tour de force* of a house, a fantastic sculpture carved in golden Ancaster stone which repudiates all thoughts of classical restraint and decorum.

The history of the Elizabethan country house is liberally sprinkled with picturesque characters. Francis Willoughby is no exception. Yet another connection of the Seymours, he was a wealthy landowner from an established family who responded with zest to the entrepreneurial spirit of the age, an industrialist who mined coal on a colossal scale, with interests in ironworks, shipping and glass. He was also a devout, almost fanatical, Protestant; he wrote sermons for his chaplain to preach to him, and among his personal collection of books is a *Life* of St Thomas

Becket in which every reference to the Pope has been carefully obliterated. His mistrust of his friends and family verged on paranoia, and his first wife left him after ten years of marriage, tired of his persecution. However, his paranoia seems to have had some roots in reality where his second wife was concerned: she was described by a contemporary as a 'whore . . .[who] stripped him both of goods and lands and left him nothing but what hangs upon his back'.

The house that Smythson created for Willoughby was no less picturesque than the man. The plan and much of the ornament for Wollaton Hall drew on various Continental pattern books – Sebastiano Serlio's *L'Architettura* and works by Vredeman de Vries and Jacques Androuet du Cerceau in particular – but everything was tempered with such a strong dash of English Gothic that, seen from a distance, Wollaton resembles nothing so much as a fairytale castle, with towers at each corner and a great keep rising from behind high curtain walls. But the walls are made of glass. The towers are capped not with crenellations and embrasures, but with strapwork cresting, obelisks and clusters of chimneys. And the 'keep' is in fact a massive central hall, lit by a clerestory and topped by a tourelled prospect room which gives magnificent views over the surrounding countryside, a belvedere rather than a watchtower, a lantern sending out its beams of stately and curious workmanship across the county.

For Wollaton was clearly intended to impress: its height, its excess of Flemish ornament, its hilltop situation, its sheer theatricality, all command attention. The four symmetrical façades and balanced plan – a central great hall, flanked by twin great chambers at first floor level – owe a great deal to the Renaissance. But in its conception the house owes even more to the mock-medieval pageantry of the annual Accession Day tournaments, those extravagant displays of loyalty to the Virgin Queen at which courtiers in elaborate armour jousted or stormed pasteboard castles to rescue damsels in distress. In many respects Wollaton is a pasteboard castle made real, a homage to the Elizabethan penchant for mythologising the past.

Later houses that have either been attributed to Robert Smythson or are clearly the work of his followers tend to be rather more austere than Wollaton.[1] (An exception is his son John's magnificently eccentric designs for the Little Castle at Bolsover in Derbyshire (*c*.1612–*c*.1621), which suggest that a fondness for novelty and whimsicality ran in the family. With its battlements and cross-loops the Castle is more of an architectural conceit than a house, a piece of Spenserian theatre which recalls the fictional days of chivalry even more deliberately and self-consciously than Wollaton.) Hardwick Hall, for example (1590–7; see page 80), is tall and compact like Wollaton, but possesses none of its flamboyance. Hardwick holds itself in, hiding behind its expanses of glass, whereas Wollaton lets itself go in a riot of ornament.

---

[1] After completing Wollaton in 1588, Smythson seems to have given up his career as a mason; instead, he stayed on as a sort of land agent and business manager with the Willoughby family until his death in 1614. There is, however, some evidence to suggest that during the 1590s and early 1600s he provided drawings for a number of houses, of which Hardwick Hall in Derbyshire is the most important. His monument in Wollaton church describes him as 'architect and surveyor unto the most worthy house of Wollaton and diverse others of great account'.

No less important than the group of late Elizabethan and Jacobean houses designed by the Smythsons and their imitators – a group which includes Pontefract Hall in Yorkshire (1591), Doddington Hall, Lincolnshire (1593–1600), Gawthorpe in Lancashire (1600–5) and Fountains Hall, Yorkshire (c.1611) – were the great prodigy houses of the period. William Cecil's houses at Burghley in Northampton-shire and Theobalds in Hertfordshire, and Sir Christopher Hatton's vast palace at Holdenby in Northamptonshire, were, like their Jacobean progeny, Hatfield in Hertfordshire and Audley End in Essex, much more than private country houses. They were built with the intention of honouring and entertaining the monarch, as Hatton made plain in a letter to Sir Thomas Heneage in September 1580, in which he wrote that he had not yet visited his new house, and meant to leave this 'shrine, I mean Holdenby, still unseen until that holy saint may sit in it, to whom it is dedicated'.

Courtiers like Cecil and Hatton must have viewed a visit from Elizabeth with a mixture of fear and anticipation: anticipation, because royal favour could greatly increase one's standing and, in consequence, one's income; and fear, because the upheaval involved in such a visit could be formidable. Elizabeth went to Theobalds thirteen times, 'lying there at his lordship's charge sometimes three weeks or a month, or six weeks together'. Each visit was said to cost Cecil two or three thousand pounds. He had to move his table from the great chamber; his steward gave up his lodgings to the royal plate; and his servants ate in the joiners' workshop and slept on pallets in a converted storehouse.

It was worth going to any lengths, though, to remain in the Queen's good favours – as the example of Sir Thomas Gresham shows. Gresham hosted a royal visit at Osterley Park (Middlesex) in the 1570s, during which Elizabeth happened to mention that his new house might be improved if the large central courtyard were divided in two: 'What doth Sir Thomas, but in the night time sends for workmen to London (money commands all things), who so speedily and silently apply their business, that the next morning discovered the court double, which the night had left single before.' The Queen was said to be delighted with this display of loyalty, although members of her court used it as an excuse for some rather laboured wit: referring to family problems that Gresham was having, they suggested that it was easier to divide a house than to unite it.

The great builders of the period all seem to have discussed their projects among themselves. They examined each other's drawings and plans, packed off their masons and surveyors to study each other's houses, and offered and received advice and criticism. Bess of Hardwick visited both Wollaton and Holdenby in the summer of 1592 while her new house was in the process of being built, presumably on the lookout for ideas. And Christopher Hatton invited Cecil's criticisms of his new building, since 'as the same is done hitherto in direct observation of your house and plots of Theobalds, so I earnestly pray your Lordship that by your good corrections at this time, it may appear as like to the same as it hath ever been meant to be'. The Lord Treasurer went to Holdenby in 1579, and was duly impressed: 'I found a great magnificence in the front or front pieces of the house, and so every part answerable to the other, to allure liking. I found no one thing of greater grace than your stately ascent from your hall to your great chamber, and your chamber answerable with largeness and lightsomeness.'

Cecil's remarks neatly encapsulate some of the major differences between the late Elizabethan and Jacobean country house and its medieval predecessor. By the second half of the sixteenth century every turret and window and decorative detail had to have its companion, so that each façade was composed as a harmonious grouping of elements within the whole, echoing the Roman architect Vitruvius' statement that 'since nature has designed the human body so that its members are duly proportioned to the frame as a whole, it appears that the ancients had good reason for their rule, that in perfect buildings the different members must be in exact symmetrical relations to the whole general scheme'. Symmetry was an expression of the divinely ordained order of things, and it was thought fitting that the proportions of a building should strive to mirror that order.

While there was much less emphasis on internal symmetry, sixteenth-century planning also differed substantially from that of earlier periods, as we noted in the introduction to Chapter 2. With very few exceptions (Wollaton and Hardwick among them), the great hall was still placed at right angles to the main axis of the house and entered through screens from a cross-passage at its lower end. But the fact that the owner held state in his great chamber on the floor above the hall had two consequences. The stairs which led from the hall to the great chamber now formed part of Cecil's 'stately ascent' along which important visitors had to travel in order to be received by the lord. As a result, Elizabethan and Jacobean staircases were wider, more richly decorated and generally more impressive than their predecessors. And a growing reluctance to eat in state, except on special occasions, led to the lord and his family moving into separate lodgings altogether, leaving a set of state lodgings – great chamber, withdrawing chamber and best bedchamber, often with a gallery attached – whose primary function was to act as a expression of an owner's wealth and status, a public focus for his pride and ambition.

In 1613, the year after Cecil's son Robert had put the finishing touches to Hatfield House, the young Inigo Jones was touring Italy in the service of the Earl of Arundel. There he carefully compared his copy of Palladio's *Quattro Libri dell'Architettura* with its author's villas and palaces, developing the reasoned and carefully integrated architectural harmonies which, when they found their expression in buildings like the Queen's House, Greenwich, and the Banqueting House at Whitehall, would eventually render the less controlled extravagances of the Elizabethan and Jacobean country house obsolete. In any case, by the 1620s a courtier's pride and ambition were finding other, more subtle, outlets than the building of the biggest, grandest and most heavily decorated heap that he could possibly afford.

But for all their brashness and naïveté – or perhaps because of it – there is something endearing about Wollaton and Burghley and their like, something captivating about their bewildering silhouettes, their 'stately and curious workmanship'. The period 1550–1630 was in many ways a glorious coming-of-age for English architecture, an era of passion and imagination that were to be curbed and mastered by the architects and designers who came after. And the man who is master of his passions is reason's slave.

DE' CINQVE ORDINI, CHE VSARONO
gli Antichi.   Cap. XII.

CINQVE sono gl'ordini de' quali gl'Antichi si seruirono, cioè il Toscano, Dorico, Ionico, Corinthio, e Composito. Questi si deono così nelle fabriche disporre, ch'el più sodo sia nella parte più bassa: perche sarà molto più atto a sostentare il carico, e la fabrica venirà ad hauere basamento più fermo: onde sempre il Dorico si porrà sotto il Ionico: il Ionico sotto il Corinthio; & il Corinthio sotto il Cóposito. Il Toscano, come rozo, si vsa rare volte sopra terra, fuor che nelle fabriche di vn'ordine solo, come coperti di Villa: ouero nelle machine grandissime, come Anfitheatri, e simili: lequali hauendo più ordini questo si ponerà in luogo del Dorico sotto il Ionico. Et se si vorrà tralasciare vno di questi, come sarebbe, porre il Corinthio immediate sopra il Dorico; ciò si potrà fare, pur che sempre il più sodo sia nella parte più bassa per le ragioni già dette. Io porrò partitamente di ciascuno di questi le misure, non tanto secondo che n'insegna Vitruuio, quanto secondo c'hò auuertito ne gli edificij Antichi: ma prima dirò quelle cose, che in vniuersale a tutti si conuengono.

DELLA GONFIEZZA, E DIMINVTIONE DELLE
Colonne, de gli Intercolunnij, e de' Pilastri.   Cap. XIII.

LE Colonne di ciascun'ordine si deono formare in modo che la parte di sopra sia più sottile di quella di sotto, e nel mezo habbiano alquanto di gonfiezza. Nelle diminutioni s'osserua, che quanto le colonne sono più lunghe, tanto meno diminuiscono, essendo che l'altezza da se faccia l'effetto del diminuire per la distanza: però se la colonna sarà alta fino a quindeci piedi; si diuiderà la grossezza da basso in sei parti e meza, e di cinque e meza si farà la grossezza di sopra: Se da xv. a xx. si diuiderà la grossezza di sotto in parte vij. e vj. e mezo sarà la grossezza di sopra: similmente di quelle, che saranno da xx. fino a trenta; si diuiderà la grossezza di sotto in parti viij. e vij. di quelle sarà la grossezza di sopra: e così quelle colóne, che saranno più alte; si diminuiranno secondo il detto modo per la ratta parte, come c'insegna Vitruuio al cap.ij. del iij. lib. Ma come debba farsi la gófiezza nel mezo, non habbiamo da lui altro che vna semplice promessa: e perciò diuersi hanno di ciò diuersamente detto. Io sono solito far la sacoma di detta gonfiezza in questo modo. Partisco il fusto della colóna in tre parti eguali, e lascio la terza parte da basso diritta a piombo, a canto l'estremità della quale pongo in taglio vna riga sottile alquanto, longa come la colóna, ò poco più, e muouo quella parte, che auanza dal terzo in suso, e la storco fin che'l capo suo giunga al púto della diminutione di sopra della colonna sotto il collarino; e secondo quella curuatura segno: e così mi viene la colonna alquanto gonfia nel mezo, e si rastrema molto garbatamente. E benche io non mi habbia potuto imaginar altro modo più breue, & espedito di questo, che riesca meglio; mi son nondimeno maggiormente confermato in questa mia inuentione, poi che tanto è piaciuta a messer Pietro Cattaneo, hauendogliela io detta, che l'ha posta in vna sua opera di Architettura, con la quale ha non poco illustrato questa professione.

   A, B, La terza parte della colonna, che si lascia diritta a piombo.

   B, C, I due terzi che si vanno diminuendo.

   C, Il punto della diminutione sotto il collarino.

Gli intercolunnij, cioè spatij fra le colonne si possono fare di vn diametro e mezo di colonna, e si toglie il diametro ne la parte più bassa della colonna; di due diametri; di due, & vn quarto; di tre, & ancho maggiori:

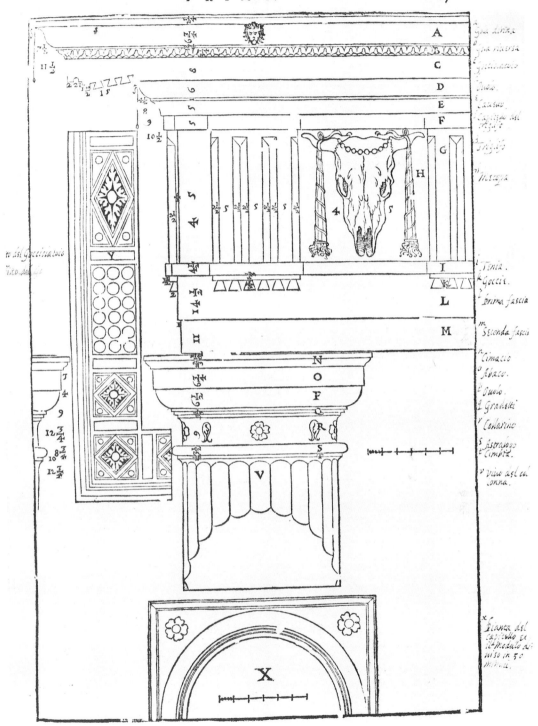

Pages from the 9th Earl of Northumberland's copy of Palladio's *Quattro Libri dell'Architettura*, with annotations in the Earl's own hand. Many Elizabethan and Jacobean courtiers took an active interest in architectural matters. (*The Lord Egremont*)

Little Moreton Hall

CHESHIRE

Little Moreton Hall lies 4 miles south-west of Congleton. Begun in the mid-fifteenth century for Sir Richard de Moreton, it was gradually extended by the Moreton family over the next 150 years.

'Times change, and we change with them,' said William Harrison, in his *Description of England*. And it is perhaps as well for us to remember that many country houses have been just as subject to changing fortunes, changing patterns of social behaviour, changing ideas of convenience and propriety, as their inhabitants. Over the years, good marriages and bad offspring, driving ambition and the need for modern comforts, even – often – a simple, if not entirely laudable desire to keep up with the neighbours, have meant that buildings that are protected today with all the reverence of shrines were arbitrarily knocked about, extended and altered, refurbished and remodelled. To their owners, they were not monuments. They were homes.

Quite apart from its role in the public consciousness as one of the most famous timber-framed buildings in England – its windows staring out blindly from innumerable calendars and jigsaws and chocolate boxes – Little Moreton Hall in Cheshire is also a remarkably coherent example of a series of architectural responses to changing circumstances. The 150 years during which it grew were years of innovation and reform; a period of transition between the communal lifestyle of the Middle Ages and the conspicuous displays of wealth exhibited by the late Elizabethans. Little Moreton made that transition.

The oldest parts of the house – the great hall and those chambers immediately to the east of it – were built around 1450 by Richard de Moreton, whose family had been landowners in the area since at least the early thirteenth century. The craftsmen responsible for the work are unknown, but are quite likely to have been local carpenters, who cut and fitted the sections of framing in their own yards before dismantling them and having them taken by cart to the site, where they would be re-assembled. In the sixteenth-century chapel it is still possible to see the marks made by the carpenters on several timbers to facilitate this re-assembly process.

As originally built, the east wing housed domestic offices. There must also have been additional lodgings elsewhere on the site, including Richard's own solar or great chamber, and it is possible that these may have been situated in a corresponding wing at the other end of the hall. However, if this was the case, that west range was evidently pulled down about thirty years later, in 1480, when Richard's grandson William built a new wing in its place and reversed the arrangement of rooms so that the kitchens and other service rooms occupied this new west wing, with lodgings to the east. At the same time William created a projecting porch giving access into the courtyard and leading to a cross-passage opening into the hall, with a gallery over it at first-floor level. A wooden screen would have concealed the doorways through to the service rooms and protected the occupants of

Little Moreton Hall, Cheshire. (*NTPL/Mike Williams*)

the hall from draughts. The gallery was closed in with a partition when an extra floor (since removed) was inserted in the hall in the sixteenth century, and the screen has disappeared, perhaps because it was not fixed as was usual in medieval houses, but free-standing and movable, like the ornate example that survives at Rufford Old Hall.

However, it is still possible to imagine William Moreton and his household, or 'family' as he would have called them, on important occasions eating in the great hall in the late fifteenth century. The maintenance of the old hierarchical way of life may well have been particularly important to William – one of the few facts that we have about him is that in 1513 he quarrelled with a neighbour 'concerning which of them should sit highest in church and foremost go in procession'. But already by the time he remodelled Little Moreton, the practice of communal eating in the hall was on the wane, and he would have been more likely to be served in his great chamber, which may have been on the first floor of the east wing of the house.

However, the present arrangement and decoration of the private apartments in the east wing date mainly from the next major alterations to be made to Little Moreton as a result of changing fashions and the pursuit of increased comfort. Those alterations, which took place during the second half of the sixteenth century in the time of William's son, William II, and grandson John, are threefold: the addition of two great bay windows, to the hall itself and to a withdrawing chamber in the east range; the extension of that east range southwards, to provide additional accommodation and a chapel; and the decoration of several of the interiors, plus the creation (or replacement) of a south range, with a long gallery over it.

The inscription recording that William Moreton made these bay windows in 1559, and that his carpenter was Richard Dale. (*NTPL/John Bethell*)

With the two bay windows, we finally have the name of one of the craftsmen responsible for the splendours of Little Moreton. William's inscription on the windows, which dates them to 1559, reads 'God is Al in Al Thing: This windous Whire made by William Moreton in the yeare of our Lorde M.D.LIX'; while underneath is a second inscription: 'Richard Dale Carpeder made thies windous by the grac of God'. Little else is known of Richard Dale, but it is probable that he and his son, who also worked in the county in the early seventeenth century, completed most of the Elizabethan alterations at Little Moreton. Certainly in his will of 1563, William II asked that the new works at the Hall should be completed 'according to the device thereof devised betwixt me and Richard Dale the head wright and workman of the same frame'.

The sixteenth-century alterations and additions to the house show how the emphasis had shifted since Sir Richard de Moreton's time from the great hall as a centre of activities towards a more materialistic concentration on the display of wealth. To be sure, the hall was still important, as the addition of the bay window demonstrates; but its glittering and extremely expensive panes of glass, like those of its companion in the withdrawing chamber, do more than provide a brightly lit sitting area for William and his family. They proclaim its owner's ability and readiness to pay for such luxuries. Function is subordinated to show.

It is not only the architecture of the Elizabethan additions to Little Moreton – the fenestration, the extra accommodation, the long gallery for promenading and

Destiny holding a sphere and dividers, an allegorical device in the long gallery, adapted from Robert Recorde's *The Castle of Knowledge* (1556). (*NTPL/Jeremy Whitaker*)

exercising (an early seventeenth-century tennis ball was found behind one of the panels) – that expresses both a more leisured lifestyle and an emphasis on externals as a social indicator: the increased sophistication of the interior decoration tells the same story. Open hearths and braziers give way to elaborately carved chimney-pieces inset with heraldic panels. Panes of glass showing emblems and rebuses, including the wolf's-head crest of the Moretons and a pun on the name – a gaping wolf's maw above a barrel, or tun – figure in several of the windows. And the warm panelling in the withdrawing chamber and the long gallery have their counterpart in the beautiful (and, in 1979, beautifully restored) walls of the parlour in the east wing, painted to represent panels, and with a heavily didactic frieze in which illustrations from the Apocryphal story of Susanna and the Elders alternate with black-letter 'captions'. In common with earlier commentators, the Elizabethans saw the story as a simple allegory of the triumph of chastity over temptation, although no doubt it also held other connotations for them: there is a thoroughly Protestant emphasis on the importance of individual conscience, while it is tempting to see Susanna as a metaphor for the Virgin Queen herself.

The Elizabethan love of allegorical devices can be seen elsewhere in the house, notably in the long gallery, where painted plaster figures at either end represent Destiny and Fortune. Almost certainly taken from the frontispiece to the 1556 edition of the mathematician Robert Recorde's work on the sphere, *The Castle of Knowledge*, they, like the story of Susanna and the Elders, have been used not only as decoration but as statements of the Moretons' views on life in general. Destiny, who holds a sphere and a pair of dividers, is accompanied by a text adapted from Recorde, which reads, 'The Speare [sphere] of Destinye whose Rule is Knowledge'; while blindfolded Fortune's motto is 'The Wheels of Fortune whose Rule is Ignorance'. This early version of the Protestant ethic would have been clear to the Moretons' contemporaries – life is what you make it, and individual advancement comes from individual effort.

The long gallery was almost the last major addition to Little Moreton. Structural evidence suggests that the south range of which it forms a part was built by Dale in the 1560s. It contained its own garderobes and – after the addition of a domestic block in the early seventeenth century – its own kitchen and servant quarters, and was probably intended as accommodation either for guests or for another member of the family. But the gallery itself, perched up on the second floor, seems to have been added some years later as an afterthought. At a time when anyone who was anyone had to have a long gallery, the Moretons clearly didn't want to be left out.

Fortunately for posterity, the Moretons' programme of almost continuous modernisation petered out after 1600. Sash-windows were inserted in the parlour at some stage during the eighteenth century, when coal-burning fireplaces were also installed in that room and in the withdrawing chamber. But although the Hall, with its distinctive ornamental timbers and its lanterns of patterned glazing, became more and more famous, a place of pilgrimage for artists, antiquarians and tourists from all over the country, the Georgian Moretons spent little time in Cheshire, preferring to live in the south of England and either letting Little Moreton or leaving it in the hands of estate managers. No doubt they, like many of their contemporaries, thought of it as a picturesque, romantic monument, but hardly a suitable country seat. By 1806, when John Sell Cotman made some drawings of the house for John Britton's *Architectural Antiquities of Great Britain*, there were chickens scratching around in the great hall, and forty years later many of the main rooms were being used for storage. (The chapel, for example, had become a coal cellar.)

When Elizabeth, the last of the Moretons, inherited the Cheshire estate from her sister in 1892, she did what she could to preserve the house, which had by now been neglected for more than a century. According to her cousin Charles Abraham, Bishop of Derby, she 'lavished ... far more than all the income on its stability and maintenance, rescued, visited and loved every corner', before leaving the house to him in 1912. He continued the preservation work that she had begun, as well as opening Little Moreton to the public at 6d a time ('teas provided'). In 1938 he and his son handed over the Hall to the National Trust.

Hardwick Hall

DERBYSHIRE

Hardwick Hall, $9\frac{1}{2}$ miles south-east of Chesterfield, was built for Elizabeth Talbot, Dowager Countess of Shrewsbury, between 1590 and 1597, to designs by Robert Smythson.

Elizabeth Hardwick, Countess of Shrewsbury. This portrait, hanging in the long gallery at Hardwick, was painted in the 1590s, during the years of her final widowhood and the building of the house. (*NTPL/John Bethell*)

For the motorist unfamiliar with that stretch of the M1 which runs through the industrial landscape between Derby and Chesterfield, the sight of Hardwick Hall comes as a delightful surprise. The tall house perches precariously on a wooded hilltop, looking down arrogantly at the constant stream of traffic passing by in the valley below. Its vast expanses of glass glitter in the sun, and ES monograms crowning each of its six towers commemorate its builder: Elizabeth Talbot, Countess of Shrewsbury, better known to posterity as Bess of Hardwick.

Bess's story is well known: Horace Walpole's summary – 'four times the nuptial bed she warmed,/And every time so well performed,/That when death spoiled each husband's billing,/He left the widow every shilling' – is true to the spirit, if not the letter, of that formidable lady's rise to power. The daughter of a Derbyshire gentry family, born in 1527, she did indeed warm four nuptial beds. Each bed was more richly appointed, each husband of a higher social standing than the last, and while those husbands may not have left her *every* shilling, her share of their considerable estates combined with good advice and astute business management to turn Bess into the richest woman in northern England.

When one considers that successful marriages were the key to her wealth, it is ironic that Hardwick was the indirect consequence of a failed marriage – her fourth and last, to George Talbot, Earl of Shrewsbury. In 1583, after years of quarrelling, the couple parted, and in spite of attempts at reconciliation their relationship deteriorated to the point where Shrewsbury's agents were riding 'up and down the country ... having daggers, guns and appointed in warlike sort', and terrorising Bess's tenants into paying their rents directly to him. Since Shrewsbury believed that Chatsworth in Derbyshire, where Bess had devoted nearly half of her life to creating a massive mansion as the focus for her dynastic ambitions, belonged to him under the terms of their marriage settlement, he made quite sure that those same agents made life at the house impossible for his wife and her two youngest sons by a previous marriage, William and Charles Cavendish. On top of this, her eldest son, Henry Cavendish, had taken his stepfather's side – and Chatsworth, into which Bess had poured so much of her own and her husbands' money, was entailed on Henry.

In July 1584 Bess decided to move back to Hardwick, where she had been born some fifty-seven years before. The family home, which she had bought the previous summer, had fallen into decay during the occupancy of her late and improvident brother James. She immediately ordered improvements, and then, as the breach with Shrewsbury and Henry widened, she began in earnest to turn Hardwick into a country house fit to be the residence of her second son William, who became her designated heir and on whom most of her hopes now rested.

But the remodelled old Hall can't have given Bess much pleasure. The alterations were hurried and inconvenient, so that the house grew in almost medieval fashion, with haphazard additions to either side of a transverse great hall (probably the legacy of James Hardwick's time). Parts of the exterior were built in broached ashlar, while others were rough-cast. Each wing contained a set of state apartments – one to the west of the hall for William Cavendish and his family, the other to the east (which stood at a 15 degree angle to the main block) for Bess – but the Countess's withdrawing room was on the cold north side of the house, with her bedchamber awkwardly placed on the floor below. William fared even worse. His great chamber had no supporting suite of bedchamber and withdrawing chamber; his private rooms were placed directly over the kitchen, and were thus subject to all the noise and smells which such a situation entailed; and the stone stairs which led up to his apartment took the visitor straight past the kitchen servery.

At some point in 1590, with the Hall far from finished, Bess evidently decided that no amount of tinkering could transform her birthplace into the sort of residence that was both convenient to live in and a suitable expression of her wealth and status. There was nothing for it but to start again.

The site chosen for this second Hardwick Hall was just a few hundred yards from the first. To draw up the plans, Bess almost certainly consulted Robert Smythson, who already had a considerable reputation in the Elizabethan building world, and many of whose previous clients were connected with the Countess in some way. As already noted, he had worked as master-mason at Longleat for Sir John Thynne, whom Bess knew well enough to ask for the loan of 'your plasterer that flowereth the hall' when she was building Chatsworth in 1560 (and who in 1566 had been mooted as a possible fourth husband). Sir Francis Willoughby (for whom Smythson created Wollaton Hall in the 1580s) was a friend and business colleague of Bess's. And Smythson had also been employed by the Earl of Shrewsbury – and possibly Bess herself – designing Worksop Manor in Nottinghamshire some time in the early 1580s. At the new Hardwick, his role was probably to provide plans and elevations. In line with usual Elizabethan practice, the task of realising – and as the occasion demanded, modifying – those drawings went to Bess's Flemish overseer of works, John Balechouse.

From late in 1590, when the foundations of the second Hall were dug, Hardwick must have swarmed with activity as the old Hall was completed and the new building rose up close by. Ponies hauled their heavy panniers of stone up the hill from quarries on the estate; wagons pulled by teams of oxen dragged heavy timbers nine miles from sawpits at Crich; lead for the roofs and pipework came in from William Cavendish's workings at Bonsall, Aldwark and Winster, fourteen miles away; and iron and glass were sent from Bess's own furnaces at Wingfield. The temporary wooden lodgings put up by the craftsmen leaned against the new walls; scaffolding, made of wooden poles and woven hurdles, encased each new stage of the building; and smoke from the nearby lime kilns mixed with the smell of sweat and the shouts of workmen.

Throughout the 1590s Bess of Hardwick progressed between the old Hall, London, and her two other Derbyshire houses, Wingfield and Chatsworth, her marital difficulties having been largely resolved in November 1590 – a few weeks after building work on the second Hall had begun – by the timely death of her husband. Finally on Tuesday, 4 October 1597, with music playing, the Dowager Countess of Shrewsbury moved into her new home.

That home was – and is still – a masterpiece of design and planning, the crowning

'Hardwick Hall, more glass than wall'. (*NTPL/Mike Williams*)

achievement of Bess's building career. Its simple, compact form, which looks out proudly over the Derbyshire hills, exploits to the full the contemporary desire for harmony and balance; while its uncomplicated composition – six towers projecting at regular intervals from a rectangular main block, and rising above the roof-line – presents a constantly shifting silhouette, an architectural conceit of the sort so dear to the hearts of the Elizabethan intelligentsia.

At the same time the exterior represents a move away from the self-conscious Renaissance detail of Longleat, the theatrical exuberance of Wollaton. For Hardwick is restrained, almost puritanical, stripped of extraneous ornament save for the Tuscan colonnades which run along the entrance and garden fronts, the classical consoles supporting the windows, and the cresting and balustrading. The house relies almost entirely on its fenestration to express both the wealth of its owner and the relative importance of the rooms within it.

The domestic offices, most of which lie on the ground floor, are lit by relatively low, two-light windows. On the first floor, where most of the family living accommodation was situated, the ceilings are a little higher, the windows deeper. And on the second storey the windows are massive, four lights deep. Finally, the towers themselves, increased in height by John Balechouse during the course of building, combine with the gradually elongating windows to create a house which seems to reach for the sky, drawing the viewer's eye upward to the imperious ES cresting which surmounts the towers – the triumph of a local girl who had made good in a spectacular way.

Internally, one of the most intriguing features of the layout is the great hall. In contrast to the accepted plan, it runs at right angles to the main axis of the house, cutting it in two at ground- and first-floor levels – a feature which may have been borrowed from the old Hall, but one with which Smythson was in any case already familiar through reading the works of du Cerceau and Palladio. As we noted in Chapter 2, the hall served a dual function, as imposing entrance to the house, and dining room for the lower servants. So, in 1601, when an inventory of the contents of Hardwick was drawn up, its hall contained three long tables and six benches, together with some candlesticks and wall sconces. But, as befits an entrance hall, it was – and still is – dominated by another declaration of ownership, this one in the form of a great plasterwork overmantel of the Hardwick family crest, two stags wearing collars of eglantine supporting Bess's coat of arms and coronet.

To the left of the hall lay the kitchens, scullery and larders, while the rooms to the right consisted of the pantry, nurseries (presumably for William Cavendish's children) and an assortment of unspecified 'chambers'. On the first floor were Bess's own suite of rooms – withdrawing chamber, bedchamber and closet – linked by a gallery passage over the hall to a low great chamber where she probably dined in the summer, and a little dining room for winter use.

In 1601 Bess's bedchamber contained a bed, hung with 'three curtains of scarlet striped down with silver lace and with silver and red silk button and loops', and equipped with a mountain of woollen blankets and sheets to keep out the cold; an assortment of chairs and stools; and a bewildering array of coffers, chests and desks – twenty-five in all – which presumably contained documents and valuables. Her

The great staircase and half landing, the final stage in the processional route from hall and kitchen to the High Great Chamber.
(*The National Trust*)

withdrawing room was a similar confusion of chests, chairs, benches and cushions, and, as was the case throughout the house, colour was provided by a distinctly uncoordinated collection of textiles. There were elaborate Flemish wallhangings; cushions of crimson velvet and red damask, with delicately embroidered covers in russets and blues; a violet fire-screen fringed with black lace; and chairs upholstered in gilded black leather or cloth of gold with red and gold silk fringe.

But if Bess's living quarters were something of a jumble, they were at least meant to be private – or as private as the bedroom and sitting room of an Elizabethan aristocrat could be. (Her maid, for example, slept on a mattress by her mistress's door.) The public face of Hardwick, with the exception of the entrance hall, was on the second floor, and there Bess's craftsmen took pains to ensure that the decoration was on a scale and of a quality that was bound to impress the distinguished visitor.

The by now mandatory arrangement of state rooms – great chamber, withdrawing chamber and bedchamber, together with an adjacent long gallery – are all placed up on this second storey. There were several distinct advantages to such an arrangement: the whole floor could be sealed off when not in use; the views obtained from the high windows were more spectacular; and the processional route from the entrance was correspondingly longer and more imposing. Lord Burghley's reaction to Sir Christopher Hatton's Holdenby – 'I found no one thing of greater grace than your stately ascent from your hall to your great chamber' – could equally well be applied to Hardwick. One can picture the response of the visiting dignitary at his or her first sight of the wonderful meandering staircase which threads its way up and out of sight, across landings and through mezzanines, until it finally arrives at the door to the High Great Chamber.

A plaster panel in the High Great Chamber, showing Diana and the death of Actaeon. (*NTPL/John Bethell*)

This room, like the rest of the state apartments, was first and foremost a showpiece, the setting for a display of wealth and majesty. Here Bess presided over her guests and favoured members of her household, who would be seated on elaborately upholstered benches and stools at a long table of white wood, while she sat on her 'chair of needlework with gold and silk fringe' beneath a great canopy of state. Looking down on the proceedings was a veritable menagerie of elephants, camels, lions and monkeys, peering out from behind trees in the plaster frieze which surrounded the upper walls. At their centre was Diana, the virgin huntress, and her court, probably an allusion to Elizabeth the Virgin Queen, although the force of the image – nature commanded and conquered by a female figure surrounded by attendants – can't have been lost on those who were privileged to enter the chief room of state where Bess herself held court.

And so it was at Hardwick that Bess passed her last years, walking – when her rheumatism allowed – in the long gallery; discussing finance with Timothy Pusey, her steward and business adviser; watching the Queen's Players perform for her in the High Great Chamber; being read to by one of her ladies in her bedchamber, perhaps from one of the books listed in the 1601 inventory, Solomon's proverbs, or Calvin, or 'a book of meditations'. After her death in 1608, Hardwick Hall went to William Cavendish. But by a curious twist of fate William subsequently bought his brother Henry's interest in Chatsworth, which became the family's principal residence, as Bess had originally intended. As a result, the Hall has remained relatively unaltered, although much of its furniture dates from the later seventeenth and eighteenth centuries. The house, park and estate, together with the principal contents, were transferred in 1959 from the Dukes of Devonshire, Bess's descendants, to the National Trust via the National Land Fund.

Two of Bess of Hardwick's children who visited her in her eightieth year, shortly before her death, recorded that she was 'a lady of great years, of great wealth, of great wit, which yet still remains'. That wit may have long since been extinguished, but Hardwick Hall remains a monument to her ambition and wealth, and one of the greatest of all Elizabethan country houses.

Montacute House

SOMERSET

Montacute House, 4 miles west of Yeovil, was built in the last years of the sixteenth century for Edward Phelips, a wealthy lawyer. The architect is thought to have been William Arnold.

In February 1610 the recently-widowed Dorothy Wadham, of Merifield near Ilminster in Somerset, wrote to her half-brother Lord Petre concerning the arrangements for building a new Oxford college in accordance with her late husband's wishes. Dorothy urged Lord Petre, one of the executors of Sir Nicholas Wadham's will, to allow her to 'employ one Arnold in the work, who is an honest man, a perfect workman, and my near neighbour, and so can yield me continual contentment in the same'; Arnold, she went on to say, 'has been commended unto me by my good friend and loving neighbour Sir Edward Phelips.'

It is partly on the strength of this letter, and partly on stylistic grounds, that the new house that Edward Phelips built at Montacute in the last years of Elizabeth's reign has been attributed to William Arnold, one of the most talented provincial mason-architects working during the late sixteenth and early seventeenth centuries. A member of a family of craftsmen – his father was probably Arnold Gonerson, the chief joiner at Longleat in the 1550s, and Edmund and Thomas Arnold, who may have been his brothers, are both recorded as working as masons on Wadham – William was employed 'in the provision of timber and stones' for the new college, as well as 'for drawing of a plott [plan] and for the building of it'. He is also known to have worked between 1608 and 1612 on the lodge at Cranborne in Dorset where Robert Cecil entertained James I; at Dunster Castle, Somerset, for George Luttrell in 1617; and at Lulworth Castle, also in Dorset, and the Hall at Bradford-on-Avon, Wiltshire (although in both of these last cases there is a chance that he was working as master-mason to designs supplied by Robert Smythson). In fact, Arnold was so successful and so much in demand as a mason, a sculptor and an architect, that Sir Edward Hext, referring to the new works at Wadham, told Lord Petre: 'If I had not tied him fast to this business we should hardly keep him; he is so wonderfully sought being indeed the absolutest and honestest workman in England.'

Arnold's patron at Montacute was just as successful, although in a rather different sphere. Edward Phelips was the youngest of the four sons of Thomas Phelips, a Somerset landowner whose family had owned or rented property in the area since at least the mid-fifteenth century. Called to the Bar in 1579, at a time when the law was rapidly becoming a boom industry – in the early 1590s, for example, Bess of Hardwick was spending nearly four times as much on legal business as she was on the building of Hardwick Hall – he soon became one of the richest and most powerful lawyers in England. Under James I he also achieved important public office. In 1603, the same year that he and his eldest son, Robert, were knighted by the King, he was appointed Serjeant-at-Law and King's Serjeant; while as Speaker of the House of Commons (from 1604) he opened the indictment against Guy Fawkes in

1606. A sober, rather severe man, with cold, hard eyes (if his portrait at Montacute is anything to go by), he was fiercely anti-Catholic, once condemning a man to death for 'entertaining a Jesuit'; and he was said by a contemporary to be somewhat 'over-swift in judging'. Phelips reached the peak of his career in 1611, three years before his death, when he became Master of the Rolls, one of the most important – and profitable – legal posts in the country.

But all of this was still in the future in 1587, when Thomas Phelips made over his Montacute property together with 'my capital and mansion house' jointly to Edward and his first wife Margaret, perhaps as a marriage gift. Little is known of the old house, which stood near the present stable block until its demolition at the end of the seventeenth century, although one can obtain some idea of it from a surviving letter in which Thomas complains of being unable to escape the attentions of a tedious neighbour and relation:

> [He] followed me through the hall, using these words, he would not leave me so. [I went] through the court into the parlour where I do customably rest and lie; [he] ever continuing his prittle prattle, drove me for my quietness to go up into the chamber over where I do lie, you do know, the stairs narrow and dark . . .

Like so many of his contemporaries, Edward Phelips's response to his rising fortunes was to build. Montacute, which was probably begun sometime in the 1590s and – assuming that the date carved over one of the doorways marks its completion –

finished by 1601, is a superb example of that late Elizabethan penchant for self-advertisement. The three-storey composition is assertively, almost aggressively, tall, its verticality stressed by the relative narrowness of the two wings which project to either side of the main block, each capped with curving Flemish gables. At the beginning of the seventeenth century, when the Ham Hill stone used to build the house was still garish and had not yet mellowed to its present honeyed golden colour, the new mansion must have possessed even more of that brash arrogance noted by Spenser in the passage quoted in the introduction to this chapter: Edward Phelips had indeed 'lifted up his lofty towers .../That they began to threat the neighbour sky'.

Compact like Hardwick, with no internal courtyards, Montacute consists of the orthodox H-shape plan used in a large number of houses of this period, such as Wimbledon in Surrey (begun 1588), Condover in Shropshire (1598) and Ham House, also in Surrey (1610). William Arnold's handling of the exterior – and in particular the east façade, which was the entrance until the late eighteenth century, when a later Edward Phelips remodelled the house and made a new drive to the west – shows an ingenuous but ingenious use of Renaissance motifs. The classical entablatures separating the three storeys, the segmental pediments surmounting the projecting bays to either side of the entrance and on the two wings, the shell-headed niches below the ground-floor windows and the circular recesses above (presumably intended to take antique busts like those at Longleat and Wollaton) – all show Arnold eager to embellish the new house with elements drawn from a Renaissance vocabulary learned, in all probability, from the pattern books that were flooding into England from France and Flanders during the last half of the sixteenth century. Even the rather naïvely carved Nine Worthies of medieval lore who look down from above the entrance and between the first-floor windows (three Old Testament heroes – Joshua, David and Judas Maccabaeus; three from antiquity – Hector, Alexander, Julius Caesar; and three from the Middle Ages – King Arthur, Charlemagne and Godfrey of Bouillon, an eleventh-century crusader and conqueror of Palestine) – are all clad in Roman dress.

But this somewhat slap-happy use of classical decoration is evidence not so much of Arnold's provincialism as of the innocent gay abandon shown by most Elizabethan masons when it came to working with classical ornaments, which were, in John Summerson's words, 'adopted for the intrinsic pleasure they gave rather than from any sense of apprenticeship to foreign achievements greater than their own'. Arnold's brief was to create an appropriately splendid façade, a piece of 'stately and curious workmanship', and not a scholarly and carefully integrated sequence of Renaissance quotations. He succeeded.

If more proof were needed of William Arnold's architectural sophistication, one need look no further than the composition of the east court. Before the main approach was shifted to the west, this court was entered via a gatehouse between the two garden pavilions, exquisite little banqueting rooms where Phelips and his family could take shelter from the sun and enjoy refreshment after a stroll in the garden (although by the 1630s they were somewhat improbably furnished as bedrooms). While we don't know what form the gatehouse took, the overall effect of the east court must have been – as indeed it still is – to evoke an image of a highly stylised medieval fortification, with the pavilions taking the place of corner towers, and a curtain wall whose crenellations have been distorted and stretched into a series of obelisks, all set against the backdrop of a towering main block, its heavily glazed high walls glittering in the sun.

Turning to the internal layout and decoration of Montacute, one sees the same blend of tradition and sophistication. Both the cross-bar and the uprights of the H-plan are only one room deep (or were, until the house was altered in the eighteenth century), producing a series of spacious well lit interiors. On the ground floor, a central cross-passage gave access to the kitchens, buttery, pantry and other offices to the south, and to a great hall in the conventional position, reached through screens to the north. The most intriguing feature of the hall is a large early seventeenth-century plaster panel at the upper end, which shows a man being beaten by his wife for taking a drink while minding the baby, and then, as a result, being made to 'ride the skimmington' or 'ride the stang' – a form of public humiliation in which a hen-pecked husband was carried round the village on a pole, or 'stang'. The practice was known in England, Scotland and Scandinavia – and even in Spain, according to Hofnagel's *Views of Seville* (1591) – and is referred to in Sir Walter Scott's *Fortunes of Nigel* and Thomas Hardy's *Mayor of Casterbridge*. Assuming that the panel is in its original position, it would have been almost the first thing a visitor would see when he or she entered Montacute. It does seem to be a singularly bizarre subject for such a location. Sadly, we know nothing of Phelips's married life.

Beyond the hall the ground floor of the north wing was taken up by the parlour – an informal panelled family eating-room – and what is now the drawing room but was originally a 'parlour chamber', according to an inventory of 1638. On the first floor, and reached by a monumental stone staircase in the north-west angle, which – seven feet wide and decorated with more of Arnold's shell-headed niches, winds its way up through the full height of the house – were the lodgings of state: the great chamber (called the dining room in 1638, and now the library), the withdrawing chamber and the 'best chamber'. In the early seventeenth century this last room, the state bedchamber, contained a 'great looking glass', a 'gilt bedstead with its furniture of purple satin embroidered with ships, the curtains and counterpart [counterpane] of wrought satin faced with gold lace', and chairs and stools embroidered 'suitable to the tester of the bed'.

The great chamber itself was elaborately decorated. Its windows were set with brightly coloured heraldic stained glass, not only tracing the genealogy of the Phelips family but also paying tribute to – and advertising Edward's connections with – a variety of courtiers and statesmen, friends and neighbours. Panelled walls are topped with an ornate plasterwork frieze. (The original ceiling, like those in the rest of the house, was plain – the present one was installed in the 1840s, when the panelling was altered, too.) And the whole is dominated by a spectacular

The east front, with the Nine Worthies in their niches, ranged along the top storey. (*NTPL/Rupert Truman*)

Sir Edward Phelips's lodgings of state, the great chamber with its heraldic glass and Portland stone chimneypiece. (*The National Trust*)

chimneypiece of Portland stone. Resting on coupled Corinthian columns, it consists of a heavy strapwork cartouche above a strapwork frieze, with shell-headed niches to either side. A watercolour of the early 1830s shows these niches filled with two well rounded naked female figures, but they have since disappeared, having apparently proved too well rounded for Victorian sensibilities. In 1638 the great chamber held eight 'arras hangings', which suggests that some of the panelling, at least, may have been a later introduction. It also contained '1 green high velvet chair' – presumably Edward Phelips's chair of state – and no fewer than eight other chairs and twenty-four stools, most of which were also upholstered in green velvet. In addition there were tables, sideboards and sixteen pictures in the room.

The final chamber in any Elizabethan lodgings of state was the long gallery, with its combination of functions. Primarily for exercise and, like all the other public rooms, for the display of status, it was also used for games and dances, masques and plays, and, of course, as a vantage point from which to admire the view. The gallery at Montacute is on the second floor, above the other state rooms. In fact, to all intents and purposes it *is* the second floor. At 172 feet – the longest gallery in England to survive relatively unscathed – it extends the full length of the house and slightly beyond it, into oriels at either end. The wings once housed four secondary bedrooms: on the west front, the wainscot chamber and the white chamber, which contained a 'silvered bedstead, head and valance of cloth of silver embroidered and fringed with gold curtains and quilt of white taffeta'; and to the east, the blue bedchamber and the primrose chamber. Originally bare and sparsely furnished – the gallery held four high chairs, twelve stools, four low stools and 'one map' – the second floor now displays a National Portrait Gallery exhibition of sixteenth- and early seventeenth-century paintings.

Edward Phelips divided the last years of his life amongst Montacute, his London town house in Broad Street, the Rolls House in Chancery Lane (where he died in 1614), and a second country seat, Wanstead in Essex, which he rented from the Blunt family. Sadly, the generations of Phelipses who succeeded him had neither his driving ambition, nor his luck. Most of the original state furniture had to be sold to pay off debts in 1651, and by the early eighteenth century the builder's great-great-grandson was lamenting 'the present mean condition of the place of our ancestors'. The decline in the family's fortunes was halted by Edward Phelips V (1725–97), who, partly through astute business management and partly as a result of inheriting property from both an aunt and a nephew, was able to carry out some judicious remodelling and restoration to Montacute. In 1787, at a time when Elizabethan architecture was held by many people to be 'the bad taste that came between the charming venerable Gothic, and pure [ie, Palladian] architecture', as Horace Walpole wrote – 'Vast rooms, no taste', was his comment on Hardwick Hall – Edward carried out a remarkably sympathetic conversion of the old buttery into a dining room, installing a splendid neo-Elizabethan chimneypiece which incorporates a 1599 plasterwork panel taken from elsewhere in the house.

But the fifth Edward's most important work at Montacute involved the remodelling of the exterior. In December 1785 he formed a drive to the west, and began to dig foundations 'for the new west front which were very great and arduous undertakings at my advanced season in life'. His intention was to create a new entrance façade between the wings some ten feet or so to the west of William Arnold's original building, to accommodate corridors at ground-floor and first-floor levels. The Elizabethan practice of providing access to the various rooms in the house via other rooms was unacceptable to eighteenth-century notions of privacy.

One might have expected Edward to opt for a façade in either a castellated Gothick, or an Adamesque neo-classical. However, an entry in his diary for 2 May 1786 shows that he had other plans in mind: 'My wife and self attended the sale of the materials of Clifton House then pulling down we bought ... the porch, arms, pillars and all the ornamental stone of the front to be transferred to the intended west front of Montacute.'

Phelips incorporated into his new west front the ornamental carvings from the entrance of this 'Clifton House' – Clifton Maybank, near Yeovil in Somerset, which was built in the mid-sixteenth century for Sir John Horsey. The result is a façade perfectly in keeping with the character of the original Montacute, or perhaps even improving on it – the quality of the Clifton carving is much more assured than Arnold's rather clumsy Nine Worthies to the east. For its time, Phelips's work represents an extraordinarily tactful solution to the problem of modernising an inconvenient old building.

Further alterations were made to Montacute in the 1800s, including the introduction of the ornamental ceiling in the great chamber and the redecoration of the drawing room, which had been upgraded from its role of informal 'parlour chamber' during the eighteenth century. In the 1930s the novelist and essayist Llewelyn Powys remembered childhood visits to the house forty years before, when his father was vicar of the parish. One winter evening he had looked down from one of the windows

> to find that in the courtyard below all was as bright as day. In that one glimpse through the small glass panes I received an impression of the enchantment of moonshine that has remained with me all my life – the fountain, the dovecot, the stone flags, the very weeds in their crevices edged with an exact hoarfrost whiteness.

Moonshine wouldn't pay the bills, though. The agricultural depression, falling rents and a long period of neglect resulting from the mental illness of one of the Phelipses led in 1895 to the sale of family silver and many of the pictures, and to the subsequent dismemberment of the estate. After leasing the house between 1911 and 1929, Gerard Phelips decided that he would have to sell up: but there were no buyers, and in 1931 Montacute was valued at £5,882 – for scrap.

Fortunately for Montacute – and for us – in the same year Ernest Cook, the wealthy grandson of the travel operator Thomas Cook, offered £30,000 to the Society for the Protection of Ancient Buildings to enable them to buy and maintain the property. The secretary of the SPAB was A. R. Powys, brother of Llewelyn, and it may be that his childhood memories led him to interest Cook in the house. In any event, Montacute was bought by the SPAB in 1931, and on 11 June 1932 it was handed over to the care of the National Trust.

Knole

KENT

Knole stands at the southern end of the town of Sevenoaks. Dating from the middle of the fifteenth century, it was substantially remodelled for Thomas Sackville, 1st Earl of Dorset, between 1603 and 1608.

Thomas Sackville, 1st Earl of Dorset; a portrait attributed to J. de Critz which hangs in the great hall. (*Courtauld Institute of Art*)

The west front. (*NTPL/Rob Matheson*)

'When men sought to cure mortality by fame', wrote Francis Bacon, 'buildings were the only way'. But in spite of its massive scale and its labyrinthine grandeur, Knole stands apart from the other great 'prodigy houses' of the period – Longleat and Wollaton, Hardwick and Montacute, Burghley and Audley End and Hatfield – in that its owner Thomas Sackville chose to retain his medieval house and to adapt it to the needs of a Jacobean courtier and his household. As a result, Knole has little of the height and symmetry – and even less of the arrogance and pride – which typify its contemporaries. But what it loses in external integrity is more than compensated for by the force and splendour of its interiors, while the sense of organic, centuries-long development, which was so little valued by Sackville's peers, is just the quality which, to twentieth-century eyes, makes the house one of the most attractive in England.

Much of the fabric of Knole dates from the second half of the fifteenth century. On 30 June 1456 William Fiennes sold the estate for £266 13s 4d to Thomas Bourchier, Archbishop of Canterbury (and for a brief period in 1455–6, Lord Chancellor of England). Between that date and his death in 1486 Bourchier built himself a substantial but relatively austere palace grouped around a series of courtyards, and containing all of the elements that one would expect to see in the house of an important medieval prelate – a great hall with a day parlour and first-floor solar at one end and kitchens and domestic offices at the other, a chapel, and lodgings for his large household.

When Bourchier died – at Knole – he left the estate to the See of Canterbury, and it functioned as an archiepiscopal palace until 1538, when Henry VIII bullied Thomas Cranmer into presenting it to the Crown. The King considerably enlarged the house by building three new ranges of lodgings and a turreted and crenellated gatehouse in front of the Archbishop's original gatehouse, thus forming what is now known as the Green Court, the main entrance court at Knole. After his death, the house went through a rather confused series of occupancies. Edward VI assigned it to John Dudley, Duke of Northumberland, who for some reason returned it two years later. Mary I granted it to Cardinal Pole for life in 1556; when he died in November 1558 (on the same day as the Queen) it reverted to the Crown. Elizabeth granted it to John Dudley's son, Robert, Earl of Leicester, who promptly sublet it, before returning it, still sublet, in 1566. In June 1566 the Queen presented the estate to Thomas Sackville, under whom Knole finally settled down to a more stable period of ownership – one which was to last nearly 400 years.

Although only thirty years of age, Sackville was already a courtier of some standing and a favourite of the Queen (who made him Lord Buckhurst the year after she gave him Knole). The son of a wealthy landowner whose acquisitiveness earned him the nickname of 'Fillsack', he was also a talented poet, whose place in literary history today is chiefly and somewhat unfairly due to his co-authorship with Thomas Norton of *Gorboduc*, the first tragedy in English, and probably the most wearisome. His other extant works – a few sonnets, the 'Induction' to *A Mirror for Magistrates*, and 'The Complaint of Henry Duke of Buckingham' – do much more to justify Edmund Spenser's tribute to his fellow-poet:

> In vain I think, right honourable lord,
> By this rude rhyme to memorise thy name,
> Whose learned muse hath writ her own record
> In golden verse worthy immortal fame.

During the last decades of the sixteenth century Sackville served as a diplomat in France and the Low Countries; entertained Elizabeth as Chancellor of Oxford University; was appointed to the commission which tried Mary Queen of Scots – it was he who was given the task of breaking the news of the sentence to Mary; and became Lord High Treasurer and Lord High Steward of England. He was, in fact, just the sort of wealthy and powerful courtier whom one might expect to build himself a new house, if only to echo William Cecil's oft-quoted words to Sir Christopher Hatton on the reasons for the two courtiers' own building schemes: 'God send us both long to enjoy her for whom we both meant to exceed our purses in these.'

But throughout his career as one of Elizabeth's chief advisers, Sackville was unable even to live at Knole himself, still less to replace the old Archbishop's palace with a Theobalds or a Holdenby for his Queen's entertainment. Although he had been granted the house and estate in 1566, it was thirty-seven years before he was able to take over the property from the Lennard family, tenants who had moved in as the Earl of Leicester handed the property back to the Crown. When he did finally gain possession in 1603, he chose to retain Bourchier's house. He was in his late sixties; Elizabeth's reign was at an end; and – although James I quickly confirmed his position as Lord Treasurer, and went on to create him Earl of Dorset early in the following year – he may have felt that the uncertainties of old age and a new reign made it an unpropitious time to build. Or perhaps, unlike his fellow-courtiers, he felt with Francis Bacon that 'it is a reverend thing to see an ancient castle or building not in decay'.

Although Sackville decided against sweeping away the medieval building entirely, his reverence for the venerable structure was not too great to deter him from immediately setting about turning it into the sort of place that was appropriate for someone of his standing. The exterior was brought up to date by, among other things, the addition of distinctively Jacobean shaped gables, decorated with obelisks and topped with leopards (the Sackville family crest). These appear on Henry VIII's entrance court, to either side of Bourchier's inner gatehouse (where they surmount projecting bays flanking the Archbishop's original entrance), and in the Stone Court beyond, where they overlook an open Doric colonnade (now carrying a later balustrade) erected by Sackville to provide a covered entrance to the main part of the building.

Some, if not all, of this work must have been completed by 1605, to judge from the date on the lead rainwater-heads in the Stone Court. It has been tentatively attributed to John Thorpe (c.1565–c.1655), once thought to be the leading architect of the period – and the designer of Longleat, Wollaton, Montacute, Audley End and almost every other substantial Elizabethan and Jacobean country house. Thorpe's reputation stemmed largely from the survival of a book by him (preserved in Sir John Soane's Museum, London) which contains more than 150 drawings, mainly of country houses. Most of them are now known to have been surveys of existing buildings, or copies taken from other architects, and there is little firm evidence of any original architectural work, with the exceptions of Dowsby Hall in Lincolnshire (for Richard Burrell, 1610) and a gallery on the south front of the old Belvoir Castle in Leicestershire (for the 6th Earl of Rutland, 1625–7). However, Thorpe is known to have carried out quite a lot of work at Buckhurst, the Sackville family house in Sussex; and it is possible that Thomas Sackville employed him to produce rough plans, or even more detailed designs, for the remodelling of Knole.

That remodelling involved much more than the cosmetic addition of some fashionably curved gables and a liberal sprinkling of Sackville leopards about the place. For if the modernisation of Knole's exterior was somewhat superficial, most of the main interiors were completely transformed, and to walk from the Stone Court into the great hall is to step back, not into the stark communal living-area which it must have been in Archbishop Bourchier's day, but into a splendid and quintessentially Jacobean entrance space, one of the grandest in England.

Some of that grandeur stems from the geometrical patterned ceiling and the arcaded plasterwork frieze, both of which were executed in 1607–8 by the King's Plasterer, Richard Dungan; in Sackville's day much more stemmed, no doubt, from his new fireplace with its massive and ornate strapwork overmantel – removed, unfortunately, at the end of the eighteenth century. But the main focal point, then as now, must have been the spectacular screen which rises up the full height of the hall and is covered with grotesque and distorted versions of Renaissance ornament in the style of the German Wendel Dietterlin's pattern-book, *Architectura* (which William Portinton, the King's Master Carpenter responsible for carving the screen, probably used as the basis for some of the details). This *tour de force* – vulgar, perhaps, yet undeniably impressive – dominates the hall, and would have dominated it even more in the early seventeenth century, when it was probably brightly painted from top to bottom. As music floated eerily down from behind its lattice screens, where the old courtier's private orchestra sat hidden and 'often [gave] me after the labour and painful travels of the day much recreation and contentation with their delightful harmony', it must have looked like some monstrous Mannerist jukebox.

The staircase leading off Thomas Sackville's hall is, in a rather different way, just as awe-inspiring. Late-Elizabethan builders like Bess of Hardwick, and Edward Phelips at Montacute, relied heavily on bare stone and sheer distance to provide the required *gravitas* and sense of anticipation on the ceremonial route from their hall to their great chamber, as well as hangings to provide the colour and variety. At Knole, on the other hand, Sackville's craftsmen – Dungan again, and the Master Painter Paul Isaacson – created a light and highly decorated single space, with the stair situated in an open well, and treated, for perhaps the first time, as an exhibit in its own right. Every inch of that space has something to tempt the eye. Looking down from the first-floor landing through an arch painted with strapwork and supported by Ionic columns, one sees a bewildering array of geometrical shapes, from the curving ribs of Dungan's ceiling to the windows set with heraldic glass and the allegorical and mythological figures worked in grisaille, the grotesque and rather sinister faces peering out from contorted Mannerist strapwork and the display of *trompe l'oeil* balusters against the walls. The whole effect is theatrical, overpowering – and perfectly calculated to impress the visitor with its magnificence and its curiosity.

At the top of the staircase are the rooms of state. The first and grandest is Sackville's great chamber (now called the ballroom). This room, which Archbishop Bourchier used for much the same purpose – for receiving and entertaining important visitors – is embellished with Dungan's most ornate ceiling. The walls are panelled and decorated by William Portinton with a wealth of curious carvings, including winged horses, chimeras and mermaids; and there is a remarkable chimneypiece made of alabaster and black, white and grey marbles, and decked with strapwork, acanthus scrolls and garlands of musical instruments and flowers, which has been described as 'among the finest works of Renaissance sculpture in England'. The artist responsible for this masterpiece has not been identified: it may have been Cornelius Cuer, who in 1607 was paid £26 10s 'for stones for a chimney piece in the withdrawing chamber at Knole'.

The other state rooms consisted of a number of lodgings, again decorated by

The great Jacobean staircase: perfectly calculated to impress the visitor with its magnificence and its curiosity. The Sackville leopard duly makes his appearance. (*NTPL/Horst Kolo*)

Dungan and Portinton. Several were provided with their own galleries, functioning both as withdrawing chambers and as display areas for paintings. Like most late-Elizabethan and Jacobean noblemen, the Sackvilles collected pictures not only for their aesthetic qualities but as souvenirs of relations, friends, and important men and women of their day – as Lord Herbert of Cherbury discovered, when, although unacquainted with the Earl, he was invited to the Sackvilles' London home, Dorset House, and brought into the gallery there: 'Showing me many pictures, he at last brought me to a frame covered with green taffeta, and asked me who I thought was there; and therewithal presently drawing the curtain, showed me my own picture.'

After putting a fortune into the remodelling and furnishing of Knole – in the last ten months of his life alone he spent well over £4,000 on buildings, materials and stock – Thomas Sackville died in harness, succumbing to an apoplectic fit while sitting at the Privy Council table in Whitehall in April 1608. His son Robert survived him by only one year, having married as his second wife a Spencer of Althorp, of whom it was said that her 'tempestuousness in domestic conversation was greater than flesh and blood could endure'. So it was left to Richard, 3rd Earl of Dorset (Robert's son by his first marriage), to enjoy the fruits of his grandfather's labours. This he did, living at Knole in almost medieval state. Among his 111 servants, most of whom were male, there were gentlemen ushers, yeomen and grooms, huntsmen and armourers, a barber, a scrivener, a falconer and a bird-catcher. Lord and Lady Sackville and their family ate 'at my Lord's table', which was presumably in the great chamber; senior servants, including the steward, the chaplain, the gentleman of the horse, and Matthew Caldicott, 'my Lord's favourite', ate 'at the parlour table'; and most of the others ate at three tables in the great hall. Kitchen menials and scullions – who included the improbably named Diggory Dyer and Marfidy Snipt, and John Morockoe, 'a Blackamoor' – ate separately, as did the nursery staff.

Keeping state like a medieval warlord was expensive, though, and Richard Sackville had neither the talent nor the inclination to follow his grandfather into lucrative government office. He preferred, as his wife Anne recorded sadly in her diary, to go 'much abroad to cocking and bowling alleys, to plays and horse races . . . [while] I stayed in the country, having many times a sorrowful and heavy heart'. By the time of his death in 1624 he had sold most of the family's London property and mortgaged Knole, yet still managed to leave behind him debts amounting to a staggering £60,000.

Knole suffered further during the Civil War, when as a result of the 4th Earl's support for the King the house was seized by Parliamentarian troops, and many of the paintings and furnishings brought together by Thomas Sackville forty years before were lost.

However, that loss was to be made up in spectacular fashion before the century was out, when through his post as Lord Chamberlain of the Household to William III, the 6th Earl of Dorset – Alexander Pope's 'Blest peer! his great forefather's every grace/Reflected and reflecting in his race' – acquired what is perhaps the finest collection of seventeenth-century furniture in the country. One of the Lord Chamberlain's privileges was the right to any of the furnishings of the royal palaces that were reckoned to be worn or out of date, and the 6th Earl took full advantage of that privilege to equip Knole with everything, it seems, that he could lay his hands on. Chairs of state from Whitehall and Hampton Court; Brussels tapestries; the fabulous suite of gilded and silvered bedroom furniture probably made by Louis XIV's upholsterer Jean Peyrard to celebrate the marriage of James, Duke of York, to Mary of Modena; even brass lock plates showing William III's monogram and a royal close stool – all these the 6th Earl brought to Knole. The house that had been built by a medieval Archbishop of Canterbury and decorated by an Elizabethan courtier-poet was now furnished by courtesy of a king.

Later generations of Sackvilles made their own contributions to Knole, adding to the collections, making alterations here and there. But the house that Thomas Sackville transformed in five short years at the beginning of the seventeenth century remains, in some indefinable way, his own. The great rooms of state with their heavy and sumptuous decoration still bear the stamp of his time and his personality; and, whether or not he set out to 'cure mortality by fame', he has done just that.

But perhaps the last word should be left to Vita Sackville-West, whose childhood was spent at Knole, whose uncle gave the house to the National Trust in 1946, and whose *Knole and the Sackvilles* manages so well to capture the spirit of the place:

> At sunset I have seen the silhouette of the great building stand dead black on a red sky; on moonlight nights it stands black and silent, with glinting windows, like an enchanted castle. On misty autumn nights I have seen it emerging partially from the trails of vapour, and heard the lonely roar of the red deer roaming under the walls.

Blickling Hall

NORFOLK

Blickling, 10 miles south of Cromer, was bought by Sir Henry Hobart in 1616. His architect Robert Lyminge extensively remodelled it between 1619 and 1629. Further major alterations were carried out in the 1760s and 1770s by Thomas and William Ivory, for John Hobart, 2nd Earl of Buckinghamshire.

Blickling was the last of the great Jacobean prodigy houses. When Sir Henry Hobart began building in 1619, the three great Lord Treasurers' houses of James I's reign – the Earl of Dorset's Knole, the Earl of Salisbury's Hatfield and the Earl of Suffolk's Audley End – were all complete, and two of their builders, Dorset and Salisbury, were already dead. So too was Robert Smythson, the architect of Wollaton and Hardwick. Inigo Jones had been Surveyor-General of the King's Works for nearly four years, and was already designing what would be his greatest work – not some vast, flamboyant palace, but the restrained Palladian Banqueting House at

Whitehall. Times were changing, and the costly and elaborate mansions which had been such a feature of the architectural scene during the previous seventy years – Longleat, Wollaton, Burghley, Theobalds, Holdenby – were fast becoming dinosaurs, leviathans whose time had passed.

But Henry Hobart was an old man in 1619, and their times were his times. Born around 1560 into an established legal family (his great-grandfather had been Attorney General to Henry VII), he had exploited to the hilt the growth of the law as a profession under Elizabeth. With James I's accession in 1603, he reached the peak of a successful career, replacing his fellow-Norfolkman Edward Coke first as Attorney General in July 1606, and then, in November 1613, as Chief Justice of the Court of Common Pleas.

The building mania of the late sixteenth and early seventeenth centuries seems to have passed Hobart by. Although he was ready enough to put his money into land – he owned extensive estates, including some property in Blickling parish itself – his three houses in Smithfield and Highgate in London, and in Norwich, were all leased or rented. But in 1616 he took the plunge and bought the Blickling estate for £5,500 from the Clere family, relatives of the Boleyns who had held the estate in Tudor times. And once committed, he quickly set about transforming the medieval moated house which had stood on the site since the 1390s into the sort of palace that he must have seen and dreamed of during his rise to power. On 18 December 1618 he held a meeting in London with three master-craftsmen to discuss his new house. They were given an advance payment of £100, and the following spring building began.

The three men who contracted for the work made quite a formidable trio. Thomas Thorpe (d.1625/6) was a master-mason, almost certainly the brother of the great surveyor John Thorpe and son of the Thomas Thorpe who was responsible for building the remarkable Renaissance-inspired Kirby Hall in Northamptonshire for Sir Humphrey Stafford in 1570. He had worked for the Crown in 1603–4 at Eltham Palace, London, and in 1606–9 on the Banqueting House at Whitehall (which burned down in January 1619, thus paving the way for Inigo Jones's building). Thomas Style, also a mason, is a rather more mysterious figure, but he is known to have contracted for the masonry at the King's Lodging in Newmarket, Suffolk, which was executed in 1614–17 (and rebuilt in 1668–71 by William Samwell).

But the most important member of the Blickling triumvirate was not a mason but a joiner, Robert Lyminge or Lemyng. Lyminge is first heard of in 1607, when he was working as a carpenter for Robert Cecil, Earl of Salisbury, on some almshouses at Theobalds in Hertfordshire. When in the same year the Earl agreed with James I to exchange Theobalds for the royal palace at Hatfield, and then decided that he wanted a completely new house on higher ground some way from the palace, Lyminge played an important part in the design of the building. Simon Basil, Inigo Jones's predecessor as Surveyor-General of the King's Works, was also involved; so too was Jones himself, to judge from the fact that he visited Hatfield in 1609 and was subsequently paid £10 'for drawing of some architecture'. And advice was sometimes sought, and more often given, by Salisbury and his clerk of works, Thomas Wilson. His patron's constant interference, largely in relation to the rising costs of the scheme, provoked an exasperated Lyminge to assert his artistic integrity in decidedly undeferential terms. Responding to one of the Earl's cost-cutting proposals, he wrote: 'it will be very deformed for the uniform of the build, both within and without, which I will never agree to'.

Hatfield was more or less complete by the time of Lord Salisbury's death in 1612, and nothing more is known of Lyminge until, with Thorpe and Style, he contracted for the shell of the new building at Blickling in December 1618. That work shows such close affinities with Hatfield – the capped angle-towers, the shaped gables and the use of an entablature as a visual link to pull together the various elements of the composition – that there can be little doubt that Lyminge was putting to good use the lessons that he had learned during his work on the earlier house. In fact Thorpe and Style left Blickling in September 1621, once the shell had been erected, and Lyminge, who is referred to as 'your lordship's surveyor', 'the contriver of your lordship's works' and – in the entry in the Blickling parish register which records his death early in 1629 – 'the architect and builder of Blickling Hall', stayed on to supervise the fitting out of the house.

From the outset, Lyminge and his colleagues were faced with an awkward problem, caused by Hobart's decision to retain as much of the original house as possible. In effect, this ruled out a conventional Jacobean treatment of the exterior. The old buildings were grouped around two courtyards, and the main entrance into the great hall which divided those two courts was only accessible by passing over the moat surrounding the site and crossing the outer court. Such an arrangement meant that a Hatfield-type U-plan, or a Montacute H, with all of the possibilities that they presented for both for a compact set of state lodgings and a spectacular approach, was out of the question.

As far as the internal arrangement of lodgings was concerned, Lyminge didn't really solve the problem. He retained the original position of the Tudor great hall on the north side of the outer court, and inserted an elaborately carved wooden staircase of the type introduced at Knole ten or fifteen years earlier into the north-east angle of the court, leading off the dais end of the hall. (At the lower end, the Tudor west range containing the kitchens, sculleries, buttery and pantry was retained in a modified form.) The staircase hall opened into a ground-floor day parlour in the south-east corner of the court, and ascended to the state lodgings, which comprised the usual group of great chamber, withdrawing chamber, best bedchamber and long gallery, on the floor above.

In order for the long gallery to be of a sufficiently grand length, Lyminge had little choice but to site it to the north of the staircase landing, running down one side of the building. This left the other chambers in the apartment to range round the outer court in such a way that they would all look out either into the outer courtyard or on to the main approach to the south.

Partly, perhaps, to provide a rather more stately view, but primarily to bestow some grandeur on this narrow main front, Lyminge added the two great gabled ranges, each 225 feet long, which flank – and, indeed, form an important visual element in – the entrance façade. That on the west was primarily a service wing, while its companion to the east housed additional lodgings, and 105 feet of stables elaborately furnished with Doric pillars and moulded arches, its fittings 'not much

Blickling Hall, Norfolk: the entrance front. (*NTPL/Eric Crichton*)

differing from your honour's stable at Highgate'. By emphasising the two wings and deliberately making them an integral part of the entrance façade, Lyminge created a massive formal forecourt, at once a splendid setting for, and a fitting introduction to, the grandeurs within.

Between the spring of 1619, when the remodelling of the old house began – although Hobart's contract with Lyminge, Thorpe and Style probably dates from December 1618, construction work was seasonal and it is unlikely that much was done until the following March or April – and Lyminge's death ten years later, the old house at Blickling was transformed into the palace that Hobart wanted.

Of the two main display façades, both of red brick with stone dressings, that to the east, in which deep projecting bays topped with pierced cresting alternate with smaller pedimented windows, is perhaps the more impressive, if only because of its great length. Seen from within the stately court formed by the two service wings, the south front is rather more restrained than one might expect of a Jacobean entrance façade, inviting rather than awe-inspiring. Instead of the three-storey centrepiece which towers over the entrance to Hatfield, there is a relatively modest composition consisting of Doric columns flanking the entrance to the first of the two courtyards, with Ionic pilasters above and, where the crowning Corinthian order should be, a simple balcony topped with statues of Justice and Prudence. The design of the entrance front was clearly a matter which exercised the minds of Lyminge and Hobart. Not only were the service wings added to strengthen the effect, but an

104

original scheme for the centrepiece (which had involved no more than the first tier of Doric columns) was revised during the building. And Lyminge held out against a plan for a battlemented brick wall to the moat, on the grounds that it 'will be very lumpish and will take away the prospect of the lower part of the house in the view of the court'. His alternative, a pierced stone balustrade which was removed in the early eighteenth century, won the day.

In the early years, when the shell was going up, Blickling must have seethed with activity as the vast quantities of building materials poured in, at such a rate that no fewer than sixty-six local men were involved in their carriage. Bricks – nearly 1.5 million between 1619 and 1622, and a million more for the service wings in 1623–4 – were fired on the estate and carted to the site. Dressed stone, perhaps from the Thorpe family quarries in Northamptonshire, would have come down the River Welland to King's Lynn and then round the coast to Cley before being carried in wagons the last twenty miles of its journey. The timber for floor joists and roof trusses came initially from 'the park and wood and other grounds', but as supplies ran short it was necessary to look further afield, to Swanton Morley, ten miles to the south-west of Blickling, and Langley, twenty miles away on the other side of Norwich. More specialised materials travelled much greater distances: the lead came from Derbyshire, iron from Sussex, and glass from Newcastle; and the paving stones for flooring were brought by sea all the way from Purbeck in Dorset to Yarmouth, and thence up the River Bure to Coltishall and overland to Blickling itself.

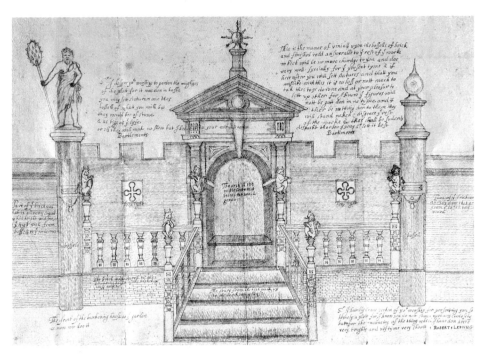

Robert Lyminge's design for a 'banketting house' in the garden, the only surviving drawing by the architect of the Jacobean house. (*The National Trust, Lothian Collection*)

During the main phase of the building work Lyminge was paid a weekly wage of 2s 6d over and above his contract fee, for his part in supervising the running of the project. He was also responsible for both overseeing and designing parts of the interior decoration – the staircase at Blickling, with its elaborate carving and its somewhat stiff newel figures, is so close in tone and style to that at Hatfield that it must be by Lyminge, probably in collaboration with a specialist carver. He certainly designed at least one chimneypiece, that in the great chamber. And the fact that Rowland Buckett, a gilder who had worked with him at Hatfield, was employed on the great long gallery chimneypiece (since removed) suggests that he had a hand in commissioning – or at least recommending – suitable craftsmen. It is tempting to speculate that when he visited Hatfield in company with Lady Hobart in September 1623 he was either showing her some feature that he wished to emulate at Blickling, or introducing her to the work of an artisan whom he wanted to employ.

Elsewhere it is harder to establish Lyminge's contribution. When in August 1620 Edward Stanyon contracted for the plasterwork ceilings in the state lodgings and the day parlour, that contract stated that they were to be executed 'according to such plots and workmanship as now or hereafter shall be drawn by Mr Robert Lyminge his lordship's surveyor of the said works'. Interestingly, though, the word 'drawn' was altered to 'directed' before the contract was signed, suggesting that Stanyon was working to a rough brief supplied by Lyminge, perhaps produced in collaboration with Henry Hobart himself.

This was almost certainly the case with Stanyon's finest work at Blickling, the ceiling of the long gallery, in which intricate and heavily embossed ribs surround panels of strapwork, heraldic achievements – and an astonishing collection of

Sir Henry Hobart by Daniel Mytens. This portrait hangs in the state bedroom. (*NTPL/Horst Kolo*)

J. C. Buckler's view of the great hall in 1820, showing Thomas and William Ivory's eighteenth-century remodelling of the Jacobean staircase. (*NTPL*)

twenty-six *impresi*, or emblematic devices. The five senses and Doctrina (learning) alternate with the Hobart arms in the centre of the ceiling, while bizarre and obscure emblems – a naked virgin astride a dragon beneath the motto '*pulchritudo feminae*' (the beauty of woman), a rhinoceros as a metaphor for the poet (who must be equally thick-skinned) – are ranged down either side.

With the exception of the five senses, these devices were taken from one of the most popular emblem books of the period, Henry Peacham's *Minerva Britanna*. As Peacham pointed out, they were intended to 'feed at once both the mind, and eye, by expressing mystically and doubtfully, our disposition, either to love, hatred, clemency, justice, piety, our victories, misfortunes, griefs, and the like; which perhaps could not have been openly, but to our prejudice revealed'. As such they were not merely a witty and instructive form of decoration, but also a personal expression of their owner's outlook on life. Perhaps more significantly, they also represented an opportunity for Hobart's friends and acquaintances both to admire their host's wit and ingenuity and to display their own erudition in interpreting the symbols. According to Paolo Giovio, author of another popular emblem book in circulation at the time, one of the prerequisites for a good *impresa* was that it 'should not be so obscure as to need the Sybil for its interpreter, nor so transparent that every mean mechanic might understand it'.

Sir Henry Hobart had little opportunity to enjoy his new house. He rarely visited

Blickling during the early 1620s, preferring to pursue his legal career in London. After his death in March 1626, it was left to his son John (1593–1647) to complete the fitting-out of the building, buying in new furniture, paintings and hangings, and settling down to the life of a wealthy squire.

Of the many architectural changes which Blickling has undergone since Robert Lyminge's time, changes which range from neo-classical to muscular High Victorian Gothic, perhaps the most significant was the major restoration programme carried out in the 1760s and 1770s for John Hobart, 2nd Earl of Buckinghamshire, by the local father-and-son team of Thomas (1709–79) and William Ivory (1746–1801). Their re-facing of the Tudor west range provoked the comment that 'the new part is very inferior and looks more like a hospital than a nobleman's residence', and was later found to have been carried out 'without a single bond stone or brick being introduced into the old wall'. Nevertheless, although they had their limitations, the Ivorys showed what was for the time a remarkable sympathy for Jacobean architecture, a sympathy which must have stemmed from Buckinghamshire's own tastes – discussing part of the proposed alterations with his aunt, the Countess of Suffolk, he vowed: 'Gothic it was, and more Gothic it shall be, in spite of all the remonstrances of modern improvers and lovers of Grecian architecture'. The Ivorys' treatment of the north façade of the house, which seems to have been left by Lyminge as an unresolved jumble of Tudor gables and Jacobean turrets, is good enough to pass for genuine early seventeenth-century brickwork; while in moving Lyminge's staircase to the great hall and enlarging it, they went to great pains both to use as much of the original timber as possible and to reproduce the spirit of the original in the new work. That they succeeded can be judged from Christopher Hussey's comment in 1930 that Lyminge had produced 'the earliest English example of the free-standing, dividing staircase developed thirty years later by Roger Pratt ... at Coleshill into the type of Palladian ascent'.

The Earl of Buckinghamshire had no sons, and on his death in 1793, which according to Horace Walpole was caused by his thrusting his gouty foot into a bucket of ice-cold water, Blickling passed to his second daughter Caroline, his eldest daughter Harriet having incurred her father's disapproval by first marrying and then divorcing Armar Lowry-Corry, 1st Earl of Belmore and builder of Castle Coole in County Fermanagh (see page 212). Harriet then married the Earl of Ancrum, later to become the 6th Marquis of Lothian; and since Caroline's own marriage to the 2nd Lord Suffield was childless, the estate eventually passed to the Lothians. In 1941 it came to the National Trust under the terms of the will of the 11th Marquis, who had done so much in the 1930s to fight for the preservation of the English country house, and whose efforts had resulted in the Trust's Country Houses Scheme.

Chapter Four

Pomp and Circumstance

1630-1720

Architecture here has not received those advantages which it has in other parts, it continuing almost still as rude here as it was at the very first.

Roger Pratt, 1649

To Roger Pratt (1620–85), a young lawyer just returned from six years of travel and study in France, Italy and the Low Countries, the great prodigy houses which had dominated the architectural scene during James I's reign must indeed have seemed clumsy and gauche. Proud, ambitious heaps like Hatfield and Blickling were hardly to be compared with the sophistication and restraint exhibited by the villas of Palladio and Scamozzi, the châteaux of François Mansart, or Jacob van Campen's Mauritshuis in The Hague. Only Inigo Jones's Queen's House at Greenwich (completed in 1630–5) and the south front of the Earl of Pembroke's Wilton, built in the late 1630s by the French architect and landscape gardener Isaac de Caus (perhaps with advice from Jones), showed the sureness of touch and the command of the classical Renaissance vocabulary that Pratt had admired in Europe.

But neither the Queen's House nor Wilton was really representative of contemporary English architecture. Jones himself was nowhere near so great an influence during his lifetime as he was to be after his death; few masons or surveyors emulated his work, except for a small number inside his immediate circle – and to all intents and purposes this meant John Webb (1611–72), who had in his own words been 'brought up by his uncle Mr Inigo Jones upon his late Majesty's command in

The grand staircase at Petworth House, Sussex, with Laguerre's mural showing the Duchess of Somerset riding in a triumphal chariot attended by her children. (*The National Trust*)

111

Queen's House, Greenwich, begun by Inigo Jones for James I's consort, Anne of Denmark, but completed for Queen Henrietta Maria in the early 1630s. (*National Maritime Museum*)

the study of architecture', and whose masterly reconstruction of de Caus' fire-damaged state lodgings at Wilton in 1648–50 was almost certainly carried out in consultation with Jones.

Stylistically, most country houses built between 1630 and 1650 tended to fall somewhere between the innocent exuberance of the early seventeenth century and the symmetry and proportion of Jones's court work. Traditional planning (involving the asymmetrically placed great hall entered via a screens passage) was cloaked in the splendidly overblown Mannerist ornament which was becoming more and more popular with artisans as they gained access to Flemish and Dutch pattern books – the sort of details described by a Flemish contemporary as 'a heap of craziness of decorations and breaking of the pilasters in the middle, and adding, on the pedestals, their usual coarse points of diamonds and such lameness, very disgusting to see'.

There were some trained craftsmen who were capable of working in the European idiom that Pratt admired: the master bricklayer Peter Mills (1598–1670) showed a commendable restraint in the designs that he made for Oliver St John's Thorpe Hall in Northamptonshire in 1654, a pretty Dutch doll's house of a building which derives from the plates in Rubens' *Palazzi di Genova*. But any list of the designers who shaped the development of the country house during the second half of the seventeenth century would contain the names of very few artisans drawn from the traditional building trades that had produced the Smythsons and Arnolds and Lyminges of the previous decades.

Such a list would largely be made up, not of masons and joiners and bricklayers, but of that type of 'ingenious gentleman' who, in Roger Pratt's words, 'has seen much of that kind [of building] abroad and been somewhat versed in the best authors of architecture: viz Palladio, Scamozzi, Serlio'. It would include Pratt himself, who came from a Norfolk gentry family and trained, like his father, as a lawyer; Hugh May, seventh son of a Sussex landowner, who served in the Duke of Buckingham's household and spent the later 1650s in exile with the court in Holland; and William Winde, whose grandfather was Gentleman of the Privy Chamber to Charles I, and who, like his father, served as a soldier in the Low Countries during the Commonwealth. It would include the lawyer William Samwell and the Dutch courtier and diplomat Balthazar Gerbier; Robert Hooke, the physicist and curator of experiments to the Royal Society; the anatomist and Professor of Astronomy Christopher Wren; and the playwright and captain of marines John Vanbrugh.

None of these men received any formal training in building design, but all were brought up within the seventeenth-century tradition of the virtuoso, the type of gentleman-scholar to which Francis Bacon had referred in 1605 when he talked of men who 'entered into a desire of learning and knowledge, sometimes upon a natural curiosity and inquisitive appetite; sometimes to entertain their minds with variety and delight; sometimes for ornament and reputation'. A consuming curiosity about all branches of learning was a mark of the virtuoso – modern lines of demarcation between disciplines simply did not exist, and Christopher Wren's contemporaries would have found nothing unusual in, for example, the fact that he could inject opium into a dog's leg to test his ideas about the circulation of the blood one day, lecture on planetary motion the next, and design the Sheldonian Theatre in Oxford the next. Anatomy, astronomy and architecture were all branches of learning, and all equally deserving of the virtuoso's attention.

Inevitably, of course, some found architectural design more engrossing than others, even within the group of enthusiastic gentleman-amateurs mentioned above. At one end of the scale were the interested dabblers who largely confined themselves to the theory rather than the practice: men like John Evelyn, who published a translation of Fréart's *Parallel of the Ancient Architecture with the Modern* in 1664 – although Evelyn did casually note in his diary that he and Hugh May 'designed a handsome chapel' during a visit to the Earl of Clarendon's Cornbury House in Oxfordshire in the same year. At the other end there were May, Wren and Vanbrugh, all of whom occupied important posts in the Office of Works and for whom building became a career. And in between these two extremes were figures like Gerbier, Pratt and Hooke, who retained other interests and who often did no more than provide designs which were then adapted as necessary and implemented by the mason-contractors and surveyors who were actually working on site.

If one excepts Balthazar Gerbier (1592–1663), whose position as artistic adviser to George Villiers, 1st Duke of Buckingham, in the 1620s had apparently involved him in alterations to several of Buckingham's houses and who really belonged to an earlier generation, Roger Pratt was the first of this group to apply himself to the practice rather than the theory of architecture. As far as he was concerned, Jones was the only architect, and the Queen's House, the Banqueting House at Whitehall and the 56ft-high Corinthian portico which Jones had added to the west front of

Coleshill, Berkshire: in a break with convention, Pratt's staircase rose directly out of the great hall. (*Country Life*)

St Paul's Cathedral were the only English buildings of any worth. Having thus voiced his disappointment with the state of English architecture in 1649, in the following year he was consulted by his cousin, Sir George Pratt, about the design of a new house at Coleshill (to the east of Swindon in Wiltshire). The early building history of Coleshill is rather obscure: one story has it that Sir George's old seat had just burned down; another says that he had inherited a partly built house from his father, who had died before he had been able to complete it. Whatever the truth of the matter, Pratt advised his cousin to start again on a fresh site, and agreed to provide him with the design. The new house was completed by about 1662.

Coleshill's basic form was what Pratt called a 'double-pile' – that is, a compact rectangular block consisting of two ranges of rooms placed back to back, rather than grouped around a courtyard or series of courtyards. Eminently practical, he thought this arrangement

> of all others to be the most useful, first for that we have there much room in a little compass, next that the chambers may there be so laid out, as to be only of use to each other; . . . it is warm, and affords variety of places to be made use of both according to the diverse times of the day, and year also, as shall be most requisite, besides that herein a little ground is sufficient to build upon and there may be a great spare of walling, and of other materials for the roof.

The two main floors were raised on a low platform formed by a rusticated half-basement; they stood behind plain astylar façades, framed by stone quoins and carried up into tall, slender chimneys. An attic storey was lit by dormers projecting from a hipped and balustraded roof, with a cupola above.

The simplicity which characterised the exterior of Coleshill extended to the interior planning. The core of the house was a group of rooms centrally placed on the main east-west axis: a two-storey entrance hall out of which a double staircase ascended to a first-floor great chamber, with a parlour below. On both floors Pratt placed two apartments to either side of this main group. Each consisted of a large chamber with two smaller rooms attached, an arrangement which he recommended in his notebooks: '[a chamber should] have a closet, and a servant's lodging with chimney, both of which will easily be made by dividing the breadth of one end of the room into two such parts as shall be convenient'. Corridors giving independent access to these apartments ran from north to south on each floor, with back stairs at either end, 'so . . . that the ordinary servants may never publicly appear in passing to and from for their occasions there'. Kitchens, larders, pantries and cellars were in the basement, together with an eating chamber for the servants, who were displaced from their traditional position in the hall.

Coleshill represents a landmark in the history of the country house; its virtuosity is such that until the publication of Pratt's notebooks in 1928 it was assumed to be the work of Jones and Webb. However, none of its features was wholly original. The Elizabethans had made occasional use of the double-pile, and it had been taken up both by Jones himself at the Queen's House, and in other buildings such as Forty Hall (1629–33) and Boston Manor (1622–3), both in Middlesex; the latter also contained a cross-corridor. Hardwick had already broken with the tradition of an asymmetrically placed hall in the 1590s, and had also made use of a secondary service stair; Burghley and Longleat both had cupolas and roof-top walks. The double stair may have been derived from the Venetian church of San Giorgio Maggiore, where one was installed by Longhena in 1643–5; and the rusticated basement came perhaps from Jones, or perhaps, like the hipped roof, from French or Netherlandish sources.

But what *was* original was the blend of elements, the brilliant way in which Pratt combined so many features so neatly in one house. And the result was a handsome and perfectly proportioned building ideally suited to the needs of an English country gentleman; it was the embodiment of what the Jacobean courtier and scholar Henry Wotton had described as the three conditions necessary for good building – 'commodity [ie, convenience], firmness and delight'. When Coleshill was destroyed by fire in 1952, just as negotiations were being concluded for its transfer to the National Trust, the country lost one of its greatest houses.

Pratt designed only four other houses (including the Trust's Kingston Lacy in Dorset), none of which has survived in anything like its original form. But other gentleman-architects were drawing both on Pratt's ideas and on their common source, the French and Dutch versions of classicism which they – and their patrons – had seen and admired during the 1650s. The Earl of Craven's Ashdown in Oxfordshire, probably designed by Balthazar Gerbier and William Winde (d.1722),

Clarendon House, Edward Hyde's London house in Piccadilly, designed by Sir Roger Pratt in 1666, and one of the most influential designs in English architectural history. (*Fotomas Index*)

clearly shows how French and Dutch practice was influencing English design in the years immediately following the Restoration. And Belton in Lincolnshire, again probably by Winde, is a good example of a house that drew directly on Pratt's work – not Coleshill, but the grander and, because of its prominent position, more influential Clarendon House in Piccadilly in London.

In 1668 Pratt married and retired to the estate at Ryston in Norfolk that he had recently inherited from another cousin, Edward. Although he retained an interest in architecture (he rebuilt Ryston), he now devoted most of his time to his studies and to the running of his estate. Others of his circle, such as Hugh May (1621–84), developed their private interests into successful careers. As we have seen, May spent the later 1650s with the court in exile in Holland, in the household of the Duke of Buckingham. On 29 June 1660 – just one month to the day after Charles II had returned to London – he was rewarded for his loyalty by being appointed Paymaster of the King's Works, an administrative post in which he supervised the financial side of the overhaul of the royal palaces which took place in the early 1660s. But unlike other Royalists who were given government posts in recognition of their services to the Crown – one thinks of the cavalier poet Sir John Denham, who was made Surveyor of the Works, and whose verse was considerably more competent than his

Pratt's design for Kingston Lacy in Dorset, 1663–5. (*The National Trust*)

architectural skills – May did not see his job as a sinecure, and was soon actively engaged in building. Eltham Lodge in Kent, which he designed for Sir John Shaw in 1663, is a splendid essay in the sort of homely classicism that May must have become familiar with during his time in The Hague: a redbrick double-pile, with a frontispiece consisting of a stone pediment above four stone Ionic pilasters, it is simple, elegant and compact.

Such is the impact – and the lasting appeal – of Coleshill, Ashdown, Eltham Lodge and their like, that they seem to dominate the architectural scene during the last half of the seventeenth century, and certainly the style that had been perfected by gentleman-architects in the 1660s was being taken up by local masons and master-builders around the country well into the late 1690s and early 1700s. William Stanton (1639–1705), the mason-contractor who in 1685–7 executed Winde's designs for Belton House, produced an adaptation of those designs for Denham Place, Buckinghamshire, built between 1688 and 1701; the bricklayer and surveyor William Smith of Warwick (1661–1724) designed Stanford Hall, a charming hipped-roofed double-pile on the Coleshill-Clarendon House model which was begun in 1697 for a Leicestershire baronet, Sir Francis Cave; and Nether Lypiatt in Gloucestershire, clearly influenced by both Coleshill and Ashdown, was designed by an unknown mason in about 1700. (His client was a judge, John Coxe, of whom little is known except for the legend that the smith who was making the gates for his new forecourt was sentenced to death for some crime, and reprieved by Coxe – but only until he had finished his work.)

Almost all of the houses belonging to this group were built for the gentry, who kept relatively small households and who had neither the money nor the inclination to live in the sort of state expected of, and by, the aristocracy. (The two exceptions are Clarendon, effectively a town house; and the Earl of Craven's Ashdown, which was little more than a lodge – the Earl owned three other houses, all considerably larger.) The nobility needed something grander, and as the reign of Charles II progressed they too looked to the Continent for inspiration, and in particular to the baroque splendours of France and Italy.

During the 1650s and 1660s, when Dutch and Flemish architecture was still fresh in the minds of recently exiled Royalists, there was a certain amount of mistrust of modern French and Italian buildings. In a swingeing criticism of John Webb's Gunnersbury House, Middlesex (1658–63) – to modern eyes a remarkably restrained exercise in Palladianism – Pratt had recommended caution, saying that we must 'by no means to proceed to a rash and foolish imitation [of Italian models] without first maturely weighing the condition of the several climes, the different manners of living, etc, and the exact dimensions and other circumstances of the building, especially the lights, etc, in all which things the Hall and Portico at Gunnersbury are very faulty'. And, during his remodelling of Lamport Hall in Northamptonshire in 1655–7, Webb himself had advised against importing foreign craftsmen:

> As for your French workman I desire always to employ our own countrymen, for by employment those grow insolent and these for want thereof are dejected, supposing they are not accounted able to perform when indeed it is only want of encouragement makes them negligent to study because a better conceit of foreigners as had they of themselves.

But as links between the French and English courts grew, helped along by both family ties – Charles II's mother Henrietta Maria was French, and his sister was married to the Duke of Orleans – and the King's alliance with Louis XIV in 1670, a number of theatrically grand country houses appeared, houses whose primary function, like that of their French progenitors (as well as their Elizabethan predecessors), was to impress by their scale and by the opulence of their decoration.

One of the earliest of these French-inspired palaces was the 1st Earl of Arlington's Euston Hall in Suffolk (c.1670), sometimes attributed to William Samwell (1628–76). In October 1671 John Evelyn spent what was by all accounts quite a wild fortnight with Arlington and the King at Euston: 'It was universally reported that the fair Lady – was bedded one of these nights . . . I acknowledge she was for the most part in her undress all day, and that there was fondness and toying with that young wanton; nay, 'twas said I was at the former ceremony, but 'tis utterly false.' He later described the house as 'a very noble pile, consisting of four pavilions after the French, beside the body of a large house'.

Another house with 'pavilions after the French' was Boughton in Northamptonshire (1683–1709), inspired – externally at least – by Versailles and built by an unknown architect for the 3rd Lord Montagu, who, having been Charles II's ambassador at the court of Louis XIV, had returned to England imbued with a love of all things French. In 1675–9 Robert Hooke (1635–1703) had already designed for Ralph, 1st Duke of Montagu a London house – 'a fine palace, built after the French pavilion way', according to John Evelyn. It was destroyed by fire in January 1686, and the Duke was said (by the architect Colen Campbell in 1715) to have brought over an otherwise unknown French architect called Pouget (or Bouget) to rebuild it in an even more thoroughly Gallic style.

What began as a trickle of European craftsmen into England in the 1670s turned into a flood in the following decades. Montagu House was decorated by a team of Frenchmen under Charles de la Fosse, and the great hall ceiling at Boughton was painted with the *Marriage of Hercules and Hebe* by Louis Chéron, a young French Protestant refugee.

Continental decorative painters were particularly in demand, as the delicate plasterwork flowers and swags which characterised early Restoration interiors gave way to the baroque fashion for vast allegorical murals which the Italian Antonio Verrio, who had assisted Charles Le Brun at Versailles, introduced at Windsor Castle in 1678 (and which were described by the contemporary diarist and traveller Celia Fiennes as 'so lofty it's enough to break one's neck to look on them'). Among other commissions, Verrio (1639–1707) also worked for the Duke and Duchess of Lauderdale at Ham House in Surrey; for William and Mary on the refurbishment of Hampton Court; for the 1st Duke of Devonshire at Chatsworth in Derbyshire, where he painted the ceiling of the great chamber with what Walpole called 'heathen gods, goddesses, Christian virtues, and allegoric gentlefolks'; and for the 5th Earl of Exeter at Burghley in Northamptonshire. Here Celia Fiennes again voiced her disapproval, saying that Verrio's gods and goddesses 'were all without garments or very little, that was the only fault ... especially in My Lord's apartment'.

Others followed Verrio: Jean Tijou the ironsmith, whose balustrades decorate Hampton Court, Kensington Palace and Chatsworth; his son-in-law Louis Laguerre, who came to England from Paris in the early 1680s with his assistant Antoine Ricard, and quickly established his reputation as one of the leading mural-painters of his day, working at Chatsworth, Sudbury, Burghley, Petworth and Blenheim; the Danish carver Caius Gabriel Cibber; the garden-designer Grillet; the Huguenot cabinetmakers Gerrit Jensen and Jean Pelletier. By the 1690s interior decoration was firmly in the hands of Continental craftsmen, and Englishmen had to follow their lead – Englishmen like James Thornhill, whose masterly staircase murals of scenes from the life of Achilles at Hanbury Hall, Worcestershire, show that native artists were more than capable of adopting the new style. By 1702, the stuccadore Edward Goudge was lamenting the decline of plasterwork, and attributing that decline in part at least to the vogue for painted murals.

But the situation with regard to architecture was rather different. Here the field was dominated by native designers, most of whom worked under Christopher Wren (1632–1723), who was Surveyor-General of the King's Works from 1669 until his

Castle Howard, Yorkshire: the baroque at its full-blown best, as seen from a balloon.
(*Angelo Hornak*)

dismissal at the age of eighty-six in 1718. Wren himself was too occupied with his official duties to undertake more than a handful of private commissions – what estate agents used to call the 'Wren-style' house should in fact be called the 'Pratt-style', although perhaps the phrase doesn't have quite the same ring to it. But his position as Surveyor-General – and court arbiter of taste – meant that while the designers who served with him at the Works (most notably his three Comptrollers, Hugh May, William Talman and John Vanbrugh) developed their own individual versions of the baroque, Wren's influence is always there in the background.

Of those Comptrollers, May has already been mentioned; and Talman, whose most important contribution to the development of the country house was perhaps his designs for the south and east fronts of Chatsworth (1687–96), is discussed in connection with Dyrham Park, Avon, part of which he also designed (see page 152). But when one thinks of the baroque in England, it is inevitably the third member of the trio, John Vanbrugh (1664–1726), who comes to mind.

Vanbrugh's magnificently palatial schemes for Castle Howard in Yorkshire (1700–26), and Blenheim in Oxfordshire (1705–16; completed by Nicholas Hawksmoor, 1722–5), epitomise the style at its full-blown best – majestically larger than life, impossibly grandiose, calculated to inspire awe in its beholders. The baroque country house is essentially public architecture, and it is at its most public in Vanbrugh's designs for Blenheim. The palace, a national monument intended as a reward to a national hero, aims to impress upon outsiders the eminence of its owner the Duke of Marlborough, victor over the French and Bavarian armies at the Battle of Blenheim in the War of the Spanish Succession.

A giant Corinthian portico opens into the great hall with a ceiling by Thornhill depicting Marlborough showing his battle-plan to Britannia, who offers him a laurel crown; this in turn leads on the central axis to the great chamber or saloon, which is painted by Louis Laguerre with the peoples of the world. (Thornhill was to have decorated the saloon, but he quoted a price of 25s a yard, which the Duchess of Marlborough thought too expensive – 'Poets, painters and builders have very high flights,' she wrote, 'but they must be kept down.') Radiating out in straight lines to either side, Vanbrugh planned two opulently decorated state apartments, which were to extend beyond the house itself in formally arranged vistas, so that both the palace and the surrounding landscape could be seen to emanate from the Duke eating in state in his saloon.

Unfortunately, the royal grants which were to have financed the building of Blenheim ceased after the Duchess of Marlborough's quarrel with Queen Anne in 1710, and although they recommenced when George I came to the throne four years later, the Duchess mistrusted Vanbrugh's extravagance and he was dismissed in 1716, before the building was finished. ('You have your end, madam, for I will never trouble you more,' the architect wrote, referring to her later as 'That B B B B old B the Duchess of Marlborough'.) It was left to Vanbrugh's collaborator and colleague at the Office of Works, Nicholas Hawksmoor (1661–1736), to complete the project in the 1720s. But by that time a reaction to the baroque was already setting in, and a purer, less ostentatious architecture was beginning to make its presence felt – the Palladianism of Colen Campbell and Richard Boyle, 3rd Earl of Burlington.

Ham House

RICHMOND, SURREY

*Built for Sir Thomas Vavasour in 1610,
Ham House was altered between 1637 and
1639 by William Murray, a connoisseur
and friend of Charles I, and extended and
remodelled in the 1670s by Murray's
daughter Elizabeth and her second husband,
John Maitland, Duke of Lauderdale.
Their architect was William Samwell.*

Ham House is remarkable – one is tempted to say unique – not only because it represents a marvellous opportunity to trace changing fashions in court architecture and design from the time of James I to the last years of Charles II's reign, but because, unlike the vast majority of Stuart country houses, it has remained relatively unscathed by subsequent changes in taste. As a result, it is perhaps the most complete seventeenth-century house to survive in Britain.

Ham is the product of three consecutive generations of Stuart courtiers. The first was Sir Thomas Vavasour, Knight Marshal of the King's Household to James I, who in 1610 built for himself a typically Jacobean H-shaped house in the meadows by the Thames below Richmond Hill, within easy reach by water of London and the riverside royal palaces. As was usual at this time, external symmetry masked an orthodox Tudor arrangement of rooms – 'uniform without, though severally partitioned within', as Francis Bacon put it – consisting of a great hall, which filled most of the cross-bar of the H, with an entrance via screens at the lower end; domestic offices which occupied the ground floor of one upright; and day rooms and a staircase squeezed into the other upright. On the first floor, the stair opened on to lodgings for Vavasour and his family, with his great chamber over the hall, and a long gallery taking up the whole of one wing.

Vavasour didn't occupy his new house for long: it soon passed to the Earl of Holderness, and after his death in 1626 it was occupied by William Murray, gentleman of the bedchamber to Charles I. In 1637 Murray acquired Ham outright – its lease was in the gift of the Crown – and over the next two years proceeded to modernise what must already have seemed a rather dated series of interiors to its new owner, who was acquainted at first hand with the court style of Inigo Jones and was a member of the Whitehall Group of *cognoscenti* which gathered round the King in the late 1620s and 1630s.

Vavasour's staircase was replaced by one which, with its carved and pierced panels representing martial trophies, gave due weight to the role of the staircase as grand introduction to the suite of state rooms on the first floor. Those state rooms were also redecorated, possibly under the supervision of the court painter and designer Franz Cleyn. The great chamber (known at Ham in the seventeenth century as the great dining room, and now called the round gallery) was given a Jonesian ceiling by Joseph Kinsman, who also produced the plasterwork in the adjoining withdrawing room, where Cleyn painted the inset pictures over the doors

Ham House, Surrey: the entrance front. (*Victoria & Albert Museum*)

and chimneypiece, and the joiner, Thomas Carter, was responsible for the panelling. Carter also installed the panelling in the long gallery next door.

All of these state rooms exhibit the more opulent approach to interior decoration that was coming into fashion in the 1630s and that would reach its peak in the apartments created by Inigo Jones and John Webb at Wilton House in 1648–50. And all remain more or less intact, with the exception of the great chamber, the floor of which was pierced around 1690 to form a first-floor gallery to the hall below. But perhaps the most remarkable survival is the final room in the state suite – the green closet, a seventeenth-century 'cabinet of curiosities'.

The closet of rarities, or cabinet of curiosities, had its roots in the Kunstkammern, Wunderkammern and studioli of sixteenth-century Renaissance princes. The grandest were attempts to re-create the world in microcosm, symbols of the owner's dominion over all things natural and artificial. Such cabinets (which often occupied several rooms, and occasionally whole floors, of a palace) contained works of art, fossils, antique sculptures, gems, coins, manuscripts – anything, in fact, that was curious or rare. They were originally private collections, intended to be seen only by their owners and a few chosen initiates, but by the later sixteenth century these collections had become more public. Henry Peacham, writing in 1634 on the acquisition of classical antiquities, noted that 'the possession of such rarities, by reason of their deadly costliness, doth properly belong to princes, or rather to princely minds'. And by that time, quite apart from the joy of ownership and any scholarly motives, one element in the putting-together of a cabinet of curiosities was to enhance one's status, to demonstrate one's ability to amass such items in spite of 'their deadly costliness'.

Seventeenth-century inventories show that Murray's cabinet housed around fifty miniatures and small paintings. The green closet's position in the state apartments – not leading off a bedchamber, but accessible from both the withdrawing chamber and the long gallery – suggests that his collection was intended as a quasi-public display area, open to family and important guests. A discriminating virtuoso who acquired original works by Italian and Flemish masters as well as copies of masterpieces admired in his day, Murray seems to have been aware of both the aesthetic and the social value of the items in his cabinet.

Murray was created Earl of Dysart by Charles I in August 1643. However, during the troubled years of the Commonwealth he seems to have thought it prudent to drop his title, and he and his wife lived at Ham as plain Mr and Mrs Murray until his death in about 1654. After the Restoration his daughter Elizabeth was allowed to succeed to the earldom in her own right, becoming Countess of Dysart. But there were more changes to be made to the house, and the third chapter in the story belongs to Elizabeth and her second husband, John Maitland, Duke of Lauderdale.

Elizabeth Murray was, as her portraits show, a great beauty: in 1644, when she was just eighteen, one of her father's friends described her as 'a jewel . . . She seems to be a very good, harmless, virtuous, witty little babe.' Subsequent events proved this to be rather wide of the mark. Witty she may have been, but she was neither very good nor harmless, and her virtue was open to question. In 1647 she married Sir Lyonel Tollemache of Helmingham Hall, Suffolk, by whom she had eleven children; during the Commonwealth she worked clandestinely for the Sealed Knot, a secret Royalist organisation, and was said to have been on such good terms with Oliver Cromwell that she was able to persuade him to spare the lives of several Royalist prisoners.

One of those prisoners was John Maitland, confined to the Tower of London after being captured at the Battle of Preston in 1651. Maitland, then the Earl of Lauderdale, was freed in the months leading up to the Restoration, and immediately left England for The Hague. He returned with Charles II, when, according to Gilbert Burnet, Bishop of Salisbury, Elizabeth 'thought that Lord Lauderdale made not those returns that she expected [and] they lived for some years at a distance'. Whatever their relationship during the early 1660s, by the time of her husband's death in 1669, and possibly for some years before, Elizabeth Murray and Lauderdale (who was married) were lovers. By 1671 he was living with her at Ham, and in spite of the advice of his friends he married her in February 1672, just six weeks after the death of his wife – which, it was alleged, he had hastened. Three months later he was created Duke of Lauderdale.

The Lauderdales were not an appealing couple. Elizabeth was still counted a great beauty, and Bishop Burnet, who was no friend of hers, could admit that she had 'a wonderful quickness of apprehension, and an amazing vivacity in

The green closet, which William Murray used as a cabinet of curiosities in the 1630s. The walls would have been hung with miniatures and small paintings. (*Victoria & Albert Museum*)

conversation. She had studied not only divinity and history, but mathematics and philosophy'. However, he went on to qualify his praise: 'She was violent in every thing she set about, a violent friend, but a much more violent enemy. She had a restless ambition, lived at a vast expense, and was ravenously covetous; and would have stuck at nothing by which she might compass her ends.' She was, in other words, a Caroline rival to Bess of Hardwick.

Her husband has come down to posterity with scarcely any redeeming features. Charles II's Secretary of State for Scotland, who ruled that country as autocratically as any monarch, he was described by Pepys as 'a cunning fellow'. Edward Clarendon called him 'proud, ambitious, insolent, imperious, flattering, and dissembling', proclaiming him 'without impediment of honour to restrain him from doing anything that might gratify any of his passions', while Burnet painted perhaps the most uncomplimentary picture of all:

> He made a very ill appearance: he was very big: his hair red, hanging oddly about him: his tongue was too big for his mouth, which made him bedew all that he talked to: and his whole manner was rough and boisterous, and very unfit for a court . . . He was haughty beyond expression, abject to those he saw he must stoop to, but imperious to all others. He had a violence of passion that carried him often to fits like madness, in which he had no temper . . . He was the coldest friend and the most violent enemy I ever knew.

However, it was the Duke and Duchess of Lauderdale who embarked on the greatest programme of modernisation at Ham. Elizabeth may well have been the driving force behind this remodelling. Lauderdale himself showed little interest in building until her influence began to exert itself a few years before their marriage, after which he not only spent a great deal on Ham – an inventory drawn up at his death in 1682 states that he 'bestowed upon buildings and reparations at Ham and gardens thereto belonging sixteen thousand pounds sterling', excluding furniture and pictures – but commenced on new works at his three Scottish houses – Thirlestane, Brunstane and Lethington.

Between 1672 and 1675 the Lauderdales greatly altered Ham. They employed William Samwell, John Aubrey's 'excellent architect, that has built several delicate houses', a gentleman-architect in the same mould as Roger Pratt and Hugh May; and like the buildings of Pratt and May, most of his houses have been altered or destroyed. They included Grange Park in Hampshire; the west wing of Felbrigg Hall in Norfolk, completed in 1686, ten years after Samwell's death; and the King's House at Newmarket, Suffolk, which Evelyn saw in 1670 and criticised as being 'mean enough, and hardly capable for a hunting house. Many of the rooms above had the chimneys placed in the angles and corners, a mode now introduced by his majesty which I do at no hand approve of.' The richly decorated white closet at Ham, part of the Duchess of Lauderdale's apartment, contains just such a corner chimneypiece.

Samwell did not produce the original designs, however. In 1671, the year before their marriage, Elizabeth had already consulted her cousin, the architect William Bruce, and proposals were drawn up in that year by a German engineer and

Sir Peter Lely's portrait of the Duke and Duchess of Lauderdale: he 'the coldest friend and the most violent enemy', she 'would have stuck at nothing by which she might encompass her ends'. An attractive couple. (*NTPL/John Bethell*)

surveyor called John Slezer, and the Dutch artist Jan Wyck. With minor modifications, this was the scheme which Samwell executed. It provided for a virtual doubling in size of the original house. This was achieved by filling in the space between the two wings on the south or garden front of the house and adding side-bays, to form two ground-floor apartments, consisting of antechamber, bedchamber and private closet, arranged, in the best French fashion, on an east-west axis to either side of a central great parlour, the marble dining room. On the first floor a state apartment, again consisting of antechamber, bedchamber and closet, ran parallel to the old great chamber and withdrawing chamber, while the Duke built a library and library closet which led off to the west of the long gallery. For all his faults, Lauderdale was a well-read man, 'very learned, not only in Latin, in which he was a master, but in Greek and Hebrew'; he had 'read a great deal of divinity, and almost all the historians, ancient and modern'. In a letter dated 21 September 1670, his first wife had complained that their Highgate house was threatened with collapse owing to the weight of the books stored in it, and the library at Ham ranks as one of the earliest purpose-built country house libraries in Britain.

Work probably began on the new additions early in 1672, around the time of the Lauderdales' marriage; and under the supervision of Arthur Forbes, the Duke's clerk of works, the shell of the new south front reached roof-level by early in the following year. Most of the bricks were made on site – the main contractor, Thomas Turner, manufactured 1.5 million between 1672 and 1674, at a cost of 8s 6d per thousand. Masons, led by John Lampen, cut the windows and the central doorcase of Portland stone, and laid the marble paving in the new great parlour, while several of the principal rooms were fitted with 'Scotch marble' chimneypieces ferried down by water. In exchange, the Duke ordered some of the earlier chimneypieces to be sent up to his Scottish houses.

The chief joiner, Henry Harlow, supplied panelling and doors, fittings for the Lauderdales' new chapel in the north-east wing, and parquet flooring for the state bedchamber and closet – the most expensive items in his account, ranging from 16s a yard to 35s for the most ornate sections, which were composed of cedar inlaid with walnut. Harlow was also responsible for making a number of changes in the old part of the house, opening up new doorways and altering some of the panelling put in in Murray's time, and installing sash-windows – one of the earliest instances of their use

The Duke of Lauderdale's library, one of the earliest purpose-built country-house libraries in Britain. (*NTPL/John Bethell*)

(another being at the Duke's lodgings in the Palace of Whitehall in 1672–3). They were obviously rather draughty, since the glazier, Augustine Beare, was paid for double-glazing several, including those in the Duchess's closet.

Most of the decorative carving was carried out by a London joiner, John Bullimore, whose accounts show that he was paid 2s a foot for carving 'bunches of leaves about the doors' of the new marble dining room, and 4s a foot for more complicated work, such as the 'two pieces of fruit two feet long' which still hang to either side of the chimneypiece in that room. By May 1674 plasterers, painters and gilders were in the house, putting the finishing touches to the new works. Meanwhile the Duke and Duchess were commissioning or buying furniture – several pieces were brought from Amsterdam in 1672 – and paintings. The court artist Antonio Verrio supplied at least one ceiling mural, *Wisdom Presiding over the Liberal Arts*, in the Duchess's white closet; and the four pictures in the panelling of the Duke's bedchamber are by Willem van de Velde the younger, who had come over from The Netherlands to work for Charles II.

In the two or three years following their marriage in 1672, the Lauderdales transformed Ham into one of the most luxurious and fashionable houses in England. There were still minor adjustments to be made, one of the most curious being that by 1675 the Duke and Duchess had for some reason swapped bedchambers, but not apartments, so that the Duke's antechamber and closet flanked the Duchess's bedchamber, and vice versa. Sometime between 1679 and 1683 the state apartment was redecorated in preparation for a visit by Catherine of Braganza, following which the suite became known as the antechamber to the Queen's chamber, the Queen's bedchamber and the Queen's closet. And the floor of the great chamber, which dated from Vavasour's day and had been refurbished by Murray, was pierced in about 1690 to form a picture gallery opening into the hall below.

John Evelyn, who visited at the end of August 1678, was impressed with the changes that the Lauderdales had wrought. 'After dinner,' he wrote, 'I walked to Ham, to see the house and garden of the Duke of Lauderdale, which is indeed inferior to few of the best villas in Italy itself; the house furnished like a great prince's; . . . and all this at the banks of the sweetest river in the world, must needs be admirable.'

The Duke died four years after Evelyn's visit; the Duchess stayed on at the house, taking over the whole of her husband's apartment, until her own death in 1698. They had no children, and her eldest son by her first marriage inherited Ham and the earldom of Dysart. He found himself faced with huge debts – largely the result of his mother's extravagance – and as a result pursued a course of 'downright stinginess', to quote one contemporary. Over the following centuries, and in spite of improving family fortunes, Ham became widely known as a house where time had stood still. Horace Walpole, who visited in 1770, wrote: 'the old furniture is so magnificently ancient, dreary and decayed, that at every step one's spirits sink, and all my passion for antiquity could not keep them up'. More than a century later, the travel-writer Augustus Hare remarked that 'no half-inhabited château of a ruined family in Normandy was ever so dilapidated as this home of the enormously rich Tollemaches'.

In 1948 Sir Lyonel Tollemache and Cecil Tollemache, descendants of Elizabeth, Duchess of Lauderdale, presented Ham to the National Trust. The contents of the house, including large quantities of fabrics, furniture and paintings dating from the time of Murray and the Lauderdales, were bought by the government and entrusted to the Victoria and Albert Museum. And with the help of a series of extremely detailed inventories a programme of careful restoration and reconstruction was initiated, covering both the house and its elaborate formal gardens. That programme continues today, (with the main emphasis being placed on the Lauderdale period), and as a result Ham and its surroundings are slowly being restored to their full seventeenth-century glory.

Ashdown House

OXFORDSHIRE

Ashdown House, 3½ miles north of Lambourn, was built in the early 1660s for William, 1st Earl of Craven. There is no documentary record of its architect, but circumstantial evidence points to either Balthazar Gerbier or William Winde.

No doubt the medieval tradition of courtly love, whereby a knight sublimated his more earthly feelings for an unattainable woman by heroic deeds and gallant acts in her service, was more prevalent in literature than in real life, and the notion finds its most enduring expression in the Arthurian romances of Malory and the *chansons* of the French troubadours. Occasionally, however, life mirrors art; and it is appropriate that the first decade of the seventeenth century, which with its elaborate tournaments and pasteboard castles witnessed a deliberate attempt to revive the ideals of the age of chivalry, also saw the birth of a knight who would devote his life to a great lady. That lady was Elizabeth Stuart, Queen of Bohemia, and the gallant knight was William, Earl of Craven, the builder of Ashdown House.

William Craven was born in 1608. His father, a lord mayor of London, died when the boy was only ten, but his mother Elizabeth worked to consolidate the family's already considerable fortunes, buying estates at Combe Abbey in Warwickshire and Hamstead Marshall in Berkshire. In 1625, the year after her death, Craven (or rather the trustees of his estate, since he was still a minor) bought further lands in Berkshire, including Ashdown Park, some seventeen miles from Hamstead Marshall; he also owned Drury House in London and an estate at Caversham, near Reading.

While still a teenager Craven was already learning the profession that he was to follow for most of his life – soldiery. He was knighted at Newmarket in Suffolk in 1626 after serving under Henry, Prince of Orange, in The Netherlands, and created Lord Craven of Hamstead Marshall in 1627, at the early age of nineteen. During the years that followed he spent much of his time engaged in various military expeditions on the Continent, and it was while he was in Holland in the late 1620s

Elizabeth of Bohemia, known as the Winter Queen (left) and William, 1st Earl of Craven, her champion (right). Portraits by Gerard von Honthorst. (*NTPL/John Gibbons*)

with Prince Maurice of Orange that he first met Frederick V, Elector Palatine and King of Bohemia, and his wife Elizabeth, the 'Winter Queen' (so-called because her husband reigned for just one year). The couple had been in exile in The Hague since the disastrous Battle of the White Mountain in 1620, when Frederick's Protestant army had been decisively defeated by a Catholic force under the Emperor Ferdinand, and the King had lost his crown, his kingdom and his Palatinate.

Elizabeth was the sister of Charles I, and something of that rather tragic sense of magnificence in adversity which surrounds both her brother and her grandmother, Mary Queen of Scots, seems also to cling to her. Known to contemporaries as the 'Queen of Hearts', and described by Henry Wotton as 'a princess resplendent in darkness', the Winter Queen spent half of her life in exile: after her husband's death at Mainz in 1632 she continued to hold court in The Hague, facing increasing financial, political and domestic difficulties with varying degrees of fortitude.

Craven, who seems to have fallen quickly under her spell, spent the next three decades doing everything that he could to alleviate those difficulties. Motivated by a desire to restore Elizabeth's German estates, he commanded the English forces under Gustavus Adolphus in 1632; he raised £30,000 to help her son Prince Rupert in his campaign to recover his father's lands in Bohemia. And during the Commonwealth, when he was himself in exile, his own estates sequestrated by Parliament, he provided her with money and did his best to mediate between the Winter Queen and her estranged son Charles Louis, who had been restored to part of the Palatinate by the Treaty of Westphalia in 1648 but who, according to a letter from Elizabeth to her champion, 'means to starve me out . . . as they do blocked towns'. When she finally left The Hague in 1661 – not for Heidelberg and the Palatinate, but for England – it was Craven, by now restored to his estates, who brought her over, placing his London house at her disposal. She died in February of the following year, bequeathing her papers and pictures to the faithful soldier who had spent so much of his time and money in her service. Created Earl Craven of Craven in 1664, he died unmarried in 1697.

Given Craven's single-minded devotion to the Winter Queen and her cause, it is perhaps inevitable that tradition should link her with the building operations on which he embarked, like so many Royalists returning from exile, after the Restoration. According to Evelyn, his estate at Caversham was 'in ruins, [its] goodly woods felling by the rebels' in 1654, and no doubt his other estates had also suffered, if not from the depredations of Parliamentarians, then at least from years of neglect during the Commonwealth. Combe Abbey was let, but in 1662 work began on the remodelling of Hamstead Marshall (which was reputed, without much foundation, to have been based on the Winter Queen's palace at Heidelberg). And at about the same time, Craven commissioned the building of Ashdown. The story goes that the house was intended as a refuge for Elizabeth from the plagues which were sweeping the capital in the early 1660s, and that after her death it was consecrated to her memory. Too little is known about the genesis of Ashdown for this to be taken as more than an attractive legend, and it may well be that the house was originally planned simply as a country retreat for Craven during the building operations at nearby Hamstead Marshall. Whatever the truth of the matter, Ashdown is beautiful enough, and eccentric enough, to stand alone without the help of romantic associations.

And stand alone it certainly does. Perched high on the Berkshire downs, its sense of isolation is increased by both its fierce verticality – softened only by the two long and relatively low pavilions, which were added in the 1680s – and its sheer incongruity: it is as if a tall and impossibly pretty Dutch doll's house has been uprooted from a giant nursery and deposited by some freak of nature in the middle of the English countryside.

The identity of the architect responsible for this doll's house remains something of a mystery, although two names stand out as likely candidates. The first is Balthazar Gerbier, the Dutch courtier, miniaturist and friend of Rubens, who, as mentioned earlier, was employed by the Duke of Buckingham and then by Charles I. His half-hearted loyalty to the King, who knighted him in 1638, was matched only by his equally half-hearted loyalty to the Commonwealth. His Royalist sympathies returned with the Restoration, but owing to the fact that he had both dedicated a lecture on military architecture to the Parliamentarian general Thomas Fairfax, and proposed to decorate the Palace of Whitehall with paintings commemorating the 'memorable achievements' of the Parliament, he found that his presence was not required at the court of Charles II. In 1662 Lord Craven, in whose regiment Gerbier's son had served as a captain, commissioned him to remodel Hamstead Marshall – and, conceivably, to design Ashdown, which was described as a 'new house' in the hearth-tax returns of 1664.

The east front of Ashdown House. (*NTPL/Nick Meers*)

However, Gerbier died in 1663, and Hamstead Marshall was completed by his assistant, William Winde, the second and more likely candidate for the authorship of Ashdown. The son of a Royalist refugee and soldier who had died in Bergen op Zoom in The Netherlands in 1658, Winde was an ensign in command of English troops at Bergen in that year. Soon after his arrival in England in 1660 his interest in military architecture, doubtless acquired in the Low Countries, widened to include country houses. As well as completing Hamstead Marshall (which was destroyed by fire in 1718), he produced a design for the garden at Caversham in 1663, rebuilt parts of Combe Abbey in the 1680s, and was probably also responsible for some unspecified work at Drury House, Craven's London home. Belton House in Lincolnshire is also attributed to him (see page 143). According to Craven's will, Winde was his godson: it was probably due to his influence that the young captain was made gentleman usher to the Winter Queen in 1661.

If Winde was indeed the architect responsible for Ashdown House, he achieved a remarkable adaptation of new form in the service of old function. In its position – at the junction of four rides through what was originally a thickly wooded and impaled deer park – and its height, Ashdown owes much to the Tudor hunting lodge, which traditionally served both as a sort of grandstand, from the upper storeys and roof of which spectators could view the chase in comfort, and as a set of temporary lodgings, where the owner, his family and a few servants could stay whilst hunting, and during the annual audit (when the household broke up for a while and the main residence was given a thorough spring-cleaning). Ashdown probably fulfilled this role for Craven: it was used as a rather grand holiday cottage for short periods during the year, rather than as a major residence.

In other respects, however, Ashdown is far from traditional. With its steeply pitched roof, dormer windows, balustraded roof and cupola surmounted by a gilded globe, it belongs to that genre of gentry house which was established by Roger Pratt and Hugh May in the 1660s. It can be no coincidence that Coleshill, which Pratt had just completed for his cousin and which was to serve as the prototype for so many smaller country houses during the second half of the seventeenth century, stood just eight miles away across the downs. Ashdown's compact proportions, on the other hand, may have been influenced by the tall town houses seen by both Craven and Winde during their time in The Netherlands, although it has also been suggested that Balleroy in Normandy, a house designed by François Mansart in 1626 which shows a number of startling similarities to Craven's lodge, may have provided the model for Winde's design.

That design is charmingly simple. Based on a forty-foot square, each façade – of dressed chalk, with quoins, string courses and mouldings of Bath stone – is five bays wide and four-and-a-half storeys high. On both of the main fronts a small stone balcony projects over the doorway, and the central first-floor window is surmounted by a pediment. Internally the space is divided into two equal halves by a spine wall, and then into quarters. A small entrance hall opens on to the massive and robust staircase (the only part of the interior to survive relatively intact from Craven's time), which occupies the whole of one of those quarters and rises up the full height of the house, finally giving access into the octagonal cupola and thence to the balustraded roof. Until the two pavilions were built, at least, there were presumably domestic offices in the half-basement and accommodation for servants in the attics, with the three remaining floors being used as lodgings for Craven and his guests.

Ashdown is the only one of Craven's buildings to have survived in anything approaching its original state; and by a curious twist of fate, it has become that shrine to the memory of the Winter Queen that it never was in the Earl's lifetime. The house was given to the National Trust in 1956 by Cornelia, Countess of Craven, but none of its seventeenth-century contents had survived. Then in 1968, when the Craven picture collection was dispersed, the Treasury bought twenty-three portraits, many of which had been left by Elizabeth of Bohemia to her protector three centuries before, and gave them to the Trust to hang at Ashdown. Today, the Winter Queen's children and relations look down from the staircase, while in the entrance hall Gerrit van Honthorst's painting of Elizabeth herself hangs beside that of her champion. He is suitably clad in shining armour.

Sudbury Hall

DERBYSHIRE

Sudbury Hall, 6 miles east of Uttoxeter,
was built and decorated for George Vernon
between the early 1660s and 1691.
The architect is unknown, but was almost
certainly Vernon himself.

Sudbury Hall is something of an enigma – a house which is Jacobean in conception, yet which dates from the reign of Charles II; a house which contains carvings, plasterwork and murals worthy of any courtier's palace, yet which was built by a member of a modest county family who couldn't even get into the House of Commons at his first attempt, let alone the House of Lords. And yet in spite of – perhaps because of – its curious origins, its pretensions, its polyglot character, Sudbury remains one of the finest and most interesting of all Caroline country houses, a testimonial to the ambitions and enthusiasms of its builder, George Vernon (1636–1702).

There had been Vernons at Sudbury since 1513, when Sir John, a younger son of Sir Henry Vernon of Haddon, inherited the manor through his wife, Ellen Montgomery. The family used the village rectory as a residence until around 1605 when, after years of bitter legal wrangling over which of two cousins, Edward or Margaret, should inherit, the dispute was settled by marrying them to each other, and Edward's mother Mary built a manor house for the young couple.

Edward Vernon lived at Sudbury until his death in 1657; his son Henry, whose relations with his father were rather strained, made his home on his wife's estate at Haslington in Cheshire. On succeeding to Edward's Derbyshire properties, he seems to have toyed with the idea of replacing his grandmother's Sudbury manor house, but in March 1659, before anything could be done, he too died, leaving his twenty-two-year-old son George to expand upon his father's plans.

We can only speculate over the reasons for George Vernon's decision to build on a scale that was matched by neither his status nor his income. His marriage in 1660 to an heiress, Margaret Onely, perhaps provided both the occasion and the initial capital, although his estates were heavily encumbered with debts and he was forced to borrow money from relatives and friends. Perhaps he was eager to enhance his prestige: Sudbury's prominent position close to what was then a major road, and the grandeur of its decoration, both suggest a strong desire for recognition.

Another possible clue to Vernon's motives lies in his political activities. Described by a contemporary in 1662 as 'loyal and very orthodox, a prudent young man, sober and active', he played an energetic part in county affairs during the early years of the Restoration: he was a commissioner for restoring ejected ministers in 1660, and High Sheriff in 1663. After unsuccessfully standing as parliamentary candidate for Derbyshire in 1670, he was returned for Derby Borough three times between 1678 and 1681, and again in 1698. Sudbury Hall may have been intended as a grandiose power base for a man who was set on making a bid for political power in the south-west of the county.

Jan Griffier's bird's-eye view of the south front of Sudbury, *c*.1682. (*The National Trust*)

Whatever the motives behind the making of Sudbury Hall, once he had resolved, sometime in the early 1660s, to build a new house, Vernon needed to decide upon a design. A seventeenth-century gentleman in his position had several options open to him. If he was not too ambitious, he might employ a local master-builder, who would draw up the plans for him and execute the work. If he wanted something rather grander, he could go follow Roger Pratt's counsel, quoted in the introduction to this chapter, and 'get some ingenious gentleman who has seen much of that kind abroad'. But if such ingenious gentlemen were hard to find, or if the landowner subscribed to the virtuoso Roger North's view that 'a professed architect is proud, opinionative and troublesome, seldom at hand, and a head workman pretending to the designing part, is full of paltry vulgar contrivances', he could take North's advice, and 'be your own architect, or sit still'.

Unable or unwilling to sit still in his great-grandmother's manor house, Vernon took the former course. Though perhaps helped by William Fowler, a surveyor who worked for the family during this period, he almost certainly designed Sudbury himself, and his account books show that he was personally involved in the day-to-day negotiations over the purchase of bricks, tiles, stone and glass, as well as dealing directly with the decorative craftsmen and local workers employed on the site.

Because those account books also refer to other work that Vernon was carrying out on his estate during the 1660s, including a complex of outbuildings, and new houses, walling and an inn in Sudbury village, it is quite difficult to chart the first phase in the building of the Hall with any accuracy. However, by 1670, when he was contracting with the Leicestershire sculptor William Wilson to 'make, cut, polish and set up the alabaster chimneypiece' in his great chamber, and to 'finish me the two frontispieces of my house', the main structure had certainly been completed.

And his account with John Ball, plumber and glazier, shows that by May 1673 he was able to reckon up 'the total of the glazing my new house'.

At this stage, that 'new house' must have looked decidedly old-fashioned. Built in diapered red brick to a conventional Jacobean E-plan with two projecting wings and a central porch, its main concession to modernity was its hipped roof and cupola on the Coleshill model. Much of the external decoration was out of date before it was even installed. The diapered brickwork, perhaps a punning reference to the fret on the Vernon coat of arms, would be more at home in the late sixteenth or early seventeenth century, as would the strapwork frieze above the ground-floor windows; while even Wilson's massive frontispiece is Jacobean in its conception, if not in its design.

The arrangement of rooms shows a similar unfamiliarity with contemporary practice. The house is divided in two across its long axis by a central passage, which opens into a great hall running along the western side of the entrance façade, just as one would expect in an Elizabethan or Jacobean house. Most of the state rooms are on this hall side of the house – the kitchens, domestic offices and informal living rooms occupied most of the eastern half. A staircase leads off the upper end of the hall, rising to what Vernon called his 'great stairhead chamber', sited exactly where one would expect a great chamber to stand in a Tudor house. (This is now known as the Queen's room, after Queen Adelaide, who leased Sudbury in the early 1840s.) Most remarkable of all, there is a first-floor long gallery which runs along the full width of the south front; a commonplace feature at the beginning of the century, but decidedly unusual in a Restoration country house. And faced, like the Jacobeans, with the problem of squeezing an asymmetrical arrangement of state rooms and family accommodation behind symmetrical façades, Vernon adopted a thoroughly Jacobean solution, using blind windows and mezzanines in an attempt to reconcile the two. It is scarcely surprising that until recently, most historians explained Sudbury as being essentially his great-grandmother Mary Vernon's manor house, which George had either completed or remodelled.

However, the real reason for Sudbury's anachronistic appearance is not that its core is actually Jacobean – in fact, the Vernon family continued to live in the old manor house while their new mansion was being built nearby – but that at the outset George was simply unaware of what was going on in progressive architectural and artistic circles. The design is the work of a man whose experience of formal domestic architecture had been gained not in London, Paris or The Hague, but in an English shire far enough away from court life to be still unfamiliar with the changes which were being brought about closer to the capital by Roger Pratt and Hugh May. Vernon learned as he went along, and in consequence the house is strangely disconcerting, a weird synthesis of the most conservative Jacobean planning and the very latest in Caroline and baroque decoration.

The very latest, because as the time came for the decoration of the state apartments at Sudbury, George Vernon's tastes had already moved on, as the thoroughly Restoration roof-line suggests. The first rooms to be decorated, the great chamber and Vernon's own room on the ground floor (now the library), were the work of local craftsmen, the sculptor William Wilson mentioned earlier, and Samuel

Edward Pierce's great staircase, with plasterwork by Robert Bradbury
and James Pettifer. (*The National Trust/Mike Williams*)

George Vernon, the builder of Sudbury. J. M. Wright's portrait in the saloon has a magnificent surround carved by Edward Pierce. (*NTPL/Jeremy Whitaker*)

Mansfield, a Derby plasterer. But by 1674 Vernon had begun to draw upon craftsmen of an entirely different order, chief among whom were the plasterworkers James Pettifer and his assistant Robert Bradbury, and the wood carver and mason Edward Pierce. Relatively little is known of Bradbury and Pettifer, although the latter was working on several London churches towards the end of the century: Pierce, on the other hand, was already a busy and important name in the Caroline building world. His commissions had included work for Roger Pratt at Horseheath Hall in Cambridgeshire, the Guildhall in the City of London, and Wolseley in Staffordshire, where a contemporary wrote that 'of all the joiner's work I have met with in this county there is none comparable to that of the new dining-room . . . done by one Pierce'. He went on to work for Wren on the rebuilding of the London churches after the Great Fire, and in his will left the pick of his 'closet of books, prints and drawings' to his 'very good friend' William Talman, architect of Chatsworth and Dyrham Park.

Between 1674 and 1680 Pierce, Bradbury and Pettifer created a series of state rooms worthy of any courtier's house. Pierce carved the decoration for the parlour, and the balustrade of the great staircase, which must rank as one of the great achievements of Restoration craftsmanship. The long gallery, the staircase, the parlour and the drawing room adjoining it, with its exquisite Grinling Gibbons overmantel, were all plastered by Bradbury and Pettifer. Their delicate swags, garlands and acanthus scrolls, swirling foliage which resolves itself here into the Vernon arms or a caricature of a Roman emperor, there into a dragon, a horse, a boar or a grasshopper, seems so light, so accomplished in contrast to the earlier Jonesian designs of Samuel Mansfield, that one can only feel sorry for the local craftsman whose work, while competent enough, was never meant to be compared with anything of this stature, and who, after the arrival at Sudbury of Bradbury and Pettifer, was relegated to plastering the walls.

As Sudbury approached completion, Vernon began to buy furniture and fittings for his new house. His first wife Margaret had died in 1675, after giving birth to at least two sons and six daughters. Pierce carved her monument in Sudbury church. Early the next year Vernon married Dorothea Shirley, sister of Lord Ferrers of Staunton Harold in Leicestershire, and in 1679 he took his wife and family on what seems to have been an extended shopping expedition to London. Vernon was combining parliamentary business with pleasure, buying furniture and pictures for the new house as a prelude to moving in, and it is possible that the old manor house which had been his home for twenty years was finally demolished during his stay in the capital. But the trip was marred by tragedy: the accounts contain a payment to a midwife on 18 March 1680, followed on 24 March by references to mourning coaches. Parliament was still sitting and, although he was newly widowed, Vernon stayed on in London, buying chests of drawers, an organ, an altarpiece and communion cloth for his chapel at Sudbury (since removed), paintings and frames, tables and chairs.

By 1682 Sudbury was to all intents and purposes furnished and complete, with elaborate formal gardens. A bird's-eye view of house and grounds painted in that year by Jan Griffier shows the south front, complete with its original wooden roof-balustrade, looking on to an attractive formal arrangement of gravel walks and fountains laid out around the short central axis of the house, the walls lined with pots containing the myrtles, oranges, pomegranates, tulips, 'greens and other trees' that Vernon had bought in London the previous year.

Inside that house, the by now considerable Vernon family – George fathered at least fifteen children, although five died before reaching adulthood – lived in the rather cramped family apartments. In 1681 he married his third and last wife, Catherine, the daughter of his kinsman Thomas Vernon, a wealthy City merchant. During the 1680s and 1690s the household's numbers were often swelled by some of the army of in-laws and cousins that he had acquired in the course of his three marriages.

But Vernon was not quite finished with the Hall: by now more sensitive to fashion, in the early 1690s he brought in another carver called Young, to make the parlour doorcase at the foot of the great staircase. At about the same time he also commissioned the painter Louis Laguerre, then working at Chatsworth for the Devonshires, to add a baroque touch to the state rooms in the shape of a set of murals for the staircase, the *Four Seasons* in the central dome of the parlour, and an *Allegory of Industry and Idleness* to be placed over the fireplace in the great hall.

It would be nice to know what George Vernon thought during his last years about the house that had taken up so much of his energy and money. As he entertained his wealthy Vernon in-laws in his magnificent state apartments, or strolled through the long gallery looking out over his new gardens, did he ever wish that he had done things differently, calling in an 'ingenious gentleman' to produce a more unified and modern design? Did he look enviously to Winde's Belton, or Hooke's still-unfinished Ragley, or Chatsworth, where Talman was busy bringing conservative Derbyshire back into the architectural mainstream? One hopes not. Bizarre Sudbury certainly is, but its owner deserved to feel proud of his creation.

George Vernon died in 1702. His grandson through his third marriage was created Baron Vernon of Kinderton in 1762. Several proposals were put forward to remodel the house in a variety of styles during the nineteenth century – mercifully, all were rejected, although between 1876 and 1883 George Devey added an unusually sympathetic servants' wing to the house. Sudbury came to the National Trust in 1967, following the death of the 9th Lord Vernon.

Belton House

LINCOLNSHIRE

Belton House, 3 miles north-east of Grantham, was built for Sir John Brownlow in 1684–8. The design, probably by William Winde, was executed by the mason-contractor William Stanton.

'Young' Sir John Brownlow, the builder of Belton House. This portrait by John Riley, *c*.1685, hangs in the saloon. (*NTPL/Roy Fox*)

'See the vicissitude of earthly things!' wrote John Evelyn, after spending an afternoon in August 1683 watching the 'sad demolition' of Clarendon House. Only seventeen years earlier Evelyn had been to see the spectacular new palace at the top of St James's Street, Piccadilly, in London, which Roger Pratt had designed for Chancellor Edward Hyde. He thought it 'without hyperbole, the best contrived, the most useful, graceful, and magnificent house in England ... Here is state and use, solidity and beauty, most symmetrically combined together.' A few days afterwards Samuel Pepys also visited the site, 'hearing so much from Mr Evelyn of it', and confirmed that Clarendon House was indeed 'the finest pile I ever did see in my life'. Now Hyde was dead and disgraced, and the most magnificent house in England was being pulled down so that the site could be redeveloped by 'bankers and mechanics'.

But the part that Clarendon House played in the history of English architecture extended far beyond its short life. Although many of its features had already appeared elsewhere (most notably at Pratt's Coleshill – see page 114), its prominent position and its powerful owner ensured that it was seen, admired and emulated all over the country. And its basic form – an astylar, two-storeyed double-pile with a central pediment and rusticated quoins, broad eaves, a hipped roof, pedimented dormer-windows and a balustraded roof-platform, all surmounted by a cupola – became a pattern for large numbers of country houses during the later seventeenth century. One can see echoes of Clarendon at Sudbury Hall (c.1665–91); at Holme Lacy in Herefordshire (1674), built for the 2nd Viscount Scudamore by a mason who had worked on an earlier Pratt house, Horseheath in Cambridgeshire; at William Smith of Warwick's Stanford Hall, Leicestershire (1697); at Hanbury Hall, Worcestershire (1701); and, in its purest and arguably its greatest incarnation, at Belton House in Lincolnshire.

Sir John Brownlow (1659–97), for whom Belton was built, had in 1679 inherited a substantial fortune from his great-uncle, 'Old' Sir John Brownlow: besides the Lincolnshire estate, that fortune included an income of £9,000 a year and around £20,000 in cash. ('Old' Sir John seems to have been quite a hoarder – during the Great Fire his servants had to retrieve some sixty-six sacks, each containing £100 in coin, from his London house.) While still only twenty, Brownlow found himself a very rich man, and he and his equally young wife and cousin Alice immediately began to live up to their newly acquired status. (The couple had been married at the age of sixteen, three months after 'Old' Sir John added a codicil to his will expressing his 'earnest desire that a marriage should be effected' between them 'in case they shall affect one another'.) After spending £5,000 on a London town house in fashionable Southampton (now Bloomsbury) Square, they turned their attention and wealth to the creation of a suitable country seat.

Like so many houses of its type and period, the design of Belton was traditionally assigned to Wren: H. Avray Tipping explained its prominent position as the first house in the first volume of his *In English Homes* (1904) by saying that it 'bears upon its face all the characteristics of the great architect who designed it, as his mind was expressed in his domestic creations. That architect was Sir Christopher Wren.' However, we now know that like Inigo Jones, who also fell victim in the nineteenth and early twentieth centuries to large numbers of rash and careless attributions,

The north front. (*NTPL*)

Wren designed very few country houses. His *oeuvre* currently stands at three – Tring Manor in Hertfordshire (since demolished), Easton Neston in Northamptonshire, and Winslow Hall, Buckinghamshire – and there is even yet some doubt about Wren's role in the design of all of them.

There is certainly no evidence at all to suppose that Christopher Wren had a hand in the design of Belton. It is much more likely to have been the work of the soldier-architect William Winde, who had been involved with the Earl of Craven's Ashdown House in the 1660s, and who in the early 1680s was engaged on remodelling another of Craven's houses, Combe Abbey in Warwickshire. Both Combe and Belton derive from Pratt's Clarendon House, but similarities between the two buildings, in particular the proportions of the central features and the detailing of the windows, suggest a closer link than might be explained by their simply having a common ancestor. The presence at Belton of several craftsmen who worked with Winde at Combe Abbey – the carpenter Edward Willcox, and Edward Goudge, the plasterer whom Winde later recommended to his cousin, Lady Mary

Bridgeman, as 'the best master in England at his profession, as his work at Combe, Hamstead [Hamstead Marshall in Berkshire, another Craven house], and Sir John Brownlow's will evidence' – add further weight to the idea that Winde was involved in the project.

However, the extent of that involvement probably amounted to no more than the supply of plans and elevations. The execution and supervision of the works was the responsibility of the mason-contractor William Stanton, a member of a famous family of masons and sculptors with a yard near St Andrew's Church in Holborn in London (which in 1684 he contracted to rebuild with Edward Pierce – another of Winde's collaborators). Stanton was primarily a monumental sculptor – he is credited with carving some thirty funerary monuments between 1665 and his death forty years later – and he probably came to 'Young' Sir John Brownlow's notice in 1681, when he set up the monument to 'Old' Sir John and his wife in Belton parish church. But in common with many seventeenth-century mason-sculptors, he not only undertook building work but was also prepared to act as clerk of works and general site supervisor when the occasion arose. The large sum of money which he received at Belton – nearly £5,000 – indicates that he and his assistant John Thompson (who went on in 1688 to work as contractor for Wren on St Paul's) played a central role in both the organisation of the scheme and the construction of the house.

How much Belton owes to Winde and how much to Stanton, it is impossible to say. It is an extraordinarily logical and straightforward house, and in both plan and elevation it shows how pervasive Roger Pratt's influence had become by the 1680s. As at Coleshill and Clarendon House, the main storey is set above a half-basement, echoing Pratt's advice that 'an ascent is most graceful with such a basement for it looks like a thing complete in itself, and this adds to the height and majesty of a building; and a prospect is more pleasant to a house than where none, as must necessarily fall out where we cannot see over the top of our out-walls'. By siting the kitchen, buttery, larder, servants' hall and other domestic offices in this basement, Winde and Stanton left the two main floors free to be devoted to family lodgings and state apartments, with the servants' lodgings placed up in the attic storey and reached via sets of back stairs at either end of the house.

The visual and ceremonial focus of the house was the group of four chambers at its centre, emphasised on both of the main façades by three-bay pedimented projections. On the ground floor an entrance hall at the south front led into a great parlour to the north; and above them a great chamber, called the 'great dining room' in an inventory of 1688, stood back-to-back with the state bedchamber and its closet. ('Let the fairest room above,' wrote Pratt, 'be placed in the very midst of the house, as the bulk of a man is between his members'.) The other main rooms, including the Brownlows' own lodgings on the first floor and a series of reception rooms below, were symmetrically disposed to either side of this group, the only jarring note being the placing of the main staircase to the east of the single-storey hall, rather than rising out of it as at Coleshill. The two wings contained the chapel and kitchen to the north, with lodgings for Lady Alice's relations and nurseries for the Brownlows' daughters to the south.

Regular payments to William Stanton began in March 1685, at about the same time that Brownlow's steward 'gave the mason to drink at laying the first stone on the new house, 5s'. Preliminary operations to clear the site had been under way since the previous year, when both the old Belton Manor and Ringston House (another Brownlow property at Rippingale, fifteen miles south-east of Grantham) were demolished and their materials – stone, wood, slates, glass and lead – were carted to the new site for re-use. New limestone for the building came from the nearby Heydour quarries of Samuel Marsh, whose son had recently been employed by the Duke of Newcastle as builder-architect at Nottingham and Bolsover Castles and Welbeck Abbey in Nottinghamshire; the quoins and keystones came from Ketton, outside Stamford in Lincolnshire.

Once begun, the building work progressed quite quickly. Stanton had the shell erected by the autumn of 1686, and decoration and finishing were more or less complete by November 1688, when the Brownlows moved into their new house. The balustrade and cupola were put up by the carpenter Edward Willcox, and the interior plasterwork was by Edward Goudge, whose ceilings at Belton rank among his finest. The chapel, in particular, is a *tour de force*: lush garlands and scrolls of acanthus leaves, fruit and flowers, all swirl around putti who cavort with baroque exuberance among foliage, grapes and flowers, while four trios of chubby – and somewhat surly – cherub heads sing out from high-relief panels. The scene is presided over by two further putti who perch precariously inside a broken segmental pediment on top of a magnificent Corinthian reredos, probably the work of William Stanton (who provided the marble pavement and altar steps) and the local carver Edmund Carpenter.

Carpenter, whose only recorded work was at Belton, was responsible for much of the woodcarving in the house. His 1688 bill specifically mentions three chimney-pieces, including one 'in the great parlour with fruit and flowers' for which he was paid £18, and another costing £26, a 'very rich chimneypiece in the withdrawing room to the great parlour done with varieties of fish and shells with birds, foliage, fruit and flowers'. (Many of the Belton carvings have since been rearranged – this probably refers to the overmantel now standing in the entrance hall.) Other carvings have traditionally been assigned to Grinling Gibbons, but although Gibbons has suffered from the same indiscriminate wave of attributions that afflicted Inigo Jones and Christopher Wren, claims concerning his putative work at Belton cannot be dismissed quite so lightly. For example, Carpenter's overmantels in the great parlour (now the saloon) and the entrance hall both have partners that are clearly not by his hand: these are much bolder and more finely executed, and certainly show close affinities with Gibbons' authenticated work.

The inventory drawn up in 1688, when the Brownlows moved into their new house, shows that Belton was furnished in a simple but modern manner – there is, for example, no evidence to suggest that any of the oak chairs and chests from the old house were installed in the new building. The hall, with its black-and-white marble floor supplied by Stanton, contained 'two marble cisterns with cocks', a rather daunting set of twenty-eight paintings of kings and queens of England from William the Conqueror to William of Orange, and 'one dozen rush armchairs'. Since the hall

was essentially a grand introduction to the other apartments rather than a living area, these would have been for the use of visiting gentry or those who had business with Sir John. The parlour was furnished with 'two very large seeing glasses', 'three crimson sarcenet curtains fringed about', eighteen more rush chairs and two japanned tables. The first-floor state bedchamber contained 'one fine bedstead with green damask curtains and valance ... twelve green velvet armchairs ... and three pieces of Moses tapestry hangings'.

By 1698, when a second inventory was taken, Sir John and Lady Alice had had time to install some more opulent and more fashionable decoration. In August 1691, for example, Brownlow had commissioned John Vanderbank, the Chief Arras Worker of the Great Wardrobe, to make a set of hangings for the drawing room adjoining the family gallery in the chapel, which were 'to be of Indian figures according to the pattern of the Queen's which are at Kensington and to be finished as well in every kind'. These hangings, which are still at Belton, were modelled on Mogul miniatures which had recently been brought back from India; Vanderbank's set of four 'Indian' tapestries for Queen Mary's withdrawing room at Kensington Palace constituted his first royal commission, in 1690.

The richer decorative scheme of which Vanderbank's tapestries formed a part was carried through into the rest of the house, if the newly named rooms listed in the 1698 inventory are anything to go by. Now there was a 'green damask drawing room', a 'white varnished drawing room' and a 'white gilt closet'; a 'white and green painted chamber', a 'blue and white painted chamber' and – as at William Blathwayt's Dyrham Park, which was being fitted out at the same time – a 'Scotch plaid room'.

But by 1698 Sir John Brownlow was dead. The serious, rather smug young man, shown complete with double chin in John Riley's portrait of about 1685, had done everything expected of a wealthy county gentleman. He had built himself an appropriately grand new house; he had served as High Sheriff of Lincolnshire and MP for Grantham; he had even, on 29 October 1695, entertained his king at Belton, giving William III such a good time that he 'sent up for [Brownlow] to London to honour him the more and to require him for his kindnesses'. According to the diarist Abraham de la Pryme, 'the king was exceeding merry and drank freely which was the occasion that when he came to Lincoln he could eat nothing but a mess of milk'. Everything seemed set for Brownlow's further advancement, perhaps even a peerage. But in July 1697, while he was staying at his uncle's house in Dorset, he shot himself – 'the reason not known', wrote a contemporary.

Brownlow's widow stayed on at Belton until her death in 1721, spending her time in arranging advantageous matches for their five daughters. According to her monument by Christopher Horsnaile the elder in Belton church, 'she was chiefly employed in their education: three of them she disposed in marriage to three noble peers of the realm [the Duke of Ancaster, the Earl of Exeter and the Earl of Guilford] and the fourth to the husband's nephew, out of respect to his memory'. And, the

The chapel, with its magnificent Corinthian reredos, probably made by William Stanton. (*NTPL/Mark Fiennes*)

inscription might have added, out of respect for that nephew's inheritance – on Sir John's death Belton passed to his brother William, whose son, another John, succeeded in 1702.

Belton itself escaped the 'vicissitude of earthly things' which afflicted Clarendon House, although it did suffer a number of quite dramatic changes during the eighteenth and nineteenth centuries, when first James Wyatt and then Jeffry Wyatville were called in to impart a more classical air to both the exteriors and the interiors, and the cupola, balustrade and dormer pediments were removed. But much of Winde's original scheme was painstakingly reinstated by the 3rd Earl Brownlow in the 1870s. The exterior was restored to its former glory, and the great parlour was given a magnificent plasterwork ceiling in the style of Edward Goudge by the London firm of George Jackson & Sons.

Others, too, sought to reproduce that glory. Like its progenitor, Clarendon House, Belton became an archetype, a model for others to emulate – a process which began in 1688, when William Stanton designed a near replica at Denham Place in Buckinghamshire for Sir Roger Hill, and ended across the Atlantic in the early years of the twentieth century when Edith Wharton built herself a miniature version of Brownlow's house, complete with pediment, dormers, balustrade and cupola, in Massachusetts. For many, Belton is the finest example of what is arguably the greatest, and certainly the most amiable, period in English country house building.

In 1984 the 7th Lord Brownlow gave the house, the garden and some of the contents to the National Trust; a grant from the National Heritage Memorial Fund enabled the Trust to buy the park and further contents, and to establish an endowment to maintain the property.

Dyrham Park

AVON

Dyrham Park, 8 miles north of Bath, was built in two stages between 1692 and 1704, incorporating parts of an earlier house. The west front is the work of Samuel Hauduroy; the east front is by William Talman. Their client was William Blathwayt.

The history of the country house in the later seventeenth and early eighteenth centuries is littered with flamboyant, even eccentric, autocrats. There is the 1st Duke of Devonshire, pleading poverty as an excuse for not paying his workmen at Chatsworth, while gambling – and losing – £2,000 in a single day at Newmarket races; the ridiculously snobbish 'Proud Duke' of Somerset at Petworth, insisting that his children stand in his presence, and disinheriting a daughter who dared to sit down for a moment when he fell asleep in his chair; and the Duke of Manchester, who remodelled Kimbolton Castle in Huntingdonshire, and of whom the French complained that while at the court of Louis XIV 'his Excellency blows his nose in the napkin, spits in the middle of the room, and laughs so loud and like an ordinary body

Dyrham Park in Avon: William Talman's east front. (*NTPL*)

that he [is] not thought fit for an Ambassador'. At times it seems as if that hauteur and ostentation which informed so much English baroque was matched by the hauteur and ostentation of its sponsors, art and architecture expressing a patron's personality as much as his status.

We can only be grateful that this theory doesn't hold water when it is applied to Dyrham Park. At times peevish and petulant, too often cautious to the point of meanness, William Blathwayt seems the antithesis of baroque values: fortunately his house, if somewhat restrained, has little in common with its builder.

The very lack of flair and flamboyance which characterised Blathwayt's life led to a successful career as an able administrator and an efficient civil servant. Born in about 1649 to a London lawyer who died when William was still a small child, he was brought up by his uncle Thomas Povey, who was, unlike his nephew, a rather inept civil servant. Samuel Pepys found him 'the most ignorant man I ever met with in so great a trust as he is', but he was nevertheless a cultured virtuoso and a convivial host with important connections at court. Probably on account of Povey's influence, in 1668 Blathwayt became Secretary to Sir William Temple during the latter's embassy at The Hague; and in 1672 he was in the service of the Duke of Richmond in Denmark, for whom he travelled to Sweden, Germany, Italy and France, returning home to England at the end of 1673.

Over the next thirty years Blathwayt steadily accumulated one government post after another. After being made Surveyor and Auditor-General of Plantations Revenues in 1680, he bought the Secretaryship at War for £2,000 in 1683, was elected to Parliament for Newtown, Isle of Wight, in 1685 – he lost his seat four years later, but then sat for Bath between 1693 and 1710 – became Clerk of the Privy Council in 1686, and a member of the Board of Trade in 1696. As Secretary at War he accompanied James II in November 1688 on his march to Salisbury, following William of Orange's landing at Torbay. But in spite of his loyalty to the old king, William III retained his services, partly because of Blathwayt's command of his native tongue, acquired during his time at The Hague, but more importantly because of his proven administrative abilities, which, combined with an apparent indifference to politics, made him the archetype of the hard-working – and safe – civil servant, who would competently conduct affairs of government without interfering in them. As a result it was Blathwayt, rather than the King's two statutory Secretaries of State, who accompanied William on his annual European campaigns against the French during the 1690s, acting not only as Secretary at War, but also as temporary Secretary of State.

Before this, though, William Blathwayt's thoughts were turning to marriage, and in September 1686 he was told of a possible match: the thirty-six-year-old Mary, daughter of a landowner named John Wynter whose seat was a Tudor house at Dyrham in Gloucestershire. In spite of the fact that the last of Mary's three brothers had died a few months earlier, leaving her heiress to a considerable estate, William at first showed little interest. However, his friend and colleague Sir Robert Southwell, the Secretary of State for Ireland – whose Kings Weston estate north of Bristol made him a near-neighbour of the Wynters, and whose son Edward would marry Blathwayt's daughter thirty years later – arranged for him to visit Dyrham. His enthusiasm fired either by Mary or by the estate, or by both, William proposed, and after a long and complicated marriage settlement had been carefully negotiated the couple were married in Dyrham church that Christmas.

Characteristically, Blathwayt's first reaction to Dyrham and his prospective bride was to calculate how much the match would cost him. He reckoned that he would have to lay out at least £2,000 on linen and plate for his new household, and, as he wrote to Southwell, he was 'afraid there will be a necessity of building a new house at Dyrham or being at a very great expense in repairing this'. John Wynter's Royalist sympathies had cost him dear during the Commonwealth, and his finances had been further depleted by a lengthy lawsuit; as a result, both the early sixteenth-century house and its surrounding estates were run down and ramshackle.

In 1686, of course, Blathwayt's idea of building a new house at Dyrham was no more than a project for the future. He had his official lodgings at Whitehall and a house near Hampton Court in Middlesex, where John Evelyn dined with him in June 1687, recording afterwards that 'this gentleman is Secretary of War, Clerk of the Council, &c having raised himself by his industry from very moderate circumstances. He is a very proper, handsome person, and very dextrous in business, and besides all this, has married a great fortune.' That fortune came to William the following year, with the death of John Wynter. And in November 1691, the two remaining Dyrham Wynters, his mother-in-law and his wife, also died. Blathwayt was left with two sons, a daughter – and sole possession of a considerable country estate. To quote James Lees-Milne, 'regarded as a business venture, [the marriage] proved as successful as any ambitious man verging on middle age could wish for'.

In February 1692, just three months into his widowhood, William began to remodel the old house at Dyrham. Before leaving on the first of his annual expeditions to Flanders with the King, he commissioned a two-storey range of apartments to the west of the Tudor great hall, a project which was completed by 1694. The new façade thus formed consists of a fairly plain two-storey central block of nine bays, flanked by two shallow three-bay projections. Beyond this, two pavilions are linked to the main house by single-storey galleries, one of which forms a covered walk to the parish church of St Peter, while the other gives access to what was, in Blathwayt's time, a nursery wing for his three young children. The overall composition owes more to the town than to the country: the raised and enclosed terrace, reached via a straight double stairway, echoes the arrangement of a French *hôtel*, with its lodgings forming three sides of a court opening on to the street through a central gateway. There were several precedents for the form in this country, including such London town houses as Robert Hooke's Montagu House (1675–9; see page 119).

Blathwayt's architect for this new work was a Huguenot, Samuel Hauduroy. He is not known to have designed any other buildings, although Louis Hauduroy and Mark Antony Hauduroy, presumably relations, worked in England as decorative painters at this time. Louis was responsible for the decoration of the staircase at Culverthorpe Hall in Lincolnshire in 1704–5, and of Thomas Archer's pavilion at Wrest Park, Bedfordshire, in 1712, while Mark Antony decorated several rooms at Knole for the 1st Duke of Dorset in 1723–4. Samuel Hauduroy himself was involved in marbling and graining the wainscot at Dyrham in 1694, suggesting that he too may have been primarily a painter. The reason for Blathwayt's choice of a relative unknown remains a mystery, although economy seems to have played a part. In his only surviving letter, Hauduroy complained that since his employer's return from campaigning in Europe late in 1692 he had been forced to work from two hours before dawn until two in the morning, and all for ten guineas, four of which had been spent on travelling back and forth to Dyrham.

During the 1690s Blathwayt's career continued to thrive. By 1696 the annual income from his various posts came to over £5,000, an amount that may well have been more than doubled by the bribes and perquisites which were part and parcel of government office in seventeenth-century England. It is an indication of this increasing status and wealth that when he decided to remodel the east front of Dyrham in 1698, effectively sweeping away the last vestiges of the Tudor house (with the exception of the great hall, which was retained as a link between the two new ranges), he went not to a Huguenot refugee who would do as he was told for a pittance, but to a man who was one of the leading country house architects of his day – William Talman, the Comptroller of the King's Works.

Talman (1650–1719) was a gifted if somewhat eclectic designer, as much at home with the work of his Caroline predecessors as he was with contemporary French and Italian architecture. Uppark in West Sussex, for example, built about 1690 for the Earl of Tankerville and almost certainly Talman's work, looked back to the Dutch-inspired conventions which Pratt had established at Clarendon House, Piccadilly, twenty-five years earlier. And his abortive scheme for Welbeck Abbey in Nottinghamshire (1703) shows the influence of the Italian baroque, while his masterly south range at Chatsworth (1687–96) – which, with its tall rectangular façade raised on a rusticated basement storey and topped with a balustrade decorated with stone urns, broke with the English tradition of hipped roofs and dormer-windows – derives from an engraving by Jean Marot of Bernini's unexecuted design for the Louvre.

The new works at Dyrham began in 1700, nearly two years after Talman was first consulted. The architect and his master mason, Benjamin Jackson, visited the site in 1699, by which time the remains of the old building had presumably been pulled down and cleared away, and foundations were being laid. For the new east range Talman adopted a similar, if rather less monumental, scheme to that which he had used at Chatsworth (where he had just been sacked by the Duke of Devonshire – he was an extraordinarily argumentative man, and it is ironic that Blathwayt, who was himself more than usually difficult to please, should be one of the few clients with whom Talman failed to quarrel). The rectangular façade is taller, longer and altogether grander than Hauduroy's west front. The rusticated horizontal bands on the ground floor, and the quoins to the two projecting wings, frame the *piano nobile*, which is further emphasised by pediments, blind balustrades and swags, and strapwork panels in the manner of engravings from Rubens' *Palazzi di Genova*. A flat, balustraded skyline is topped with heavy stone urns at the angles of the wings, while an eagle perches on a rock (the family crest) in the centre; and a long orangery, perhaps based on that at Versailles and probably also by Talman, leads off to the south, effectively hiding from view the stabling, kitchens and domestic quarters which were put up in 1698 by Edward Wilcox, Talman's foreman.

Blathwayt was rarely at Dyrham during both phases of the construction work: he was either abroad with William III, or hard at work in his Whitehall office. However, his absence did not prevent him from taking an active interest in both the building operations and the spectacular and elaborate formal gardens which were being laid out by Thomas Hurnall, his head gardener, during the 1690s and early 1700s. Accounts were sent up to London each week for his approval, and his many letters, first to Robert Henley, who acted as his agent or clerk of works during Hauduroy's time, and then to Charles Watkins, who supervised the Talman wing and the completion of the pleasure grounds, show him constantly chivvying and complaining and bullying: 'these people [ie, the workmen] want stirring up roundly and not to be overfed with money'; 'I know the aversion mankind has at Dyrham for *finishing* anything'; 'I don't find there is much riddance of idle fellows at Dyrham'.

Blathwayt emerges from these exchanges as a rather unendearing character,

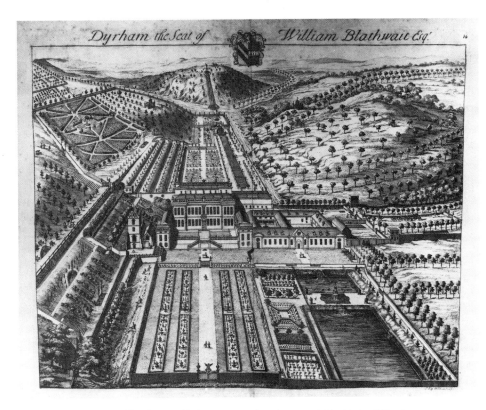

Kip's bird's-eye view of Dyrham, with its water garden, in 1712. (*The National Trust*)

pedantic and, in spite of his considerable wealth, forever trying to cut corners. In reply to a letter from Watkins, he reluctantly agreed to the installation of window shutters on a side of the house where they would serve no practical purpose, 'for uniformity's sake', but stipulated: 'I would have them all of deal (to be painted) except that one side that appears of the window shutter when it lies in the wall which is one fourth part of the whole and no more and is to be veneered with walnut.' He also decided that the solder to seal the lead sheets of his bath-house would be prohibitively expensive, and that the workmen should simply lay the lead with overlapping edges. Watkins patiently explained that the bath would leak.

By July 1702, when the Blathwayt eagle was hoisted into position over Talman's east front – 'without prejudice to the house, walls and glass windows,' commanded its owner – the building work was virtually complete and the interiors were being decorated and furnished. Both the west and the east ranges were served by substantial staircases – the former of Virginian walnut, with panelling grained to match, and the latter of American cedar, with walnut treads, grained dado, soffits, doors and window cases and marbled walls. (One of Hauduroy's early designs, showing intricately carved balusters, was rejected by Blathwayt on the grounds that 'this will harbour dust very much'.) Hauduroy's range was largely given over to family apartments and business rooms. On the ground floor there was a family parlour or eating room, and a waiting room for servants: this last contained twenty-four leather fire buckets and, according to an inventory of 1710, 'an elephant's snout'. William Blathwayt's own apartment was on the first floor.

Talman's grander east range, on the other hand, was intended to house the main display rooms, which were 'more for state than use except upon extraordinary occasion', according to Blathwayt's nephew and clerk, John Povey. There were two state apartments. That on the ground floor, which opened off to the south of a central vestibule decorated with embossed and painted leather hangings, consisted of a tapestried antechamber, a bedchamber hung with damask, and a cabinet or closet lined with panels of yellow striped satin, all with their doorways aligned to form an enfilade. On the first floor, a second state apartment led off a great chamber at the head of Talman's staircase, hung with gilt leather and furnished with gilt leather chairs.

In a house of this date one might expect the state apartments to be disposed to either side of the main axis, as at Ham House, providing that symmetry and centrality that was fundamental to late-Caroline and baroque planning. As it was, the area to the north of the vestibule below, and the great chamber above, was taken up with Talman's staircase, a reception room (known in Blathwayt's time as 'the plod room' from its plaid or check furnishings), and a secondary bedchamber. However, on the ground floor at least, the sense of balance was provided in a novel way. During the 1690s Blathwayt bought a number of pictures and books from his uncle Thomas Povey, including a remarkable and much admired perspective painting by Samuel van Hoogstraeten, *A View Down A Corridor*. This was hung in a closet beyond the plod room, in line with the enfilade of the apartment across the vestibule, so that when viewed from that apartment it created an illusion of depth, as though a second, balancing suite of rooms did indeed exist to the north of the main axis. (The Duke of Devonshire used a similar device at Chatsworth, where a massive pier-glass hung in the saloon produced a mirror image of the state enfilade.)

By the time that William Blathwayt's new house was finished in 1704, the rather

petty and distinctly unbaroque economies that he was constantly urging on the hapless Watkins had gained some point, as his career in government began to slip into decline. With the death of William III in March 1702, his post as acting Secretary of State came to an end; and, since Blathwayt was no match for the political intriguers and manipulators who were jockeying for power around the new queen, his other offices were taken from him one by one. He was dismissed from the Secretaryship at War in 1704, and lost his place on the Board of Trade in 1707 and his seat in Parliament in 1710. Angry, embittered and determined that his two sons should not enter politics and suffer his fate, he retired to his country house, dying in 1717 at the age of sixty-eight.

Dyrham Park remained relatively unaltered, apart from the removal and rearrangement of some of the furnishings and the sweeping away of the formal garden at the end of the eighteenth century. The Blathwayt family continued to hold the house until 1956, when, together with the contents and eleven acres of the grounds, it was bought through National Land Fund procedures by what was then the Ministry of Public Buildings and Works; it was transferred to the National Trust five years later, following an extensive restoration programme. In 1976 two hundred and sixty-three acres of parkland came to the Trust via the Department of the Environment, again through the National Land Fund.

Petworth House

WEST SUSSEX

Petworth House, in the centre of the village of Petworth, was rebuilt after 1688 for Charles Seymour, 6th Duke of Somerset, almost certainly with advice from William III's Huguenot architect Daniel Marot. It was partly remodelled after a fire in 1714, and further altered later in the eighteenth century by Matthew Brettingham, father and son; and in 1869–72 by Anthony Salvin.

Petworth House: a limewood carving by Grinling Gibbons of musical instruments. This forms part of the magnificent surround to the portraits of Lord and Lady Seymour of Trowbridge, grandparents of the Proud Duke, in the Carved Room. (*NTPL/Jeremy Whitaker*)

If his elder brother had behaved himself in church, Charles Seymour might never have been in a position to rebuild Petworth, and the world would never have known one of the greatest baroque houses of the seventeenth century.

Petworth had been owned since the early Middle Ages by the Percy family, and there had been some sort of mansion there before 1309, when Henry, Lord Percy, was granted a licence to crenellate an existing manor house. The political careers of the Earls of Northumberland, as the Percys became in 1377, were rarely happy, and seven of the eleven earls were killed in battle, executed, murdered or imprisoned. In 1615, after studying architecture whilst languishing in the Tower of London as a result of his suspected involvement in the Gunpowder Plot, the 9th Earl – another Henry Percy, whose interest in alchemy earned him the nickname of the 'Wizard Earl' – drew up plans for a new mansion to the north-west of the present house. Although the Wizard Earl was released in 1621 (after paying a fine of £11,000), whereupon he began to build some of the service ranges, the new house came to nothing, and on his death in 1632 Petworth still consisted basically of the ancient cruciform manor house that had stood on the site for centuries. Few other changes had been made to the old building when in 1670 Henry's grandson, Joscelyn, the 11th Earl, died, leaving an only daughter as heiress to Petworth and the considerable Percy fortune.

This daughter, Elizabeth, was as unlucky in wedlock as her ancestors had been in politics. When she was scarcely twelve, her ambitious grandmother married her to Lord Ogle, who died a year later, in 1680. She seems to have been a precocious adolescent: her second husband, Thomas Thynne of Longleat, was murdered in Pall Mall, London, in February 1682 by her lover, Count Charles Königsmarck.[1]

Which brings us to Charles Seymour (1662–1748) and the indecorous behaviour of his elder brother. As the younger son of the 4th Duke of Somerset, Charles was a member of a family every bit as illustrious and long-lineaged as the Percys. It could trace its roots back to the Norman St Maurs, taking in on the way a lord protector of England, the 1st Duke, and a queen, Jane Seymour. During a tour of Italy in 1678 Charles's brother, the 5th Duke, was apparently rather rude to some ladies in a church at Lerice. Horatio Botti, the husband of one of those ladies, took exception to the Duke's behaviour and followed him to his inn, where he shot him dead on the doorstep, thus unwittingly elevating Charles to the dukedom.

For Elizabeth – and her grandmother, eager to see the young heiress enter into a more lasting marriage than before, with a suitably eligible nobleman – it was a case of third time lucky. Within a few months of Thynne's murder, a match was arranged between the Wizard Earl's great-granddaughter and the new 6th Duke of Somerset, and later that year the couple were married.

---

1 Königsmarck escaped justice, but several of his accomplices were hanged. John Evelyn describes with ghoulish relish seeing the body of one, a Colonel Vrats, who was embalmed 'by a particular art invented by one William Russell, a coffin-maker, which preserved the body without disembowelling … The flesh was florid, soft, and full, as if the person were only sleeping. He had now been dead near fifteen days, and lay exposed in a rich coffin lined with lead, too magnificent for so daring and horrid a murderer.'

Charles Seymour, 6th Duke of Somerset – the Proud Duke – in a portrait by Closterman,
hanging in the Carved Room. (*Courtauld Institute of Art*)

For five or six years, the Duke and Duchess seem to have done little to modernise Petworth, except for wainscoting some of the main rooms in 1686 'according to the work in his majesty's great and new gallery at Whitehall', which Wren was then remodelling for James II. But when Elizabeth came of age in 1688, so gaining access to the whole of her considerable inheritance, they decided to make Petworth their principal seat, and began in earnest to turn the rambling old house into a palace.

Perhaps because it was cheaper, perhaps because of a desire to retain the architectural evidence of his wife's long pedigree, the Duke opted to remodel the existing building, retaining the original internal walls wherever possible, rather than starting afresh. The back of Petworth remains a patchwork jumble of medieval, Tudor and Jacobean work. The Duke's efforts were concentrated on creating a magnificent west front with a 320 foot façade, which both housed a series of state apartments and effectively disguised the irregularities that lay behind it.

His accounts show that he employed a number of craftsmen associated with the King's Works. The project was supervised by the master mason Samuel Foulkes, who had worked for Christopher Wren on the building of Winchester Palace until 1685, when Charles II's death effectively brought building operations to a halt. John Scarborough, Clerk of the Works at Greenwich Palace and a man often employed by both Wren and Robert Hooke as a measuring clerk, spent a week surveying the new works at Petworth in 1690, a task for which he was paid £10 15s. The bricklayer Edward Dee, and John Hunt the glazier, both worked for the Crown at Hampton Court, as did the plasterer Edward Goudge. Grinling Gibbons was Master Carver in Wood to the King. Only the mason John Selden, who was responsible for much of the external and internal decoration – including the 'keystones with carved wings' (the Duke's crest) which appear above each window – was a local man without any record of working for the Crown.

With such a prestigious assembly of workmen, one might expect that the designs for the new building would also have come from the Office of Works, perhaps even from Wren himself. But the fact is that we simply don't know who built Petworth, although several names have been proposed, including Wren (on the strength of a resemblance between the west front and his scheme for Winchester Palace) and William Talman, Comptroller of the King's Works from 1689 and designer of Dyrham Park. Talman's designs for the south front of Sir John Germaine's Drayton House in Northamptonshire (1702) bear some resemblance to Petworth.

But the original proportions and treatment of both the façade and several of the interiors suggest that the creative mind behind the new house had a first-hand knowledge of contemporary French architecture which went beyond anything encountered in the designs of either Talman or Wren. A painting of the house in the possession of the Duke of Rutland shows that Petworth originally had high, exposed mansard roofs, with the projecting three bays at each end separated to give the appearance of pavilions. And the centre of the façade was emphasised by a square section dome crowned with a balustrade and by statues on the parapet below. Such Gallic touches imply a Gallic designer.

One candidate is the 'Monsieur Pouget' or 'Bouget', said to have been responsible for the francophile 1st Duke of Montagu's town house in Bloomsbury in London.

Petworth in about 1700, showing the west front and part of George London's formal garden.
(*Country Life, collection of the Duke of Rutland*)

There are strong similarities between that building, Petworth and Montagu's country house, Boughton in Northamptonshire. For example, Montagu House also boasted a squared dome, and such a dome still caps the stable block at Boughton. Since Montagu was married to the widowed Countess of Northumberland, Elizabeth's mother, it seems possible that Pouget or Bouget was recommended to the Duke by his father-in-law, who had perhaps become acquainted with him during his time as ambassador at the French court.

A second and more likely candidate is Daniel Marot, a Huguenot who fled to the Low Countries after the revocation of the Edict of Nantes in 1685 and subsequently became architect to William of Orange; and here there is some documentary evidence, albeit tantalisingly vague, to support the attribution. The Duke of Somerset's personal account book for 1693 records an unitemised payment of £20 to a 'Mr Maro', while a note in his library catalogue records that at some unspecified point in the early 1690s 'Monsieur Marot' borrowed a copy of Montaigne's essays.

However, the most convincing argument for Marot's involvement in the design of Petworth is the house itself, as Gervase Jackson-Stops has shown in his book *The Country House in Perspective*. Square domes appear in several of Marot's designs, such as his scheme for the Hôtel Wassenaar-Obdam at The Hague. And the brackets carved with masks over the windows of the pavilions, the busts in panels below them, and the handling of the great hall of state in the centre of the west front, all have parallels in works which Marot executed for William III. The staunchly Protestant Duke of Somerset was one of that group of noblemen who invited William and Mary to take the throne in 1688, and it is tempting to speculate that, eager to emulate his new king, the Duke of Somerset sought both a designer and a group of master-craftsmen who would build him a house which both demonstrated his allegiance and advertised his links with the Crown.

Not that those links were as close as Somerset would have liked. Although he entertained William III at Petworth in 1693, he failed to achieve the high office that he felt was his due. And as time wore on, the 'Proud Duke', as he became known, developed an exaggerated sense of his own importance which amounted almost to an obsession. He used to come down to breakfast at 8am each morning in full ceremonial dress. And he ate in almost medieval state each day, although he rarely had guests, since, according to Jeremiah Miles who visited Petworth in 1743, he 'treats all his country neighbours, and indeed everybody else, with such uncommon pride, and distance, that none of them visit him'.

The baroque, of course, was perfectly suited to express such an autocratic personality. Subsequent internal alterations have changed and softened Petworth's character, but enough survives to show us what it was like at the end of the seventeenth century. The hall of state, with its chimneypieces on which the Duke's heraldic supporters, a bull and a unicorn, balance precariously, looks much as it did in the 1690s. So too does the chapel, the main focus of which is not the reredos and altar at the east end, but the elaborate family pew to the west, which stands beneath a gigantic proscenium of carved and painted 'drapery' on which the Proud Duke's arms and coronet are held aloft by winged angels. And the Carved Room, in which a collection of Gibbons and Selden wood-carvings from around the house were assembled in the late eighteenth century, gives us some idea of the opulent decoration of many of the state rooms.

But one of the finest baroque interiors to survive at Petworth dates not from the 1690s, but from the period immediately following a disastrous fire at the house in 1714. The staircase, which leads up to the Duke's great chamber over the hall, is dominated by a set of awe-inspiring murals by Louis Laguerre. On an upper wall the Duchess of Somerset sits in her chariot, attended by the Three Graces (and her pet spaniel), while above her the Muses direct one's gaze up to the ceiling, painted with an assembly of the gods. The lower scenes show the story of Prometheus, who was chained to a rock on Mount Caucasus while vultures fed on his liver, as a punishment for having stolen fire from the chariot of the sun, and who was eventually rescued by Hercules. The choice of subject is an apt one, operating simultaneously on several different levels: it is at once a reference to the recent fire; an allusion to the Proud Duke's crest, a phoenix rising from the flames; and an allegory of the Duke himself, 'liberated' by William III, who was often depicted as Hercules.

The Proud Duke remained until the end of his life a prisoner of his own arrogance. By the time of his death in 1748 he was a rather pathetic figure, clinging desperately to his noble status and long pedigree in a world which had moved on from the autocratic absolutism of the late seventeenth century, leaving him behind.

Somerset was succeeded by his eldest son, Algernon, who died without male heirs in 1750. His estates and titles, including the earldoms of Northumberland and Egremont (granted to him by George II in 1749), were divided: his son-in-law, Sir Hugh Smithson, changed his name to Percy and became first Earl, and then Duke of Northumberland, while his nephew Charles Wyndham inherited Petworth and other estates as the 2nd Earl of Egremont. Wyndham, a member of the Society of Dilettanti, amassed a considerable collection of antique statues, and commissioned

Matthew Brettingham the elder to design a gallery to house that collection in 1756–63, as well as making other changes to the house. Brettingham's eldest son, also Matthew, modified the west front in 1774–9; and in the early nineteenth century the 3rd Earl extended his father's gallery, using an unknown architect. The last major building phase was in 1869–72, when Anthony Salvin added a *porte-cochère* and rebuilt the south-east part of the house.

In 1947 Charles Wyndham, 3rd Lord Leconfield, passed Petworth to the National Trust; the greater part of the furniture and pictures were transferred to the Trust from the Treasury.

Antony House

CORNWALL

Antony House lies 5 miles west of Plymouth, just across the tidal area known as the Hamoaze. It was built to replace an earlier house between 1718 and 1729 for Sir William Carew. Traditionally attributed to James Gibbs, the house is almost certainly the work of another, unidentified architect; the master-mason in charge was John Moyle of Exeter.

The seventeenth century started well for the Carews of Antony. In 1602 Richard Carew (1555–1620), whose family had lived since the end of the fifteenth century in the medieval house which then stood on the estate, finally published the *Survey of Cornwall* on which he had been working since the 1580s. A friend and admirer of William Camden, Sir Philip Sidney and William Cecil, Carew was one of the greatest, and most readable, of the Tudor topographers. His classic account of all things Cornish was only the second county survey to be written (following William Lambarde's *Perambulation of the County of Kent*, which appeared in 1576). Simultaneously scholarly and anecdotal, Carew's book covers everything from tin-mining, agriculture and the pilchard industry to the language, the sports and games – and even the rats: 'Of all manner of vermin, Cornish houses are most pestered with rats, a brood very hurtful for devouring of meat, clothes and writings by day; and alike cumbersome through their crying and rattling, while they dance their gallop galliards on the roof at night.'

Little is known of Richard Carew's Antony. It probably stood at some distance from the present building – perhaps half a mile away to the east – but nothing of it has survived. The topographer John Norden describes the house of this man 'whose learning and diligence hath brought forth very memorable things of his native country in history' simply as 'profitably and pleasantly seated', noting that its owner had created a salt-water pond below the house, and stocked it with sea fish. No doubt Richard's feelings about the place were somewhat ambivalent. As someone with such a strong sense of place and history, he must have loved it as his family's

Antony House, Cornwall: the north front. (*NTPL/John Bethell*)

home while regretting that it kept him away from the company of like-minded friends. In 1605 he wrote to his fellow-antiquarian Sir Robert Cotton, describing his 'grief that my so remote dwelling depriveth me of your sweet and respected antiquarian Society', referring to the group of friends – Camden, John Stow, Lambarde and others – who met at intervals in Cotton's Westminster house to discuss their researches.

Richard died in 1620 and during and after the Civil War the Carews, who continued to live for the most part at Antony, suffered more than most families in consequence of the hostilities. The topographer's son Richard – who obviously inherited his father's literary inclinations but not his talent, if his pamphlet describing the 'excellent helps really found out, tried, and had, . . . by a warming-stone' is anything to go by – seems to have sided, albeit half-heartedly, with Parliament, despite having been made a baronet twelve months before Charles I raised his standard at Nottingham in August 1642. He died the year after the outbreak of war, leaving nine children, two of whom, at least – Alexander, who succeeded him, and John, his half-brother – also came out against the King.

Neither Alexander nor John fell in battle, but both met tragic ends as a result of the war. Alexander's early enthusiasm for the Parliamentarian cause wavered fatally in 1643, when, as governor of St Nicholas Island in Plymouth Sound he lost his nerve in the face of a wave of Royalist successes in the West Country which threatened Plymouth, and offered to change sides, bringing the island and its fort with him. Rather unwisely, as things turned out, he refused to surrender until a promised pardon from the King arrived. In the meantime, his shifting sympathies were discovered by the staunchly Parliamentarian citizens of Plymouth. He was arrested and taken to London, where he was tried and, on Monday 23 December

1644, beheaded on Tower Hill. There is a story that his portrait, which hangs in the library at Antony, was torn from its frame by Royalist relatives when he declared for Parliament, only to be replaced when he changed his allegiance: true or not, the picture has certainly been crudely stitched together at some point in its history.

John Carew fared little better than his older half-brother. Unlike Alexander, though, who according to Edward Clarendon was 'sottishly and dangerously wary of his own security (having neither courage to obey his conscience, nor wickedness enough to be prosperous against it)', John was an earnest and committed radical ideologue, confident enough of the rightness of his cause to put his name to Charles I's death warrant. He was also a Fifth Monarchist, believing in the imminent coming of Christ; after accusing Cromwell of having 'taken the Crown off from the head of Christ and put it upon his own', he spent two years as a prisoner in Pendennis Castle.

At the Restoration the order for his arrest as a regicide reached him in Cornwall, and in spite of being given the opportunity to flee the country he set off for London,

ABOVE: Alexander Carew: legend has it that this portrait was torn from its frame by Royalist relatives when he declared for Parliament, to be replaced when he returned his allegiance to the Crown. (*The National Trust*)

LEFT: The entrance hall: Edward Bower's portrait of Charles I hangs over the fireplace. (*NTPL/John Bethell*)

saying 'that he had committed both his life and estate to the Lord, to save or destroy, as he thought meet'. After a trial during which he was denied the advice of counsel and one of the judges gave evidence against him, he was sentenced to be hanged, drawn and quartered. John Carew was executed on 14 October 1660, although only after his unrepentant twenty-minute sermon from the scaffold had been curtailed by his increasingly impatient attendants: 'Mr Sheriff interrupted him, saying, "Tis desired that you spend the rest of your time preparing yourself". Another said, "You spend yourself, Sir, in this discourse". Another said, "It rains".'

One might suppose that the examples of John and Alexander would have been enough to discourage the Carew family from any further involvement in politics. However, Alexander's grandson, Sir William, who inherited Antony in 1692, also inherited the family penchant for choosing the losing side. A Tory and a Jacobite, he conspired in 1715 to raise Devon and Cornwall for the Pretender James Edward Stuart, earning himself a spell of preventive custody in the Citadel at Plymouth while George I dealt with James's forces in the north. Deterred, perhaps, from playing a more active role in affairs of state, Sir William retired to Antony, where he put his energies, and his wife's money – in 1713 he had married Anne, the only child of Gilbert, 4th Earl of Coventry, who brought with her a substantial dowry and an even more substantial inheritance on her father's death in 1719 – into rebuilding the house.

Since at least 1814, when Samuel and Daniel Lysons referred to the designer in their *Magna Britannia*, Sir William Carew's Antony has been associated with the name of James Gibbs (1682–1754), the gifted architect of St Martin-in-the-Fields and St Mary-le-Strand in London, and the Radcliffe Camera in Oxford. The attribution may have been given some force by the fact that as a Tory, a Scot and a Catholic, Gibbs had been a victim of anti-Jacobite feeling, being dismissed in January 1716 from his post as surveyor to the Commissioners for building Fifty New Churches in London. (His first important patron had been a fellow-Catholic – John Erskine, 11th Earl of Mar, who fled into exile after being defeated at the head of the Pretender's Scottish forces at Sheriffmuir.

In fact the main block at Antony bears little relation to Gibbs's other designs, and is almost certainly by another architect. But the colonnades and pavilions which flank the house do correspond closely to plate 57 in *A Book of Architecture*, a collection of 150 executed and unexecuted designs published by Gibbs in 1728 (with Sir William Carew as one of the subscribers), which went on to become one of the most widely-used pattern books of the eighteenth century. At 101 feet, the façades at Antony are precisely the same width. If it weren't for the fact that the house was begun in 1718, ten years before the appearance of *A Book of Architecture*, one might assume that Gibbs's published design had simply been adapted by a local architect. As it is, there are several hypotheses: that Antony was designed by one of Gibbs's pupils; that it was created in two stages, with Gibbs being responsible for the colonnades and pavilions after the main house was finished; or that Gibbs provided the initial plans in 1718, and that these were then considerably modified by a local man.

If the name of the architect of Antony is still open to dispute, that of the actual builder (who may, conceivably, also have provided or adapted the plans) is not: he was an accomplished and successful West Country mason, John Moyle of Exeter in Devon, who in 1718 contracted with Sir William 'for building the shell of a house . . . according to a draught agreed upon', at a cost of £1260 excluding materials. As 'John Moyle of the City of Exeter, Bricklayer', he had already worked at Antony some five years previously, when he built a garden wall for the old house. And during the 1710s and 1720s he is known to have carried out works at Powderham Castle to the south of Exeter for William Courtenay, and at Boconnoc House near Lostwithiel in Cornwall, where he added an east wing for Thomas Pitt.

The mellow grey Pentewan stone with which Antony is faced (and which hides a carcase of the same brick as that used for the wings) was probably brought the thirty miles from St Austell Bay by sea. Both the garden front to the north and the entrance front (which is sadly disfigured by a heavy *porte-cochère* put up during the second half of the nineteenth century) are of nine bays, the middle three projecting slightly below a triangular pediment; both are astylar, with quoins and a simple string course. The attics are lit by two groups of dormers with alternating triangular and segmental heads, and the whole is raised over a basement storey. In fact, the house that Sir William Carew built as an outlet for his frustrated revolutionary tendencies is uncomplicated and restrained – and none the worse for that.

That simplicity is carried through to the interior planning. An enfilade on the ground floor running along the central spine of the house links the principal rooms: an entrance hall and saloon in the centre, with reception rooms and staircase hall grouped to either side. On the first floor an east-west corridor performs the same function. The rooms themselves are also restrained, with walls wainscoted with oak, except in the library, where the bare deal panelling was originally painted.

The oak panels form a perfect backdrop to the remarkable collection of paintings and memorabilia accumulated over the centuries by the Carews – and the Poles, for in the nineteenth century Antony was inherited by Reginald Pole, the great-great nephew of Sir William, who accordingly adopted the name of Pole-Carew. In the library is the patched portrait of the hapless Alexander Carew. A picture of Sir Watkin Williams-Wynn hangs over the chimneypiece in the dining room, given to Sir William Carew to commemorate a pact between the two men whereby Sir Watkin would raise Wales for the Pretender while Carew pledged Devon and Cornwall. And in the hall, Michael Dahl's portraits of Sir William and Lady Anne look out from either side of the entrance onto Richard the topographer, and the West Country artist Edward Bower's picture of Charles I, said to have been taken from sketches made during the his trial in Westminster Hall. The sad and sombre image of the defeated king is given an added poignancy from the knowledge that it rests in the home of the family who suffered imprisonment and death both to defend the Stuarts and to see him dead.

Sir William Carew died in March 1743, some fourteen years after the completion of his new house. In the early nineteenth century Reginald Pole-Carew consulted Humphry Repton on the landscaping of the grounds (the great north lawn and the radial vistas to the River Lynher date from this time). And in Victorian times Reginald's son William, who added the unfortunate *porte-cochère* to the entrance front, added an equally unfortunate Italianate wing to the east of the main block. Then at the beginning of this century William's son, another Reginald, had that east wing enlarged in an entirely unsuitable heavy Jacobethan style, encased in brick with stone dressings and Flemish gables. The work was carried out while he was away in Ireland, and on his return he is said to have been horrified at the result. The whole wing was demolished after the Second World War, restoring Antony to its original simple symmetry.

Antony House was given to the National Trust by Sir John Carew Pole in 1961, together with twenty-nine acres of the immediate grounds and an endowment. A further thirty-four acres of parkland were given in 1965.

Chapter Five

The Grandeur that Was Rome

1720-1820

'Architecture has its political use,' wrote Christopher Wren in 1665. 'It establishes a nation.' So it does, but an architecture that is too closely bound to a particular political ideology is guilty by association when that ideology is replaced by another – as Wren found to his cost.

To the generation of Whig landowners who came to power with the accession of George I in 1714, the baroque, in spite of having flourished in the aftermath of the Glorious Revolution of 1688, had too many links with both the bad old days of Charles II and the absolutist monarchism of Louis XIV. Already in the early years of the eighteenth century, when Chatsworth was less than a decade old, when Vanbrugh's great mansions at Castle Howard and Blenheim were still half-built, the 3rd Earl of Shaftesbury was criticising the type of 'sumptuous palace' whose

Nicholas Revett's Ionic portico at West Wycombe Park, Buckinghamshire. Revett based his design on the Temple of Bacchus at Teos, which he had surveyed in the 1760s when he and James Stuart were preparing for publication *The Antiquities of Athens*. (*NTPL/John Bethell*)

169

opulence and ostentation had no foundation in an acceptable moral code:

> What pains! study! science! Behold the disposition and order of these finer sorts of apartments, gardens, villas! ... with all those symmetries which silently express a reigning order, peace, harmony, and beauty! But what is there answerable to this, in the minds of the possessors? What possession or propriety is theirs? What constancy or security of enjoyment? What peace, what harmony within?

And Shaftesbury was only one among an increasing number of thinkers and architects who saw in the buildings of Wren, Vanbrugh and their ilk a lack of order, the sort of arbitrary hauteur that recalled the tyrannies of the Stuarts. The architect Colen Campbell (1676–1729) dismissed the baroque as 'parts ... without proportion, solids without their true bearing, heaps of material without strength, excessive ornaments without grace, and the whole without symmetry'. Alexander Pope showed his contempt for the style in his account of Timon's villa, the archetypal baroque palace 'Where all cry out, "What sums are thrown away!"/So proud, so grand; of that stupendous air,/Soft and agreeable come never there'; and poured scorn on the heavy decoration of its interiors: 'On painted ceilings you devoutly stare,/Where sprawl the saints of Verrio or Laguerre'. To replace what was seen as the debased and corrupt architecture of the preceding generation a new style was needed; an enlightened and authoritative style, based on reason and rules; a national style, too – for the Whigs, like Wren, believed that 'architecture ... establishes a nation'.

That style was found in the works of the sixteenth-century Italian Andrea Palladio (1508–80). Palladio's *Quattro Libri dell'Architettura*, which had first appeared in 1570, methodically explored and reconstructed the buildings of ancient Rome. It expounded on the system of rules governing the creation of those buildings, which had been handed down by Marcus Vitruvius Pollio (fl.46–30BC) in his *Ten Books of Architecture*, the only complete architectural treatise to survive from antiquity. And it provided illustrations, in the form of Palladio's own designs for villas, palaces and churches, of a way in which the early Georgians might interpret those rules to create an architecture both sanctioned by classical tradition – the yardstick by which all civilised activity was measured – and sufficiently different from the baroque to represent the clear break with the immediate past that they so desperately wanted. As a result, the influence of Palladio – and of his first English interpreter, Inigo Jones – was to grow until it dominated the whole of English architecture.

The opening shot in the campaign to ensure the adoption of Palladianism was fired in 1715, with the publication of the first volume of Colen Campbell's *Vitruvius Britannicus*. Although ostensibly a general survey of recent British architecture, the book praised 'the renowned Palladio' and 'the famous Inigo Jones', and included a large number of the latter's designs, making it abundantly obvious that in Campbell's view these were the role models for modern architects to follow. The following year Giacomo Leoni (c.1686–1746) published the first instalment of his English edition of the *Quattro Libri*. (The title-page actually says 1715: Leoni seems

Giacomo Leoni's Lyme Park in Cheshire, 1725: a mixture of Palladian principles and baroque flamboyance. (*NTPL/Mike Williams*)

to have falsified the date of publication because he didn't want to be seen to be following Campbell.) The book contains a splendid allegorical frontispiece by Sebastiano Ricci: Father Time unveils a bust of Palladio, which is illuminated by beams of light cast from the star of the Garter held aloft by a flying putto; the winged figure of Fame lies beneath the bust, while Britannia, accompanied by two putti bearing the royal arms, looks on. Again the message is clear: it is for England and King George to reveal Palladio's glories once more.

Leoni's own buildings, which include Lyme Park, Cheshire (1725, for Peter Legh) and Clandon Park in Surrey (c.1731, for Thomas Onslow), borrow freely from both Palladio and Jones, but they still retain a hint of baroque flamboyance. In

Leoni's marble hall at Clandon Park in Surrey, *c*.1731. (*The National Trust/Jeremy Whitaker*)

fact Leoni took a fairly pragmatic view of the master's work. In his preface to the *Quattro Libri* he blithely announced that he had 'made ... many necessary corrections with respect to shading, dimensions, ornaments, etc'; and in reproducing Palladio's designs in his translation, he was quite happy to add a dome here, or a pediment there.

The third of the early eighteenth-century pioneers of Palladianism, Richard Boyle, 3rd Earl of Burlington (1694–1753), was rather more of a purist. Influenced by both Leoni and Campbell (who in 1718 remodelled the Earl's town house in Piccadilly in London), the young Burlington developed an interest in building and design. In 1719 he travelled to Italy, where he sought out the villas of Palladio and his pupil Scamozzi, and saw how classical architecture might have its contemporary counterpart. He bought up every edition of the *Quattro Libri* that he could find (including at least four copies of the original 1570 edition), acquired an important collection of original Palladio drawings, and, in short, determined to lead an English architectural renaissance of classical values.

During the 1720s Burlington established himself as the arbiter of architectural taste, the high priest of a movement which saw itself as the spiritual heir not only of Palladio, but of ancient Rome itself. 'You shew us, Rome was glorious, not profuse,' wrote his friend Alexander Pope in the fourth of his *Moral Essays*, 'Of the Use of Riches', which was dedicated to Burlington:

> ... Make falling Arts your care,
> Erect new wonders, and the old repair;
> Jones and Palladio to themselves restore,
> And be whate'er Vitruvius was before.

This is just what Burlington set out to do, not only by patronising like-minded designers such as Campbell and William Kent, but by erecting 'new wonders' himself. In the grounds of his estate in Chiswick, London, close by the Jacobean mansion that stood there, he built in 1725–9 a 'temple of the arts', a meeting place where he could gather his disciples. Chiswick is modelled in the main on Palladio's Villa Capra, with some additional borrowings from Scamozzi and a number of chimneypieces copied from Jones and John Webb. It is a square block just 68 feet across, and consists of a low rusticated ground storey with a much taller domed *piano nobile* above – relative proportions that were to hold good for much of the eighteenth century. A grand Corinthian portico reached via an elaborate double staircase defines the first-floor entrance, and inside nine main chambers are grouped around the octagonal saloon, which rises to the full height of the dome. One of the most significant features of the detailing is the inclusion on the garden front of three 'Venetian' windows, triple openings in which the central one is arched and wider than the others. This was a design that Burlington found among Palladio's drawings (although they actually derive from an illustration in Sebastiano Serlio's *Architettura* (1537)), and was to become a familiar motif in eighteenth-century architecture. One can see a Venetian window peering out even from among the half-timbering of the medieval Ightham Mote, a rather curious Georgian attempt to impart a contemporary flavour to the ancient manor house. And should anyone fail to realise

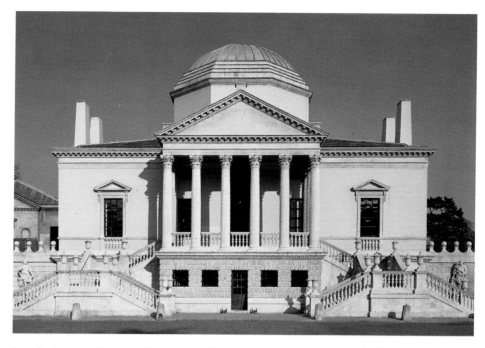

Lord Burlington's Chiswick Villa, London. 'Possessed of one great hall of state,/Without a room to sleep or eat,/How well you build let flattery tell,/And all mankind how ill you dwell.' (*English Heritage*)

where its owner's architectural loyalties lay, Chiswick has two statues by Michael Rysbrack flanking the stair – Palladio on the left, with Inigo Jones on the right. The whole was 'a model of taste', as Horace Walpole said decades later – even if it was 'too little to live in, too large to hang on a watch'.

And 'taste' was what mattered to the early Georgians. The rule of taste applied in architecture and in art, in literature and in life. And 'that faculty or those faculties of the mind, which are affected with, or which form a judgment of, the works of imagination and the elegant arts', as Edmund Burke defined it, was argued about and written about and disputed so often that by the 1750s one commentator was driven to complain:

> The fine ladies and gentleman dress with taste . . . the painters paint with taste, and, in short, fiddlers, players, singers, dancers, and mechanics themselves are all the sons and daughters of taste. Yet in this amazing superabundance of taste few can say what it really is, or what the word signifies.

What it did *not* signify was an individual's subjective response to the arts. The eighteenth century's obsession with rules and systems excluded subjectivity: a judgement about a palace or a painting or a poem was a way of exhibiting one's knowledge of accepted aesthetic criteria, eternal ideas derived from antiquity.

Indeed, such criteria went beyond aesthetics into the realms of social behaviour, so that the writer James Forrester, in his account of how to make friends and influence people, the splendidly titled *Polite Philosopher, or, An Essay on that Art which makes a Man happy in himself, and agreeable to others* (1734), was able to equate the classically sanctioned forms of Palladianism with polite manners:

> That true politeness we can only call,
> Which looks like Jones's fabric at Whitehall;
> Where just proportion we with pleasure see,
> Though built by rule, yet from all stiffness free.
> Though grand, still plain, magnificent, not fine,
> The ornaments adorning the design.
> It fills the mind with rational delight,
> And pleases on reflection, as at sight.

The idea that 'just proportion', building by rules, and plain grandeur are the qualities that engender 'rational delight' leaves little room for the spontaneity of freely expressed emotion, either in architecture or in life. (And the point is tellingly made in Lord Chesterfield's famous letter warning his son against laughter – 'I am sure that, since I have had the full sense of my reason, nobody has ever heard me laugh'.) But spontaneous expression was not what Burlington, Campbell and their associates in the other arts were seeking: they looked for the Ideal, for perfection, for a system of eternal truths that could be unlocked and used to mould a brave new world that was rational, regular and codified. That system was to be found in the buildings and writings of the ancients – and Palladio held the key.

There were dissenting voices, of course. In James Miller's *Man of Taste* (1735) a servant, Martin, impersonates Lord Apemode, who is in need of a new house to accommodate the collection of paintings and statues that he has just brought back from Italy:

> They are all huddled together for the present, for want of apartments proper to place 'em in; but I have sent my builder over to Venice, to bring home a score or two of models, and then I shall immediately fall to building. 'Tis building! building, madam! by which a man must now manifest his taste.

And in his famous epigram on Chiswick Villa, Lord Hervey highlighted a frequent criticism of Burlingtonian Palladianism – ironically, the same criticism that Pope made of the baroque in his fourth *Moral Essay* when he said that ''Tis use alone that sanctifies expense':

> Possessed of one great hall of state,
> Without a room to sleep or eat,
> How well you build let flattery tell,
> And all mankind how ill you dwell.[1]

---

1   Wit turned to malice in another of Hervey's epigrams, in which he alluded to Lady Burlington – 'Dame Palladio' – and her infatuation for the Duke of Grafton, giving her husband cuckold's horns in the shape of Ionic scrolls: 'Her worn-out huntsman frequent may she hold,/Nor to her mason-husband be it told/That she, with capital Corinthian graced,/Has finished *his* in the Ionic taste.'

But Chiswick was never intended as a dwelling: the everyday business of living went on in the family mansion, and the villa was given over entirely to the state rooms on the *piano nobile* and Burlington's own private library on the floor below. However, the relatively small-scale designs such as the Villa Capra which Palladio had produced for the gentlemen-farmers of Vicenza proved to be attractive models for the houses of the Georgian gentry, and one can see a series of influential villas appearing in the 1720s, such as Marble Hill, Twickenham (1724–9), built by the Earl of Pembroke and Roger Morris for George II's mistress Henrietta Howard; Colen Campbell's Stourhead, Wiltshire (1721–4, for Henry Hoare; see page 179); and Campbell's Mereworth Castle in Kent (1722–5, for John Fane), a Villa Capra derivative which Walpole found 'so perfect in the Palladian taste that it has recovered me a little from the Gothic'.

There is a sense in which these villas and their descendants, which appeared in increasing numbers from the 1740s onwards, were the Palladian equivalents of the gentry houses built by Roger Pratt and Hugh May in the previous century. But the great baroque palaces also had their Palladian counterparts. Campbell's Wanstead House in Essex (1714–20, for Sir Richard Child; demolished 1822), while not conforming closely to any of Palladio's designs, showed that it was possible to create grandeur without lapsing into any of those Vanbrughian excesses which so disgusted the man of taste. The house consisted of a central block projecting from between two long flanking wings. There was little external ornament, except for the prominent portico and the rustication which defined the ground storey, the platform on which the *piano nobile* rested. And the whole effect was one of restrained magnificence and decorous splendour.

Wanstead was the forerunner of a series of grand and massive 'houses of parade' designed in the middle years of the eighteenth century by the next generation of architects, men who had been raised on the Palladianism of Campbell, Burlington and their circle. All begun in the 1730s, they included Holkham Hall, Norfolk, designed by William Kent (?1685–1748); Wentworth Woodhouse in Yorkshire, designed by Henry Flitcroft (1697–1769); Prior Park, Bath, by John Wood the elder (1704–54) for Ralph Allen, and intended as a spectacular advertisement for Allen's Bath stone quarries; and Nostell Priory, Yorkshire, designed for Sir Rowland Winn by James Moyser (c.1693–1753) and built by James Paine (1717–89).

In spite of their often vast size – if one includes its outlying wings, the east front of Wentworth Woodhouse extends a full 606 feet – these houses all exhibit a stately restraint wholly at odds with the dramatic Vanbrughian interplay of forms which had characterised Castle Howard and Blenheim. Equally importantly, Palladio and Burlington or Campbell all figure somewhere in their intellectual pedigrees. Burlington, who was William Kent's patron, may well have been involved in the design of Holkham; Flitcroft's allegiance to the Earl was such that he was nicknamed 'Burlington Harry'; Ralph Allen had links with the Burlington circle through his friendship with Pope. And at Nostell – loosely based on Palladio's unexecuted designs for the Villa Mocenigo on the River Brenta – James Moyser was on the fringes of the Burlington circle, and Campbell may well have been commissioned to execute the designs, with Paine being brought in after his early death in 1729.

By the second half of the eighteenth century a model for the larger country house had emerged, a model which derived ultimately – and inevitably – from Palladio. The porticoed central block linked to flanking pavilions, a type which recurs in the *Quattro Libri*, seemed admirably suited to English needs. The *piano nobile* of the main building could house the state apartments, which were by now primarily galleries and function rooms reserved for grand entertaining and the display of art-objects. The two wings (or occasionally four, as at Holkham and in Matthew Brettingham's original designs for Kedleston in Derbyshire, 1758) might contain kitchens, private apartments, a chapel, a library, an orangery – even stabling; and the ground-floor rustic could be filled with ordinary day-rooms or domestic offices. Sometimes the pavilions were simply linked by screen walls, as at Basildon Park, Berkshire, built in 1776–83 by John Carr of York (*c*.1742–1821). Sometimes they were connected by curving corridors, as at Kedleston and Mario Asprucci's Ickworth in Suffolk, a device which enabled the central block to be set back and framed by its wings. And sometimes they were no more than slightly lower extensions of the main body of the house, perhaps two rooms deep, as in Samuel Wyatt's remodelling of Shugborough in Staffordshire in the 1790s.

But by this time the search for rules and precedents had stretched back beyond Palladio and the Renaissance, back to antiquity itself. In an echo of early-eighteenth-century Palladianism, the first signs of this more scholarly approach to classical architecture were marked (in England, at least) by a series of publications, the most notable of which were Robert Wood's *Ruins of Palmyra* (1753) and *Ruins of Balbec* (1757); James Stuart's and Nicholas Revett's *Antiquities of Athens*, the first volume of which appeared in 1762; and Robert Adam's *Ruins of the Palace of the Emperor Diocletian at Spalatro in Dalmatia* (1764).

Each of these books was produced by men who had not only been to Italy to study Renaissance interpretations of classicism (although they had all done that as well) but, intent on adding to their countrymen's knowledge of antiquity, had travelled further, exploring and recording sites in Syria, the Greek archipelago and Dalmatia. The results of these expeditions helped English architects to broaden their vocabulary. Two examples can serve for many: both William Chambers' Temple of the Sun at Kew Gardens in Surrey (1761) and Henry Flitcroft's Temple of Apollo at Stourhead in Wiltshire (1767) derive from an engraving in Wood's Balbec book, a copy of which Flitcroft's patron, Henry Hoare, had bought when it appeared ten years before. More importantly, such travels taught designers that there were other equally interesting sources besides Palladio and his contemporaries.

Of these pioneer archaeologists, Robert Wood (1716–71), who was a gentleman-adventurer rather than an architect, took up a career in politics, eventually becoming an under-secretary of state. Nicholas Revett (*c*.1721–1804) also had private means, although he did undertake a few architectural commissions, including the Ionic portico at West Wycombe Park in Buckinghamshire, modelled on the Temple of Bacchus at Teos, which he had measured during a second Greek expedition in 1764–6. James Stuart (1713–88), who had bought out Revett's interest in their *Antiquities of Athens* before publication, achieved both wealth and celebrity when the book appeared. He produced some interesting work, including garden buildings like the Triumphal Arch at Shugborough (1764–7), based on the Arch of Hadrian in Athens, and the Temple of the Winds at Mount Stewart, County Down, before wasting what might have been a promising career in drink and dissolution.[2]

Robert Adam made rather better use of his time abroad, and it is interesting to see history repeating itself in the dedication to George III of his *Ruins ... at Spalatro*, which reproduces the message contained in the frontispiece to Leoni's edition of the *Quattro Libri*. Referring to Diocletian's palace as 'the favourite residence of a great emperor, who, by his munificence and example, revived the study of architecture, and excited the masters of that art to emulate in their works the elegance and purity of a better age', Adam goes on to ram home the point:

> Architecture, in a particular manner depends upon the patronage of the great. At this happy period, when Great Britain enjoys in peace the reputation and power she acquired by arms, your Majesty's singular attention to the arts of elegance promises an age of perfection.

But Adam was far from advocating Burlingtonian Palladianism – indeed, he no doubt agreed with the opinions of his brother James, recorded in his journal during a stay in Vicenza in 1760. Of 'the different buildings of Palladio with which this city abounds' James declared himself 'no admirer ... his private houses are ill-adjusted both in their plans and elevations'.

To Adam, the search for an ideal architecture, so important to the first generation of eighteenth-century classicists, seemed pointlessly limiting. While he agreed that the buildings of the ancients should 'serve as models which we should imitate, and as standards by which we ought to judge', he also held that 'rules often cramp the genius and circumscribe the idea of the master'.

In other words, Adam's thinking on architecture, while still rooted in classical principles, had moved on from the Palladian quest for eternal truths to a more flexible and ultimately more creative response to the past: a response expressed in the masterly group of country houses that he designed and decorated during the 1760s and 1770s – houses like Kedleston, Osterley, Saltram. Here he was not afraid to draw on Burlingtonian Palladianism, on French neo-classicism, on archae-ological discoveries from Italy, Syria or Greece, or on Renaissance figures such as Michelangelo, Raphael and Domenichino. Just how far removed he was from the Palladians can be judged from his remarks on the reviled Vanbrugh. In the preface to the *Works in Architecture of Robert and James Adam*, published in 1774 as an advertisement for the brothers' practice, he says:

> We cannot ... allow ourselves to close this note without doing justice to the memory of a great man, whose reputation as an architect has long been carried

---

2   In 1780, when Stuart was working on Elizabeth Montagu's house in Portman Square, London, he exasperated his client with his lies, drunkenness and unreliability. 'I have found out that in dealing with Mr Stuart great caution is necessary,' she wrote; 'Since he began my house he has been for a fortnight together in the most drunken condition.'

down the stream by a torrent of undistinguishing prejudice and abuse. Sir John Vanbrugh's genius was of the first class; and in point of movement, novelty and ingenuity, his works have not been exceeded by anything in modern times.

The new scholarship, and its corollary, a new eclecticism, signalled the end of Palladianism. There was no return to the baroque, of course – even Adam, while admiring the picturesque massing of Vanbrugh's palaces, dismissed the 'barbarisms and absurdities' of his detailing. But the mere fact that Adam and those who came after him could recognise a plurality of styles meant that the utopian vision of Campbell and Burlington, the Whig dream of a national style of architecture which would recreate the grandeur that was Rome, was over. The stage was set for the great nineteenth-century wave of revivals.

Stourhead

WILTSHIRE

Stourhead, 3 miles north-west of Mere, was designed by Colen Campbell in 1721–4 for Henry Hoare, a London banker. The flanking pavilions were added by Sir Richard Colt Hoare in 1792.

Henry Hoare the Elder, holding an elevation of the east front of Stourhead: this 1722 portrait by Michael Dahl now hangs in the hall.
(*NTPL/Charlie Waite*)

If the House of Lords had believed William Benson when in 1719 he tried to convince them that their chamber was in danger of collapsing, London and the British nation might have been provided with a splendid new Palladian Parliament building. On the other hand, Benson's assistant Colen Campbell might never have had the time to design Stourhead.

Benson (1682–1754) was a wealthy West Country landowner, patron of literature and amateur architect, whose house, Wilbury in Wiltshire (1710), was directly inspired by John Webb's nearby Amesbury Abbey, then thought to be by Inigo Jones. It thus stands (or rather stood, since it was altered later in the eighteenth century) as one of the first serious attempts to revive Jonesian Palladianism. However, Wilbury House apart, Benson's fame – if fame it can be called – rests chiefly on the fact that he was the man who in 1718 persuaded the government to dismiss the ageing Christopher Wren from his post as Surveyor of the King's Works, and to appoint him in his stead.

An enthusiastic proponent of Palladianism – and a scandalously corrupt and machiavellian politician – Benson managed, during his fifteen-month tenure in office, to sack his most capable subordinates, to alienate most of his colleagues, and to line his pockets to such an extent that Nicholas Hawksmoor accused him of having 'got more in one year . . . than Sir Christopher Wren did in forty years for his honest endeavours'. With the architect Colen Campbell, whom he had appointed as his Chief Clerk and Deputy Surveyor in September 1718, he also concocted an extraordinary scheme to convince the Lords that their chamber was in such a dangerous state of disrepair that it should be vacated and dismantled. Apparently the two men, fired perhaps by Shaftesbury's *Letter concerning Design* (1712) which called for a new Parliament and royal palace to proclaim 'united Britain the principal seat of the Arts', planned to replace the Houses of Parliament with a magnificent Palladian building. A less biased survey showed Benson's assessment to have been economical with the truth, and in July 1719 both men were dismissed, the politician to follow his literary, architectural and financial interests, and the architect to pursue by more orthodox means the task of convincing polite society of the rightness of the Palladian style.

In spite of his dismissal from the King's Works (which seems to have done little harm to his professional reputation), by the early 1720s Campbell had established himself as the leading advocate of Palladianism in Britain. The publication of *Vitruvius Britannicus* (1715, 1717, 1725), which artfully blended his own designs, both executed and unexecuted, with those of Inigo Jones and other famous architects, showed him to have been an accomplished self-publicist. At the same time, his condemnation in *Vitruvius* of the theatrical exuberance of the baroque struck a chord with the Whigs. For him, and for them, Palladio's classicism provided an architecture whose basis in antiquity meant that it was perfectly suited to the new enlightened renaissance that they sought to bring about.

Campbell's houses were just as influential as his polemic. Wanstead in Essex, as we noted in the introduction to this chapter, was to be the prototype for the great 'houses of parade' which would appear later in the century. And with his more modest schemes, Campbell produced a pattern for the Georgian villa, adapting Palladio's published designs to meet the needs of those among the gentry and nobility who had neither the money nor the inclination to build a palace.

It was undoubtedly William Benson who brought Campbell to the notice of one who may have had the money, but certainly didn't have the inclination for palace-building – his brother-in-law, Henry Hoare (1677–1725). A successful banker who lived at Quarley in Hampshire, a few miles from Benson's Wilbury House, Henry was the second son of Richard Hoare, a London goldsmith who had moved into banking in the late seventeenth century, and who had prospered by it. The family bank, in which Henry was a partner, still operates today from the site of Richard's premises at the sign of the Golden Bottle in Fleet Street.

Henry Hoare had recently bought the Stourton estate in Wiltshire, which had at its core a house that had once been the rather grand seat of a rather grand recusant family. In the mid-sixteenth century the antiquary John Leland described it as 'magnificent, and high embattled castle-like', and 150 years later John Aubrey noted 'a great open-roofed hall, and an extraordinary large and high open-roofed kitchen', all conjuring up 'the time of the old English barons'. But both the house, which had been sacked and badly damaged by Parliamentarian troops during the Civil War, and the Stourton family, who had suffered for their Catholicism, had fallen on hard times. The heavily mortgaged estate had passed in 1714 to Sir Thomas Meres, whose son John sold it to Henry Hoare three years later. Henry pulled down what remained of Stourton, spent four guineas on 'Mr Campbell's book' (*Vitruvius Britannicus*), and commissioned the architect to build a new house on a site nearby. He named it Stourhead.

Stourhead was begun in about 1721, with Nathaniel Ireson (1686–1769), a former apprentice to Francis Smith of Warwick, as the main contractor. It was probably more or less completed by 1724, although later payments to Robert Taylor for chimneypieces, to Thomas Johnson for ironwork, and to Campbell's assistant Roger Morris (who was also responsible for Marble Hill in Twickenham) suggest that work continued on the interiors after Hoare's death in 1725. Campbell's designs for Stourhead were published in 1725 in the third volume of *Vitruvius Britannicus*.

Derived from the the house that Palladio had built at Fanzolo in the 1560s for Leonardo Emo (illustrated in Book 2 of the *Quattro Libri dell'Architettura*), those designs show a five-bay, two-storeyed, rectangular building in the villa style, raised on a rusticated half-basement containing the kitchens and other domestic offices,

Colen Campbell's design for the east front of Stourhead, from the third volume of his *Vitruvius Britannicus*, 1725. (*The National Trust*)

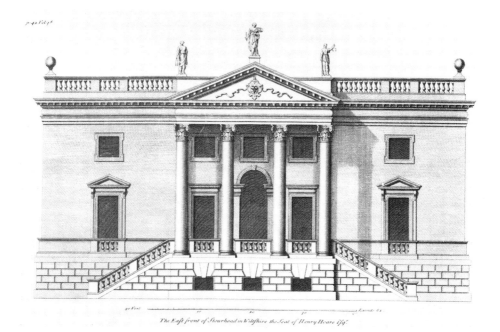

The East front of Stourhead in Wiltshire the Seat of Henry Hoare Esq.

Stourhead from the north-east; a watercolour by J. C. Buckler, 1817.
(*NTPL/John Bethell*)

and topped with a balustrade. The *piano nobile*, which is reached via a simple double stair on the east front leading to a pedimented tetrastyle portico, consists of entrance hall, staircase hall and chapel – a slightly unusual departure from the expected sequence of hall-staircase-saloon – centrally grouped along the main east-west axis, and flanked by reception chambers and apartments. The garden front to the south is dominated by a Venetian window in its centre, with a cartouche above. There are no wings, and the late-seventeenth-century ideal of a formal enfilade of state rooms is replaced by a tight grouping of interconnected rooms.

The overall effect is of a building that is compact without being mean; elegant rather than ostentatious; stately, but not stiff and formal: a building that exemplifies proportion, grace and symmetry, those very qualities that Campbell found to be lacking in baroque architecture. On the east front, the entrance hall is a 30-foot cube, and the two rooms flanking it (now the music room and the cabinet room) measure 30 by 20 feet; they in turn connected with chambers measuring 25 by 20 feet. Campbell had learned the lesson of the master well. He understood that in Palladian terms beauty is, in the words of Sylvio Belli, Palladio's friend and fellow member of the Accademia Olimpica, 'a correspondence of all parts arranged in their proper place', and that proportion is 'the very source of just distribution, of beauty and of health'.

In fact Stourhead differed in a few important details from Campbell's published

The saloon in 1901. After a fire in 1902, E. Doran Webb destroyed its classical proportions, concealing two bedrooms above a heavy Wrenaissance ceiling. (*The Ladies' Field*)

designs, as one can see from Michael Dahl's portrait of Henry Hoare, which shows him holding an elevation of the east front as built. The most significant modifications related to this front, and detracted somewhat from the dramatic qualities of the original scheme: the double stair leading up to the projecting portico was jettisoned in favour of a rather heavy single flight, while the portico itself gave way to an engaged frontispiece with pilasters rather than detached columns. Perhaps Campbell himself made these changes, although they leave the façade looking rather too subdued and flat when compared with the *Vitruvius Britannicus* engravings. Or perhaps it was Ireson, or Morris, or even William Benson, who certainly took an active interest in his brother-in-law's new house, but whose precise contribution remains something of a mystery.

Henry Hoare left Stourhead to his widow Jane, Benson's sister, who continued to live there. In the meantime his son Henry (1705–85) enjoyed what he later described as a 'gay and dissolute style of life', before buying his uncle's house at Wilbury and settling down to banking and 'the pursuit of that knowledge which distinguishes only the gentleman from the vulgar'. When his mother died in 1741 Henry II moved into Stourhead, where in about 1744 he employed Henry Flitcroft to make a number of alterations to the house. These included the conversion of his father's chapel into a great saloon with a coved ceiling, and the addition of a projecting central bay to the west front, with a Venetian window on the *piano nobile*

and a triangular pediment above – all in a restrained Palladian style which harmonised well with Campbell's original scheme.

Flitcroft was also responsible for much of the building work in the pleasure grounds which Henry II began in 1743 and which he continued to develop for the rest of his life – the landscape garden which is the main source of Stourhead's fame:

> Prepare the mind for something grand and new;
> For Paradise soon opens to the view! . . .
> The wond'ring rustics, who this place explore,
> Feel sentiments their souls ne'er felt before;
> And Virtuosi with amazement own
> They never thought such wonders were in stone!

The justifiable fame of those wonders in stone – the Pantheon, the Temples of Apollo and Flora, the Grotto – and the perfection of their lakeside setting has to a certain extent eclipsed Colen Campbell's achievement at Stourhead. And later alterations took the house ever further away from the original conception. The library and picture gallery which Henry II's grandson Richard Colt Hoare built in flanking pavilions in 1792, although outstanding Regency interiors in their own right, effectively destroyed Campbell's south front – the library juts out to one side of the central Venetian window. They also lessened the impact of the original entrance façade; a fault only partially rectified by the projecting portico that was finally added – with an attic storey above which broke the regularity of the original roofline – by Charles Parker in 1838–9.

But the most devastating blow to Campbell's Stourhead occurred in 1902, when a disastrous fire gutted the main block. It started on an upper floor and spread slowly, so that it was possible to save most of the contents – but the Palladian interiors were totally destroyed. Henry Hugh Arthur Hoare consulted a local architect, E. Doran Webb, who had laid out the south terrace beside the house some five years previously – an unfortunate choice, since Webb's sympathies clearly lay, not with Campbell and Palladio, but with the Wrenaissance. He squeezed a miniature version of Roger Pratt's great Caroline double staircase at Coleshill into the central inner hall where Campbell's single stair had stood, and destroyed the proportions of the saloon by both lengthening it and lowering it, concealing two bedrooms above a heavy neo-baroque ceiling. In addition, Webb created on the west front a bizarre, faintly classical façade which, in the words of the National Trust guidebook to the house, 'must be considered an aberration'. As if this weren't enough, when the work was approaching completion in 1905 the roof timbers began to sag, and Webb and the Hoares parted company. Sir Aston Webb, the designer of Admiralty Arch and the east front of Buckingham Palace (and, understandably, no relation to E. Doran Webb) was called in to remedy the situation.

Stourhead – the house and its contents, the pleasure grounds, and some 2,500 acres – was given to the National Trust in 1946–7 by Henry Hugh Arthur Hoare.

The portico on the entrance front, added by Charles Parker in 1838–9. (*NTPL/John Bethell*)

The later alterations all have their own intrinsic merits, but none of them compares with the scale of Campbell's achievement. By providing a model which would be followed by generations of eighteenth-century designers, his Stourhead helped to change the course of English architectural history.

THREE ADAM HOUSES

In spite of the fact that the National Trust owns more country houses by Robert Adam than by any other architect (five in all,[3] plus the Templetown mausoleum in County Antrim), the decision to devote almost half of this chapter to the work of a single designer seems, on the face of it, to give undue weight to one individual's contribution. True, Robert Adam belongs to that very small and select band of architects – Inigo Jones, Wren, and perhaps Edwin Lutyens – who have become household names. But aren't these household names merely figureheads, the personifications of complex movements, ideas, the expression of social and cultural values? Isn't architecture about practice rather than personalities?

Yes and no. Yes, because no act of creation takes place in isolation. No, because in Adam's case, at least, it is possible to argue that one individual made a greater, more significant and more direct contribution to the history of the country house than any of the other architects mentioned in this book. Between the late 1750s and the 1770s he 'brought about, in this country, a kind of revolution in the whole system of [the] useful and elegant art' of architecture. That this assessment of his achievement comes from the man himself does nothing to lessen its truth, although it does shed light on his character – arrogant, massively ambitious and a master of the art of self-advertisement. He was also a genius, whose ability to take classical motifs, to abstract them and refine them and turn them to the needs of his clients, influenced generations of architects and changed the course of country house design.

Robert Adam was born at Kirkcaldy in Fife on 3 July 1728, the son of William Adam, a successful Scottish architect and building contractor. Two or three years after entering Edinburgh University in 1743, he left without a degree to work in his father's drawing office; and after William's death in 1748 he carried on the practice in partnership with his elder brother John. By 1754 Robert had amassed enough capital – more than £5,000 – to enable him to embark on a Grand Tour, with the intention of studying the monuments of antiquity at first hand. His ambition was to equip himself with fresh architectural ideas and eventually to establish himself in London, which he did on his return from Europe in January 1758.

---

3 Hatchlands, Surrey (1758–61, for Admiral Edward Boscawen); Kedleston Hall, Derbyshire (c.1760–70, for Sir Nathaniel Curzon; see page 188); Osterley Park, Middlesex (1763–80, for Robert Child; see page 195); Nostell Priory, Yorkshire (1765–85, for Sir Rowland Winn); and Saltram House, Devon (1768–79, for John Parker; see page 201). Like most of Adam's work, all involved the remodelling or completion of an existing building.

Robert Adam; a portrait by George Willison, *c*.1770–5. (*National Portrait Gallery*)

For the next twenty years Adam was perhaps the most influential – and certainly one of the busiest – designers in the country. His ability to draw on a variety of classical sources produced a new and extensive vocabulary of ornament; his confident and undogmatic response to antiquity made Burlingtonian Palladianism seem stiff and conventional. And his integrated approach to interior decoration, in which everything from ceilings and chimneypieces down to carpets, door furniture and candlesticks was regarded as an element in an overall decorative scheme, revolutionised contemporary attitudes. Within a few years every architect and builder was striving to emulate the Adam style.

The three houses described in the following pages exemplify British design at its most elegant, its most urbane. They show the monumental extent of Adam's achievement in single-handedly bringing about an architectural revolution. But by 1782, when Saltram, the last of them, was complete, his career was already on the wane, his reputation overshadowed by a new generation of architects led by James Wyatt. His last years, until his sudden death on 3 March 1792, were spent mainly on country house commissions in his native Scotland.

Kedleston Hall

DERBYSHIRE

Kedleston Hall, 3 miles north of Derby, was built for Nathaniel Curzon, 1st Baron Scarsdale. It was begun in 1758 to designs by Matthew Brettingham. Brettingham was almost immediately superseded by James Paine, who was himself replaced as architect by Robert Adam in 1760.

Nathaniel Curzon, 1st Lord Scarsdale, and his wife, Lady Caroline Colyear. This portrait, painted in 1761, hangs in the state boudoir at Kedleston. (*NTPL/Simon Corder*)

Visiting Derbyshire in the summer of 1778, the travel-writer Richard Sulivan was enjoying a leisurely, if uninspiring, stroll round the manufactories of Derby with some friends, when his ancient and garrulous local guide suddenly broke off the tour and cried, 'Come, come, gentlemen, if you have a mind to see Lord Scarsdale's, you must go directly. It is now noon, and travellers have no admittance but from ten till two.' The party accordingly got back into their carriage and drove the three miles

The south front of Kedleston. The interplay of forms and planes is a perfect example of Adam's conception of architectural 'movement'. (*NTPL/Mike Williams*)

north to Kedleston, where Sulivan was given good cause to thank the old man. The entrance front of the new house was 'sufficiently large to admit of every idea of grandeur and magnificence'; but even so, it did little to prepare the tourists for their first sight of the interior:

> Here, indeed, the senses become astonished... In one word, the whole strikes you as if it were designed for a more than mortal residence... Altogether this house is really magnificent: the hand of taste is evident in every part of it (nor can it be otherwise, when known to be the work of Messieurs Adam); nor does any cost seem to have been spared in rendering it complete.

Sulivan was not the only Georgian traveller to be impressed with Kedleston. 'Of all the houses I ever saw,' said William Bray after his visit there in 1777, 'I do not recollect any one which so completely pleased me as this.' 'The most perfect, that I ever saw,' wrote another visitor. 'All is consistent and uniform, and all is in the most elegant style.' And Horace Walpole, who saw the house in September 1768, described it as 'magnificently finished and furnished', as well as remarking, intriguingly, on the 'indecent carving in ivory' in the privy.

In fact, as a piece of contemporary architecture, Kedleston drew more accolades than perhaps any other building of the second half of the eighteenth century. It was open to the public even before it was finished, and tourists thronged to see it from all over the country. Such was the demand that Curzon built an inn 'for the accommodation of such strangers as curiosity may lead to view his residence', published a catalogue to the contents, and, as Sulivan discovered, was forced to restrict admission to between the hours of 10am and 2pm. His housekeeper Mrs Garnett, whose job it was to show visitors over the Hall, became quite a local celebrity: a portrait of her, catalogue in hand, still hangs in the house.

Sir Nathaniel Curzon, Bt (1726–1804), the proud builder of this eighteenth-century wonder – the 'Glory of Derbyshire' – was a perfect example of that new breed of Georgian landowner who rejected more traditional pastimes in favour of the pursuit of taste and sensibility. The Curzons had held lands at Kedleston since the twelfth century, and when Nathaniel inherited the estate in November 1758 he found himself the owner of the latest in a succession of Curzon residences: a redbrick Queen Anne house designed for his grandfather by Francis Smith of Warwick in about 1700. There were formal gardens to the south, which had been laid out by Charles Bridgeman in the early 1720s, and the village of Kedleston straggled along a public road that ran just 150 yards away to the north.

Curzon immediately began to plan a more modern mansion, a suitable setting both for his growing collection of pictures and for the peerage to which he aspired. (After some intensive lobbying, he was created Baron Scarsdale of Scarsdale in April 1761.) With the example of Thomas Coke's Holkham Hall in mind, he called in Matthew Brettingham, Coke's executive architect under Burlington and Kent, to supply designs for a house to be based, like Holkham, on Palladio's Villa Mocenigo, in which a rectangular block was connected by curving corridors to four pavilions. At Kedleston the main block holds the state rooms – hall and saloon disposed along a central north-south axis, with drawing rooms, library, dining room and state bedchamber to east and west – while the north-east and north-west pavilions contain the family apartments and the kitchens, respectively. The two pavilions on the south front were to accommodate a music room and a chapel, but Curzon ran out of money, or momentum, or both, and these were never built.

Early in 1759 Brettingham began work on the family wing, while the old Queen Anne house was still standing; but within a matter of months he had been replaced by James Paine. Paine was a Palladian architect in the tradition of Burlington and Kent, whose extensive and successful practice led a contemporary to remark that he and Sir Robert Taylor 'nearly divided the practice of the profession between them, for they had few competitors till Mr. Robert Adam entered the lists'. By April 1760 Paine had completed the kitchens and started on the north corridors and the eastern end of the main block. And then Mr Robert Adam did indeed enter the lists.

The marble hall: 'Here, indeed, the senses become astonished.' (*NTPL/Andrew Haslam*)

In fact, Adam had been involved with the new works at Kedleston since the project began. Writing to his brother James in December 1758, a few days after being introduced to Curzon, Adam said that he had

> got the entire management of his [ie, Curzon's] grounds put into my hands with full powers as to temples, bridges, seats and cascades... You may guess the play of genius and scope for invention. A noble piece of water, a man resolved to spare no expense, with £10,000 a year, good tempered and having taste himself for the arts and little for game.

During the summer of 1759 he spent some time at Kedleston, drawing designs for various features in the grounds: as a result, the road running past the house was re-routed, the village was demolished and re-sited a few miles away; and the three-mile path known as the Long Walk was laid out.

Then, in the spring of 1760, Adam replaced Paine as architect to the house. The older man, who was to be deposed by Adam three more times, at Nostell Priory, Alnwick and Syon, wrote some years later that he was so busy with other commissions that he had begged to be excused, and that 'the noble owner placed this great work in the hands of those able and ingenious artists, Messrs. Robert and James Adam'. This may well be true – Paine certainly was very busy, and he remained on good terms with Adam – but the young Scotsman's growing reputation must also have contributed to Curzon's decision to dispense with Paine's services.

Whatever the reason, Adam took over the direction of the whole project. He retained Brettingham's and Paine's original concept of a central block with connected pavilions – indeed, it was too late for him to do anything else. But he modified the north front and built the south front to his own design, introducing a triumphal arch, based on the Arch of Constantine in Rome, as the external expression of the magnificent domed saloon which stands behind it, the central focus of the house.

The interplay of forms – the domed roof of the saloon which recedes from the four detached Corinthian columns of the arch, each carrying its own piece of projecting entablature supporting classical figures, the curves of the horseshoe stair leading up to the principal floor, the niches containing lead statues of Flora and Bacchus and the unrealised quadrant corridors leading in Adam's design to a music room and a chapel – exemplifies what Adam described as 'movement' in architecture:

> The rise and fall, the advance and recess with other diversity of form, in the different parts of a building, so as to add greatly to the picturesque of the composition ... That is they serve to produce an agreeable and diversified contour, that groups and contrasts like a picture, and creates a variety of light and shade, which gives great spirit, beauty, and effect to the composition.

In spite of the absence of the two pavilions, Adam's painterly response to the façade still manages to combine the elegance of a classical vocabulary with a baroque vitality: the result is one of the masterpieces of English architecture.

The saloon, whose coffered dome was inspired by the Pantheon in Rome. (*NTPL/Andrew Haslam*)

If Adam's designs for the exterior of Kedleston were constrained by his predecessors' schemes and his patron's reluctance to spend more money on completing the house, there were no such curbs on his plans for the interior. Paine had intended a sequence arranged along the central axis, consisting of a columned entrance hall lit by windows looking on to the park, and leading into a staircase hall which in turn would have led to a circular drawing room projecting through the south front. Adam did away with Paine's windows and central stair. His top-lit hall was meant to conjure up associations with the open courtyard, or atrium, of a Roman villa, which was, he wrote, 'consecrated to their ancestors, and adorned with their images, their arms, their trophies, and other ensigns of their military and civil honours'. But it was also meant to impress. When Samuel Johnson, one of Kedleston's few critics, commented on this room's apparent uselessness, it was his common-sense utilitarianism that prevented him from realising that it did indeed have a use, and a very important one: the conspicuous display of its owner's taste and wealth. (It took the more perceptive Horace Walpole to remark on the disparity between display and reality: he noted that Curzon had had the house designed 'in the best taste, but too expensive for his estate'.)

The functional nature of the medieval and Elizabethan great hall has disappeared completely at Kedleston: no one would dream of actually *doing* anything here, except marvelling at the scale and monumental nature of the decoration. The twenty Corinthian columns and pilasters which surround the central space, carved from a striking green-veined alabaster and each twenty-five feet high; the vast open floor of Hopton Wood stone inlaid with Italian marble; the grisaille panels around the walls, depicting sacrificial and martial scenes – all are meant to produce an initial response of awe, wonder and admiration at such a spectacular expression of the owner's taste and culture. And this was exactly the response that they evoked in Sulivan, when he wrote that 'here, indeed, the senses become astonished'.

The atrium of a Roman villa would open on to the vestibulum, which was, Adam tells us, 'sacred to the gods'. By replacing Paine's staircase with two flights in aisles to either side of the hall, he was able to reproduce this arrangement at Kedleston. The hall opens directly on to the domed, 62-feet-high rotunda of the saloon, inspired by the Pantheon in Rome. Originally a sculpture gallery – another quasi-public display space, sacred to art and antiquity – the saloon was altered and furnished in the 1780s, providing a setting for the county balls which were so much a feature of late Georgian society. Its decoration was clearly intended to reinforce the bond that Curzon felt with the past. Grisaille panels by Biagio Rebecca (1735–1806), showing scenes from medieval and Tudor history, remind the spectator of the family's long lineage, while William Hamilton's four paintings of Roman ruins over the doors perhaps symbolise not only Curzon's taste and scholarship, but also his feeling of kinship with his spiritual forebears in antiquity, and the desire of eighteenth-century connoisseurs to build another civilisation that would rival the grandeur of Rome.

Kedleston was more or less complete by the end of the 1760s with the exception of the hall, the ceiling and chimneypieces of which were executed to the designs of George Richardson, one of Adam's assistants, in 1776–7. The house was given to the National Trust in 1986 by Viscount Scarsdale, direct descendant of the builder.

Osterley Park

MIDDLESEX

Osterley Park near Isleworth was built for Sir Thomas Gresham before 1576. It was bought by the Child family in 1711, and was remodelled, probably between 1756 and 1759 by William Chambers for Francis Child, and between 1763 and 1780 by Robert Adam for Francis's brother Robert.

The early 1760s were Robert Adam's most active period. In the short time since his return from Italy in 1758 he had become the most fashionable architect in England, having persuaded polite society that he, and he alone, was qualified to interpret the classical past with accuracy.

Designs for interiors and furniture, remodelled façades and garden buildings, executed with the aid of a team of highly skilled draughtsmen, streamed from his London office, to be implemented by the group of artists and craftsmen who were gathering round him. These included the carpet-maker Thomas Moore; Matthew Boulton, described by Josiah Wedgwood as 'the first and most complete manufacturer in England of metal'; the brilliant stuccoist Joseph Rose; and painters such as Giovanni Battista Cipriani, Antonio Zucchi, Angelica Kauffmann (whose desire for social status led her to marry a count, only for her to find out after the wedding that he was really a Swedish valet) and Biagio Rebecca, whose embarrassing propensity for practical jokes ran to painting a black kettle on Lady Howard de Walden's white satin chair at Audley End. In one year alone – 1763 – Adam had country house projects in hand at Shardeloes in Buckinghamshire, Harewood House in Yorkshire, Kedleston in Derbyshire, Bowood in Wiltshire, Compton Verney in Warwickshire, Witham Park in Somerset, Mersham-le-Hatch in Kent, Syon in Middlesex, Ugbrooke in Devon, Moor Park in Hertfordshire and Audley End in Essex – although only two of these, Mersham and Witham Park, involved him in creating entirely new houses, and Witham was destined to be abandoned unfinished at the death in 1770 of its owner.

It was also in 1763 that Robert Child (1739–82) inherited Osterley Park in Middlesex. Fifty years before, his grandfather Francis – an extremely wealthy London banker – had bought the Elizabethan mansion, not as a residence, but because its substantial underground vaults provided a useful and relatively secure spot to store the bank's cash.

With a view to modernising the redbrick house, which consisted of a central block and two projecting wings forming three sides of a courtyard, Robert's brother (another Francis) had carried out some alterations in the 1750s, probably to the designs of William Chambers. These included the remodelling of both the Tudor long gallery and a chamber at the front of the house which became the breakfast room; the design of some furniture and chimneypieces; and possibly the recasing of the exterior. Chambers' alterations obviously did not go far enough for Francis Child: in 1761 he asked the man of the moment, Robert Adam, to produce a design

The entrance front of Osterley Park, Middlesex: Adam's double portico is a brilliant solution to the problem of providing an Elizabethan house with a classical façade. (*Victoria & Albert Museum*)

for a more fundamental remodelling. Adam planned to retain the central block, but would have shortened the two wings by some 25 feet and created a Corinthian portico opening directly from the house on to the courtyard. His schemes were never executed, perhaps because of Francis's death at the age of only twenty-eight.

But Francis's younger brother Robert, who inherited both the family banking business and Osterley, had seen enough to be sure that Adam was the right man to finish off the job begun by Chambers a few years before. With his natural banker's caution, he rejected the Scotsman's radical proposals for changing the house, and asked him to produce designs that would incorporate the earlier alterations but would at the same time classicise the entrance façade and provide a magnificent series of state rooms.

At Osterley, as at so many other houses where Adam was called upon to modify existing schemes, the truth of Stravinsky's dictum that artistic freedom means operating within constraints is amply demonstrated. Faced with the problem of how to bring the rather narrow U-shaped layout up to date without significantly altering its structure, Adam hit upon the spectacular solution of creating a double portico which would link the two wings of the house, forming a fourth side to the courtyard while at the same time creating an uncompromisingly neo-classical entrance which would advertise its owner's espousal of the cult of the antique. The idea derived ultimately from the Portico of Octavia in Rome, although Adam may have been inspired by James Gibbs' unexecuted design for a similar portico at Witham Park, Somerset, which was published in Colen Campbell's *Vitruvius Britannicus* in 1717. Whatever the source, it was a bold and imaginative stroke which obviously overcame any misgivings that Child may have felt at the prospect of alighting from his carriage in wet weather and having to walk up a flight of steps, under the portico, and then across a slippery courtyard to reach the entrance hall on the opposite side.

That entrance hall is a startling introduction to the interiors at Osterley. The grey and white colour scheme, the stucco panels on the walls containing trophies of arms (a neo-classical re-interpretation of the medieval practice of hanging weapons and armour in the great hall), the coffered apses at each end containing Roman statues, all combine to create a cold, austere beauty – impressive, certainly, but hardly welcoming. Only the grisaille paintings over the two fireplaces (attributed to Cipriani) contain echoes of an older, more hospitable function, with their representations of Ceres, goddess of the corn, and Bacchus, god of wine.

But if the hall was not a place for visitors to linger, it was undoubtedly a room in which they were invited to admire the way in which Adam managed to bring together the various elements in his decorative scheme. The concentric ovals of the ceiling are echoed – though not exactly mirrored – in the slate inlay of the stone floor, while his attention to the smallest detail meant that the firegrates as well as the chimneypieces, the brass door furniture as well as the doors themselves, were all made to his designs.

The same is true of the eating room at Osterley, where lyre-back dining chairs, sideboard, pier-glasses and urns on pedestals were all designed by the architect. Like the hall, the eating room was meant first and foremost as a showpiece. There was no dining table to distract from the decoration: instead, the chairs were all arranged round the walls, leaving the central space open, and several mahogany gate-leg tables were kept in the passage outside, to be brought in as necessary. The emphasis on stucco and the absence of damask and tapestries may be traced to Adam's eminently commonsensical remarks on the dining room at Syon, of which he wrote that stucco, statues and paintings were a more fitting form of decoration for such a room, since 'they may not retain the smell of the victuals'.

Most of the state rooms – the hall, eating room, library and drawing room – had been completed by 1773, when Horace Walpole drove over from nearby Strawberry Hill to pay the first of two visits to Osterley. He liked what he saw:

> On Friday we went to see – oh, the palace of palaces! – and yet a palace sans crown, sans coronet, but such expense! such taste! such profusion... The old house I have often seen, which was built by Sir Thomas Gresham; but it is so improved and enriched, that all the Percies and Seymours of Sion must die of envy. There is a double portico that fills the space between the towers at the front, and is as noble as the Propyleum of Athens. There is a hall, library, breakfast-room, eating-room, all chefs-d'oeuvre of Adam, a gallery one hundred and thirty feet long, and a drawing-room worthy of Eve before the Fall.

However, on his second visit to the house, in 1778, Walpole's reaction was not so unreservedly positive. In the intervening five years Adam's schemes for the final three rooms in the state apartment – an antechamber known as the tapestry room, the state bedchamber, and a dressing room – had been finished. While Walpole was delighted with the tapestry room, praising it as 'the most superb that can be imagined, and hung with Gobelin tapestry, and enriched by Adam in his best taste',

The state bed: 'What would Vitruvius think of a dome decorated by a milliner?' asked Horace Walpole. (*Victoria & Albert Museum*)

The Etruscan room: a remarkable expression of the mid-Georgian craze for Greek ceramics.
(*Victoria & Albert Museum*)

he was less impressed with the domed state bed, festooned with artificial flowers. He proclaimed it 'too theatric, and too like a modern head-dress ... What would Vitruvius think of a dome decorated by a milliner?' And as for the final chamber in the sequence, the Etruscan dressing room, he was even less restrained in his condemnation:

> [It] is painted all over like Wedgwood's ware, with black and yellow small grotesques. Even the chairs are of painted wood. It would be a pretty waiting-room in a garden. I never saw such a profound tumble into the Bathos. It is going out of a palace into a potter's field... and it is called taste to join these incongruities!

With the benefit of hindsight we can safely say that the old connoisseur overreacted to Adam's later work at Osterley. True, the state bed *does* look more like a Covent Garden set than a haven of rest – but then it was intended as a display piece rather than as a sleeping place for Mr and Mrs Child. True, the transition from bedchamber to Etruscan dressing room *is* rather abrupt, but Adam's free interpretation of the motifs found on Greek (not, as the Georgians supposed, Etruscan) vases and urns, and his use of these motifs as a decorative theme, showed the architect at his most experimental. He was taking a contemporary craze for Greek ceramics – Josiah Wedgwood had named his new works 'Etruria', and in 1768, seven years before Adam's designs for the Etruscan room, had declared that his London agent was 'mad as a March hare for Etruscan vases' – and creating something both striking and original – a *tour de force* rather than a work of art.

Of more interest is the fact that Walpole had noticed the change in style between Adam's monumental, muscular early period – the period of broad, sweeping designs and unfussy details which lasted until around 1770 – and his later work, characterised by a more fragile delicacy of execution and possessing a strongly two-dimensional quality, in contrast to the bold reliefs of the 1760s. Osterley is perhaps the best of his surviving buildings in which to compare these two styles, both of which have a great deal to tell us about his approach to country house design; it is also one of the most complete and intact collections of Adam interiors in the country.

Osterley was finished by 1780, but Robert Child did not live long to enjoy his 'palace of palaces', to use Walpole's phrase. He died in 1782 at the early age of forty-three, his end reputedly hastened by his distress at the scandalous behaviour of Sarah Anne, his only child. The eighteen-year-old Sarah Anne had fallen in love with John Fane, the 10th Earl of Westmorland, but her parents had other suitors in mind for her. One evening over dinner, 'Rapid' Westmorland asked Child what he would do if *he* were in love with a girl and her parents refused to consent to the match. Child rashly replied that he would 'run away with her, to be sure!' The couple took his advice, and in the early hours of the morning of Friday 17 May 1782 they eloped to Gretna Green. Child and his wife gave chase, but after Westmorland, urged on by Sarah Anne, had shot the horse out from under the banker's groom, and had prevailed on an old army friend whom they met on their way to slow down the pursuit by ordering his detachment of dragoons to carry out 'manoeuvres' on the road, they gave up and returned home. The young lovers were married at Gretna the next day.

Faced with a fait accompli, the Childs arranged for the couple to undergo a second, more conventional marriage. But shortly before his death two months later, Robert altered his will to leave Osterley and the bulk of his fortune to Sarah Anne's *second* son, or failing such a son, the eldest daughter, in the hope of preventing the senior branch of the Westmorlands from benefiting from the elopement. Sarah Anne herself seems to have been motivated as much by pragmatism as by passion. Asked by her mother why she was so quick to marry when there was the chance of more advantageous matches, she is said to have replied, 'Mamma, a bird in the hand is worth two in the bush.'

Robert's will achieved its desired effect: Osterley was inherited by Sarah Anne's daughter, Sarah Sophia, who married the 5th Earl of Jersey. The 9th Earl gave Osterley to the National Trust in 1949.

Saltram

DEVON

Saltram, just over 3 miles east of Plymouth, was remodelled for the Parker family by an unidentified architect in the 1740s. Robert Adam created a saloon and library for John Parker between 1768 and 1772, and converted the library to a dining room between 1779 and 1782. Further alterations were made in 1818–20 by John Foulston.

John Parker, Lord Boringdon: 'as dirty, as comical and talking as bad English as ever'. This portrait by his friend, Sir Joshua Reynolds, hangs in the morning room at Saltram. (*NTPL*)

'We went this evening to Mr Parker's ... We walked ourselves tired, and I had the pleasure of finding Parker as dirty, as comical and talking as bad English as ever.' Georgiana, Duchess of Devonshire's account of a visit to John Parker's house at Saltram in July 1782 calls to mind the jolly but uncultivated country squire epitomised by Alexander Pope half a century before, the sort of boor who

> With his hounds comes hallooing from the stable,
> Makes love with nods, and knees beneath a table;
> Whose laughs are hearty, though his jests are coarse,
> And loves you best of all things – but his horse.

And, at first sight, John Parker's career seems to bear this out. A hard drinker who could lose £1,000 in one night's play at Boodles, a keen hunting and shooting man who devoted much of his time, energy and fortune to the creation of a successful racing stable, he does indeed seem to have sprung straight from the pages of *Tristram Shandy* or *Tom Jones*. A small full-length portrait painted in 1769 confirms the impression: gun in hand, Parker lolls, dishevelled, complacent and portly, against a five-bar gate.

But on delving a little deeper into his career, one soon realises that there was rather more to the man than hock, hounds and horses. That portrait, for example, is by Joshua Reynolds, art adviser to Saltram's squire, a regular visitor to the house and a close family friend. His gambling crony at Boodles was the 2nd Earl of Shelburne, George III's principal secretary of state and a noted connoisseur. And Parker's tastes and ambitions were wide enough to encompass not only success on the turf (his 'Saltram' won the 1783 Epsom Derby), but also the best in art and architecture. He commissioned a series of beautiful interiors for Saltram from

The south front. (*NTPL/John Bethell*)

Robert Adam, and amassed a picture collection which included some eleven or twelve paintings by Reynolds, Van Dyck's *Bolingbroke Family*, landscapes by de Loutherbourg, and works by Stubbs, Angelica Kauffmann, and a wide range of Italian, Dutch and Flemish masters. Dirty and comical John Parker may have been, but he was also a discriminating collector and patron of the arts.

He was born in 1734, the son of John Parker of Boringdon, two miles away. His grandfather had bought the Saltram estate in 1712, although the family continued to live at Boringdon until the 1740s, while the quadrangular Tudor house with its late seventeenth-century additions was let. There is a somewhat macabre tradition that John's mother, Lady Catherine, daughter of the 1st Earl Poulett, set about modernising Saltram when her husband was dangerously ill and she thought that she would soon be in need of a dower house. However, against all expectations John Parker senior recovered, and he and Lady Catherine decided to leave Boringdon and to make Saltram their family home.

Lady Catherine may well have planned a grand neo-classical mansion at Saltram. An undated, unsigned design for a 370-foot façade, consisting of a domed and porticoed main block flanked by pavilions, still hangs in the house, and is inscribed 'To the Rt Hon the Lady Katherine Parker at Saltram'. The scheme came to nothing, but the Parkers did their best to draw a thoroughly Palladian veil over the old house, grafting a series of Burlingtonian façades on to the east, west and south sides. Tradition ascribes this work to Lady Catherine herself, although the name of John Sanderson (d.1774) has also been suggested. Whoever was responsible, it must be said that their treatment is only partially successful: the outline of the Tudor building peers over the eighteenth-century work here and there, tumbling out into the open on the north side, while the five-bay seventeenth-century block is clearly discernible in the middle of the west front.

But if the exterior handling of Saltram represents some sort of reluctant concession to the past, the interiors that survive from Lady Catherine's time show no such element of compromise. The south-east quarter of the house is filled with splendidly exuberant rococo plasterwork and carving, ranging from the elaborate life-size figure of Mercury which gazes down from the ceiling of the entrance hall, to the musical quartet of putti who cavort, complete with instruments, among the clouds in the morning room. Considering the fine quality of the plasterwork, it is surprising that the identities of the stuccadores, like that of the architect, are still unknown: Francesco Vassali, Thomas Stocking of Bristol, and Charles Stanley and Thomas Roberts of Oxford, have all been proposed as likely candidates.

John Parker senior died in 1768, having made such a complete recovery from his near-mortal illness that he outlived Lady Catherine by ten years. The next year their son married for the second time, taking as his wife the Hon. Theresa Robinson, daughter of the 1st Lord Grantham. (His first marriage, to Frances Hort in 1764, had ended tragically when his new bride died suddenly in Naples on their honeymoon.)

In spite of having inherited a house that had been so recently modernised, John and Theresa quickly set about putting their own imprint on Saltram. Even before their marriage, and perhaps inspired by evenings spent in the superb Adam drawing room of the Earl of Shelburne's Lansdowne House in Berkeley Square, London, John commissioned Robert Adam in 1768 to remodel the rooms on the east range, altering the drawing room and creating a library and a saloon which would be a formal and social focus for the whole house.

Adam's library in the north-east corner stood for less than ten years before being converted into a new dining room. His work in the drawing room was largely confined to designing the giltwood side-tables and pier-glasses which flank the doorway into the saloon, preparing the eye for the rather startling transition from the heavier rococo interiors of the 1740s to his own more restrained neo-classicism. The contrast between the two styles remains, nonetheless, and one is unprepared for the sheer beauty of the saloon, with its magnificent ceiling by Joseph Rose, the intricate Thomas Whitty carpet which mirrors its design, the pale-blue damask walls and the Chippendale furniture. Most of Adam's established team of artists and craftsmen brought their talents to bear on finishing this room – not only Rose and Whitty, but Antonio Zucchi, who painted the ceiling roundels with the seasons and mythological scenes; Thomas Carter the younger, who carved the chimneypiece (and whose father was responsible for some of the earlier rococo stone carvings in the house); and Matthew Boulton, who produced the bluejohn candelabra which stand in the four corners of the room. A set of history paintings by Angelica Kauffmann was moved from here to the staircase hall in the early nineteenth century.

In 1771, two years after their marriage, Theresa wrote to her brother Lord Grantham: 'The Great Room is well finished indeed!' – and asked him to look out for suitable pictures and bronzes. (Grantham was just then taking up his post as ambassador in Madrid.) The Van Dyck already hung there, and John Parker was negotiating with Reynolds to buy two Claude landscapes. However, the deal fell through when Parker offered £800 and Reynolds refused anything less than £2,000.

The saloon was clearly intended as the chief room of state at Saltram: it was to be a fashionable – and very public – 'room of parade', containing the most elaborate and elegant furnishings and decoration, where the best pictures were to be hung, and where the family could hold balls, concerts and other entertainments. On such occasions visitors would be received in the entrance hall, shown through into the morning room and drawing room, and then led into the candle-lit 'Great Room' itself, where seating was carefully arranged around the walls to display the impressive central space to best effect. An orchestra would play, either in the adjoining library or outside the windows of the saloon. Forty years later, Frances, wife of John and Theresa's son Jack, described such an event, a ball held in 1810:

The Saloon was prepared for the dancing and looked quite brilliant and beautiful – We lighted it by hanging lamps over the windows and putting a quantity of candles over the doors, the places in which they were fixed being concealed by large wreaths and festoons of leaves and flowers beautiful to behold. The floor was chalked after an exquisite design of my own, by a celebrated artist from Plymouth – out of the great window we had a temporary place erected for the North Devon Band which played the dances all night – round the room we had two rows of seats affording comfortable anchorage for about 200 persons.

Judging from Theresa's frequent letters to her brother in Madrid, the Parkers seem to have lived happily at Saltram during the early 1770s, although the constant round of socialising sometimes taxed Theresa's patience. In October 1772 she was telling Grantham: 'we expect a good deal of Company this week ... You may guess how agreeable it will be; how far I shall think so, I may as well keep to myself.' And to her other brother, Frederick, she confessed: 'Don't betray me about the County, but really they are for bad, though to anyone else I must only speak of them as worthy respectable Country Gentlemen.' Nevertheless, entertaining friends and neighbours, going up to their London house – John served as MP for Devon from 1762 to 1784 – and caring for their young son, born in 1772, occupied much of the Parkers' time. Reynolds painted them both. Indeed, he painted Theresa twice, once leaning rather self-consciously against a pedestal, and, in her own words, 'drawn feeling my pulse'; and then seated, with her son, who was in fact added to the picture in 1775, several years after its completion.

It was in September 1775 that Theresa gave birth to their second child, also called Theresa. Just over a month later, aged only thirty-one, she was dead of complications arising from the delivery, leaving John a widower for the second time. In a tribute to her, Reynolds wrote that 'her amiable disposition, her softness and gentleness of manners, endeared her to everyone', and went on to praise her artistic judgement: 'she seemed to possess by a kind of intuition that propriety of taste and right thinking, which others but perfectly acquire by long labour and application'. Although his first reaction to his wife's death was to quit Saltram and his two children, spending time on one of his Somerset estates, Parker eventually returned to Devon and picked up the threads of his life, with Theresa's sister Anne acting as a housekeeper-cum-governess to his son and daughter.

The Parkers had contemplated a new dining room at Saltram when Adam first worked there. The earlier rococo work seemed outmoded in comparison to his more

Adam's saloon. (*NTPL/Rob Matheson*)

elegant decorative schemes, as Grantham was already pointing out during a visit in 1769: 'the two new rooms are very forward, they are highly finished . . . the stucco in the other parts of the house is not in a good taste'. However, as he went on to say, it was 'still much too good to destroy'. But when in 1778 a fire devastated the old laundry and brewhouse in the north range, John Parker took the opportunity to ask Adam to remodel the west and north sides of the house. His designs provided for a complex of service rooms to the north – an idea in part dictated by the existing layout, but also symptomatic of a growing trend towards placing the servants in a separate wing of their own rather than in a basement underneath the main block. On the west, Adam suggested an imposing oval dining room with a curved portico breaking through the centre of the façade and connected to the saloon by a 60-foot gallery with screens at each end and niches for displaying statuary.

Perhaps because he was faced with mounting debts, perhaps because as a widower he lacked the motivation to embark on another large-scale building project, Parker rejected the design. Instead, he commissioned a new kitchen from a 'Mr Parlby, the chief builder of the Dock [at Plymouth]' and Richard Stockman, the estate carpenter who had already put up several buildings in the grounds, including the orangery and the chapel. But Parker did ask Adam to convert the new library in the east range into a dining room, replacing the bookcases with pictures, blocking up several windows and introducing new furniture.

Apart from this, the original decoration remains – the ceiling by Joseph Rose (with distinctly literary paintings by Zucchi, which include *Plato and His Pupils* and *Virgil Reading the Aeneid*), the Whitty carpet and the Carter chimneypiece, all executed to Adam's designs. Completed by about 1781, the new dining room formed part, together with the drawing room and the saloon, of the public suite of rooms. It would not have been used for everyday meals: the family ate either in the morning room on the south front or upstairs in what is now the Chinese Chippendale bedroom. Nor would it have contained a large dining table: when Parker entertained in here, portable tables would have been brought in for the purpose, as happened at Osterley. Otherwise it remained relatively empty, a display room like the saloon.

In 1784, two years after the Duchess of Devonshire's visit to Saltram, John Parker was elevated to the peerage as Lord Boringdon. In the years leading up to his death in 1788, he was increasingly plagued by ill health and money worries. No doubt he remained dirty and comical; no doubt he talked 'as bad English as ever'; and no doubt he continued to exhibit that curiously attractive synthesis of connoisseur and country squire. Reynolds' portrait of him is a fitting memorial to the one side of his character; Saltram is a monument to the other.

John Parker's son, who was created Earl of Morley in 1815, commissioned the Plymouth-based architect John Foulston (1772–1842) to make a few further alterations to the house, including the addition of the rather heavy single-storey Doric portico on the entrance front. After the death of the 4th Earl in 1951, the 5th Earl and the National Trust negotiated with the Treasury to accept Saltram, its principal contents and 291 acres of parkland in payment of death duties. The house was eventually transferred to the Trust by the Treasury in 1957.

Berrington Hall

HEREFORD & WORCESTER

*Berrington Hall, 3 miles north of
Leominster, was built in 1778–81 for
Thomas Harley. The architect was Henry
Holland, and the grounds were landscaped
by Holland's father-in-law, Lancelot
'Capability' Brown.*

The peace and quiet of the Berrington estate, with the Black Mountains of Wales and the Brecon Beacons in the distance, must have come as a welcome relief to Thomas Harley (1730–1804). When he bought the estate in 1775, the third son of the 3rd Earl of Oxford was reeling from a rather eventful fourteen years in London politics, as MP for the City, alderman, Sheriff and Lord Mayor.

During that time his implacable opposition to 'Wilkes and Liberty' had earned him the contempt of the mob. He had been pelted with wood and dung when, as Sheriff, he presided at the Royal Exchange in December 1763 over the public burning of John Wilkes's *North Briton* after his prosecution for libel; he had been dragged from his carriage and beaten up, and had the windows of his house smashed on several occasions. He was regarded by some as an 'enemy of the people', and his effigy had been beheaded by a chimney sweep on Tower Hill. Small wonder that in 1774, when Wilkes was himself elected Lord Mayor and the crowd celebrated by smashing Harley's windows again, he took to the hills, resigning his City seat and standing for Hereford – unsuccessfully, although he had better luck two years later. Then, in 1775, he decided to buy the Berrington estate, on safe and familiar territory in Herefordshire and not far from the Harley family seat at Eywood.

It may have been while he was staying at Eywood with his brother, the 4th Earl of Oxford, that Thomas Harley was introduced to Lancelot Brown, who was engaged in making some improvements to the Earl's gardens. Certainly Brown accompanied Harley on one of his frequent rides over to Berrington, and, besides laying out the grounds, he probably also advised on the choice of site for Harley's new house. Looking down over a wide valley, through which flows a tributary of the River Lugg, it was a position of the sort much favoured by the landscape gardener, and the scene was completed by the creation in the foreground of an artificial lake of nearly fourteen acres encircling a four-acre island.

Perhaps Brown was also consulted on the designs for the house. Having originally turned to architecture because of 'the great difficulty ... in forming a picturesque whole, where the previous building had been ill-placed or of improper dimensions', he had acquired quite a reputation as an architect – Humphry Repton later bore witness to the 'comfort, convenience, taste and propriety of design in the several mansions ... which he planned'. But by the late 1770s he was tending increasingly to leave the building side of the business to his young son-in-law, Henry Holland. And it was Holland who in 1778 submitted an estimate for 'The several works proposed to be done in Building a new house for the Rt Honble Thomas Harley'.

Henry Holland (1745–1806) was the son of a successful master-builder, at whose yard in Fulham, London, he learned his trade. Unlike Robert Adam, he didn't study abroad, and the refined vocabulary of French neo-classicism that became a hallmark of his style seems to have been acquired through a careful analysis of contemporary French engravings, and, later in life, from employing French assistants and craftsmen.

In 1771, with financial backing from his father, Holland embarked on a speculative building project to provide housing on an 89-acre site in Chelsea, London, known as Hans Town, which included Sloane Street and Cadogan Place. It became enormously popular, attracting residents such as Jane Austen, Mary Russell Mitford and Lady Caroline Lamb. And in the same year Holland entered into a loose partnership with Lancelot Brown, a friend of his father's, whose daughter Bridget he married in 1773. While they both continued to take on individual commissions, the two men collaborated on a number of country houses until shortly before Brown's death in 1783. These included Claremont in Surrey (1771–4, for Robert Clive), where they replaced a Vanbrugh house with a solid, compact classical block in which the state rooms on the *piano nobile* were grouped around a central staircase hall; Benham Place, Berkshire (1774–5, for the 6th Lord Craven); and Cardiff Castle (1777–8), where Lord Mount Stuart invited the pair to remodel and extend the medieval fabric, after rejecting a rather too grandiose scheme from Robert Adam.

But Holland's most important individual commission in the 1770s, in that it opened the door to a tremendously successful career, was Brooks's club-house in St James's Street, London (1776–8). Brooks's brought him into contact with the Whig noblemen who gathered at the club, and who in the 1780s and 1790s were to become his chief patrons. It also brought him to the attention of the Prince of Wales. The Prince was made a member of Brooks's in 1783; and so impressed was he with Holland's treatment of the building that he chose him to remodel Carlton House, his London residence, in the same year, and in 1786 commissioned him to build the Marine Pavilion at Brighton.

However, in 1778, when he produced his designs for the Tory Thomas Harley's house at Berrington, Holland's career as a Whig favourite and architect to the Prince of Wales was still in the future. Little is known about the building history of Berrington – indeed, the only documentary evidence to survive is the estimate mentioned above, which was for £14,500, to include making the bricks, quarrying the stone, supplying and erecting the scaffolding, and providing all materials, travel expenses and lodging for the craftsmen. The estimate shows the concern for practical comfort and convenience which Holland had no doubt learned from Brown: 'the partitions in bed-chambers and garrets to be partly noggined and part filled with sawdust . . . a strong counter-floor laid to prevent noise and fire . . . one pair stairs to have mahogany sashes, glazed crown glass double hung . . . 2 water closets with marble basins and mahogany seats'.

In fact, it is scarcely an impression of comfort that one receives from a first glance at the exterior. In what amounts almost to an inversion of the concept of flanking pavilions linked by quadrants to the centre, Holland built two simple, gabled service ranges behind the house, connected by short quadrant screens both to the main

Berrington Hall, Hereford & Worcester: the solid and excessively plain entrance façade.
(*NTPL/John Bethell*)

block and to a third service range to the north, thus creating an enclosed court.
(Three of these screens have since been altered, and one was removed in the
nineteenth century.) As a result, the solid and excessively plain entrance façade to
the south – two principal storeys raised on a low basement and topped with a low
attic behind a balustrade – seems to stand quite alone looking down over the valley,
while its massive tetrastyle Ionic portico pushes itself forward aggressively, as
though the whole house were straining to distance itself from the domestic offices
lurking in the background. The hard, reddish sandstone with which Berrington is
faced (quarried a mile away at Shuttocks Hill), combined with the almost total
absence of ornament, presents an image of a neo-classical simplicity verging on
barracks-like severity – an impression that is accentuated rather than diminished by
the irregular arrangement of the portico columns: the two central ones are widely
spaced so as to give uninterrupted views over the valley from the hall windows, and
this adds to the squat, rather louring aspect of the façade.

But if the exterior of Berrington is rather plain, the interiors are a delight, a
wonderland of marble floors, delicately modelled and painted ceilings and elegant
chimneypieces, with one of the finest staircase halls of the period anywhere in
England. Their civilised opulence – which must have far exceeded Holland's
original £14,500 estimate – is a testament to the architect's vision, and to the skills of
the largely unknown group of craftsmen who executed his designs. The likely
explanation for such luxuriance, though, is rather more prosaic. In April 1781
Thomas Harley married his daughter Anne to George, eldest son of Admiral
Rodney, one of the most distinguished naval commanders of the day; and since

The drawing room ceiling, attributed to Biagio Rebecca, which commemorates the marriage of Thomas Harley's daughter to the eldest son of Admiral Rodney. (*NTPL/John Bethell*)

Anne and her new husband were likely to inherit Berrington, it seems probable that to celebrate the union Harley opted for a more lavish – and more expensive – decorative scheme than he had at first envisaged. The precise sequence of events is uncertain, but the decoration must date from either around the time of the wedding, or from a year later, when the admiral, following his brilliant victory over the French under the Comte de Grasse off Dominica in April 1782 during the War of American Independence, was created Baron Rodney.

In plan, the *piano nobile* at Berrington consists of a series of rooms grouped round a central staircase hall, as at Claremont. The square entrance hall, with an elaborate floor of black, white and grey marble – as opposed to the 1778 estimate, in which 'hall and staircase are to be paved with stone' – provides the first, startling intimation that the interiors of the house promise a lighter, more urbane experience than the stark exterior. As with Adam's treatment of the hall at Osterley, panels with armorial trophies on the walls echo the medieval practice of hanging arms and armour here; but the ceiling is a simpler composition than Adam might have used, relying on segments over the walls and spandrels springing from each corner to create a sense of airy movement.

The staircase hall: a Soanesque exercise in spacial drama. (*Country Life*)

In contrast, the ceiling of the drawing room to the west is much more elaborate: against a lavender background, painted roundels linked by plaster putti and sea horses surround a central medallion of Jupiter, Venus and Cupid which, with the roundels, is tentatively attributed to Biagio Rebecca, who worked for Adam, for James Wyatt, and certainly for Holland himself later in the 1780s. The choice of subject – and the sea horses – make it easy to see in the ceiling a reference to the Rodney marriage.

And such references are to be seen all over the house. The little boudoir beyond the drawing room has a ceiling, less ornate than that in the drawing room, in which bands of blue and pink frame an oval of Venus on a cloud playing with cupids. The superb chimneypiece in the dining room on the east front contains two inset marble panels, one of which depicts a classical figure holding what seems to be a crane, with a battleship in full sail in the background, while the other shows another figure with Britannia's shield and trident at her feet. The frieze in the staircase hall is decorated with entwined dolphins. Berrington seems filled with decorative features that advertise and celebrate the union – and, of course, the status-enhancing family connection with an acclaimed war-hero.

But Harley's new house is much more than a curious collection of nautical and nuptial memorabilia: it is a testament to Holland's developing powers as a neo-classical architect of genius, and nowhere is this more apparent than in the staircase hall at the heart of Berrington. A succession of sweeping arches beneath a great ribbed glass dome in the centre of the stairwell provides dramatic contrasts of light and shade, while the lyre-motif balustrade of the staircase itself leads the eye up towards a series of galleries at first floor level, defined by scagliola columns on three sides, and pilasters against an alcoved wall on the fourth. The result is a pure, awe-inspiring exercise in spatial drama, reminiscent of John Soane who worked in Holland's office as a young man – so reminiscent, in fact, that some have detected Soane's hand at work here, although he left England before the designs for Berrington had progressed very far. The hand is almost certainly Henry Holland's, and if he learned from his pupil, so much the better for Harley – and for us.

The staircase hall is a masterpiece, as is Berrington itself. The striking contrast between the austere, even forbidding exterior (an unconscious response, perhaps, to the over-exuberance of the London mob) and the spacious treatment of the interiors; the dignity and grace of the detailing; the confident handling of a neo-classical vocabulary: all combine to make the house one of the most attractive expressions of late eighteenth-century classicism. In June 1784 the inveterate tourist John Byng, who was usually sparing with his praise for contemporary architecture, pronounced it 'gay, just finished and furnished in all the modern elegance, commanding beautiful views, a fine piece of water, and ... throughout a scene of elegance and refinement'. And so it is.

After Thomas Harley's death in 1804 Berrington Hall passed to his son-in-law, who on the death of his father in 1792 had become Lord Rodney. In 1901 the 7th Lord Rodney sold the estate to Frederick Cawley, who was created Baron Cawley in 1918; and in 1957, after the death of the 2nd Lord Cawley, the house and park were transferred to the National Trust via the National Land Fund.

Castle Coole

COUNTY FERMANAGH

Castle Coole lies 1½ miles south-east of Enniskillen. The house was designed by James Wyatt and built for the 1st Earl of Belmore between 1790 and 1797. Most of the furnishings were added by the 2nd Earl between 1807 and 1825.

Castle Coole possesses none of that 'lived-in' quality so prized by travel writers and tourists alike. There is little that is intimate or homely about its austere façades and restrained interiors. Yet it possesses an exquisitely awe-inspiring, cold beauty, stemming directly from that austerity and restraint, a beauty which makes it without doubt the greatest neo-classical country house in Ireland and, in the words of James Lees-Milne, 'for sheer abstract beauty the most successful composition of

[James Wyatt's] to survive'. The appeal of its severe splendour was summed up by Bougrenet de la Tocnaye, who, shown over the brand-new mansion in 1797 by its proud owner the 1st Earl of Belmore, agreed that it was 'a superb palace' – yet added that 'temples are fit only for the gods'.

James Wyatt (1746–1813), the creator of this 'superb palace', was the most prolific of all eighteenth-century architects, with more than two hundred projects to his name – and perhaps also the most vilified. His early success, which followed his brilliant neo-classical designs for the Pantheon in Oxford Street, London, an assembly room which was completed in 1772 when he was only twenty-six, aroused a great deal of professional jealousy, not least from Robert Adam, whom Wyatt supplanted as polite society's favourite architect. His ability to design with equal facility in a range of styles, from Palladian to Greek Revival to Gothic, alienated the purists, and his over-enthusiastic 'restorations' of the cathedrals at Lichfield, Salisbury, Hereford and Ely earned him the enduring nickname of 'Wyatt the Destroyer' as well as the loathing of the nineteenth-century Gothicists. A. W. Pugin called him 'this monster of architectural depravity – this pest of cathedral architecture', and pronounced that 'all that is vile, cunning and rascally is included in the term Wyatt'.

As if such unrestrained condemnation were not enough, Wyatt's total lack of organisational skills and his neglect of his many clients have become legendary. 'Where, infamous beast, where are you? What putrid inn, what stinking tavern or pox-ridden brothel hides your hoary and gluttonous limbs?' stormed William Beckford, infuriated at the architect's delays and evasions during the building of Fonthill Abbey in Wiltshire. (Fonthill's central tower later collapsed because Wyatt hadn't been on hand to ensure that the builder incorporated the necessary supporting arches.) After his appointment in 1796 as Surveyor-General of the Office of Works he spent so little time at his post that his cleaning woman was able to run a girls' school in his Whitehall office. And at the time of his death the operations of the Office of Works itself were in such disarray that the whole system had to be reorganised, and the post of Surveyor-General was abolished so that no one man could ever be in such a position of power again.

But in spite of the controversies which surrounded, and still surround, his chaotic professional life (and an equally chaotic personal life, in which drink and women played rather too large a part), during his lifetime Wyatt was acknowledged to be one of the best designers – if not *the* best – of country houses in Great Britain. When Armar Lowry-Corry, then Baron Belmore, decided in the late 1780s to replace his grandfather's Queen Anne house on the Castle Coole estate with a mansion that would be grander than his brother-in-law's recently remodelled house a few miles away at Florence Court, Wyatt was the natural choice.

He was not, however, the first choice: initially Belmore went to the Irish architect Richard Johnston, talented designer of the assembly rooms in Dublin (now the Gate Theatre) and older brother of the more famous Francis Johnston, whose country houses in both neo-classical and castellated styles show the influence of Wyatt. The site, halfway up a hill overlooking Lough Coole and the old house, was levelled in 1788, and Richard's earliest drawings are dated 14 October 1789. But by

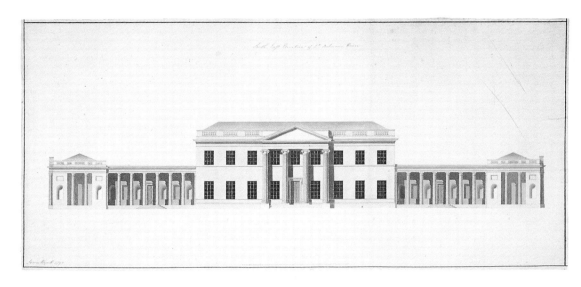

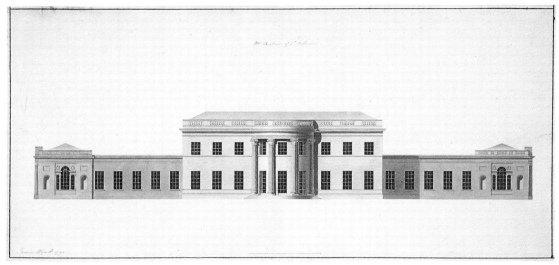

James Wyatt's designs for the house, dated 1790: the entrance front (top)
and the garden front (bottom). (*The National Trust*)

May of the following year, and probably after work had already begun on the
foundations of the house, he had been replaced by Wyatt.

The circumstances of Johnston's dismissal aren't known, but it was not
uncommon for a patron to change architects mid-stream: Robert Adam had
supplanted James Paine at Kedleston, for example, when the building was at quite
an advanced stage. Belmore's decision to employ the much more celebrated Wyatt
may well have been connected with the fact that in December 1789 he was created
Viscount Belmore – perhaps he felt that his new status required a rather grander,
more sophisticated residence.

Wyatt's designs, produced between 1790 and 1793, show a conventional plan not
dissimilar to Johnston's original drawings – a fact which adds weight to the idea that
work had begun on the building by the time that the English architect appeared on

the scene. But the overall effect is more compact, more concentrated, with fewer details to distract attention from the main composition. Two low, colonnaded wings containing family living accommodation flank a central nine-bay block which houses the state rooms. These consist of an entrance hall on the south, approached through a high but shallow portico, and leading into an oval saloon (which breaks out in a characteristic Wyatt bow on the garden front), with library, staircase hall and drawing room on the west, and breakfast room, secondary stair and dining room to the east. Domestic offices and servants' rooms occupy a basement storey running the full length of the building.

Work began on the construction of the basement in June 1790. As the house took shape, Portland stone for the external cladding was shipped from Dorset to a purpose-built quay at Ballyshannon in County Donegal, then brought by barge and cart up Lough Erne to Enniskillen. The west wing, main block and east wing were roofed in 1791, 1792 and 1793 respectively, and the portico was erected in twelve days during June of the next year. Then came the task of fitting out the rooms.

Throughout, the architect avoided inflicting the frustrations felt by his other clients at his infrequent and long-delayed site visits by the simple expedient of sending his drawings to Belmore, and not visiting Castle Coole at all. This was a tactic employed not only by Wyatt – who in spite of a flourishing Irish country house practice only ever came to Ireland once, to consult with the 3rd Lord Conyngham over the building of Slane in County Meath in 1785 – but also by Adam, whose designs for Headfort House (also in County Meath) and Castle Upton (County Antrim) were executed at second hand, and by William Chambers, whose several Dublin houses, including the brilliant neo-classical Casino at Marino House, were similarly supervised by native Irish architects.

At Castle Coole, this mail-order approach to country house building was also followed by several of the fashionable English craftsmen employed by Belmore. In a letter dated 2 July 1793 the stuccoist Joseph Rose, who was responsible for most of the ceilings in the state rooms, wrote from London to thank his employer for accepting his cancellation of a proposed site visit, 'for indeed I have got so much business in this country at present, that it would have hurried me a good deal to have taken so long a journey'. He went on to advise Belmore on how to proceed:

My Lord, you will want a man to do the ornamental parts – I mean the parts that must be done by hand on the ceilings – if I can engage with one must I send him to Castle Coole? . . . I think my Lord I can get some parts of the work modelled in London (under my own inspection), I mean only those parts that are the most difficult – and send them by the wagon to Liverpool and from thence to be sent to the care of Mr Ellis (in Stafford Street Dublin) to be forwarded to Castle Coole.

And so Lord Belmore's great new house gradually took shape, with Wyatt's designs being implemented – and often altered – either on site by the clerk of works, Alexander Stewart, or back in London where Joseph Rose and the sculptor Richard Westmacott, who carved several of the state room chimneypieces, were producing many of the decorative details and shipping them off to Ireland. During the summer of 1794 carpenters were at work on the screen of wooden Doric columns in the entrance hall, which were then coated in scagliola to represent marble, and on the sash-windows in the saloon. Chimneypieces and sections of plasterwork were arriving from London and being installed during 1795. Two years later most of the doorcases had been fitted, the doors and window shutters were hung, and furniture – some bought in, some made on the estate to Wyatt's designs – was making an appearance.

However, Lord Belmore was gradually coming to realise that his grand new country house was going to be rather more expensive than he had anticipated. Already by June 1795 the project had cost nearly £54,000, and this excluded Wyatt's fee – usually 5 per cent of the total estimated cost – and some of the more expensive items, such as Westmacott's chimneypieces. Belmore was torn between a desire for fashionable interiors and a reluctance to pay fashionable prices, and at several points during the building operations he seems to have vacillated between economy and extravagance. For example, in the summer of 1793 he rejected Wyatt's designs for the ceiling of the staircase hall as too expensive, and asked Rose to draw up estimates for a plain ceiling without decoration. Rose did as he was told. But then Belmore wrote from Bath, where he was staying at the time, ordering him to draw up a third design, a compromise that was to be neither too plain nor too ornate. This was approved when Belmore called in at Rose's London workshop on his way home – not least, one suspects, because Rose assured him that 'it will not amount to more than half of the first design' – and in March 1795 it was forwarded to Robert Shires, the senior plasterer at Castle Coole.

By 1797 Belmore had moved in to what was, structurally at least, a country house fit for a viscount – fit, indeed, for an earl, which is what he became in November of that year. The perfect proportions of his entrance hall promised elegance and splendour. His oval saloon, with its elaborate and costly plasterwork by Rose and scagliola pilasters by Domenico Bartoli, was one of the finest in Ireland. His double-return staircase provided a grand ascent to the first floor, with its spectacularly beautiful top-lit lobby – one of Wyatt's greatest achievements – the boudoir (now called the bow room) and the state bedroom. But the drawing room remained unfinished, and the suite of mahogany furniture which Wyatt had designed remained incomplete. The ornate colour schemes for the interiors remained unexecuted, and the tunnel that had been built to connect the house to a new stable block led nowhere. In spite of all the compromises, the money had run out.

Belmore died in 1802, neither the first nor the last nobleman to have built beyond his means. There the story of Castle Coole might have ended, if it hadn't been for his son, the 2nd Earl, who, on inheriting what was undoubtedly an architectural masterpiece, resolved to finish and furnish it in the manner that it deserved. New stables were built in 1817, to the designs of Richard Morrison; and between 1807 and 1825 John Preston, one of Dublin's finest upholsterers and interior decorators, was commissioned to redecorate the state rooms. In the saloon, crimson satin curtains with matching velvet draperies and gold trimmings were installed, and the old furniture – some of it designed by Wyatt, but most probably brought from the early eighteenth-century house – was replaced by new sofas, stools, tables, pier

The first-floor lobby: a perfect space. (*NTPL/John Bethell*)

glasses and lampstands, all in the rather more exuberant Regency taste that was becoming fashionable. The magnificent state bed, described in Preston's accounts as a 'full-sized bed stead ... enriched by carving of very superior design and execution ... [with] a very richly designed tester and dome, with suit of carved and gilt drapery ornaments', arrived in 1821.

In the drawing room, Preston's fabrics and trimmings alone came to more than £1,000. (For the journey from Dublin to Enniskillen, the upholsterer supplied 'a very strong dove-tailed chest to contain and preserve the saloon and drawing room and state bed curtains, inside lined with cedar secured with iron hinges with jointed plate and padlock', at a cost of £10 5s.) The room was furnished with what Preston's accounts describe, with a justifiable pride, as 'two very superb Grecian couches ... the entire executed in a very superior style', a set of some thirteen 'very superb armed chairs, seats backs and arms thickly stuffed and mattressed, French feet and arms richly carved', twelve 'unarmed chairs', and a 'large and singularly beautiful table circular top, broad behul [boulle] border ... supported by four richly carved and gilt standards upon a shaped porphyry plinth'.

Preston's Regency furnishings are some of the finest in Britain; and in the rooms where they predominate, the opulent satins and giltwood complement rather than contrast with Wyatt's stern architecture. But elsewhere – in the sparsely furnished entrance hall, or the perfect space of the first-floor lobby – the interiors of Castle Coole, like its cold façades, still belong to its architect, not Wyatt the Destroyer, but Wyatt the Creator, even Wyatt the Genius.

Castle Coole was transferred to the National Trust by the Ulster Land Fund in 1951. In 1980 the Trust embarked on a seven-year project to restore the stonework (which had been damaged over the centuries by the corrosion of the iron clamps originally used to hold the Portland stone cladding in position), at a cost of £3.2 million; and in 1986 a programme of redecoration and interior restoration was begun, and continues into the 1990s.

Ickworth

SUFFOLK

Ickworth, 3 miles south-west of Bury St Edmunds, was begun in 1795 by Frederick Hervey, 4th Earl of Bristol and Bishop of Derry, to the designs of an Italian architect, Mario Asprucci the younger, modified by two Irish brothers, Francis and Joseph Sandys. Unfinished at the 4th Earl's death, the house was completed between 1821 and 1829 by his son, the 1st Marquess of Bristol.

Frederick Augustus Hervey, 4th Earl of Bristol and Bishop of Derry. This portrait painted in Naples by his friend, Madame Vigée Lebrun, hangs in the drawing room at Ickworth.
(*NTPL/Angelo Hornak*)

He is one of the greatest curiosities alive [wrote Catherine Wilmot, a young Irish girl staying in Rome during the spring of 1803]. Such is his notorious character for profane conversation, and so great a reprobate is he in the unlicensed sense of the word, that the English do not esteem it a very creditable thing to be much in his society, excepting only where curiosity prompts. . . The last time I saw him he was sitting in his carriage between two Italian women, dressed in white bed-gown and night-cap like a witch, and giving himself the airs of Adonis.

Who was this rake who was already so mad, bad and dangerous to know when Byron was still a Harrow schoolboy? None other than the seventy-two-year-old Bishop of Derry, Frederick Hervey, 4th Earl of Bristol – connoisseur, eccentric, and builder of Ickworth, one of the most grandiose, and singular, neo-classical mansions in England.

Hervey (1730–1803) had always been given to unconventional behaviour. As Anglican Bishop of Derry, he had earned the enmity of George III by his benevolent attitude towards Roman Catholics and Dissenters alike, and his championing of the nationalist Irish Volunteers movement and the Catholic franchise. And his rather bizarre view of his ecclesiastical responsibilities led him on one notable occasion to organise a curates' foot-race, the first prize being a vacant and lucrative benefice in his diocese. His unpredictable temper – in Siena he once hurled a tureen of hot spaghetti over the procession of the Blessed Sacrament passing beneath his window, because he had 'a particular aversion to the tinkling of bells' – his whimsical dress,

The north front showing the rotunda and neo-classical porch. (*NTPL*)

which prompted at least one innocent rustic to exclaim that 'that there man cannot be a parson in them there clothes', and his penchant for foreign noblewomen of doubtful reputation – all proclaim him to be far removed from the stereotype of a Georgian divine.

And yet there is another side to the reprobate Earl-Bishop. He was also a discriminating collector, a connoisseur and patron of the arts of whom the sculptor John Flaxman once wrote that he had 'reanimated the fainting body of Art in Rome', and an inveterate builder of country houses.

The genesis of those houses – three in all – is as complex and confused as the personality of their builder. The first, Downhill, a vast mansion perched on a windswept cliff on the north coast of County Londonderry, was begun in 1775, perhaps with the £10,000 legacy left to the Earl-Bishop by his eldest brother, the 2nd Earl of Bristol, who died in that year. Both James Wyatt and Charles Cameron (who was to gain fame working for the Empress Catherine of Russia) have been suggested as architects; John Soane was consulted, although his designs were not employed; a Cork man, Michael Shanahan, was probably responsible for most of the work; and an Italian, Placido Columbani, supervised the project.

Downhill was scarcely finished when in 1787 Hervey began to build his second house, Ballyscullion, on the shores of Lough Beg, County Donegal. This time the design certainly came from Shanahan, but the work was carried out by Francis and Joseph Sandys. The model for the house was Belle Isle, a domed rotunda built in

1775 on an island in Lake Windermere in Cumbria, and, presumably under instructions from Hervey, Shanahan adapted the form to create a domed and porticoed oval main block which was to be linked to flanking pavilions by quadrant corridors. These wings would contain the Earl-Bishop's growing collection of paintings and marbles, brought together during increasingly frequent trips to Europe.

The form of the building, of interest because it was the prototype of Ickworth, derives from the ideas of the eighteenth-century engraver and architectural theorist Giovanni Battista Piranesi, although in one of those touches of absurdity which seem to envelop Hervey's life it may have been first brought to his notice in the form of a dog-kennel, John Soane's design for which, complete with rotunda and curving wings, was shown to him by the young architect in Naples in 1779. The idea may also owe something to Burke's definition of the sublime, which stipulated, amongst other things, that buildings should possess 'greatness of dimension, succession and uniformity', or that 'rotund form' which simulates infinity. 'Nothing,' said Burke, 'is more prejudicial to greatness than for a building to abound in angles.'

By November 1789 Hervey was writing to his daughter, Lady Erne: 'my house at Ballyscullion which you don't care a jot about and which I care so much about is finished'. This was rather an exaggeration, in fact, since although the rotunda was completed and furnished by the early 1790s, the wings were never built, perhaps because its builder lost interest in the project as he turned his attention to the last and greatest of his houses – Ickworth.

The Herveys had held land at Ickworth since the fifteenth century, but the 1st Earl of Bristol had pulled down the Tudor manor house in 1710, to make way for a mansion more suited to the rising fortunes of the family. Although he consulted both William Talman and John Vanbrugh about this new house, it was never built, and the family divided their time between their residence in Bury St Edmunds and Ickworth Lodge, a farmhouse on the estate which had been fitted up as temporary accommodation while the projected new house was under construction.

The 1st Earl's son John predeceased him, and on the Earl's death in 1751 the title passed to his three grandsons in succession – George, Augustus, then in 1779 Frederick, the Earl-Bishop. Two years later Hervey visited his ancestral estates, where he consulted Capability Brown about building the long-awaited new house. However, in November 1782 he abandoned his plans for Ickworth – he also abandoned his long-suffering wife, whom he left at Ickworth Lodge, never to meet her again – and returned to Ireland, where work was still in progress at Downhill.

Ten years passed before he visited Ickworth again, taking advantage of his wife's absence (she was spending the summer in Ramsgate) to select a suitable site for the new house that he had now determined to build on his Suffolk estate. There were several motives for this decision. First, his annual income of £20,000 from his Irish property, which had doubled when he succeeded to the earldom and had been rising steadily ever since, provided the opportunity. Second, he may well have seen Ickworth as a suitable base for entertaining on a royal scale, since he harboured fond – but vain – hopes of marrying his eldest surviving son to the illegitimate daughter of the King of Prussia. Third, and perhaps most importantly, he needed a suitable setting in which to display his ever-increasing collection of paintings and sculptures.

Mario Asprucci's design for the north front. A marked resemblance to one of the Earl-Bishop's other houses, Ballyscullion in County Donegal, suggests that Hervey had a close hand in the planning of Ickworth. (*Courtauld Institute, collection of the Duke of Devonshire*)

His galleries, he wrote in 1796, would 'exhibit an historical progress of the art of painting both in Germany and Italy', and 'by classing the authors under the different schools, will show the characteristic excellence of each, instruct the young mind and edify the old'.

Having decided on the site, Hervey cast around for a suitable architect. C. H. Tatham, who met the Earl-Bishop in Rome in November 1794, was invited to make a design 'for a villa to be built in Suffolk, extending nearly 500 feet including offices. The distribution of the plan is very singular, the house being oval, according to his desire.' Tatham was paid five guineas for his designs, but in the event Hervey commissioned the Italian architect Mario Asprucci, son of the curator of the Borghese collections and an influential figure in Roman artistic circles.

Asprucci's drawings show a marked resemblance to Ballyscullion, suggesting that they were produced after close consultation with Hervey. (Like the earlier building, Ickworth was to consist of a large and dramatic rotunda, flanked by curving corridors leading to two low pavilions which would house the Earl-Bishop's art collection.) The drawings were completed by early 1796, when they were taken back to England by Francis Sandys, one of the two brothers who had supervised work at Ballyscullion in the late 1780s. Sandys was in Rome with Hervey in 1794,

The dining room: 'my lungs always played more freely, my spirits spontaneously rose much higher, in lofty rooms than in low ones where the atmosphere is too much tainted with ... our own bodies'. (*NTPL/Mark Fiennes*)

and returned to England two years later, when the landscape-painter Joseph Farington recorded in his diary that John Flaxman had called on him in company with 'Mr. Sandys an architect; a young man who left Rome at the beginning of April, and is now employed, as he says, in beginning to build a palace at Ickworth for Lord Bristol'.

Francis and his brother Joseph made a number of changes to Asprucci's designs. They reduced the size of his two-storey portico and gave it a pediment, bringing it into line with the façade of Ballyscullion. Bands of bas-relief panels (which would be executed by Casimiro and Donato Carabelli from Flaxman's illustrations of the *Iliad* and *Odyssey*) were confined to the rotunda itself, instead of being carried on along the two corridors, as originally specified. And it was decided that those corridors should join the rotunda not at its centre, but towards the front, which had the effect of setting the main block back behind the façade and reducing the dramatic impact of the composition. All of these changes were incorporated into a model of the house that was constructed in 1796 and sent to Italy for the Earl-Bishop's approval.

In spite of his absence from Ickworth, Hervey took an active interest in the progress of his new palace. His surviving letters show him discussing the choice of building materials, or specifying the height of the ground-floor rooms – which was to be 30 feet, since 'my lungs always played more freely, my spirits spontaneously rose much higher, in lofty rooms than in low ones where the atmosphere is too much tainted with ... our own bodies'. They show him asking his friend, a Cambridge professor called John Symonds, to settle a disagreement between the Sandys brothers over the dimensions of the two galleries, or approving Francis's designs for the staircase balustrade. In the meantime, Hervey scoured Europe, travelling to

Dresden, Munich, Venice, Trieste, Padua, Milan, Rome, Naples, constantly searching for the works of art with which he hoped to fill his new house; and forgetting – or at least neglecting – his diocesan duties, which had failed to bring him back to Ireland since 1791.

However, Hervey's plans for his Ickworth collection were destined to fail. In April 1798 he set out from Venice for Rome, and between Ferrara and Bologna he was arrested by the French, who had invaded Italy that year. He was imprisoned in Milan for nine months, and the bulk of his collection, which was stored in Rome ready to be transported to England, was confiscated by order of the French military commander. In spite of several attempts to retrieve the 'immense property there of marbles, pictures, mosaic pavements' which he valued at around £18,000, it was never recovered, notwithstanding the efforts of the considerable artistic community in Rome, who banded together to petition the authorities for its restoration.

On his release in 1799, Hervey leased a house in Florence and continued his travels round Europe. Even the death of his wife in 1800 at the Lodge, within sight of what she described as the 'stupendous monument to folly', which was still under construction, failed to bring him home, and provoked no emotion stronger than annoyance at certain provisions in her will. By the time that the young Catherine Wilmot saw and described him in Rome in the spring of 1803, he had not set foot in Downhill, Ballyscullion or Ickworth for more than ten years.

Three months later he died, in a peasant's outhouse on the road to Albano. (The man was too scared to allow a heretic bishop, even a dying one, into his cottage.) His body was shipped back to Ickworth in a coffin disguised as a crate containing an antique statue, because the superstitious sailors refused to carry a corpse.

So Frederick Hervey never saw Ickworth. At his death the vast rotunda was still just a shell with a temporary roof and a makeshift wooden staircase, the walls of the great curving wings and the picture and sculpture galleries only a few feet above ground. It wasn't until 1821 that his son, who had seriously considered demolishing the house, finally decided to complete the corridors and pavilions, though reversing his father's original scheme by turning the rotunda into a showcase for the works of art that remained, and living in one of the wings. In 1829, more than thirty years after the Earl-Bishop embarked on his grandiose project, the family finally moved into their new mansion.

Time has not been kind to Hervey's buildings. Downhill was damaged by fire in 1851, and gutted in 1950: the ruins, and the Mussenden Temple built by Shanahan in 1783–5, are in the care of the National Trust. Ballyscullion was never completed; ten years after its owner's death, it was pulled down to avoid window tax. Having been handed over to the Trust in 1956, Ickworth alone remains intact – not a 'stupendous monument to folly', but a monument to the eccentric vision of 'one of the greatest curiosities alive'.

Chapter Six

Irregular in Parts

1820-1930

Huge halls, long galleries, spacious chambers, join'd
By no quite lawful marriage of the arts,
Might shock a connoisseur; but, when combined,
Form'd a whole which, irregular in parts,
Yet left a grand impression on the mind,
At least of those whose eyes are in their hearts.

Byron, *Don Juan*, 1823

1823 marked a turning point in the life of George Hammond Lucy. In that year he married the reluctant young heiress Mary Elizabeth Williams – 'My sweet Mary, love *will come* when you know all of Mr Lucy's good qualities,' her mother assured her. That year, too, he inherited Charlecote Park in Warwickshire, the Tudor mansion on the banks of the Avon where his ancestor, Sir Thomas Lucy, had entertained Elizabeth I and been knighted by Robert Dudley, Earl of Leicester, and where, if legend is to be believed, Shakespeare himself had been fined and flogged for poaching deer.

But in 1823 the old house was rather run down and neglected: 'You may imagine ... how much is required to be done at Charlecote,' George told Mary, 'which in time I hope we shall accomplish.' And within a few years the couple had commissioned designs for a major remodelling from the local Warwickshire architect Charles Smith, a pupil of Sir Jeffry Wyatville. Over the next four decades the house was transformed into a comfortable, modern family home.

There is nothing particularly remarkable in that, of course. The history of the English country house is full of such changes and transformations, as new money brought with it the means to create new comforts, new amenities. But what *is*

Lindisfarne Castle, off the Northumbrian coast. (*NTPL/Joe Cornish*)

The great hall at Charlecote Park in Warwickshire: 'a whole which, irregular in parts, /Yet left a grand impression on the mind'. (*Sir Edmund Fairfax-Lucy*)

interesting is the fact that George and Mary Hammond Lucy chose to rebuild their house in a period style which, like Don Juan's 'huge halls, long galleries, spacious chambers', sought to conjure up the glories of the past, to leave 'a grand impression on the mind'.

The Elizabethan gatehouse, of a mellow rosy-pink brick, was carefully preserved; so was the Renaissance porch emblazoned with the arms of Queen Elizabeth to mark her visit to the house in 1572. The great hall was given a ribbed ceiling in plaster, painted to look like timber, and a mock-Tudor chimneypiece, crowned with a bust of Elizabeth copied from her tomb effigy in Westminster Abbey. The newly built library and dining room were decorated with armorial glass and rich Jacobethan plasterwork; and an 'antique' sideboard was bought for the dining room, after the date inscribed on its back had been carefully re-carved to read '1558', the date of the original house.

On one level, such a desire to evoke past glories can perhaps be put down to George Hammond Lucy's need to reinforce his ancestral connections (he was a Lucy only through his great-grandmother). And yet there was something more in the couple's determination to re-create an Elizabethan country house. It was an expression of the late Georgian *Zeitgeist*, which by the 1820s had veered away from the cool reason of classicism towards a more romantic interest in England's past – an interest in quaint, picturesque architecture that was 'irregular in parts', in traditional styles whose visual, emotional and nationalistic appeal outweighed the classicists' claims that the buildings of the ancients should serve as the only models to imitate, the only standards by which architecture should be judged. To understand why the Lucys should cheerfully have chosen to throw out classical precepts which had governed the design of country houses for a century or more, one has to look beyond their individual circumstances, back to the roots of the Gothic Revival.

As a building style, the Gothic had never entirely disappeared. Quite apart from the provincial masons who, largely unaffected by the demands of fashion, continued to work in the style of their forefathers well into the eighteenth century, several nationally important architects were happy to use medieval forms and motifs as the occasion arose. Robert and John Smythson played with them at Bolsover Castle in Derbyshire (c.1612–c.1621); Wren employed them in adding to or remodelling existing buildings, when 'to deviate from the old form would be to run into a disagreeable mixture, which no person of good taste could relish'. And Vanbrugh had experimented with bold, romantic, medieval compositions on several occasions, most successfully at his own house at Greenwich in London, Vanbrugh Castle (c.1717), a fantastic toy fort of red brick, with round towers and pointed roofs.

However, the Gothic Revival proper may be said to have started some fifteen years after Vanbrugh Castle, with William Kent's attempts to reduce Gothic forms to classical formulae in his rebuilding of the Clock Court at Hampton Court (1732), and, in 1738 and 1742 respectively, in his designs for screens at Westminster Hall in London and Gloucester Cathedral. Kent's style enjoyed a brief vogue during the 1730s and 1740s, although, with its Palladian emphasis on symmetry and its essentially superficial use of ornament, which so often seems to have merely been glued to an impossibly rigid framework rather than growing organically out of its structure, it had little in common with true pointed architecture.

Perhaps the most famous early example of the Gothic Revival is Strawberry Hill, the 'little Gothic castle' which Horace Walpole built for himself at Twickenham, Middlesex, between 1750 and the late 1770s. Strawberry Hill certainly advanced the revival of medieval forms. In its studied irregularity, contrived to evoke the haphazard conjunction of forms so characteristic of medieval buildings, it showed the way towards the picturesque massing which would become so popular with future generations. And its literary flavour, an unscholarly delight in the display of Gothic ornament for its own sake, suggested to the eighteenth century that perhaps classicism took itself a little too seriously.

All the same, while one wouldn't go so far as to support Walpole's modest contention that 'My buildings are paper, like my writings, and both will be blown away in ten years after I am dead', it is true that his 'little Gothic castle' was only one among a number of essays in medievalism to appear during the middle years of the eighteenth century. Others include Sir Roger Newdigate's rambling Tudor courtyard house at Arbury in Warwickshire, transformed between 1750 and 1790 into a fanciful Gothic castle, all towers and finials and plaster vaulting; and Castle Ward, County Down (1762–70), one of the most bizarre of all Georgian country houses, reputedly designed by an unknown architect to reflect the different tastes of its owner Bernard Ward and his wife. The entrance façade, hall, dining room and library show Ward's conventional espousal of Palladianism, while Lady Anne's

The boudoir at Castle Ward, County Down. The house is part Palladian, part Gothic, reputedly because Bernard Ward and his wife couldn't agree on a style. They parted soon after it was finished. (*NTPL/John Bethell*)

garden front, saloon, morning room and boudoir were designed in an elaborate Gothic, with battlements, pinnacles and ogival windows. The couple parted soon after the house was built.

Paradoxically, it was the neo-classicists who really opened the doors to a revival of Gothic and Tudor forms in country house design. By recognising a plurality of styles, by suggesting that it was legitimate to look to different periods for inspiration, they effectively broke the hold that classicism had had on the architectural mainstream during the first half of the eighteenth century. It is no coincidence that Robert Adam, who created the austere classical splendours of Kedleston and Osterley, could also turn his hand to a range of castellated and Gothic designs – still doggedly symmetrical, perhaps, but happy to borrow a vocabulary of ornament from the Middle Ages. Alnwick in Northumberland (*c.*1774–80) and Culzean on the Ayrshire coast (1777–92) are just two examples. And James Wyatt, much less tied to antiquity and the rule of reason than Adam, produced neo-classical, castellated and full-blown Gothic houses with equal facility: the restrained simplicity of Castle Coole has its counterparts in the considerably less restrained Belvoir Castle in Leicestershire (1801–13), and the positively unbridled Fonthill Abbey in Wiltshire (1796–1812).

But it isn't enough to say that neo-classical designers used architectural forms that derived, however distantly, from the Middle Ages, simply because they were available. One needs to look further, to ask why those forms should have appealed to late-Georgian patrons like George Hammond Lucy, to ask why the rules of taste had changed so dramatically since the days of Burlington and Campbell.

Even when Palladianism was at its peak, and before, there had been a small band of dedicated enthusiasts, mostly antiquarians and topographers, who had sought out ruined abbeys and castles, in order both to record them before they passed away and to regret their passing. At Malmesbury Abbey, Wiltshire, in 1678, Anthony à Wood confessed to feeling 'a strange veneration come upon me to see the ruins of such a majestic and gigantic pile'. And fifty years later Thomas Gent found that the remains of Kirkstall Abbey in Yorkshire evoked an even more poignant sense of loss: '[I] came down, by a gentle descent, towards its awful ruins; which, Good God! were enough to strike the most harden'd heart, into the softest and most serious reflection.'

But by the end of the eighteenth century, medieval remains were attracting increasing numbers of eager tourists. 'The finest ruin that it is possible for imagination to conceive,' wrote one visitor to Fountains Abbey in Yorkshire in 1795: 'the grandeur of its appearance is rather aided than diminished by the upper parts of the building being somewhat broken.' 'The imagination has a free space to range in,' said another, 'and sketches ruins in idea far beyond the boldest strokes of reality.' Such monuments to the futility of human endeavour allowed one to indulge in what one tourist described as 'that pleasing melancholy musing which is always excited at the view of such venerable monuments of departed grandeur'.

But ancient abbeys, castles and manor houses offered more than the opportunity for melancholy musings on the transient nature of Man's aspirations, power-ful though that attraction was. First and foremost, they held a potent visual appeal. William Gilpin (1724–1804), whose topographical tours propounded the picturesque as a way of seeing, emphasised the attraction of roughness, variety, accident, contrast and ruggedness – precisely those qualities that were to be found in Gothic ruins. ('Picturesque beauty is a phrase but little understood,' he said in 1798; 'We precisely mean by it that kind of beauty which would look well in a picture.')

By suggesting that it was appropriate to admire such ruins Gilpin legitimised the asymmetrical lines of medieval architecture. Such irregularity had been dismissed by earlier commentators, who thought that 'both for the natural imbecility of the sharp angle itself, and likewise for their very uncomeliness, [medieval buildings] ought to be exiled from judicious eyes, and left to their first inventors, the Goths or Lombards, amongst other relics of that barbarous age'. Following Gilpin, Richard Payne Knight (1750–1824) and Uvedale Price (1747–1829) also extolled the virtues of the Gothic ruin. Price declared that 'Gothic architecture is generally considered as more picturesque, though less beautiful than Grecian'; and Payne Knight, in his poem *The Landscape* (1794), suggested:

> Bless'd is the man, in whose sequester'd glade,
> Some ancient abbey's walls diffuse their shade;
> With mould'ring windows pierc'd, and turrets crown'd,
> And pinnacles with clinging ivy bound.
>
> Bless'd too is he, who, 'midst his tufted trees,
> Some ruin'd castle's lofty towers sees;
> Embosom'd high upon the mountain's brow,
> Or nodding o'er the stream that glides below.

Indeed, so blessed were the owners of such ancient abbeys and ruined castles that those who didn't possess one took to building their own, turning for advice to men like the amateur architect Sanderson Miller (1716–80)[1]. Miller's design for an elaborate Gothic folly at Wimpole in Cambridgeshire (*c*.1749) is a perfect example of the genre – a battlemented tower rises up in the midst of broken walls and traceried windows, at once an attractive eye-catcher and a homage to the times when, to quote the caption to a 1777 engraving of the building, 'On Towers like these, Earl, Baron, Vavasor,/Hung high their Banners in the air'.

A second element in the movement towards the revival of traditional English architectural forms – perhaps less intellectually attractive than the Picturesque, but even more potent – was the late eighteenth century's fascination with British (which to all intents and purposes meant English) history. Already in the early 1700s the Whig desire to create a civilisation which would rival that of Rome – the same desire that had driven Lord Burlington to embrace Palladianism as an architectural expression of a new renaissance – had led to an increasing emphasis on, and celebration of, the Saxon and Gothic foundations of English democracy. And it was a short step from celebration to deliberate revival.

So when in the early 1740s Lord Cobham commissioned James Gibbs to design a Temple of Liberty – 'a trumpet-call of Liberty, Enlightenment and the Constitution' – for his classical gardens at Stowe, Buckinghamshire, the style chosen was a spiky, asymmetrical Gothic, with castellations, finials and pointed windows filled with tracery. A line from Corneille's *Horace* carved over the door might have become the watchword for a whole generation of later Gothicists – *Je rends grâces aux Dieux de nestre pas Romain* ('I thank the Gods that I am not a Roman'). As a statement of the freedoms enjoyed by eighteenth-century Englishmen – greater even than those of ancient Rome – the Temple was meant to celebrate the historic roots of

---

1   Miller seems to have been more of an amateur than an architect. His designs for Hagley Hall, Worcestershire (1754–60), had to be redrawn before they could be given to the workmen, and his Gothic tower at Wroxton church, Oxfordshire (1747–8), apparently 'fell down the first winter'. Even so, his work at, for example, Lacock Abbey (where he remodelled the Great Hall and built a gateway, both in the Gothic style, 1754–5), shows him to have been not without a certain flair.

A design by Sanderson Miller for a Gothic folly at Wimpole Hall, Cambridgeshire.
(*The National Trust, Bambridge Collection*)

those freedoms, which dated back to Alfred the Great (then thought to have been responsible for founding the right to trial by jury), and to Magna Carta and the establishment of parliamentary representation. What better way to express the glorious traditions of English liberty than via an architectural style that – since Cobham and his contemporaries made no distinction between Saxon and Gothic – had originally been an expression of those values?

Nor was Cobham the only patron of architecture to see the ideological possibilities of the Gothic. In the 1760s Henry Hoare raised a battlemented, triangular brick tower, 160 feet high, on the edge of the Stourhead estate in Wiltshire, in homage to Alfred the Great. Beneath a rather unsophisticated statue of the King, an inscription proclaims him to be 'a philosopher and a Christian, the Father of his People, the Founder of the English Monarchy and Liberty'. (Hoare also re-erected at Stourhead the late medieval High Cross which had once stood in the centre of Bristol.) Neither Cobham nor Hoare were fanatical Gothicists – classical architecture predominates at both Stowe and Stourhead – but it was only a matter of time before native English models were preferred over the foreign, and pagan, temples and villas of antiquity; only a matter of time, too, before early British architecture became the inspiration for rather more than whimsical follies and ideologically-inspired garden monuments.

The interest in early British history and its architectural monuments was given added impetus at the end of the eighteenth century, when the worries and uncertainties caused by the aftermath of the French Revolution of 1789, followed by the declaration of war against France in February 1793, disrupted many of Britain's links with Europe. It became extremely difficult for artists and architects to travel to Italy or Greece to study classical remains at first hand. Indeed, the whole tradition of the Grand Tour was forced to find another focus, so that the antiquary Richard

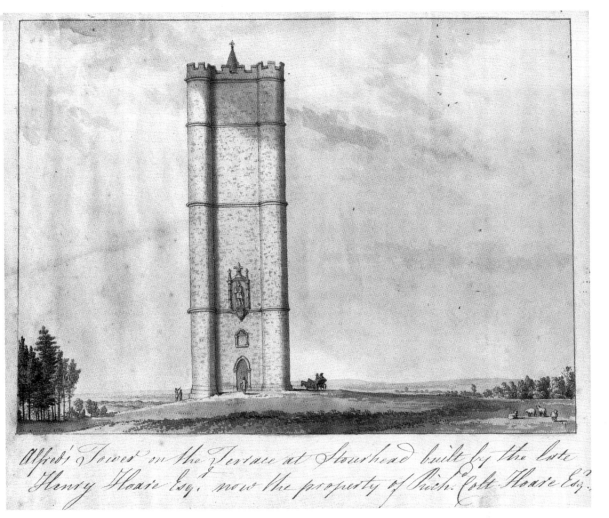

Alfred's Tower on the Terrace at Stourhead built by the late Henry Hoare Esq.[r] now the property of Rich: Colt Hoare Esq.[r]

Gough's complaint in 1780, that 'temples and palaces of the polite nations of antiquity engross our attention, while the works and memorials of our own priests and heroes have no effect on our curiosity', found its answer in William Mavor's *British Tourist* of 1800:

> Roused, at last, from the lethargy of indifference about what was in their reach, and inspired with more patriotic notions than formerly, of the pleasure and utility of home travels, we have, of late years, seen some of our most enlightened countrymen, as eager to explore the remotest parts of Britain, as they formerly were to cross the Channel, and to pass the Alps.

This imposed interest in the discovery of Britain, coupled with a Romantic sensibility which sought escape in a securer and more ordered past, only enhanced the appeal of the medieval and Tudor architecture which was that past's most obvious legacy to the Georgians. For the writer Richard Warner, exploring the Warwickshire castle of Kenilworth in 1802, 'again imagination takes fire, again she darts back with the poet into ages that are passed, into the depths of the days of chivalry, and calls up the fair form of Kenilworth Castle in its glory; the scene of mirth and gallantry'. At Hardwick Hall, tourists reverently trod in what they fondly believed were the footsteps of Mary Queen of Scots. The legend that she was held prisoner at the house – several years before its foundations were laid – is in itself another instance of the Georgian propensity to mythologise the past and to celebrate the architectural remains of that mythology. So too is the imaginative (and generally imaginary) recreation of Merry England which Walter Scott used to such effect in novels like *Ivanhoe* (1819), *Kenilworth* (1821), *The Fortunes of Nigel* (1822).

So to return – at last – to Charlecote Park: George and Mary Hammond Lucy's decision in the 1820s to remodel their house in an Elizabethan Revival style was governed by something rather deeper than the desire to confirm their links with the ancient Lucy family. They were also participating in a much wider cultural movement, which used its country houses to give expression to its love affair with the past. In their different ways, all the houses described on the following pages – irregular in parts every one – bear the marks of that love affair.

Penrhyn Castle

GWYNEDD

Penrhyn Castle at Llandegai, 1 mile east of Bangor, was built in a neo-Norman style between about 1819 and 1835 by Thomas Hopper, for the slate magnate George Dawkins-Pennant.

George Hay Dawkins-Pennant, a posthumous
miniature by C. J. Basebe, 1841.
(*Private Collection*)

Tourists visiting North Wales in the mid-nineteenth century in search of that pleasurable frisson of fear occasioned by the sight of massive mountains and awesome cataracts, would often make a detour to see the 'several immense openings ... as rude as imagination can paint' of the Penrhyn slate quarries outside Bangor. Applying a critical vocabulary learned from their eighteenth-century forebears –

Penrhyn Castle, Gwynedd: 'They want to add a *Keep* out there, Francis, I don't know what they mean by it,' said its owner, Dawkins-Pennant. (*NTPL*)

and applying it as enthusiastically to the works of man as to the works of nature – they would recall Edmund Burke's definition of sublime objects as 'vast in their dimensions . . . dark and gloomy . . . solid and even massive'. And they would agree that the quarries were indeed sublime, marvelling at how 'such yawning chasms could have been formed by any but the immediate operations of Nature'.

Such tourists would also visit and admire the quarry-owner's nearby mansion – a colossal castle every inch as sublime as the slate-works. Some 600 feet in length, with a keep 115 feet high, Penrhyn Castle is certainly vast in its dimensions, its walls are solid and massive, and the black Penmon limestone used in their construction is dark and gloomy. The building must have evoked just that sense of Romantic awe and wonder which so delighted late-Georgian and early-Victorian sightseers.

Thomas Hopper: he 'used to come in after breakfast and ask leave to add another tower'. (*National Portrait Gallery*)

But for all its heavy Romanesque details – the round towers and rounded arches, the chevron mouldings and dogtooth ornament, the vaulting springing from clusters of slender shafts – Penrhyn is no conqueror's castle, but a product of the same eighteenth-century aesthetics that governed those tourists' responses to it. The fact that it is, or pretends to be, a 'real' castle rather than a regular block embellished with turrets and battlements, proclaims its participation in an essentially literary tradition which has its roots in Horace Walpole's *Castle of Otranto* and the works of Mrs Radcliffe, rather than the *Chanson de Roland*. And its vast, sprawling, asymmetrical shape can be traced back, not to the defensive fortifications of the early Middle Ages, but to the turn-of-the-century theories of the Picturesque expounded by Richard Payne Knight – 'Component parts in all the eye requires:/One formal mass for ever palls and tires' – and Uvedale Price:

> [Symmetry] is adverse to the picturesque . . . In Gothic buildings, the outline of the summit presents such a variety of forms, of turrets and pinnacles, some open, some fretted and variously enriched, that even where there is an exact correspondence of parts, it is often disguised by an appearance of splendid confusion and irregularity.

The two men responsible for Penrhyn's own rather bizarre neo-Norman brand of 'splendid confusion and irregularity' were the slate magnate and plantation owner George Dawkins-Pennant (1764–1840) and his enthusiastic architect Thomas

Hopper (1776–1856). In 1808 George Dawkins assumed the additional surname of Pennant when he inherited property and business interests in Wales and Jamaica from his cousin Richard Pennant. That property included the Penrhyn estate, on which stood a rather curious castellated Gothick pile clad in bright yellow tiles – 'Penrhyn glitters in its yellow glory' wrote one visitor in 1791 – the result of extensive remodelling of a much earlier house some thirty years before by Samuel Wyatt, brother of James. Some of the estate income had been left to Pennant's widow for her use during her lifetime, and it wasn't until her death in 1816 that Dawkins-Pennant actually took up his inheritance.

A combination of factors led him, some three years later, to embark on a building programme that would transform his modest Welsh seat into a colossal castle many times its size. The rather half-hearted medievalism of the Wyatt house was already beginning to look old-fashioned in comparison with the more scholarly and more self-consciously picturesque wave of castles which were springing up all over the country – castles like John Nash's Luscombe in Devon (1799–1804), and James Wyatt's Belvoir in Leicestershire. Nearer to home, L. B. Hesketh was beginning a monumental castle some 480 yards long, with eighteen towers, at Gwrych, twenty-five miles along the North Welsh coast at Abergele.

Dawkins-Pennant's character and politics may also have influenced his decision to build. He was by all accounts cold and reserved in his personal dealings, and a reactionary in politics. As MP for New Romney in Kent in the 1820s, he opposed both the movement towards a widening of the franchise which led to the 1832 Reform Bill, and the efforts of Shaftesbury's Anti-Slavery Society to abolish slavery in the British Empire – no doubt motivated in the latter case, at least, by self-interest, since he had well over 700 slaves at work on the Jamaican sugar plantations which were the original source of the family's wealth. It is tempting to see the neo-Norman castle as at once an authoritarian response to social change and democracy, a harking back to a securer, more hierarchical (if largely mythical) past when the social order went unchallenged, and an attempt to create a sense of continuity and lineage on the part of an English squire whose links with North Wales, though real, were remote.

However, the choice of style and, if Dawkins-Pennant's relatives are to be believed, the vast scale of the enterprise – his son-in-law later recalled how 'Mr Hopper used to come in after breakfast and ask leave to add another tower' – may well have been due to the influence of his architect. By 1819 Thomas Hopper had established himself as a competent and successful designer, adept at working in any of half-a-dozen different genres. He once said: 'It is an architect's business to understand all styles and to be prejudiced in favour of none.' At various times he designed country houses using Greek Doric, Greek Ionic, Palladian, Tudor-Gothic and Jacobethan, and just before work began on Penrhyn, he had built for the 2nd Earl of Gosford a rather clumsy neo-Norman castle in County Armagh, reputed to be the biggest country house in Ireland, with a three-storeyed keep and a massive round tower. Gosford was probably the direct inspiration for Dawkins-Pennant's house, and it seems likely that it was Hopper, fresh from his Irish experiment in neo-Norman, who first put it forward as a suitable model.

Gosford Castle was by no means the first building in Britain to use Romanesque motifs. Architects had been tentatively exploring the potential of the round-headed arch for several hundred years. Inigo Jones had used it in his restoration work at the Tower of London in 1637, as had Hugh May at Windsor Castle in 1671 and John Vanbrugh at his own house in Greenwich in 1717. More recently, Robert Adam at Culzean (1777–92) and Seton in East Lothian (1790–1), James Wyatt at Norris Castle on the Isle of Wight (1799), and Robert Smirke at Eastnor in Herefordshire (1812–20), had all experimented with the form. But until the nineteenth century there was no real sense of Norman as a style in its own right. Well into the 1600s, most Norman building was popularly believed to have been put up by the Romans, and even when it was recognised as later work most architects drew few practical distinctions between 'Saxon' (as the style was usually called) and true Gothic, blending the two indiscriminately. At Gosford, and at its more thorough-going Norman successor, Penrhyn, Hopper no doubt saw himself not as a pioneer of a neo-Norman style, but simply as an eclectic exponent of the Gothic Revival – a notion which his cheerful if somewhat nightmarish mixture of Romanesque, Gothic, Renaissance and even Byzantine forms at Penrhyn bears out.

The earliest references to the building of the castle date from April 1819, when Dawkins-Pennant's clerk of works, William Baxter, was sent to Penmon on the island of Anglesey to agree prices for stone with a number of different quarries. By the following July, carpenters were at work on site, presumably preparing scaffolding, and parts of the shell were probably fairly well advanced by 1821. Progress was fairly slow, however: when the young Princess Victoria came to look at the castle in 1832, she reported in her journal that it was 'not near finished yet'. The internal walls weren't plastered until the spring of 1830, to judge from entries in the accounts at that time referring to the arrival of 400 bushels of cow hair and quantities of lime from the kilns at Port Penrhyn. And the delivery of 292 plates of glass in June and July of that year suggests that the main body of the house was only then nearing completion. The adjoining stable block was put up between August 1831 and June 1833, the chimneypieces were supplied in 1833–4, and doors were still being hung, and furniture made, much of it by estate workmen to Hopper's own designs, in 1835.

While all this was going on, Dawkins-Pennant seems to have been alternately fired with enthusiasm for his great house, and bewildered at the size and scope of the project. During his stays at Penrhyn he lived in what Hermann von Pückler-Muskau, visiting in 1828, described as 'a humble cottage in the neighbourhood, with a small establishment'. The German prince noted his 'building-mania', and commented that 'it appeared to give him great pleasure to show and explain everything to me, and I experienced no less from his enthusiasm, which was agreeable and becoming in a man otherwise cold'.

At the same time, there are hints that Dawkins-Pennant was to some extent swept along by Hopper's own enthusiasm for the scheme. Edward Littleton, who came to

The grand staircase, described by Christopher Hussey as 'the baroque of romantic revival architecture'. (*NTPL/Mike Caldwell*)

Penrhyn in September 1832, recorded in his journal that 'Mr Pennant has delivered himself over entirely to his architect, who delights in rearing a mass of building to his own [taste] without the slightest consideration for the comfort of the family'. And while this is no doubt an exaggeration, the story told by Dawkins-Pennant's brother-in-law Francis Maude, that the landowner once said to him, 'They want to add a *Keep* out there Francis, I don't know what they mean by it', does conjure up an irresistible image of Dawkins-Pennant as a nineteenth-century Lord Emsworth at Blandings Castle, dazed and somewhat bewildered at the turn that events were taking.

Wandering round Penrhyn, one can sympathise both with its builder's enthusiasm, and with his bewilderment. Hopper's treatment of the four elements that make up Penrhyn – the stable court, the domestic offices, the main block containing the state rooms, and the family accommodation in the keep, all linked along a roughly north-south axis – provided Dawkins-Pennant with an abundance of what Uvedale Price described as two of the most fruitful sources of human pleasure: variety and intricacy. Price defined this last as 'that disposition of objects, which, by a partial and uncertain concealment, excites and nourishes curiosity'. The determined asymmetry of the layout, with its seventy roofs and seventeen projecting towers, its battlements and bastions and barbican, accentuates the already vast scale – now hiding, now revealing, new aspects of the complex elevations, but always dominated by the massive square keep, derived from that at Castle Hedingham in Essex, where Hopper was County Surveyor for forty years.

The interiors, described by Christopher Hussey as 'the baroque of romantic revival architecture', are indeed as theatrical as any Vanbrughian palace. From the open plateau of the carriage forecourt, a forebuilding leads into a long, low, arcaded entrance corridor which opens out with a dramatic flourish into a vaulted three-storey grand hall, cathedral-like in its dimensions and embellished with pastiche thirteenth-century stained glass showing signs of the zodiac, supplied by Thomas Willement in 1835–6. Beyond the hall, and occupying the site of the original house, lies a suite of heavy and ornately decorated state rooms, the library, drawing room and boudoir. These apartments and the other principal rooms of the house – the dining room, the chapel and the state bedroom – are replete with bizarre furniture designed by Hopper: 'Norman' tables and chairs, 'Norman' chimneypieces and bookcases, even a 'Norman' cast-iron stove and a 'Norman' four-poster bed.

But the climax to this remarkable series of violent visual shocks is Hopper's grand staircase, described by one writer as a 'nightmarish conception' which 'translates into masonry the qualities relished in *The Mysteries of Udolpho* and other "novels of horror"'. This towering space is so elaborately and profusely carved that it seems almost alive with writhing, fantastic shapes, ranging from precise Romanesque geometrical patterns to sinuous Celtic interlacing, and from grotesque masks and jousting knights to the outright surrealism of the row of human hands which span the arch into the drawing room.

Some of Hopper's decoration, such as those hands, is pure personal invention, with no counterpart in either medieval or Georgian building. However, a great deal, both in the staircase hall and elsewhere, is now known to have been drawn from two published sources. The engravings of the antiquarian John Carter, whose *Ancient Architecture of England*, published between 1795 and 1814, attempted to set out 'in a regular manner' the 'orders of architecture during the British, Roman, Saxon and Norman eras', were almost certainly used for much of the decorative carving on columns and arches. (Dawkins-Pennant's own copy of the book still survives at Penrhyn.) And Joseph Strutt's *Sports and Pastimes of the English People* (1801), the illustrations of which were mainly taken from medieval manuscripts, was the inspiration for many of the figurative carvings.

The castle can stand as a consummate expression of late eighteenth- and early nineteenth-century aesthetics, or as the masterpiece of the neo-Norman Revival. But the overriding impression created by a visit to Penrhyn is not one of scholarship diligently applied. Faced with the size, the scale, the daring imaginative breadth of Hopper's castle, all thoughts of sources and models are swept aside. Describing her own impressions of the building in 1845, Louisa Stuart Costello wrote: 'To wander through the wondrous halls of Penrhyn is like struggling along in a bewildered dream occasioned by having studied some elaborate work on the early buildings of the Saxons or Normans.' And it is as a 'bewildered dream' that it is best remembered – ridiculous at times, but always sublime.

George Dawkins-Pennant died in 1840. He had no sons, and Penrhyn was left to Juliana, the elder of his two daughters (known collectively as the 'Slate Queens'), who in 1833 had married Edward Gordon Douglas, a grandson of the 14th Earl of Morton. Juliana died in 1842; Edward Douglas-Pennant, as he had become the previous year in accordance with his father-in-law's will, was created Baron Penrhyn of Llandegai in 1866. In 1951, following the death of his great-grandson, the 4th Lord Penrhyn, the castle and more than 40,000 acres of the family's Welsh estates were conveyed to the National Trust through National Land Fund procedures.

Knightshayes Court

DEVON

Knightshayes Court, 2 miles north of Tiverton, was built for Sir John Heathcoat-Amory, a lace manufacturer. Begun in 1869, it was designed by William Burges; the interiors were subsequently completed by John Diblee Crace.

Visitors to Billy Burges's rooms in Buckingham Street, off the Strand, London, were liable to be greeted by a short, rotund figure with a parrot perched on the shoulder of his hooded medieval robe, peering myopically at them through his thick pebble-glasses. (Edmund Gosse once recalled how, during a country walk, Burges had genuinely mistaken a peacock for a man.) Having negotiated the pack of poodles and terriers which guarded their master – one of which, with a healthy disrespect for architects and their nearest and dearest, had bitten Edward Godwin, Sir William

Architect and patron: William Burges, a sketch
from the *Graphic* (above), and Sir John Amory,
a portrait by John Gray showing him posing
in the hall, where the picture now hangs.
(*Nicholas Toyne, Jerome Dessain & Co. Ltd;
NTPL/John Bethell*)

Emerson's wife and J. P. Seddon's mistress[2] – they would be invited to take tea,
served in vessels of beaten gold, the cream poured out of a single onyx and the tea
itself 'strictured in its descent on account of real rubies in the pot'.

The more one learns of William Burges (1827–81), the more like a character out
of a Firbank novel he seems. His opium habit, his passion for rat-hunting, his visits to
the notorious Judge and Jury Club where salacious legal cases were re-enacted
nightly, complete with semi-nude *tableaux vivants* – all seem to have more in common
with *Valmouth* than with conventional Victorian values. Yet Burges was also a
medieval scholar with an international reputation, one of the leading architectural
theorists of his day, and a designer of genius whose buildings and decorative
schemes, furniture, sculpture and metalwork, conjured up rare and magical
Tennysonian dream-worlds which combined absolute fidelity to the spirit of the
Middle Ages with breathtakingly idiosyncratic fantasy. His houses are muscular

---

2   William Emerson (1843–1925) was one of Burges's pupils, who went on to make a name for himself
    in India as a leading architect to the Raj; John Pollard Seddon (1827–1906) and Edward William
    Godwin (1833–86) were fellow-architects and personal friends of Burges.

and confident essays in the Gothic; their interiors are equally muscular, equally confident, but gloriously eccentric, filled with chivalrous plaster knights and pious painted pilgrims, gilded ceilings, great castellated chimneypieces and grotesquely carved corbels.

It remains something of a mystery as to why, in about 1867, Burges should have been chosen to build a new house at Knightshayes for John Amory. A hunting, shooting, fishing industrialist, Amory was scarcely the sort of man one would have expected to patronise the High Victorian avant-garde; and, as it turned out, the relationship between client and architect proved not to be a happy one.

Having inherited a prosperous lace-works in Tiverton from his father in 1857, Amory was looking for an imposing yet comfortable country house to consolidate his move along the well trodden path from business to the leisurely life of a country squire. He had bought the Knightshayes estate in 1860, but soon grew discontented with the Regency house that stood there, and determined to replace it with something better. Burges may have come to his notice through two minor commissions carried out in the West Country in the 1860s: an elaborate chimneypiece depicting the legend of St Neot, designed for Colonel Charles Lygon Somers' house, Treverbyn Vean, in Cornwall; and the decoration of a house called 'The Daison' near Torquay in 1865–6. Or perhaps Amory's wife Henrietta had heard of the architect from one of her relations: Burges's papers mention that he met an Unwin (Henrietta's maiden name) in 1860.

Whatever Amory's reasons for choosing Burges, in 1867 the architect was commissioned to design a new house on the Knightshayes estate. His designs for the exterior, worked out during 1867 and 1868, were accepted, with a few modifications. On Saturday 17 April 1869 the foundation stone was laid, to the accompaniment of a hymn specially composed for the occasion – 'Architect of both creations,/Not yet is thy word fulfilled;/Pour thy spirit on the nations,/Build us up the while we build'. And by the early 1870s the shell was complete.

At this stage, the Amorys must have been pleased with the way their new house was progressing, agreeing with the verdict of *Building News* that it was 'stately and bold, and its medievalism . . . not obtrusive'. Both entrance and garden façades, in a chunky Gothic, are solid and assured. Burges's penchant for extravagant stone-carving was kept to a minimum: plate tracery quatrefoils to several windows, big gargoyles and fleurons, an angel in the central gable, and a hooded medieval figure bearing a lantern in the entrance porch. His original scheme called for a massive tower with a spire over the north-west corner of the house – a feature which would have emphasised the otherwise fairly restrained asymmetry of the composition – but this was considerably reduced in size when the house was built. The overall effect was summed up in 1872 by Charles Eastlake in his *History of the Gothic Revival*:

> Massive walls, bold gables, stout mullions . . . large and solid looking chimney shafts, corbelled from the walls or riding on the high-pitched roofs, are the principal incidents which give this building dignity and effect . . . there is a kind of sympathy between its stern unyielding nature and the robust rather than refined character of [Burges's] design.

A country seat that had 'dignity and effect', that was 'robust rather than refined', was just the sort of building that the robust rather than refined Devon squire was looking for.

In plan, Knightshayes had a traditional late-medieval layout, efficiently adapted to meet the needs of a Victorian family. On the entrance front a north-south cross-passage led through screens into an east-west great hall. The main staircase opened off the upper end of this hall, while at the lower end the masculine domain originally comprised a gun room – which also served as a smoking room until 1901, when the firm of Ernest George & Yeates was commissioned to add to the west end of the house an 'apartment specially dedicated to the use of tobacco' – a waiting room for tenants and other callers on business, and a billiard room. The garden front was occupied by reception rooms: projecting bays housed a dining room and a drawing room, with an octagonal morning room and a library sandwiched between them and separated by the cross-passage. A self-contained service wing to the east completed the scheme.

With the main structure of the house approaching completion, Burges turned his attention to its internal decoration, where the restraint that he had shown in the external detailing was notable only by its absence. The ceiling of the gentlemen's room was to be painted with a sun and signs of the zodiac, while niches below would be filled with figures 'showing the occupations of the year'. The morning room floor would be strewn with carpets of 'Turkish Persian Indian and other Eastern production'; its panelled walls were to be inset with tiles painted with birds and flowers, while above, a frieze would show grisaille figures 'illustrating the Heroes and Heroines of the Fairytales'. The first-floor boudoir was to be even more elaborate. This female enclave would be devoted to idealised images of womanhood, and dominated by a frieze portraying incidents from Tennyson's *Dream of Fair Women*. The windows were to be filled with stained glass showing scenes drawn from Chaucer's *Legend of Good Women*, a mermaid would swim across the canopied chimneypiece, and the ceiling was to be decorated with medallions showing courtly subjects from Tennyson and Chaucer, set amongst a host of little sparkling circular mirrors.

But the climax of Burges's scheme was the drawing room. Its unifying theme was to be chivalric love, a subject which, with its connotations of a high-principled pre-industrial society, fascinated not only Burges but also most of High Victorian society – including the Queen herself, who had Albert painted as her knight-in-shining-armour. Amidst green panelled walls festooned with birds and flowers set in mother-of-pearl, and topped by a frieze showing men and women who had died for love, there were to be two great chimneypieces: one, on the eastern wall, to be carved with 'heraldry and above statues of writers upon Love'; the other to be a representation of a medieval castle, the lower part marble, the upper part of 'sculptured stone coloured and gilded'.

Burges's design for the latter, adapted from a fourteenth-century German ivory mirror-case that he had exhibited at the Royal Archaeological Institution in 1857, shows *The Assault on the Castle of Love*. Knights, depicted at rather more than half life-size, sprawl along the massive mantelpiece, struggling with siege ladders and

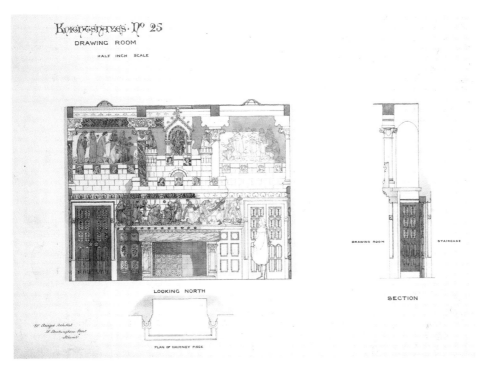

LOOKING NORTH

SECTION

DRAWING ROOM   STAIRCASE

PLAN OF CHIMNEY PIECE

William Burges's design for *The Assault on the Castle of Love* in the drawing room. (*NTPL*)

crossbows or being carried from the field of battle by their squires. Damsels, with expressions ranging from the demure to the downright brazen, look down from the battlements above. The whole composition is presided over by a winged Cupid, while to either side painted figures 'shewing the various conditions of life' offer him their hearts. And as a finishing touch Burges envisaged a gallery set behind the chimneypiece, on which, via a secret door and a spiral stair set into the wall, the ladies of the house could stand, flirting with the gentlemen below.

Burges collected all of these schemes, described by his biographer, J. Mordaunt Crook, as 'a technicolour synopsis of the High Victorian Dream', in a magnificent album of fifty-seven watercolours. The book was finished and signed on 21 November 1873, and shortly afterwards the architect presented it to his client. John Amory sacked him.

Not straight away, however. Initially the family seems to have approved of the designs, since work started on the first stage of the scheme, the stone-carving. Under the great staircase, corbels decorated with fish and ducks, a little chick breaking out of its shell, a fat frog, a cat and a monkey, demonstrate Burges's quirky imagination at work. And in the hall itself larger corbels exhibit a range of human figures – a chain-mailed soldier armed with a crossbow, a scholar, a smocked peasant bringing in the sheaves, a stonemason and a merchant clutching his bag of gold.

Elsewhere there are tantalising glimpses of what might have been: the secret staircase to the unexecuted *Assault on the Castle of Love* chimneypiece; an intricate Turkish screen separating the landing from a stone balcony which overlooks the hall; animal corbels – including Lust as an absurdly cute ram with a harp – representing the Seven Deadly Sins in the billiard room, which was also to have been decorated with 'red lines on white ground with medallions containing figures of virtues', and a painted and gilded ceiling 'with the addition of small silvered glasses' to represent stars.

It was during the second half of 1875, and before work on the interiors had progressed very far, that Burges's services were dispensed with. Perhaps, as Amory's grandson suggested years later, the squire was becoming anxious about the expense: the shell of the house had already cost well over £14,000, and Burges had few scruples about devoting vast amounts of a client's wealth to the realisation of his projects, believing with unworldly hauteur that 'Money is only a secondary concern in the production of first-rate works'. Or perhaps, as the rooms began to take shape and the practical implications of actually having to live in a Burgesian fantasy began to dawn upon him, Amory simply lost his nerve. Burges was in any case becoming increasingly preoccupied with a much bigger project – his 'restoration' of Cardiff Castle and Castell Coch, both for the Marquis of Bute, a dedicated medievalist with much more money than Amory and far fewer qualms about realising the architect's dreams. He was also devoting much of his time to designing a new London house for himself in Melbury Road, Kensington. (Several of the Knightshayes schemes were eventually reworked and used either at Cardiff or at Melbury Road.)

But at Knightshayes itself the interiors still stood in need of completion, and Amory turned to John Diblee Crace (1838–1919). In 1875 Crace, who came from a long-established London firm of architectural decorators, had just finished Italianising the state apartments at Longleat in Wiltshire. He had already come into contact with Burges on several occasions in the past, constructing a table to the architect's designs for Treverbyn Vean in the early 1860s, and being called in by the Fellows of Worcester College, Oxford, in 1874 to provide a safer, more sedate alternative to Burges's elaborate cinquecento Florentine scheme for the redecoration of the College Hall. (In fact, Burges was allowed to finish his work at Worcester, but only after the threat of being replaced by Crace had forced him to emasculate his original designs. Two examples of his Worcester College work are now at Knightshayes – a large sideboard in the billiard room, and a marble chimneypiece in the drawing room.)

Crace worked at Knightshayes from 1875 to 1882, several years after John Amory (by now Sir John Heathcoat-Amory, Bt) and his family had moved in. The decorator's treatment of the interiors was competent if conventional, but even his considerably less exuberant designs quickly proved too much for the Amorys. From the 1880s, when Burges's drawing room ceiling was hidden behind plaster panels, and the red, blue and gold stencilling of the drawing room window-mullions was covered with thick cream paint, until the 1950s, the house suffered terribly from the low esteem in which High Victorian architecture was generally held. The screens passage and its gallery were demolished. Crace's dining room, with its frieze of hearty platitudes from Burns – 'Be blest with health and peace and sweet content', 'Keep thy tongue and keep thy friends', 'Come ease, come travil, come plesur, come pain, my warst word is welcome and welcome again' – was swathed in heavy Lincrusta paper. And his watered-down version of Burges's schemes for the library, gentlemen's room and billiard room was virtually obliterated.

In 1973 the house and park were bequeathed to the National Trust by Sir John Heathcoat-Amory, grandson of the builder, and over the last two decades the Trust, with the support of his widow, has done much towards restoring the house to its Victorian splendour. Wherever possible, the Crace interiors – and the little of Burges's work that was actually executed – have been reinstated, and today the house stands as a marvellous example of High Victorian design.

In spite of the fine quality of its execution, however, Knightshayes will always be an 'if only' house: if only Billy Burges had been allowed to realise his eccentric fantasies, if only John Amory's nerve had held. Looking at the designs for the boudoir, with its frieze illustrating *The Dream of Fair Women*, it is hard not to recall some lines from Tennyson's poem:

> How eagerly I sought to strike
> Into that wondrous track of dreams again!
> But no two dreams are like.

'No two dreams are like': Amory dreamed of a comfortable house in which he could live the leisurely life of a country gentleman; Burges dreamed of a fairytale palace. The two dreams were ultimately irreconcilable, with the result that Knightshayes has a dual life, as a Victorian gentleman's residence and as a monument to a magical but unrealised fantasy.

Cragside

NORTHUMBERLAND

Cragside, at Rothbury, 13 miles south-west of Alnwick, was the home of the inventor and armaments manufacturer William Armstrong. Between 1869 and 1884 Armstrong's small weekend villa (built in 1863–6 by an unidentified architect) was remodelled and enlarged by Richard Norman Shaw. Further additions were made to the house by Frederick Waller in 1895.

'The palace of a modern magician' – the phrase was first used of Cragside in a magazine called *The World* in 1879; it was quoted in the *Newcastle Journal* in December 1900, and has subsequently appeared in almost every published account of the house, becoming a byword for one of the most spectacular Victorian mansions in Britain.

In fact, there were two modern magicians at work at Cragside. The first, and the one to whom the article in *The World* was referring, was the nineteenth-century technocrat and philanthropist William Armstrong (1810–1900), whose career reads like a case-study from Samuel Smiles's *Self-Help*. The son of a Newcastle corn merchant, Armstrong was fascinated from an early age by the potential of hydraulics: 'William had water on the brain,' his family used to say. His father

Cragside in Northumberland: 'the palace of a modern magician'.
A watercolour by an unknown artist. (*NTPL/Charlie Waite*)

insisted that he train for the law, but, while a partner in a firm of Newcastle solicitors, he was elected a Fellow of the Royal Society for developing a machine which generated electricity from effluent steam. His part in establishing a new company to supply water to the city of Newcastle was successful enough to enable him to give up his job in 1847 and set up his own heavy engineering business at Elswick on the River Tyne, producing a range of equipment including hydraulic cranes, bridges, locomotives, and – following the adoption by the army of his patent breech-loading rifled artillery in the 1860s – armaments. In spite of serious defects in the new Armstrong gun, which necessitated a temporary return to muzzle-loading ordnance (a contemporary source reported that 'gunners became nervous of a weapon which could shoot out of both ends'), W. G. Armstrong and Company went on to become one of the largest armaments manufacturers in Europe.

In 1863 this 'modern magician' began to withdraw from the day-to-day management of his industrial empire although he remained chief partner in the firm until his death in 1900. On a visit to Rothbury and the Debdon valley, where he had spent many happy childhood holidays – 'my earliest recollections consist of paddling in the Coquet, gathering pebbles on its gravel beds, and climbing amongst the rocks of the Crag' – he suddenly decided to build a small fishing lodge, which would become the heart of a country estate. His first purchase, in November of that year, consisted of no more than twenty acres, but by systematically acquiring more and more land as it became available, he eventually owned some 1,729 acres of pleasure ground and more than a score of farms.

Armstrong approached the task of turning the bare hillsides of the valley into an estate with all the vigour and application that had made him such a successful businessman. He and his wife Margaret stayed in a miller's house on the site while he personally directed the landscaping operations, the blasting, excavating and planting, damming the Debdon and installing a hydraulic ram to supply water to his gardens – and to the new lodge that he had begun to build late in 1863, 'a small house ... for occasional visits in the summertime'. His architect, whose identity is unknown, produced a rather prosaic two-storey villa with steeply pitched gables, a low central tower and mullioned windows, perched on a dramatic site halfway up a hill overlooking the Debdon. This first Cragside was finished by 1866, and for three years the Armstrongs used it as a weekend retreat, continuing to live in their Newcastle house at Jesmond Dene.

Then in 1869 Armstrong was introduced to the second 'modern magician', a young architect who, with a wave of his wand – and fifteen years' hard work – was to transform the villa into a palace. His name was Richard Norman Shaw.

Shaw (1831–1912) was one of a new generation of architects who, having learned their trade with the High Victorians – Shaw himself served a five-year apprenticeship with William Burn, worked for two years in Anthony Salvin's office, and then went as chief draughtsman to George Edmund Street – were in revolt against the reverence which their forebears felt for the Gothic. In 1863 Shaw had set up in practice with a like-minded friend from his days in Burn's office, William Eden Nesfield. Working separately, but frequently developing their ideas together, Nesfield and Shaw moved away from the strict period styles of the preceding

LEFT: William Armstrong sitting in the inglenook in the dining room at Cragside, painted by H. H. Emmerson. (*NTPL/Charlie Waite*)

RIGHT: Richard Norman Shaw, seated, with his friend and fellow-pioneer of the Old English movement, William Eden Nesfield, *c*.1873. (*The National Trust*)

generation towards a more eclectic, romantic type of architecture which did not belong to any one period but drew on a range of sources, from Gothic and Tudor through to seventeenth- and early eighteenth-century vernacular. The style became known as 'Old English', its very vagueness emphasising the essentially lyrical evocation of a hazy, mythical past that their buildings aimed for. And, by breaking with the scholarly pedantry of the High Victorians, the two men helped to revolutionise domestic architecture.

Shaw was probably brought to Armstrong's attention by the painter and Royal Academician John Calcott Horsley, whose early eighteenth-century house at Willesley in Kent he had altered and extended in the Old English style some five years earlier. In the late 1860s Armstrong bought *Prince Hal Taking the Crown from His Father's Bedside*, one of Horsley's vast historical genre paintings – so vast, in fact, that it wouldn't fit into Armstrong's Newcastle home. A new gallery was needed, and Horsley suggested Shaw as the man for the job.

So at the end of September 1869 Shaw travelled to Newcastle, where he listened politely to Armstrong – who, he wrote to his wife, 'talked of guns and engines no end' – and got the commission for the new gallery. While he was there, he was invited to spend a few days at the villa at Cragside, which Armstrong was thinking of enlarging. The story goes that the architect sketched out the whole scheme for Cragside in a few hours while the other members of the house-party were out shooting, and promptly presented it to his host on his return – an exaggeration, perhaps, although tales of his hard-sell approach to prospective clients are legion. C. F. A. Voysey used to say that when Shaw went out to dinner, he wore extra-long cuffs to his shirt, on which he could swiftly draw designs which he would use to snare rich and unwary fellow-guests.

In any event, Shaw was given the commission, and in three stages between 1869 and 1884 he more than trebled the size of Armstrong's original house. The first phase, an extension to the north-west, consisted of an inner hall, dining room and library, with a suite of hot-air, plunge and shower baths beneath, and bedrooms above. But by 1872, when these works were nearing completion, his client had decided on further additions. So Shaw then created a new east-west wing to the south of the main block, containing a new staircase, a long gallery (which originally served as a museum for Armstrong's collection of geological and scientific specimens), and the Gilnockie Tower, the design of which was based on the stronghold of John Armstrong of Gilnockie, a border raider and supposed ancestor who was hanged by James V of Scotland in 1530. Shaw also raised the tower of the original house, and crowned it with a half-timbered gable.

His third and last set of designs, carried out in 1883–5, involved the building of yet another wing, this time on a roughly north-south axis and to the east of the Gilnockie Tower. This housed a large top-lit drawing room which also served as a gallery for the display of Armstrong's growing collection of contemporary paintings.

Richard Norman Shaw's task at Cragside was certainly a difficult one: to weld the 1863 house and the additions, spanning more than fifteen years, into a unified whole would have been well-nigh impossible. Already in 1872, when the earlier designs were published in *Building News*, Edward Godwin commented that the composition lacked unity, that it looked 'as if two or three houses had been brought together and shuffled up somehow into one'. But much of the magic of Cragside stems from just this lack of cohesion, which in Shaw's treatment of the exterior translates into a dramatic tension as the different elements advance and recede, rise and fall. Gables jostle with crenellations; towers strive to outreach tall Tudor chimneystacks; cavernous Gothic arches compete with mullioned bay windows; and half-timbering stands side by side with dressed ashlar and rough stonework.

At first sight, perhaps, these juxtapositions create a feeling that Cragside has gradually evolved over centuries rather than years. But this soon fades: if anything, the building's irregularities owe more to Georgian theories of picturesque beauty than to the full-blown historicism of the Victorian Gothicists. This is the key to the success of the house. Against all the odds, Cragside succeeds precisely because all of those periods, all of those styles, have been ransacked and then ruthlessly subordinated to visual impact, to spectacle and excitement.

Given the site, the house's additive building history and Shaw's unconventional handling of the façades, one might expect that the internal planning of Cragside would be equally complex and challenging. And so it is, although here the variety and irregularity which produce such a powerful effect in the exterior can on occasion

The drawing room with W. R. Lethaby's chimneypiece, which was said to weigh ten tons. (*NTPL*)

feel confused and tiresome. The dark, narrow corridor which originally formed the spine of the 1863 house seems out of keeping with the scale of the new Cragside. And the route from the drawing room to the dining room, admittedly a feature that Victorian architects tended to make as impressive as possible, is nearly sixty yards in length. As Armstrong's guests, who included the Prince and Princess of Wales and an impressive array of foreign potentates eager to purchase warships and weaponry – the King of Siam, the Shah of Persia, the Crown Prince of Afghanistan – went down to dinner, negotiating the gallery, six flights of stairs and a long passageway, one suspects that admiration at the grandeur of their host's new house must have been tempered by the prospect of the return journey.

But while the circulation spaces at Cragside may seem to ramble interminably, the individual interiors are some of the finest of the period in Britain. The main living room was the library – an elegant high-art interior, with Morris and Company stained glass, light oak panelling, and a beautiful beamed and coffered ceiling with inset walnut panels and carved bosses by James Forsyth, one of Shaw's favourite craftsmen. Here, unlike the later interiors – the library belongs to Shaw's first set of alterations, and was completed in 1872 – the architect seems to have either selected or designed many of the furnishings. Chief among these is a set of ebonised mahogany Queen Anne chairs made by Gillow, with cane seats and leather backs stamped with a pomegranate motif.

Next door to the library is the dining room – and when Armstrong's guests finally did arrive here, their surroundings, as well as the meal, must have made the journey seem worthwhile. Heavy but somehow still intimate, it is the quintessential Old English interior, a quaint farmhouse parlour refined and stylised and enlarged until it met the requirements of a great Victorian industrialist, while still retaining an air of comfortable old-world domesticity. Ceiling and walls are panelled in light oak, with carvings of flowers, birds and animals by James Forsyth. Forsyth may also have been responsible for the richly carved stone inglenook, a feature which, with its connotations of cosy yeomen homesteads, was to appear again and again in the work of Shaw and his followers. Wooden settles stand to either side of the fireplace, and the inscription on the lintel between them reads, 'East or West, Hame's best'.

It is interesting to compare the dining room with the other great set-piece interior at Cragside, the drawing room, begun in 1883 and finished just in time for the Prince and Princess of Wales's visit in August 1884. During the twelve years which separate the two rooms, Shaw had grown in confidence and sophistication, moving away from the atmospheric intimacy of his Old English work towards a more self-indulgent opulence, an ostentation symbolised in the Cragside drawing room by the colossal Renaissance marble chimneypiece designed by his chief assistant, W. R. Lethaby. Said to weigh ten tons and smothered in elaborate carving, this brilliant but cold monument surmounts another inglenook. But, in contrast with the one in the dining room, this one is lined with fine marble, and its settees are covered in red leather. It expresses wealth rather than welcome, power rather than peace.

The drawing room was Richard Norman Shaw's last job at Cragside. Further work – competent, but lacking Shaw's flair – was carried out in the 1890s by the Gloucester architect Frederick Waller, who added a billiard room to the east of the drawing room wing. (There was no smoking room in the house and, according to a 1901 article in *The Onlooker*, before the billiard room was created it was not unusual to see 'a row of Japanese or other foreign naval officers, in charge of some war vessel building at the famous Elswick works, sitting in a row on the low wall outside the front door, puffing away for all they were worth'.) In the meantime, William Armstrong continued to turn his engineering skills to domestic use: hydraulic machinery powered lifts which moved goods and people from floor to floor, as well as the spit which turned the joints of meat in the kitchen; rumour even suggested that it rotated the heavy pots in the conservatories. An internal telephone system provided room-to-room communications. And, as a result of his involvement in Joseph Swann's experiments with incandescent light bulbs, the house was among the first in the world to be lit by hydro-electric light.

All of these wonders inevitably fuelled the Victorians' innocent delight in man's ability to tame and harness natural forces – hence Armstrong's title of 'modern magician'. But to modern eyes, the magical qualities which the house undoubtedly possesses stem not so much from the technology that dazzled his contemporaries as from the drama and tension of its design. Richard Norman Shaw, the man responsible for that drama and that tension, was the real magician of Cragside.

William Armstrong was knighted in 1859 and created 1st Baron Armstrong of Cragside in 1887. He and his wife had no children, and after his death in 1900 his house and estate passed to his great-nephew, who in 1903 was made 1st Baron Armstrong of the second creation. Cragside passed to the National Trust in 1977.

Wightwick Manor

WEST MIDLANDS

Wightwick Manor, 3 miles west of Wolverhampton, was built in 1887 for a local industrialist, Samuel Theodore Mander. The architect was Edward Ould, who also added a new east wing to the house in 1893.

Just for a second, Wightwick Manor deceives you. Just for a second, the elaborate timber-framing and the asymmetrical grouping, the tall chimneystacks and the oriel windows and the ranks of carved quatrefoils, beguile you into thinking that here on the outskirts of Wolverhampton stands another Little Moreton or a Speke, a black-and-white gentry house from the days of the Tudors.

The illusion quickly fades: the craftsmanship is rather too accomplished, the asymmetry a little too deliberate, the ornament too profuse and self-conscious. The house is clearly – and gloriously – late Victorian. But the knowledge brings with it more questions than answers. Who would want to build a half-timbered manor house in the year of Victoria's Golden Jubilee? And why?

The 'who' is straightforward enough – Samuel Theodore Mander (1853–1900). Mander was a partner in the local varnish and colour-making firm of Mander Brothers, set up by his forefathers in 1773. After being educated at London University and Clare College, Cambridge, he married Flora Paint, the aptly named daughter of a Canadian MP, and settled down to play his part in running the family business. In 1887 he bought the Wightwick estate and, while retaining most of the original buildings and giving them a facelift of brick dressings and rendered walls, commissioned Edward Ould of the Liverpool and Chester firm of Grayson & Ould to build him a new house on a site to the south-west of the old manor.

Ould was something of a specialist in timber-framed buildings. He had trained under John Douglas, who, as Hermann Muthesius noted in *Das englische Haus*, 1904, was 'born and resident in Chester, the home of true half-timbering, [and who] devoted himself most lovingly to the re-introduction of the style, mastered it down to the last detail and produced buildings of great charm'. Ould himself played a significant part in the black-and-white revival in the north-west of England. His flourishing practice included designs for a series of half-timbered villas in the area, two of which were published in the *Builder* in 1885 – Bechry, across the border in Flintshire, and Dee Hills, Cheshire (for Thomas Hughes, author of *Tom Brown's*

Wightwick Manor, West Midlands: 'No style of building will harmonize so quickly and so completely with its surroundings and so soon pass through the crude and brand-new period, and none continue to live on such terms of good-fellowship with other materials.'

(*NTPL/Kevin J.Richardson*)

Schooldays and a campaigning conservationist). In his introduction to *Old Cottages, Farm Houses, and Other Half-timber Buildings in Shropshire, Herefordshire and Cheshire* (1904), a collection of one hundred photographs taken by the architectural woodworker James Parkinson, Ould discussed the suitability of timber-framing for modern housing:

> As one who has had some experience of such building, I would say that, given a suitable client, one who is worthy of the privilege of living in a timber house ... it is an eminently suitable style ... No style of building will harmonize so quickly and so completely with its surroundings and so soon pass through the crude and brand-new period, and none continue to live on such terms of good-fellowship with other materials...

Ould's recommendation that modern half-timbered houses would harmonise quickly with their surroundings gives a clue to one of the reasons for the success of the black-and-white revival. The idea that a Penrhyn Castle or a Knightshayes Court should have been deliberately designed to merge into the natural landscape would have been greeted with bemusement, even horror, by their builders. But by the last decades of the nineteenth century, and largely as a result of the Old English work of Richard Norman Shaw, William Eden Nesfield and their followers in the 1860s and 1870s, the aggressive self-confidence of High Victorian Gothic was giving way to a softer, more intimate historicism. This was a style that looked for its inspiration to the yeomen farmsteads and rambling manor houses of the sixteenth and seventeenth centuries, so many fine examples of which still survived in the West Midlands and the north-west; a style that developed the lyrical eclecticism of Shaw and Nesfield into a cult of quaintness, a passion for the hand-crafted vernacular.

In deciding on Edward Ould and on half-timbering at Wightwick, then, Theodore Mander could simply be said to have been following a trend. The rejection of industrialisation and the dehumanising effects that it had on both workers and – via the poor aesthetic standards of mass-produced art-objects – consumers, had occupied thinkers and reformers like Thomas Carlyle, John Ruskin and William Morris. This rejection was readily transformed into a pre-occupation with the survivals of a pre-industrial culture, and an attempt to recreate or at least to evoke them.

Mander was neither the first nor the last late Victorian magnate to build his new house in a style that rejected the values of the industrial society that had made him wealthy. But the style was well suited to what we know of the man. A house which tactfully recalled the past without indulging in displays of arrogance, a house whose warm, solid, English oak evoked images of hospitality and Merry England rather than aristocratic hauteur, seems somehow appropriate for a mayor of Wolverhampton, who set up a rest home for retired governesses at Wightwick, built a village hall, and organised regular Sunday cricket matches between his firm and the village followed by supper at the Manor. Mander was a high-minded and paternalistic squire, the living embodiment of what the 7th Duke of Northumberland had described in 1880 as 'our county life, under which a body of gentlemen possessed property and, having the interests of the people at heart, took part in sports and directed the local affairs of their district, thus showing they were of use and influence in the world'.

Wightwick is the product of two quite separate building campaigns. The 1887 house, of oak, Ruabon brickwork and Madeley tiles, with some rather restrained carving by Edward Griffiths of Chester – who showed himself capable of considerably less restraint in the beasts and castles and galloping horsemen which he carved some ten years later at Dunstall Hall, Staffordshire – was practically doubled in size in 1893 by the addition of a new east wing, again by Ould, consisting of a great parlour, a new dining room and billiard room, and bedrooms for visitors above. Mander is said to have decided on the extension because he needed extra accommodation for guests attending the cricket weeks that he wanted to organise. The later work is more confident, more scholarly, and more richly decorated. The expanses of rather garish Ruabon brickwork give way to a softer and less obtrusive base course of local sandstone, encouraging the eye to dwell on the intricate oak carving by the Cambridge firm of Rattee & Kett, which skilfully quotes details from other houses: the barge boards and the dormer on the garden front derive from Little Moreton Hall in Cheshire; the oriel to the east comes from Ockwells Manor, Buckinghamshire.

In case the building should fail to conjure up the desired images of Old English hospitality, the message is reinforced by verses on the gables, from *Troilus and Cressida* – 'Welcome ever smiles, and farewell goes out sighing' – and Herrick's arcadian love-lyric, 'To Phyllis':

> Live, live with me, and thou shalt see
> The pleasures I'll prepare for thee:
> What sweets the country can afford
> Shall bless thy Bed and bless thy Board.
> Thy feasting tables shall be hills
> With daisies spread and daffodils.

And lest Herrick seem a mite too frivolous for a Victorian gentleman's residence – 'To Phyllis' does, after all, go on to promise: 'Thou shalt have ... gloves, garters, stockings, shoes and strings/Of winning colours, that shall move/Others to lust, but me to love' – there is a more pious text over the garden entrance: 'God's Providence is mine inheritance'.

Wightwick's rooms exhibit the same strain of Old English romanticism as the exterior, but it is a romanticism tempered with the concern for Art and Beauty that was then so fashionable with upper-middle-class aesthetes. The self-consciously 'artistic' interiors contain a bewilderingly eclectic but still undeniably attractive mixture of fittings and furnishings. L. A. Shuffrey's heavy neo-Jacobean plasterwork ceilings bear down on spindly chairs and textiles from Morris and Company; oak panelling (some of which was recycled from the old manor house) provides a backdrop for the blue and white ware made fashionable by Dante Gabriel Rossetti and J. M. Whistler in the 1860s; an Italian Renaissance chimneypiece has a surround of William de Morgan tiles. Everywhere one can sense the force of Walter Pater's dictum that 'beauty exists in many forms, [and] all periods, types, schools of

taste, are in themselves equal' – although some, notably pre-industrial English, are more equal than others.

Much of the present collection of furnishings and art-objects at Wightwick was assembled by Theodore Mander's son and daughter-in-law, who took over the house after his death. Nevertheless, while he was hardly the sort of precious aesthete satirised in Gilbert and Sullivan's *Patience* – 'A Japanese young man/A blue and white young man .../A greenery-yallery, Grosvenor Gallery/Foot-in-the-grave young man' – enough remains from his time to show that these later additions reflected and built upon his own tastes (and presumably those of his wife, about

ABOVE: A settle by G. F. Bodley, with paintings
by C. E. Kempe. (*NTPL/Andy Williams*)

LEFT: The great parlour.
(*NTPL/Jeremy Whitaker*)

whom much less is known). Those tastes, formed perhaps by the study of Ruskin,
whose *Seven Lamps of Architecture* Mander bought in the same year that he obtained
the Wightwick estate, seem to have been further moulded not only by Edward Ould,
but also by a rather greater talent – Charles Eamer Kempe.

Kempe's precise role at Wightwick remains something of a mystery, and one
would like to know more. He is best remembered today as a gifted and prolific pre-
Raphaelite glass-designer, and the house contains fine examples of his work – the six
painted panels in the hall, for instance, which depict female figures in medieval
dress. But Kempe also worked on occasion as an architectural decorator, and in the

grandest room at Wightwick, the great parlour – actually a two-storey living-hall in the Nesfield-Shaw tradition, complete with minstrel gallery and open-timber roof – he not only executed the painted glass, with its saints, shields, mottoes and coats of arms, but also had a hand in the design of both the polychromatic decoration of the roof and the plaster frieze telling the story of Orpheus and Eurydice (perhaps inspired by Abraham Smith's *Court of Diana* frieze in the High Great Chamber at Hardwick Hall). Moreover, Kempe had first-hand experience of the romantic half-timbered style: his own house, Lindfield Old Place in Sussex, was a genuine Elizabethan timber-framed building which he enlarged and remodelled. It is possible that he collaborated with Ould on the 1893 extension to Wightwick, a partnership which would certainly account for the more vigorous and confident handling of its exterior in comparison with the earlier parts of the house.

Theodore Mander died in 1900 at the early age of forty-seven. With remarkable foresight, and at a time when the reputation of all things Victorian was at a particularly low ebb, his son Geoffrey carefully preserved Wightwick's decoration and furnishings. Even more remarkably, he and his wife flew in the face of fashion by bringing together the superb collections of pre-Raphaelite art, textiles and furnishings that fill the house today.

Sir Geoffrey Mander offered Wightwick Manor to the National Trust in 1937. Proposing the transfer of ownership to the Trust's Secretary, Macleod Matheson, he wrote modestly that 'The place is not, of course, of historic interest, but it is a singularly attractive example of modern half-timber work in Elizabethan and Jacobean style, and the inside is as good as the outside.' Luckily for us, Matheson and his colleagues had the foresight to appreciate Wightwick's importance, even though it was scarcely fifty years old. This masterpiece of late Victorian architecture was the very first house to come to the Trust through its new Country Houses Scheme.

TWO LUTYENS CASTLES

Edwin Landseer Lutyens and Frank Lloyd Wright were both born in 1869. Both were great architects; both are still household names. But Frank Lloyd Wright is revered, quite rightly, as a pioneer of modern design, while Lutyens has come to be seen as a reactionary who, as Hermann Muthesius noted in 1904, 'propagated the view that is so widespread in England that . . . old art cannot be bettered'. Dismissed as elitist and irrelevant by the more earnest architects and historians who came after him – 'For the the first forty [years] of our century, no British name need here be mentioned,' said Nikolaus Pevsner in his *Outline of European Architecture* – it is perhaps not surprising that the man who, in his son Robert's words, 'admitted no challenge from the future' should have been rejected by the men who were moulding that future, just as the Modern Movement was itself rejected by later generations.

But Lutyens can't be dismissed quite so lightly. Like Rudyard Kipling – the poet of Empire, just as Lutyens, the designer of New Delhi, was the architect of Empire – his work exhibits a sophistication and a depth which can too easily be overlooked by

Sir Edwin Lutyens (centre) on site at Castle Drogo with his client, Julius Drewe (left), and John Walker (right), Drewe's building manager. (*The National Trust*)

those who see only its ideological implications. For all their lyrical romanticism, there is an ambivalence, a dramatic tension to so many of Lutyens' buildings. They question the status quo even while they seem to confirm it, and, far from looking backwards and losing themselves in a sterile revivalism, his houses in particular offer new and innovative solutions to the problems of shaping and expressing the values of the country house in an era of change.

Nowhere is this more apparent than at Lindisfarne and Drogo, the two Lutyens castles which belong to the National Trust. With both houses – the one a drastic remodelling of a Tudor fort, the other a completely new creation – the architect who 'admitted no challenge from the future' could so easily have retreated into the conventional language of the castle form as an emblem of a more hierarchical past, an expression of arrogance and anti-democratic hauteur; or he could simply have wallowed in nostalgia and self-consciously quaint antiquarianism. But this was not the path that he chose to follow. He preferred instead to create something wholly, starkly new, stripped bare of extraneous details. In their Spartan austerity, their bold massing, their emphasis on geometry and spatial arrangements rather than ornament, Lindisfarne and Castle Drogo are far from being islands of reaction in a changing architectural scene. They confront that change; they respond to it; and they represent a new aesthetic which had more in common with progressive twentieth-century ideas than either the Modern Movement, or perhaps Lutyens himself, realised.

Lindisfarne Castle

NORTHUMBERLAND

Lindisfarne Castle, which stands on Holy Island, 12 miles south-east of Berwick-on-Tweed, was built in the 1540s. At the beginning of the twentieth century it was bought by Edward Hudson, founder and proprietor of Country Life, and restored by Edwin Lutyens between 1902 and 1912.

Edward Hudson, the founder of *Country Life*. 'His head thrust forward when he walked, as though he were searching for something. I suppose he looked, always, for beauty.'
(*Country Life*)

One day in 1901, Edward Hudson and Peter Anderson Graham were touring Holy Island in Northumberland when they came across a lonely fortress, perched high on a crag overlooking the harbour. Intrigued, the proprietor of *Country Life* and his editor knocked at the door, and when no-one answered the two men clambered up the walls to find themselves, not in a fairytale castle, but in a deserted tumbledown complex of barracks and blockhouses littered with broken bits of furniture and other debris. Remembering that first sight of Lindisfarne some twelve years later, Anderson Graham remarked that 'few men in the conditions under which [Hudson] found it would have conceived the idea that it might be transformed into a thing of beauty'.

The castle had been built in the late 1540s to defend the strategically important harbour on Holy Island, described in 1550 as being 'sufficient for a great navy of ships to rest safely in, and very aptly for the wars towards Scotland'. The uniting of England and Scotland under James I fifty years later caused both the harbour and the fort which protected it to lose much of their importance, although a garrison of twenty-four men was maintained there during the seventeenth century. (Its governor, a Captain Rugg, achieved some local celebrity for 'his great bottle nose', which was, according to one visitor to the island in 1635, 'the largest I have seen'.) The garrison steadily dwindled during the 1700s, and was withdrawn in 1819; by the middle of the nineteenth century it was being used as a lookout station by the local coastguards.

An aristocratic early-Victorian tourist coming on the ruins of a Tudor fort like Lindisfarne might simply have admired the picturesque situation, wrinkled his nose at the forlorn squalor of the interiors, and gone home to his own romantic castle, purpose-built by Anthony Salvin or Edward Blore. But Edward Hudson belonged to a different generation and a different social class – a class connected with commerce rather than land, and a generation enabled by the railway and the motor car to escape from the cares of urban living into the wealthy Edwardian businessman's twin refuges, the countryside and the past. To live in an old house in a rural setting combined the two: *Country Life*, which Hudson had founded in 1897, owed much of its success to the dexterity with which it peddled dreams of noble halls and panelled chambers, quaint and beautiful survivals of a mythical Merry England, to stockbrokers and industrialists who were willing and able to buy those dreams. It is perhaps not surprising that Hudson, hard-headed entrepreneur though he was, should chase the same dream.

And chase it he did. Within days of his visit to Lindisfarne, he was negotiating with the Crown over the sale of the castle. Once it was confirmed, the choice of architect for the restoration was a mere formality, and in January 1902 Edwin Lutyens wrote to his wife from Scotland that he had 'just got a telewire from Hudson saying he has got Lindisfarne Castle – will I go and look at it as I am up here so I had better. It will be amusing.'

Lutyens' relationship with Hudson dated from 1899, when the pair were introduced by Gertrude Jekyll. In the same year the young architect designed for Hudson the Deanery Garden at Sonning in Berkshire, a romantic masterpiece described by Christopher Hussey as 'a perfect architectural sonnet, compounded of brick and tile and timber forms'. (No doubt both Lutyens and Hudson, who sold the house within a few years, were amused to see an advertisement for the Deanery placed by the estate agents Hampton's in *Country Life* in 1906, describing it as 'a very beautiful Elizabethan house perfectly true in character and detail'.) Hudson was one of Lutyens' most important patrons, not only providing him with four commissions – the Deanery, Lindisfarne, the Wrenaissance *Country Life* building in Tavistock Street, London (1904), and Plumpton Place in Sussex (1928) – but also publicising his work relentlessly through the pages of his magazine. Years after Lindisfarne had been completed, Lutyens' wife Lady Emily remembered Hudson as an old man at the inauguration of New Delhi in 1931, his faith in her husband so triumphantly justified, weeping and saying over and over again to himself, 'Poor old Christopher Wren! He could never have done this!'

Apart from their professional relationship, the two men became and remained close friends and were, for a time, neighbours in Queen Anne's Gate in London. The architect's daughter Mary has left a touching portrait of the publisher, 'very kind, but unattractively plain', playing with the Lutyens children in their nursery: 'We had a fire-screen in the nursery, the bottom part of which could be moved up leaving a gap at the bottom. It was perfect for playing French Revolutions, and Hudson was most obliging in kneeling on the floor and putting his head through the gap so that we could guillotine him.'

At Lindisfarne Lutyens' task was to make the most of the castle's romantic setting, and to create a series of interiors that would introduce that sense of romance where none had existed before. An obvious strategy would have been to build a castle in the air, to create a story-book fantasy complete with towers and battlements –

something like E. Finden's rather fanciful early nineteenth-century engraving of Lindisfarne. Over the border in Scotland there were plenty of contemporary precedents for such a treatment: houses like the colossal Sauchieburn Castle in Stirlingshire, finished some ten years before for the coal-owner John Maitland; Kinloch Castle on the Isle of Rhum, just built by the London firm of Leeming & Leeming for George Bullough, who had specified that his house should be as large as his yacht (he had a very, very big yacht); and the vast and vulgar Skibo Castle, which an Inverness firm, Ross & Macbeth, was currently rebuilding for the American steel millionaire Andrew Carnegie (complete with marble swimming pool, stained glass windows depicting Carnegie's rags-to-riches story, and – inevitably – a resident bagpiper).

But a flamboyant Scotch-baronial handling of the site would have been at odds with the stark and desolate simplicity which plays such a big part in Lindisfarne's appeal. Perhaps sensing this, Lutyens removed some of the more banally picturesque features – crenellation and some balustrading – choosing instead to emphasise the gaunt, sheer severity of the silhouette and its organic relationship with the crag from which it emerges, aspects which the Scottish art-nouveau architect Charles Rennie Mackintosh also recognised in the sketches of the castle that he made during a stay on Holy Island in 1901.

The entrance to the castle was reached via a long sloping ramp to the south. This led through a portcullis and up a short flight of steps into an open artillery position to the east, the lower battery. A complex of buildings lay at the heart of the site; and to the west, but on a higher level, an upper battery held the ruins of the captain's residence, reached via a stairway carved out of the rock. Lutyens retained this split-level arrangement. On the lower battery he did away with the sash-windows and cement of the central block and built a new entrance hall and kitchen, and converted the Tudor kitchen and stores on the north side of the castle into a dining room and drawing room. Bedrooms replaced a third battery on the upper level, and the whole structure was linked to the old captain's quarters – also converted into two bedrooms, one above the other – by a beamed long gallery.

In the summer of 1908 when the Prince and Princess of Wales paid a visit to Holy Island, they came to see how Hudson's castle was progressing. According to Lutyens, who was also present, the Prince was alarmed at the open stone ramp leading up to the entrance, and suggested that they should erect a wall: 'I told him we had pulled one down and that if he really thought it unsafe we would put nets out. He thought that very funny.' The Princess said that the cobbles with which Lutyens had surfaced the access ramp hurt her feet; the Duke of Northumberland, also in the party, looked thoroughly bored; and his daughters 'stole flowers out of the house and picked wild flowers in spite of notices'. Hudson and Lutyens were so drained by the experience that they both took to their beds as soon as the royal party left.

Lindisfarne was completed in 1912. In ten years Lutyens had transformed a collection of derelict blockhouses into an exciting and intricate labyrinth of reception rooms and bedrooms, reached by stone ramps and twisting passageways, wide flights of steps and narrow winding stairs growing out of the solid rock. Giant

The ship room at Lindisfarne. (*NTPL/Charlie Waite*)

fireplaces yawned cavernously out at Hudson's seventeenth-century oak furniture; wide arches and massive columns groaned under the weight of heavy vaulting like medieval undercrofts; circulation spaces opened into the rock or thrust up through it. The overall effect is atmospheric without lapsing into historicism. It was, to use Christopher Hussey's expression, 'romance without period'.

However, it was also romance without comfort. Analysing Lindisfarne's appeal in 1913, the architectural critic Lawrence Weaver wrote: 'Hudson entered with a lively enthusiasm into the spirit of the work, and did not demand that wealth of modern devices which some people insist on installing in the most ancient fabrics.' When you are chasing a dream, gas and electricity don't seem so important; candles and blazing log fires seem more romantic, more in keeping with their surroundings. But 'the magic spell soon loses its power', as one contemporary put it, 'and we regard the old times and ancient manners with qualified regret, much as we pretend to look askance at modern luxuries and conveniences'. Life at Lindisfarne – which, to be fair, Hudson had always intended as a summer holiday home, a refuge from London – could be rather spartan, as his house-guests soon discovered.

One such guest was Lytton Strachey, whose account of his stay at the castle provides us with a fascinating, if rather spiteful, glimpse of day-to-day life there in Hudson's time. In 1918 the success of Strachey's *Eminent Victorians* turned him into something of a literary lion overnight, and society hostesses vied with each other to show him off at their house parties. That summer he was the guest of Lady Astor, Lady Horner, Lady Desborough, the Asquiths – and, at the end of August, of Edward Hudson at Lindisfarne Castle.

Strachey was not impressed with Lindisfarne. He arrived late one evening in a dog-cart, splashing over the partly flooded causeway that connects the island to the mainland. (Ten years earlier Lutyens had noted with some amusement that the Prince of Wales was anxious to get away as soon as he heard that the tide was rising: 'For a sailor I thought him over nervous'.) He admitted that the castle's situation was magnificent, and the views 'extraordinarily romantic'. But as for the building itself, it was 'All timid Lutyens – very dark, with nowhere to sit, and nothing but stone under, over and round you, which produces a distressing effect – especially when hurrying downstairs late for dinner – to slip would be instant death. No, not a comfortable place, by any means.'

Apart from Strachey and his host – 'a pathetically dreary figure ... a kind of bourgeois gentilhomme' – the house party consisted of the publisher William Heinemann, endlessly reminiscing about the naughty nineties; Lady Lewis, who upset the author by constantly referring to his *Early Victorians*; Mr Fort, an ex-military man 'with a voice like a megaphone and an infinite heartiness – and a simplicity of behaviour'; Mrs Fort; and a wealthy black banjo-playing American and his wife. The group was completed by the famous cellist Guilhermina Suggia, her mother, who apparently couldn't speak a word of English, and George Reeves, her accompanist.

Hudson insisted on packing Strachey and Reeves off on dawn fishing expeditions, much to the dismay of the Bloomsbury aesthete, whose only solace was listening to Madame Suggia's music-making. She was a regular visitor to Lindisfarne, and its owner seems to have laboured under a distinctly unrequited passion for her: Strachey unkindly described him as 'a fish gliding underwater, and star-struck – looking up with his adoring eyes through his own dreadful element'. Her portrait by Augustus John, showing her playing the Stradivarius that Hudson gave her, hangs in the Tate Gallery in London. Each day, said Strachey:

> I used to go with her, her mother (a pitiable old remainder biscuit) and the accompanist, to her bedroom; she would then lock the door (to prevent the ingress of Hudson, I fancy) and practise – for hours – playing Bach suites one after the other ... until one tottered down at last to lunch (for this used to happen in the morning) in a state of ecstasy. Then in the evening after dinner she gave her full dress performances. It was really all an extraordinary joy.

Strachey spent a week at Lindisfarne, 'surrounded by cormorants and quicksands', fishing when he had to, listening to Suggia whenever he could, and getting drunk on Hudson's champagne in the evenings. Eventually he fled back to his Berkshire home, where he promptly caught shingles.

In spite of Strachey's devastating portrayal of life at the Castle, those who knew its owner remember him as a kindly, endearing character; inarticulate and gauche, perhaps – bourgeois, certainly – but a good friend and a discerning patron of the arts. He had intended to leave his dream-castle to Billy Congreve, the son of his friend, the one-armed Boer War veteran General Sir Walter Congreve; the boy had spent some time there while convalescing after a bout of diphtheria, and had grown to love the place. But Billy Congreve was killed in 1916 (Lutyens designed his memorial), and in 1921 Hudson sold Lindisfarne to the banker Oswald Falk. Falk in turn sold it to another banker, Sir Edward de Stein, who gave it to the National Trust in 1944.

Edward Hudson died in 1936. Thirty years later, Pamela Maude, who had married Billy Congreve three weeks before his death, wrote a poignant memoir in *Country Life*. 'His head thrust forward when he walked,' she recalled, 'as though he were searching for something. I suppose he looked, always, for beauty.' He may not have found comfort at Lindisfarne, but he certainly found beauty.

Castle Drogo

DEVON

Castle Drogo, 12 miles west of Exeter, was built between 1910 and 1931 by Edwin Lutyens for Julius Drewe, founder of the Home and Colonial Stores.

A revolutionary change swept through Western architecture in the years leading up to the First World War. In Germany, Walter Gropius was working towards a new aesthetic, stripped of any extraneous ornament, in the cold, hard, vertical expanses of glass which made up his Fagus Factory at Alfeld (1911). In France, Le Corbusier was experimenting with the use of reinforced concrete frames for domestic housing.

Across the Atlantic in Chicago, Frank Lloyd Wright was looking to the machine as a source of inspiration, and writing of the twentieth century as an age in which machines will 'take the place [that] works of art took in previous history'.

In England, Edwin Lutyens was building a castle.

If that were all it was, then Castle Drogo would still be interesting, perhaps, as a quaint expression of that element in English architecture which turned its back on contemporary society and escaped into a misty Tennysonian medievalism. If that were all, we could smile or frown at his prayer that 'God keep the feudal and preserve all that is best in it and the result is love and loveliness'. We could read Lutyens' romantic definition of the country house, set down as he started work on Drogo, as 'a centre for all that charity that should begin at home and [that should] cover, hen-wise, with wings of love those all near about her that are dependent, weaker and smaller', and shake our heads at his naïveté, perhaps even secretly admire his Canute-like struggle to turn back the tide of twentieth-century social change.

But Drogo is much more than an escapist fantasy, a toy fort built on the shifting sands of an outmoded historicism. Whatever Lutyens' private desires for the maintenance of a social and architectural status quo which was already beginning to fragment around him, in his designs for the last castle to be built in England he achieved a new, raw and very modern elementalism, defining the very essence of a castle, stripping it of its externals, and then reinterpreting it to suit the needs of a landed family in the twentieth century. Drogo is a dramatic and ambiguous *tour de force*, which simultaneously conjures up and repudiates the past. Its composition and materials establish links with the medieval, while at the same time rejecting the hazy, idealised romanticism of the late nineteenth century in favour of a wholly contemporary conception which is every bit as cold and hard-edged as the granite blocks from which it is built.

The idea for a castle on the Drewsteignton estate in Devon came not from Lutyens himself, but from his client, Julius Drewe (1856–1931). ('I wish he didn't want a castle,' wrote the architect to his wife in August 1910, 'but just a delicious lovable house with plenty of good large rooms in it'. He was not accustomed to having his clients tell him what to build.) Drewe was a businessman and tea importer who in 1883 had opened a grocery shop called the Home and Colonial Stores on the Edgware Road in London. By 1890 there were another 106 Home and Colonial Stores around the country, and although he was only thirty-three Drewe had made enough money to retire to the Home Counties. Here he lived first in a castellated Georgian mansion at Culverden in Kent, and then from 1899 at Wadhurst Park in Sussex, a redbrick house built in the 1870s by E. J. Tarver for a Spanish banker and friend of the Prince of Wales called Adrian de Murietta, who had gone dramatically bankrupt and had been forced to sell up.

In spite of the increasing numbers of *nouveaux riches* gaining acceptance in Edwardian society, a country estate and a long pedigree were still the goals of many

Castle Drogo, Devon: the entrance tower. Details like the battlements and the Drewe lion seem unimportant in comparison with the house's simple yet inspired geometry. (*NTPL/David Cripps*)

269

successful turn-of-the-century entrepreneurs. And, true to the spirit of his age, having once established his credentials as a member of the landed classes by buying Wadhurst and earning himself an entry in Burke's *Landed Gentry* in the process, Drewe became absorbed in the task of tracing his family's ancestry. An older brother who shared his interest consulted a professional genealogist, who told the Drewes that they were descended from Drogo or Dru, a Norman baron who had come to England with William the Conqueror, and whose descendant, Drogo de Teigne, had given his name to the parish of Drewsteignton in Devon in the twelfth century. Julius was convinced. By 1910 he had bought lands at Drewsteignton, and in that year he decided to build himself a seat on a spectacular site 900 feet above sea level and 200 feet above the wooded gorge below, a great castle which would commemorate (and publicise) his centuries-old connections with the area.

So it was that early in 1910 Drewe approached Edwin Lutyens with the commission to build Castle Drogo. His choice of Lutyens as architect was not a surprising one: there is a family tradition that he asked Edward Hudson's advice, and Hudson, always keen to champion Lutyens' cause, had proposed him as 'the only possible architect'. From his time at Wadhurst, Drewe would also have been familiar with Lutyens' early work in Kent and Sussex.

Lutyens had worked on castles before, of course: not only at Hudson's Lindisfarne, but also at Lambay, three miles off the County Dublin coast, where he restored a late sixteenth-century fortified house for Cecil Baring between 1908 and 1912, and at Howth Castle on the Irish mainland, where in 1910 he added a new tower and chapel for Gaisford St Lawrence. But in restoring an existing castle, however freely, the architect was working within a pre-defined architectural framework. He had never before been called upon to design a completely new castle: in fact, he had never been asked to build *any* country house on the monumental scale which Drewe envisaged at Drewsteignton.

The earliest plans for the house, drawn up in the late summer of 1910, proposed a massive Tudoresque manor, ranged around a quadrangle and complete with gables and tall chimneystacks. These plans were discarded later in the year, after Drewe had announced his wish for 'a large keep or commemorative tower, to commemorate the first Drogo'. From then on neither client nor architect had any doubts that the building was to be a castle, a homage to Drewe's illustrious ancestor, whom Lutyens took to including in his perspective sketches as a matchstick knight-in-armour on horseback.

A new, more severe, U-shaped courtyard scheme of April 1911 gave way to a design in which the wings of the U splayed outwards at about 20 degrees off the central north-south axis. The main block of the house formed the base, with an entrance from the north, placed centrally between the two wings, and double-height dining and drawing rooms to either side of a great hall on the south front. Work was proceeding on the foundations, when in 1912 Drewe decided that his castle was simply too big to be practical, a conclusion given added weight by his determination that Lutyens' cavity walls should give way to more authentic solid granite, thus substantially increasing building costs. As a result, the whole of the west wing and the western end of the main block were abandoned. The great hall was retained for a

One of Lutyens' early designs for Castle Drogo, complete with matchstick knight-in-armour on horseback. (*The National Trust*)

short time, and its undercroft excavated, but finally it too was dispensed with, and the undercroft was eventually converted into the castle chapel.

By 1913 only one side of Lutyens' courtyard scheme remained. He then suggested a curtain wall and a castellated barbican across the driveway, to screen the entrance and to retrieve some of a sense of moving into an enclosed area, and even went so far as to erect full-scale timber mock-ups for Drewe's inspection. These too were vetoed. However, in October 1913, three years after Lutyens had made his first drawings, Drewe's site agent at Drogo was writing with relief to the architect: 'I am pleased to hear that it is now settled what to do to complete the mansion.'

For Lutyens, who had little faith in a client's judgement at the best of times, this series of changes of mind and compromises must have been trying. But he remained on good terms with Drewe, and was, in any case, becoming increasingly occupied with the architecture of Empire during these years, first in South Africa where he was designing an art gallery in Johannesburg, and then in India, where from 1912 onwards he was working on his plans for New Delhi. This is not to say that he did not retain a close interest in Drogo, or that he felt unable to insist on a point when he felt strongly. On his return from his first visit to Delhi in 1912, for example, his instructions to the stonemasons working on the great granite blocks from which the castle was to be built caused Drewe some concern:

> May I ask *why* you have altered your opinion as to preparation of the granite facing? From the commencement you expressed your firm decision that only rough granite should be used ... [The] building should be continued to your pre-Delhi instructions. What might have happened to us if you had also seen the pyramids as well makes us quake to think about.

271

Lutyens refused to be swayed: 'The big, lumpy blocks are right for the lower courses but quite impossible to carry them up . . . it will mean a barbaric building worthy of a small municipal corporation . . . I am very keen about your castle and must "fight" you when I KNOW I am right.'

The subsequent building history of the castle was as full of incident as the early design stages. Lutyens forgot to obtain local planning permission for the castle. Rain seeped through the granite. The asphalt leaked and had to be replaced. The original budget of £50,000 for the house and £10,000 for the gardens increased threefold. ('I suppose £60,000 sounds a lot to you but I don't know what it means,' wrote Lutyens to his wife in 1910, with disarming candour.) Work was interrupted by the war, which claimed the life of Drewe's eldest son Adrian, a tragedy from which the businessman never really recovered, as his daughter recalled later: 'The joy very much went out of life as far as my father and mother were concerned, and things were very much quieter.' Drewe himself suffered a stroke in 1924, and although the family finally moved in in 1927 his health remained poor and he died in 1931, shortly after the finishing touches had been put to his great castle.

Considering Drogo's confused origins and its prolonged and often unhappy development, it is little short of a miracle that it should have survived as the coherent architectural composition that we see today. In spite of all the slings and arrows that fortune and the Drewes hurled at Lutyens' scheme, and our regrets at what might have been, the castle as built emerged as one of the masterpieces of twentieth-century country house building.

Its success rests on its immensely powerful visual impact, the stark and ultimately very contemporary regular figures and plane surfaces which characterise the main façades and many of the interiors. Drogo is not pretty; it is no fairytale castle in the air. The more obvious clichés that one might expect to find in a building intended to reverberate with the echoes of ancestral voices – crenellated towers and irregular fenestration, the 644lb working portcullis and the heraldic Drewe lion over the entrance, with the family motto *Drogo Nomen et Virtus Arma Dedit* ('Drewe is the name and valour gave it arms') – seem unimportant in comparison with the simple yet inspired geometry of the house, culminating in the masterly south front. Here the walls are progressively cut away from around the huge windows (which remain on the same vertical plane), to produce a full bay on the top storey, while the corners of the block have been retained, rising with knife-edge clarity to the parapet. The monumentality of the façade is increased, here as elsewhere around the building, by Lutyens' use of inclined or battered east and west faces to accentuate the sense of height. And the whole establishes a connection with the great keeps and tower houses of the Middle Ages without needing to resort to quotations from medieval architectural styles.

Internally, the compromises over the plan meant that the state rooms had all to be concentrated in the south wing, and the domestic offices in the north, with the Drewes' apartments and the nurseries above them. The only room to suffer in any serious way from this arrangement is the dining room on the lower ground floor, which had to be lowered to accommodate the drawing room above, producing a rather oppressive space which is not lightened by the heavy Wrenaissance ceiling.

The ceiling above the staircase: the circulation spaces at Drogo are a source of wonder and delight. (*NTPL*)

The treatment of the other state rooms is more successful, progressing from the severe plain granite walls of the entrance hall in the west tower, mellowed only by the somewhat cosmopolitan furnishings (many of which came from Wadhurst Park), through the mixture of granite and warm oak in the library, where the family used to take afternoon tea, to the elegant pale-green deal panelling of the drawing room, with its spectacular views of Dartmoor and the Teign valley.

Attractive though most of the living areas in the castle are, it is the circulation spaces – the staircases and twisting corridors, which accommodate the changes of level and direction brought about by the fact that the north wing is not only raised slightly above the south but also set at an angle to it – which capture one's imagination at Drogo. Here that same confidence in apparently simple geometrical designs and the interplay of planes which is evident in the façades appears again in Lutyens' handling of the interiors.

Surprises are everywhere. Wide passages punctuated by shallow saucer domes disappear round unexpected corners, or fade into the distance – and quite a distance it can be, since the kitchens are some fifty yards away from the dining room. Walls rear up like cliffs as the floor suddenly falls away in long flights of steps. Vaults and arches intersect like medieval undercrofts, while above the main staircase, which revolves around an apparently solid core but in fact conceals a complete servants' stair within it, the ceiling alters at each turn, changing from coffered vault to dome to arches to oak beams, but remains at its original height, so that by the time one reaches the bottom the distance from floor to ceiling is a towering twenty-seven feet. In the hands of a lesser architect, such variety would be bewildering, even irritating: here, it is a source of wonder and delight.

The more one studies Drogo, the more one comes to realise the extent of Lutyens' achievement. The almost unnatural precision of the masonry, the perfect regularity of the vaults and arches and domes, the great windows breaking through the walls and flooding the rooms inside with light, all remind us that it is a wholly twentieth-century conception. At the same time, the restrained treatment, the absence of ornament, the grim granite of the interiors, demonstrate that this is no Scotch-baronial exercise in historicism. The house is neither a 'real' castle, an anachronistic expression in stone of Lutyens' prayer that 'God keep the feudal', nor a sham folly: with Drogo, Lutyens managed against all the odds to create a building that is unashamedly modern, while still conveying that sense of timeless solidity which his client required.

On the death of Julius Drewe's son Basil in 1974, Julius's grandson and great-grandson, Anthony and Christopher Drewe, gave Castle Drogo and 600 acres of surrounding land to the National Trust. It was the first twentieth-century country house to come to the Trust – and the last great country house to be built from new in Britain.

Historic Houses
of the
National Trust

Ardress House, County Armagh: detail of a plasterwork plaque by the
Dublin *stuccadore*, Michael Stapleton. (*NTPL/Alan North*)

The gazetteer which follows gives brief details about the historic houses cared for by the National Trust. Where a house has been described in the *English Country Houses* series, in Mark Girouard's *The Victorian Country House*, or in the magazine *Country Life*, references are given at the end of the entry. More comprehensive information is available in the Trust's own guidebooks to each property, many of which contain extensive bibliographies.

Details of opening times and admission charges are contained in *The National Trust Handbook*, which is published annually. Please note that several houses (indicated in the text) are not normally open to the public, but may be viewed by prior arrangement with the Trust's tenant.

Abbreviations

ECH Caroline: Oliver Hill and John Cornforth, *English Country Houses: Caroline 1625–1685*, Country Life (1966)

ECH Baroque: James Lees-Milne, *English Country Houses: Baroque 1685–1715*, Country Life (1970)

ECH Early Georgian: Christopher Hussey, *English Country Houses: Early Georgian 1715–1760*, Country Life (1955); reprinted by the Antique Collectors' Club (1988)

ECH Mid Georgian: Christopher Hussey, *English Country Houses: Mid Georgian 1760–1800*, Country Life (1956); reprinted by the Antique Collectors' Club (1988)

ECH Late Georgian: Christopher Hussey, *English Country Houses: Late Georgian 1800–1840*, Country Life (1958); reprinted by the Antique Collectors' Club (1988)

Vict. CH: Mark Girouard, *The Victorian Country House*, Oxford (1971); 2nd edition, Yale University Press (1979)

CL: *Country Life* (Roman numerals refer to volumes; Arabic numerals refer to pages. Recent page references are preceded by the number of the issue in which they appear.)

Aberconwy House

CONWY, GWYNEDD

14th century: the oldest building in Conwy, after Edward I's great castle and the church. Two lower floors of stone support a half-timbered upper storey jettied out over the street. Aberconwy now houses a National Trust shop and an exhibition of the history of the town.

A la Ronde

EXMOUTH, DEVON

Late 18th century, for Jane and Mary Parminter, two spinster cousins. According to family tradition, the source of the curious design – a sixteen-sided block under a thatched roof – was the Byzantine basilica of San Vitale at Ravenna, known to the Parminters from a visit they made during their Grand Tour.

A la Ronde's interiors are equally curious. Walls were painted a vivid green above marbled dados and, in several rooms, superimposed with an exotic collage of shells, feathers and other materials supplied by the cousins themselves. The result is the finest surviving example of a Georgian decorative speciality known to contemporaries as 'ladies' amusements'.

CL lxxxiii, 448; xcv, 243; clxxxiv, 28.71; clxxxv, 7.38

Alfriston Clergy House

ALFRISTON, EAST SUSSEX

Built *c.* 1350, probably for a well-to-do farmer. The name 'clergy house' may stem from the fact that Alfriston was later owned by the Church. A rare intact survival of a 14th-century timber-framed house, and the first building to come to the National Trust – bought for £10 in 1896.

Angel Corner

BURY ST EDMUNDS, SUFFOLK

A Queen Anne house, which now contains the Gershom Parkington collection of clocks, watches and other timepieces.

Alfriston Clergy House,
East Sussex.
The figures ranged in
front of the house in
this photograph taken
in 1894 include the
founders of the National
Trust, which came into
being the following
year. (*NTPL*)

Anglesey Abbey

LODE, CAMBRIDGESHIRE

The chapter house and parlour of a 13th-century Augustinian priory, converted into a manor house *c*. 1600; extensively remodelled and extended in 1926–58 for the 1st Lord Fairhaven, whose architects included Sidney Parvin and Professor Albert Richardson (1880–1964).

Anglesey Abbey contains rich collections of furniture, silver, paintings, porcelain, tapestries and statuary, all assembled by the millionaire Lord Fairhaven, who bought the estate with his brother in 1926. According to James Lees-Milne, Fairhaven was always served before his guests at meals, 'in the feudal manner which only the son of an oil magnate would adopt'.

CL lxviii, 832; lxix, 110, 376; cxv, 770, 860; cxviii, 601; cxx, 321

Antony House

TORPOINT, CORNWALL

Built to replace an earlier house between 1718 and 1729, for Sir William Carew. Although traditionally attributed to James Gibbs, the house is almost certainly the work of another, unidentified architect: the master mason in charge was John Moyle of Exeter. (See p.162.)

CL lxxiv, 172, 202; cxxxiv, 978; clxxxii, 23.252, 24.162

Ardress House

PORTADOWN, CO. ARMAGH

Before 1705, for Thomas Clarke; enlarged and remodelled in the 1780s by George Ensor (d.1803) for himself; further extensions by George Ensor II (1772–1845).

The house which the Irish architect George Ensor acquired in the 1780s through his marriage to an heiress, Sarah Clarke, was a plain, five-bay gabled planter's homestead. Ensor embellished the east front with a modest portico, perhaps more suited to the town houses that he was then designing in Dublin, and added a beautiful Adamesque drawing room behind the main block, with plasterwork by Michael Stapleton (d.1801), Ireland's leading *stuccadore*. Ensor's son, the polemicist George Ensor II, extended the house further by adding a dining room and library to the west, beyond the Stapleton drawing room, and lengthening the east front by four bays.

The Argory

MOY, CO. ARMAGH

Built in the 1820s by Arthur and John Williamson for the barrister Walter McGeough Bond. The little-known Williamsons were employed on the recommendation of the talented Dublin architect Francis Johnston, and the plain, neo-classical house shows Johnston's influence, although perhaps not his flair. Lengthened centre windows to the south and west were added in the late 19th century.

CL clxx, 849; clxxiii, 1768; clxxiv, 20

Arlington Court

BARNSTAPLE, DEVON

1820–3 for Colonel John Chichester, by the Barnstaple architect Thomas Lee (1794–1834).

Arlington is a plain, even severe house in the Greek Revival style. Its exterior furnishes little evidence that Lee, who was also responsible for the National Trust-owned Wellington Monument on the Blackdown Hills in Somerset, learned a great deal during the years he spent as one of John Soane's many pupils. However, several fine interiors – especially the anteroom, with its shallow dome, segmental arches and mirrored panels – show that Lee's time in Soane's office was not wasted. Arlington was enlarged, and a north wing added, by Colonel Chichester's grandson in 1865.

CL clxix, 1178

Ascott

LEIGHTON BUZZARD, BUCKINGHAMSHIRE

A small Jacobean farmhouse, remodelled and enlarged in 1876–84 for Leopold de Rothschild. His architect was George Devey (1820–86); further additions were made after Devey's death by his assistant Isaac Williams.

It would be hard to better Mary Gladstone's description of Ascott as 'a palace-like cottage, the most luxurious and lovely thing I ever saw'. It is indeed a vast, half-timbered cottage, in a style which might be termed banker's Old English.

CL ii, 210; viii, 240; cviii, 826; clix, 662

Ashdown House

LAMBOURN, OXFORDSHIRE

Built in the early 1660s, for William, 1st Earl of Craven; designed by either Balthazar Gerbier or William Winde. (See p.130.)

ECH Caroline 137

CL xxxiii, 454; xcv, 151

Attingham Park

SHREWSBURY, SHROPSHIRE

1783–5, by George Steuart (c.1730–1806) for Noel Hill, 1st Lord Berwick; picture gallery and staircase by John Nash (1752–1835) for the 2nd Lord Berwick, 1807–10.

Hill was an MP whose loyalty to Pitt the Younger in the vote against Charles James Fox's East India Bill was bought for the price of a peerage. The motto that he chose on becoming

Attingham Park, Shropshire: John Nash's staircase. (*NTPL/John Bethell*)

Lord Berwick in 1784 – *Qui uti scit ei bona* ('Let wealth be his who knows how to use it') – aptly sums up his motives in converting the brick-built Queen Anne house into a grand new mansion. Attingham is essentially a late example of a Palladian 'house of parade' with French neo-classical trimmings. Steuart designed a massive eleven-bay main block dominated by a three-storey Ionic portico, set against a backdrop of two pavilions linked to the main house by long colonnades. In 1807 the 2nd Lord Berwick commissioned Nash to create a top-lit staircase and gallery in the centre of the house. The gallery, which housed Berwick's considerable collection of paintings, was one of the earliest to use curved cast-iron ribs (made at nearby Coalbrookdale) in the construction of its ceiling. It leaked.

ECH Mid Georgian 195

CL xlix, 158, 186; cxvi, 1350; clix, 880

Baddesley Clinton

SOLIHULL, WARWICKSHIRE

Built or remodelled by the Brome family in the 15th century, on the site of a 13th-century moated farmstead; adapted over the next 400 years by members of the Ferrers family. (See p.59.)

CL i, 20; xviii, 942; lxx, 435; lxxi, 408, 434; clxiii, 1802, 1866; clxvii, 1005

Barrington Court

ILMINSTER, SOMERSET

Built some time between 1552 and 1564 for William Clifton, a prosperous London merchant.

A typical early-Elizabethan E-plan house, built – like its neighbour Montacute – of honey-coloured Ham stone. The original entrance façade to the south consists of two long projecting wings enclosing a forecourt; a centrally-placed porch leads into a cross passage which opens into the great hall. In 1907, neglected and dilapidated, Barrington was the first country house to be acquired by the National Trust, although the Trust was unable to find the funds necessary for its repair. In 1920 it was let to Colonel A. A. Lyle, who restored the house and filled it with his fine collection of oak panelling and other interior

fittings. Barrington Court is currently let to Stuart Interiors, for the display of their period and reproduction furniture.

CL xvi, 414; lviii, 706, 799; lxiii, 370, 404; lxiv, 332; cvi, 767; cxxiii, 495; cxxviii, 184

Basildon Park

PANGBOURNE, BERKSHIRE

1776–83, by John Carr of York for Francis Sykes.

A Palladian house consisting of a three-storey central block flanked by two-storey pavilions, built for Sykes with money acquired during his time with the East India Company. The interiors were completed by J. B. Papworth (1775–1847) for the Liberal MP James Morrison, who bought Basildon in 1838. The house stood empty and neglected from 1910 to 1952. Between the wars it was acquired by George Ferdinando, who offered to dismantle it and re-erect it anywhere in America for one million dollars. There were no takers. In 1952 Basildon was bought and carefully restored by Lord and Lady Iliffe.

CL clxi, 1158, 1227, 1298

Bateman's

BURWASH, EAST SUSSEX

A modest but charming sandstone house completed in 1634. Of particular interest because of its associations with Rudyard Kipling, whose home it was between 1902 and his death in 1936.

CL xxiv, 224; lxxix, 90

Belton House

GRANTHAM, LINCOLNSHIRE

Built 1685–8 for Sir John Brownlow. The design, probably provided by William Winde, was executed by the mason-contractor William Stanton. (See p.141.)

ECH Caroline 193

CL iv, 368, 400; xiv, 614; xxx, 308; lxi, 493; lxviii, 382; cxxi, 910; cxxxi, 650; cxxxvi, 562, 620, 700

Beningbrough Hall

SHIPTON, NORTH YORKSHIRE

By William Thornton (*c*.1670–1721) for John Bourchier, *c*.1716.

William Thornton was a 'joyner and architect' who worked under Nicholas Hawksmoor at Castle Howard and on the restoration of Beverley Minster, both in Yorkshire. Little is known about the building history of Beningbrough, a redbrick house with stone dressings. But it has recently

Beningbrough Hall, North Yorkshire: a chimneypiece in the state dressing room carrying a display of late seventeenth-century Delftware and oriental china, flanked by mezzotint portraits of members of the Kit Cat Club. (*NTPL/Jeremy Whitaker*)

been suggested that Thornton – who is described as Bourchier's architect in a list of Yorkshire houses contained in a copy of *The Builder's Dictionary* of 1734 – was working to Bourchier's own designs. The strong influence of recent Italian architecture on the form and decoration of the exterior may well be evidence of Bourchier's Grand Tour of the Continent in 1704–6.

ECH Baroque 243

CL xx, 342; lxii, 772, 820; cxxiv, 997

Benthall Hall

BROSELEY, SHROPSHIRE

Built or altered in the late 16th century for the Benthalls, a family whose Catholic sympathies led them to incorporate in the house several secret places for priests. Benthall has been extensively altered over the past 400 years, and contains Jacobean and Caroline interiors (including a fine staircase of *c*.1618) and two rococo chimneypieces by Thomas Farnolls Pritchard (1723–77), the architect of the famous Iron Bridge at nearby Coalbrookdale.

CL xli, 664

Berrington Hall

LEOMINSTER, HEREFORD & WORCESTER

1778–81 for Thomas Harley by Henry Holland, whose father-in-law, Lancelot Brown, landscaped the grounds. (See p.207.)

ECH Mid Georgian 184

CL cxvi, 1952, 2102, 2182; cli, 1089

Blickling Hall

BLICKLING, NORFOLK

Extensively remodelled 1619–29 by Robert Lyminge for Henry Hobart; further major alterations carried out in the 1760s and 1770s by Thomas and William Ivory, for John Hobart, 2nd Earl of Buckinghamshire. (See p.101.)

CL iii, 112, 144; xvii, 822; xxvii, 673; li, 6, 213; lxvii, 814, 902, 936; lxxxix, 137, 160; xci, 1239; xcv, 1075; cvii, 1871; cxxvii, 323; cxli, 446; clxxxii, 11.104, 12.136, 13.128

Boarstall Tower

AYLESBURY, BUCKINGHAMSHIRE

Early 14th century; with 16th- and 17th-century alterations. The three-storey gatehouse tower is all that remains of a fortified and moated house put up by John de Handlo. Its 40ft-long top-floor chamber was probably a set of communal lodgings for the household. (Admission by appointment only.)

Bodiam Castle

ROBERTSBRIDGE, EAST SUSSEX

Built in the 1380s for Sir Edward Dalyngrigge. (See p.34.)

CL ix, 200; xxxv, 950; xl, 700; xlviii, 381; lix, 234; lxx, 509; cii, 74

Bradley Manor

NEWTON ABBOT, DEVON

A 15th- and 16th-century hall house incorporating parts of an earlier building. The interiors contain painted Tudor decoration and carving in wood and stone, and some spectacular plasterwork by John Abbot of Frithelstock (1640–1727). Parts of the exterior were gothicised in the early 19th century.

CL xcvi, 377

Braithwaite Hall

EAST WITTON, NORTH YORKSHIRE

A 17th-century gabled stone farmhouse; original features include chimneypieces, panelling and an oak staircase. (Admission by appointment only.)

Bramber Castle

BRAMBER, WEST SUSSEX

Only fragments remain of the great Norman fortress built for William de Braose *c.*1100; one of the earliest of all English stone castles, it was occupied until the 14th century, then abandoned.

Bridge Cottage

FLATFORD, SUFFOLK

A thatched cottage housing an exhibition about John Constable, several of whose paintings depict the house.

Buckland Abbey

YELVERTON, DEVON

Built as a Cistercian abbey in 1278; remodelled by Richard Grenville after 1576. Buckland has undergone many alterations since Grenville first converted it into a house, although several buildings remain to show its monastic origins, including the abbey church and a great barn. It was bought by Francis Drake in about 1581, and his family continued to live here until 1946.

CL xxxix, 328; clxxxii, 30.110

Buscot Park

FARINGDON, OXFORDSHIRE

Late 18th century, built for – and probably by – the then owner, Edward Loveden Townsend; two pavilions added by Geddes Hyslop for the 2nd Lord Faringdon in the 1930s.

A rather severe neo-classical building, Buscot Park contains some sumptuous interiors filled with Regency and Empire furniture, and Faringdon's wide-ranging art collection, which includes works by Palma Vecchio, Gainsborough, Rembrandt, Reynolds, Burne-Jones and Graham Sutherland.

CL xl, 490; lxxxvii, 502, 524

Calke Abbey

TICKNALL, DERBYSHIRE

Built 1701–4 by an unknown architect for Sir John Harpur, incorporating parts of an Elizabethan house; altered 1789–1810 by William Wilkins the elder (1751–1815), for Sir Henry Harpur.

Calke Abbey is architecturally an engaging house, both as a good example of provincial baroque and for Wilkins's classical remodelling. But its main interest derives from the reclusive

Calke Abbey,
Derbyshire:
Sir Vauncey Harpur
Crewe's bedroom –
the epitome of a house
where nothing is thrown
away. (*NTPL*)

nature of several members of the Harpur family – which first manifested itself in the early 19th century, when Sir Henry Harpur married a lady's maid and withdrew from polite society – and the tendency, amounting almost to mania, never to throw anything away. As a result Calke is a time-capsule, a vast emporium of art-objects and stuffed animals, toys and furniture and carriages and birds' eggs.

CL clxxiv, 1062, 1162, 1242; clxxxiii, 14.138; clxxxiii, 20.208; clxxxiv, 52.36

Canons Ashby

DAVENTRY, NORTHAMPTONSHIRE

An H-shaped house built in the 1550s by John Dryden, incorporating parts of an earlier farm which once stood on the site. It was extended in the 1590s by Sir Erasmus Dryden, who also commissioned some elaborate allegorical murals. The great chamber, now called the drawing room, contains a magnificent domed early Caroline ceiling, filled with thistles, pomegranates and curious heads of Indian princesses in strapwork cartouches.

Canons Ashby was altered again in the early 18th century, when Edward Dryden, cousin to the poet John, remodelled the south front and laid out a formal terrace garden. The interiors which date from this period include the painted parlour, an interesting piece of baroque *trompe l'oeil*, almost certainly executed by Edward's cousin, Elizabeth Creed (1642–1728).

CL xvi, 978; xlix, 246, 278, 306; xci, 715; cxxxi, 1506; clxix, 930, 1026; clxxv, 1856; clxxvi, 20

Carlyle's House

CHELSEA, LONDON

An architecturally unremarkable Queen Anne house, famous as the home of Thomas and Jane Carlyle from 1834 until their deaths in 1881 and 1866 respectively; still filled with their possessions.

Castle Coole

ENNISKILLEN, CO. FERMANAGH

Designed by James Wyatt and built for the 1st Earl of Belmore in 1790–7; furnishings added by the 2nd Earl in 1807–25. (See p.212.)

CL lxxx, 654, 682; cxliv, 648; clxxix, 918

Castle Drogo

DREWSTEIGNTON, DEVON

1910–31 by Edwin Lutyens for Julius Drewe, founder of the Home and Colonial Stores. (See p.267.)

CL xcv, 69; xcviii, 200, 244; cvi, 30; clvii, 779

Castle Ward

STRANGFORD, CO. DOWN

Built 1762–70 by an unknown architect, for Bernard Ward, later 1st Viscount Bangor.

Castle Ward is an eccentric house, a unique attempt at appeasement before the battle of the styles got under way in the 19th century. The entrance façade to the east and the interiors immediately behind it – the hall, dining room and library – are solidly Palladian, in accordance with Ward's wishes. However, his wife Lady Anne favoured the Gothick, and so the garden front and the rooms to the west – the saloon, morning room and boudoir – are all pointed doors and plaster vaulting behind battlements, pinnacles and ogival windows. The compromise obviously concealed deeper, irreconcilable differences: shortly after the house was completed the couple separated, and Lady Anne went to live in Bath.

CL cxxx, 1260, 1320; landscape, clxxxi, 37.130, 39.168

Charlecote Park

WELLESBOURNE, WARWICKSHIRE

Originally built in the 1550s for Sir Thomas Lucy; extensively remodelled in 1826–67 for George Hammond Lucy and his wife Mary Elizabeth. Their architect was Charles S. Smith (*c*.1790–?), a pupil of Sir Jeffry Wyatville, but Smith was not retained to supervise the work, which was carried out by the Lucys in consultation with the designer Thomas Willement (1786–1871).

Although little except the gatehouse and the Renaissance porch survives from the 16th century, Charlecote's associations with Elizabeth I, who visited in 1572, and William Shakespeare, who was reputed to have been caught poaching in the park in around 1583, have tended to overshadow the house's real architectural significance as one of the landmarks of the 19th-century Elizabethan Revival.

ECH Late Georgian 211

CL i, 46, 78; xxxv, 126; lxi, 993; lxxi, 485; cvi, 771; cxi, 1080, 1164, 1328; cxxiv, 997

Chartwell

WESTERHAM, KENT

An unpretentious redbrick Victorian house remodelled by Philip Tilden (1887–1956), and famous as the home of Winston Churchill from 1922 to 1964. Chartwell still contains a large quantity of Churchilliana, including a number of his paintings, family photographs, cigar boxes – and velvet siren suits.

CL cxxxvii, 169

Chedworth Roman Villa

YANWORTH, GLOUCESTERSHIRE

Discovered by accident in 1864, when a gamekeeper found fragments of paving and pottery on the site, the villa at Chedworth originated in the first half of the 2nd century AD, and was progressively enlarged over the next 250 years. It consisted of a series of ranges fronted by verandas and grouped round a courtyard, with the north side extending in a long wing to the east. Excavations have revealed several colourful mosaic floors, including that in the dining chamber, which depicts Bacchic scenes and the four seasons, and two mosaics in the bath complex.

The villa was abandoned some time after the early 5th-century collapse of Roman government in Britain. Towards the end of its life, the occupants seem to have been converted to Christianity, to judge from the discovery at the site of a slab inscribed with the chi-rho symbol.

Cherryburn

MICKLEY SQUARE, STOCKSFIELD, NORTHUMBERLAND

A family farm including a restored house, the birthplace of Thomas Bewick (1753–1828), the father of modern wood-engraving. Cherryburn houses a small museum devoted to his life and works, and a printing shop.

Chirk Castle

CLWYD

A border castle begun c.1295, attributed to either James of St George (c.1235–1308), Master of the King's Works in Wales, or one of his subordinates such as Walter of Hereford (d.1309). It was remodelled in 1673–8, perhaps by William Winde, and further alterations were made in the 18th century and again in 1845, when A. W. N. Pugin (1812–52) redecorated the classical Georgian interiors.

Pugin found it rather difficult to hang honest Gothic decoration on to classical interiors: 'Such a job as Chirk is enough to drive any man mad,' he wrote. 'All little things are as difficult to get properly done as the greatest. It is worse than the House of Lords.' Sadly, much of Pugin's work was swept away in the 20th century.

CL ix, 656; xxxvi, 332; cx, 896, 980, 1064, 1148; cxvi, 1261; cxxxvi, 1702; clxiv, 169; clxxii, 810

Cilgerran Castle

CARDIGAN, DYFED

Built c.1225 by William Marshall, Earl of Pembroke, on the site of an earlier stronghold. Two

great ditches, and towers which projected from a curtain wall, formed the main defence. Slighted in the 15th century, perhaps at the time of Owen Glendower's revolt in 1405 (when it was briefly held by the Welsh), the castle seems never to have been repaired. Its picturesque ruins, perched above a steep wooded gorge, inspired large numbers of Romantic artists, including Turner and Richard Wilson.

Clandon Park

WEST CLANDON, SURREY

Built c.1730–3 for Thomas, 2nd Lord Onslow, by Giacomo Leoni.

In spite of the rather unfortunate 19th-century *porte cochère* which mars the integrity of the entrance façade, Clandon is a superb example of the early 18th-century transition from baroque to Palladian. Leoni applied Palladio's theories of proportion to the dimensions of several of the main chambers. The Palladio Room to the south, for example, was so-called because Leoni created it in accordance with that architect's ideas of the perfect ratio: height = $\frac{1}{2}$ length = $1\frac{1}{2}$ width. The entrance hall is in the form of a 40-ft cube. But much of the decoration still retains the theatrical, larger-than-life qualities of the baroque, in particular the splendid hall ceiling, in which the legs of the stucco figures dangle into the cornice, deliberately breaking out of the whole composition. Most of the original contents have gone, but the house contains a fine collection of furniture and porcelain given to the National Trust by Mrs David Gubbay.

ECH Early Georgian 97

CL lxii, 366, 398, 434; cix, 1091; cxix, 1038; cxxviii, 1215; cxlvi, 1456, 1582; cxlix, 1004

Claydon House

MIDDLE CLAYDON, BUCKINGHAMSHIRE

1760s and 1770s for Ralph, 2nd Earl Verney; designed in part, at least, by Thomas Robinson (c.1702–77).

Claydon's crowning glory is the extraordinary rococo decoration carried out by the carver and carpenter Luke Lightfoot, who may also have been responsible for parts of the design. He was described by Robinson as 'an ignorant knave' and a man 'with no small spice of madness in his composition'. Lightfoot's astonishing work – in particular in the north hall and the Chinese room – bears out the second of these epithets, but not the first: swan-like ho-ho birds, perched on door surrounds, preen themselves; tiny bells hang from a pagoda-like ceiling; and winged wyverns with barbed tails strain to break free from the walls. In contrast, the saloon and staircase hall by Joseph Rose is a model of neo-classical restraint. Unfortunately, the building and decoration of Claydon ruined Verney, and after the contents of the house were sold in 1783 his niece, who succeeded him, dismantled parts of Robinson's original scheme, including a grand ballroom and an equally grand rotunda.

ECH Early Georgian 242

CL ix, 617; xxxi, 356, 394; cxii, 1278, 1400, 1480

Clevedon Court

CLEVEDON, AVON

Built *c.*1320 for Sir John de Clevedon.

In spite of later additions and improvements, Clevedon Court retains much of its medieval spirit. The manor house, which was grafted on to an even earlier building incorporating a heavy mid-13th-century watch-tower (the remains of a fort designed as protection against Welsh raids from across the Bristol Channel), contains a fine first-floor chapel (dedicated in 1321). The old kitchen houses a display of Eltonware pottery made by a late Victorian owner of Clevedon, Sir Edmund Elton, a versatile artist and inventor (and captain of the local fire brigade) who devised, among other things, the Elton instantaneously detachable dress guard clip to keep ladies' skirts out of their bicycle wheels.

CL vi, 692; cxvii, 1672; cxviii, 16

Claydon House, Buckinghamshire: carvings by Luke Lightfoot in the alcove in the Chinese room, with figures taking tea. (*NTPL/Lucinda Lambton*)

Cliveden, Buckinghamshire: the south front and terrace with the Borghese balustrade. (*NTPL/Vera Collingwood*)

Cliveden

TAPLOW, BUCKINGHAMSHIRE

1850–1 for the Duke of Sutherland by Charles Barry (1795–1860); clock tower 1861 by Henry Clutton (1819–93); internal alterations *c.*1895 for William Waldorf Astor by Frank Pearson (1864–1947) and others.

In its perfect setting on a terrace high above the Thames, Barry's three-storey Italianate palace exudes all the complacent confidence and prosperity of early Victorian Britain, in spite of a rather complex building history which involved linking the main block to two wings designed by Thomas Archer (*c.*1668–1743) in *c.*1705. The house replaced two earlier mansions. The first was put up by William Winde in *c.*1674–7 and was destroyed by fire in 1795; the second, designed in 1827–30 by William Burn (1789–1870), suffered a similar fate in 1849. A political and literary centre in the early years of this century, when the 2nd Viscount Astor and his wife Nancy entertained Kipling, Henry James and Churchill, among many others, the house is now let as a hotel to Blakeney Hotels Ltd. Three rooms and the extensive gardens are open to the public.

CL xxxii, 808, 854; lxx, 38, 68; xciii, 83; clxi, 438, 498; clxxvi, 625; clxxix, 924

Clouds Hill

WAREHAM, DORSET

A tiny brick-and-tile cottage on the slopes of Clouds Hill above Bovington Camp, which was bought by T. E. Lawrence when he rejoined the RAF in 1925; filled with his books and furniture. It was as he was returning to Clouds Hill from Bovington in 1935 that Lawrence was killed in a motor-cycle accident.

Coleridge Cottage

NETHER STOWEY, SOMERSET

The home of Samuel Taylor Coleridge for three years from 1797; substantially altered in the later 19th century.

Coleridge wrote many of his greatest poems here, including 'Frost at Midnight' and 'The Rime of the Ancient Mariner'. The cottage was also the setting for one of the most famous of all literary disasters. Having composed 'Kubla Khan' during an opium dream, the poet had begun to set it down when he was 'called out by a person on business from Porlock'. On his return an hour later, he found that the poem had 'passed away like the images on the surface of a stream into which a stone has been cast', and he was unable to remember more than a few lines.

Compton Castle

MARLDON, DEVON

A manor house built in several phases between the 14th and 16th centuries by the Gilbert family. Fortifications, including a 24ft-high curtain wall and a watch tower – perhaps a response to the threat of French coastal raiders – date from the reign of Henry VIII. Carefully restored between 1931 and 1956, Compton remains a rare survival of a late-medieval fortified house.

CL clxx, 1546

Corfe Castle

CORFE CASTLE, DORSET

Mainly built during the 12th and 13th centuries, with some later additions; slighted by order of Parliament in 1646.

Corfe was already a royal residence in the 10th century, when according to legend it was the home of Elfrida, the stepmother of King Edward the Martyr, who is said to have murdered him at Corfe in 978. The oldest surviving parts of the building are fragments of an early Norman hall which stood on the site, surrounded by a wooden palisade. Henry I replaced that hall with a stone keep; in the early 13th century King John built a range of lodgings and domestic offices, and most of the defences in the outer bailey. Henry III added Corfe's two great gatehouses. The castle's ruinous condition is due to deliberate demolition after a Royalist garrison was besieged by Parliamentarian forces during the winter of 1644–5.

CL cxvii, 1163

Cotehele

ST DOMINICK, CORNWALL

Built between the late 15th century and 1627, incorporating parts of an earlier medieval house. (See p.52.)

CL xi, 485; xvii, 822; lvi, 324, 360; ci, 367; cvi, 771; clxxxiv, 5.52

Coughton Court

ALCESTER, WARWICKSHIRE

A Tudor courtyard house, altered after being damaged during the Civil War; Gothick west front of 1780, and further alterations in 1835.

The main focus of Coughton is its great gatehouse, built in the first half of the 16th century for Sir George Throckmorton, whose family had held the estate since 1409. The Throckmortons were a prominent recusant family: Thomas Throckmorton lent his house to Sir Everard Digby in 1605, and it was here on 5 November of that year Lady Digby and Father Garnet heard that the Gunpowder Plot had failed.

CL xcviii, 236

Cragside

ROTHBURY, NORTHUMBERLAND

Originally a small villa built in 1863–6 by an unidentified architect; remodelled and considerably enlarged in 1869–84 by Richard Norman Shaw for the inventor and armaments manufacturer William Armstrong; further additions by Frederick Waller in 1895. (See p.247.)

Vict. CH 305

CL vii, 464; lxxxix, 234; cxlvi, 1640, 1694; clvi, 178; clxii, 87; clxviii, 759

Croft Castle, Hereford & Worcester: Thomas Farnolls Pritchard's Gothic staircase hall.
(*NTPL/Jeremy Whitaker*)

Croft Castle

LEOMINSTER, HEREFORD & WORCESTER

A 14th- and 15th-century castle with internal decorations by Thomas Farnolls Pritchard for Thomas Johnes, 1765.

After the rugged grandeur of Croft's massive external walls and battlemented towers, the lightness and delicacy of Pritchard's interiors – and in particular the airy Gothic staircase hall – come as a delightful surprise. Johnes was a cousin of the picturesque theoretician Richard Payne Knight, whom Pritchard was to help with the designs for Downton Castle (also in Hereford & Worcester) in 1772.

CL cvii, 1206, 1292; cxxii, 706, 1255; cliv, 303; clxxxi, 53.44

Cwmmau Farmhouse

BRILLEY, HEREFORD & WORCESTER

An early 17th-century timber-framed and stone-roofed farmhouse.

Downhill House and Mussenden Temple

CASTLEROCK, CO. LONDONDERRY

Downhill was begun in 1775 by the Cork architect Michael Shanahan for Frederick Augustus Hervey, the eccentric Bishop of Derry and later 4th Earl of Bristol. The Temple, named after the Earl-Bishop's cousin Mrs Frideswide Mussenden, was completed in 1785.

CL cvii, 34; cl, 94, 154

Dudmaston

BRIDGNORTH, SHROPSHIRE

Built *c*.1695 for Sir Thomas Wolryche; attributed to William (1661–1724) and Francis (1672–1738) Smith of Warwick. Alterations of 1826, including a new attic storey, are attributed to John Smalman (*c*.1783–1852).

Dudmaston is a modest house, with a remarkable art collection. Largely assembled by Sir George Labouchere and his wife, Rachel Wolryche-Whitmore, who inherited the property in 1966, the collection includes works by Ben Nicholson, Henry Moore and Barbara Hepworth.

CL clxv, 634, 714, 818; clxxxi, 23.228

Dunham Massey

ALTRINCHAM, CHESHIRE

An E-shaped Elizabethan house which was extensively remodelled in 1732–40 for the 2nd Earl of Warrington. After consulting 'Mr Bouget' (*see* Petworth House, p.159), the Earl chose as his architect John Norris, whose other works are unknown except for the now-demolished Atherton Hall, Lancashire (1750). The entrance front has been remodelled twice: in 1789 by John Hope of Liverpool (1734–1808); and again in 1905, when Compton Hall was commissioned to create a neo-Caroline façade loosely based on Sudbury in Derbyshire, and to provide some Edwardian home comforts.

CL clxix, 1562, 1664; clxx, 18, 106; clxxxi, 27.156

Dunstanburgh Castle

CRASTER, NORTHUMBERLAND

Built on a remote cliff-top site between 1313 and 1316, for Thomas, 2nd Earl of Lancaster and grandson of Henry III. The castle's strongest defences, to the south, took the form of a substantial curtain wall and a gatehouse keep with flanking D-shaped towers. Badly damaged in 1462 and 1464, when it was held by Lancastrians and besieged by Yorkists, Dunstanburgh was never properly repaired, and gradually declined into the picturesque ruin which stands today.

CL cv, 135; cxvi, 1150

Dunster Castle

DUNSTER, SOMERSET

A medieval castle remodelled in 1617 by William Arnold (d.c.1637) for George Luttrell; reconstructed for George Fownes Luttrell in 1868 by Anthony Salvin (1799–1881).

Dunster is a strange mixture. Several of its interiors are Jacobean, the result of Arnold's remodelling; others – notably the magnificent staircase, and the dining room ceiling in the style of Edward Goudge – show a more sophisticated Caroline touch. And the overall 'medieval' character of the house, particularly its exteriors, is entirely due to Salvin's romantic Victorian restoration.

CL xiv, 686; clxxxi, 29.124, 30.102; clxxxiv, 22.152

Dyrham Park

DYRHAM, AVON

Built in two stages between 1692 and 1704, incorporating parts of an earlier house. The west front is the work of Samuel Hauduroy; the east front is by William Talman. Their client was William Blathwayt. (See p.148.)

ECH Baroque 85

CL xiv, 434; xl, 546; cxii, 1651; cxxix, 631; cxxxi, 335, 396; clxxxii, 41.236

Eastbury House

BARKING, ESSEX

An H-shaped late Elizabethan manor house of red brick, with mullioned windows and Dutch gables. Apart from some murals, few original interior features remain. The house is let to the London Borough of Barking and Dagenham. (Admission by appointment only.)

CL lxxix, 12

East Riddlesden Hall

KEIGHLEY, WEST YORKSHIRE

Mid-17th century, for the clothier James Murgatroyd, who bought the estate in the 1630s. The house consists of a square, gabled main block with mullioned windows and an impressive, if somewhat eclectic, entrance front. This has a two-storey porch flanked by classical columns and a rose window, beneath battlements and pinnacles. The Murgatroyds are said to have been the prototypes for the Bad Baronets in Gilbert and Sullivan's *Ruddigore*.

CL xciii, 440; cxii, 107; cxxviii, 1543

Erddig

WREXHAM, CLWYD

Built 1683–7 for Joshua Edisbury by the Cheshire mason Thomas Webb; wings added 1721–4; remodelled 1773–4 for Philip Yorke to designs by James Wyatt – although the architect who actually implemented those designs was Joseph Turner of Chester (c.1729–1807). The dining room was remodelled in 1827–8 for Simon Yorke by Thomas Hopper.

Although hardly an architectural masterpiece, Erddig is a rarity – a country house that presents a well-rounded view of the lifestyles of all of its occupants, family *and* staff. One of its most intriguing – and endearing – features is the remarkable collection of portraits and photographs of the domestic staff which the Yorkes commissioned over two centuries.

CL xxvi, 742; xxxvi, 555; lxi, 992; cliii, 1153; clxi, 844; clxiii, 906, 970, 1070; clxiv, 1331

Farnborough Hall

BANBURY, WARWICKSHIRE

An old manor house remodelled in Palladian style in 1745–50 for William Holbech, perhaps to the designs of his Warwickshire neighbour, the gentleman architect Sanderson Miller. The internal alterations and stable block of 1813–16 are by Henry Hakewill (1771–1830), and the spectacular rococo plasterwork is by the Yorkshire *stuccadore* William Perritt.

CL cxv, 354, 430

Felbrigg Hall

CROMER, NORFOLK

A house with an extremely distinguished architectural pedigree. It comprises a Jacobean entrance front attributed to Robert Lyminge of Blickling (d.1628); a west wing added in 1674–86 to the designs of William Samwell, who remodelled Ham House; a service wing, Gothic library, staircase and several interiors, all of 1751–6 by James Paine. Samwell's wing contains plasterwork by Edward Goudge, who worked at Belton and Petworth; Paine's interiors were decorated by Joseph Rose. All carried out for the Windham family, who bought the estate in 1459.

Not surprisingly, considering the artists involved, Felbrigg is a masterpiece. Perhaps it is fortunate that James Wyatt, who was asked to make alterations to the house in the 1790s, never got round to the job – although the architect's dilatoriness provoked his client William Windham into a splendid display of spleen:

> It is dishonest to make engagements which you are either not able or not willing to fulfil. It is in the highest degree uncivil to receive letter after letter, containing a question, which the writer is entitled to ask, and to send no answer. Pray, Sir, who are you, upon whom engagements are to be of no force; and who are to set aside all the forms of civility, established between man and man?

CL lxxvi, 666; clxviii, 2344; clxxxiv, 14.138, 15.102

Felbrigg Hall, Norfolk: the cabinet, which was remodelled for William Windham II in 1751 to house the bulk of the pictures acquired on his Grand Tour ten years earlier. (*NTPL/Jeremy Whitaker*)

Fenton House

HAMPSTEAD, LONDON

A late 17th-century brick house, with dormers and tall stacks. It is named after the Baltic merchant who owned it in the 1790s, but nothing is known of either the architect or the family who commissioned the building.

CL cvii, 802

The Fleece Inn

BRETFORTON, HEREFORD & WORCESTER

A half-timbered farmhouse dating back to the 15th century, the Fleece became an inn in 1848.

Florence Court

ENNISKILLEN, CO. FERMANAGH

A small early 18th-century house built for Sir John Cole (and named after his wife Florence) was replaced *c*.1750 by his son, the 1st Lord Mount Florence, who built a much larger mansion, seven bays wide and three storeys high, with fine rococo plasterwork by the Dublin *stuccadore* Robert West. Open colonnades and pavilions were added in 1771, perhaps by the Sardinian architect David Ducart, for William Willoughby Cole, later 1st Earl of Enniskillen.

CL cxlii, 800; clxix, 1242, 1318

Gawthorpe Hall

PADIHAM, LANCASHIRE

Built 1600–5, for Lawrence Shuttleworth; tentatively attributed to Robert Smythson (*c*.1535–1614); altered in 1850–2 by Charles Barry for Sir James Kay-Shuttleworth.

The foundation stone of Gawthorpe Hall was laid on 26 August 1600 by the Revd Lawrence Shuttleworth, whose family had settled in Lancashire by the end of the 14th century. Shuttleworth's accounts show that the supervisor of works and master mason was one Anthony Whithead. It is on stylistic grounds that the design has been attributed to Smythson, who may have provided the plans and elevations, which were then modified by Whithead. Two hundred and fifty years later Sir Charles Barry was called in to make structural repairs. ('It will be necessary to have a new ceiling in the dining room,' wrote Sir James Kay-Shuttleworth to his wife: 'The present ceiling will fall on our heads.') Barry raised the central staircase tower by one storey and capped it with an openwork parapet; the interiors were extensively remodelled and refurnished, with contributions from A. W. N. Pugin and J. G. Crace (1809–89), both of whom worked with Barry on the Houses of Parliament.

CL xxxiii, 670; cxvii, 985; clviii, 558, 630; clxxxi, 24.96; clxxxii, 23.248

Grantham House

GRANTHAM, LINCOLNSHIRE

A town house with a central hall which dates from *c*.1380; considerable Elizabethan and Georgian additions.

Grantham House has undergone some major changes since the Middle Ages. The Hall family, wealthy wool merchants who occupied it in the 16th century, changed the entrance façade, while the garden front was remodelled by Anne, Lady Cust, soon after her husband Sir Richard bought it in 1734. Lady Cust is also thought to have panelled the drawing room and introduced from nearby Belton House three still lifes (attributed to J. B. Ruoppolo) which she inherited from her brother Viscount Tyrconnel in 1754.

CL cxxxvi, 552

Great Chalfield Manor

MELKSHAM, WILTSHIRE

Built sometime between 1467 and 1488 for Thomas Tropnell, a prosperous and acquisitive local landowner who obtained the estate from the heirs of the Percy family, owners since at least 1199.

A mural in the parlour may well depict Tropnell – if so, he seems to have had six fingers on each hand. The house consists of a great hall with lodgings at either end, which originally formed one range of a courtyard house, much of which has disappeared. John Eyre, who married Tropnell's great-granddaughter in 1550, remodelled several of the interiors, and may have been responsible for a long service wing to the west of the main house, which perhaps contained additional lodgings with a gallery of sorts above. Great Chalfield was sympathetically restored in 1905 by Harold Brakspear, using drawings made in 1836 by T. L. Walker, a pupil of Pugin.

CL xxxvi, 230, 294; xciv, 376

The Greyfriars

WORCESTER, HEREFORD & WORCESTER

A late-medieval timber-framed and tiled town house with minor additions.

The Greyfriars was built in 1480 for a Worcester brewer, Thomas Grene, on a site next to a Franciscan monastery. Although one of the two ranges running back from the street is Elizabethan, and casement windows were introduced in the early 17th century, the house remains a good example of a wealthy merchant's home of the late Middle Ages. Threatened with demolition in the 1940s, it was rescued and restored before being given to the Trust in 1966.

CL cxlvi, 1390

Greys Court

ROTHERFIELD GREYS, OXFORDSHIRE

A medieval manor house founded by the de Greys – Edward III granted the 1st Lord de Grey a licence to crenellate in 1347. Most of those fortifications are now in ruins, but the modest Tudor brick and flint house which was built in the medieval courtyard is still very much intact; an elegant classical drawing room was added *c.*1750.

CL xcv, 1080, 1124; clxxxiii, 16.198

Gunby Hall

SPILSBY, LINCOLNSHIRE

A three-storey, seven-bay rectangular block of red brick with stone dressings, built in 1700 for Sir William Massingberd. The central three bays are recessed between slightly projecting wings; and the entrance is through a doorway with a broken, scrolled pediment and a coat of arms. A north wing was added in 1873. Tennyson, who was born at Somersby, a few miles north of Gunby, described the house as 'a haunt of ancient peace'.

CL xciv, 816, 860; cvi, 769; clxxxii, 22.138

Ham House

RICHMOND, SURREY

Built for Sir Thomas Vavasour in 1610; altered in 1637–9 by William Murray; extended and re-modelled in the 1670s by Murray's daughter Elizabeth and her second husband, John Mait-land, Duke of Lauderdale. Their architect was William Samwell. (See p.122.)

ECH Caroline 65

CL vi, 144; xlvii, 372, 404, 440; lviii, 569, 998; lxi, 986; lxii, 497; lxviii, 754; lxxii, 14; ciii, 226; cvii, 1538; cxxii, 718; clxii, 1418; clviii, 902; clxix, 250, 322

Hanbury Hall

DROITWICH, HEREFORD & WORCESTER

A red-brick house with stone dressings on the Clarendon/Belton model, complete with pediment, dormers, a hipped roof and a cupola; built for Thomas Vernon, a wealthy lawyer, and finished in 1701. The staircase was painted in 1710 by James Thornhill (1675–1734).

Hanbury's genesis is something of a mystery. Three masons – James Withenbury of Worcester, William Rudhall of Henley-in-Arden, and John Chatterton – appear to have been invited *c.*1700 to submit their designs for Vernon's new house. Each depicts a front of eleven bays with three-bay projecting wings (the form of the present building), suggesting that the brief was fairly specific; but apparently none was adopted, and the designer of Hanbury remains unidentified. Perhaps Withenbury, Rudhall or Chatterton submitted a second drawing, which hasn't survived; or perhaps Thomas Vernon went to an entirely different architect. Ragley Hall in Warwickshire, designed by Robert Hooke in 1679–83, has been suggested as the prototype of Hanbury.

ECH Baroque 124

CL x, 368; xxxix, 502; cxliii, 18, 66

Hardwick Hall

CHESTERFIELD, DERBYSHIRE

1590–7 for Elizabeth Talbot, Countess of Shrewsbury ('Bess of Hardwick'); designed by Robert Smythson. (See p.80.)

CL ii, 434, 464; viii, 464; xiii, 710; xliii, 550; lvii, 229, 320, 422; lxi, 328, 661; lxiv, 806, 870, 904, 934; cvii, 1871; cxxii, 334, 346; cxxiii, 1408; cxxiv, 269; clii, 1441; cliv, 1756; clvi, 930; clxxx, 1736; clxxxiii, 6.68; clxxxiii, 10.134; clxxxiv, 28.90, 30.76

Hardy's Cottage

HIGHER BOCKHAMPTON, DORSET

The small cob and thatch cottage in which Thomas Hardy was born in 1840. It figures in *Under the Greenwood Tree*, in which a village dance is set in the parlour to the left of the porch.

Hatchlands Park

EAST CLANDON, SURREY

Built 1757–9 for Admiral Edward Boscawen, by Stiff Leadbetter (d.1766); interiors 1758–61 by Robert Adam. Alterations were made in the late 18th century by Joseph Bonomi (1739–1808), in the 1880s by Halsey Ricardo (1854–1928), and in 1903 by Sir Reginald Blomfield (1856–1942).

Hatchlands' chief architectural interest lies in the fact that several of its interiors, including the library and drawing room, represent some of the earliest of Adam's decorative schemes, designed just after his return from Italy.

ECH Mid Georgian 49

CL xxxix, 176; cxiv, 870, 1042; clxxxiii, 16.182

Hezlett House

LIFFOCK, CO. LONDONDERRY

A single-storey thatched cottage dating from *c.*1691, when it was probably built as a parsonage for the rector of Dunboe. The house is particularly interesting for its cruck construction, a form not often seen in Northern Ireland at this date.

Hill Top

NEAR SAWREY, CUMBRIA

A small, mainly 17th-century farmhouse, bought in 1905 by Beatrix Potter as part investment, part holiday home. It features in several of her stories: the 19th-century dresser figures in *The Tale of Samuel Whiskers*, and the grandfather clock was the model for the one in *The Tailor of Gloucester*.

Hinton Ampner

BRAMDEAN, HAMPSHIRE

A large Victorian house, remodelled twice in a neo-Georgian style by the connoisseur Ralph Dutton, 8th and last Lord Sherborne: first in 1936–9, and again in 1960.

Hinton Ampner is quite a rarity – a country house dating, in part at least, from the 1960s, when Dutton carefully rebuilt his home and its collections after they had been all but destroyed in a fire. The result is both attractive and revealing of post-war attitudes to interior design.

CL ci, 326, 374; cxxii, 536; cxxiii, 494; cxxxvii, 1424; cxxxix, 1240; clxxxii, 20.150

Hinton Ampner,
Hampshire:
the art deco bathroom
put in by Ralph Dutton
(*NTPL/Nick Carter*)

Horton Court, Avon: William Knight's detached Renaissance loggia in the garden. (*NTPL/Fay Godwin*)

Horton Court

HORTON, AVON

Sometime between 1100 and 1150 an ecclesiastic called Robert de Beaufeu built himself a manor house at Horton. Remarkably, the hall of that house still stands, an extraordinary survival which forms a link between the Saxon aula and the conventional medieval hall. It is connected to a later house, which was either built or extensively remodelled in the 1520s for William Knight, a diplomat who was involved in the unsuccessful negotiations with the Pope over Henry VIII's divorce from Catherine of Aragon in 1527. Knight also built the detached Renaissance loggia which stands in the garden.

CL lxxi, 122

Hughenden Manor

HIGH WYCOMBE, BUCKINGHAMSHIRE

A farmhouse converted to a gentleman's residence in 1738; remodelled in 1862 for Benjamin Disraeli, by Edward Buckton Lamb (1806–69).

After buying the Hughenden estate in 1848 – as a prospective leader of the Conservative Party he needed a suitable country seat – Disraeli continued the process of gothicising the house, which had been begun by an earlier owner, the antiquary John Norris. Gothic plaster vaults were installed in the hall in 1858 by W. G. Lacey; and then four years later E. B. Lamb was commissioned to reface the façades in his own pleasing but rather bizarre Jacobethan style. (Lamb's obituary in the *Builder* noted that 'he constantly endeavoured, even at the expense sometimes of beauty, to exhibit originality'.)

CL i, 463; cxiii, 1604, 1698; clxxi, 216

Ickworth

HORRINGER, SUFFOLK

Begun in 1795 by Frederick Hervey, 4th Earl of
Bristol and Bishop of Derry, to the designs of an
Italian architect, Mario Asprucci the younger, as
modified by two Irish brothers, Francis and
Joseph Sandys. Unfinished at the 4th Earl's death,
the house was completed 1821–9 by his son, the
1st Marquess of Bristol. (See p.218.)

ECH Mid Georgian 239

CL xviii, 870; lviii, 668, 698; cxvii, 678; cliii, 1362

Ightham Mote

SEVENOAKS, KENT

The core of the house dates from the 1340s;
significant additions were made in the late 15th,
16th and 17th centuries. (See p.46.)

CL i, 406; vii, 336; xxi, 414; lxi, 987; lxxi, 240

Kedleston Hall

NR DERBY, DERBYSHIRE

For Nathaniel Curzon, 1st Baron Scarsdale;
begun in 1758 to designs by Matthew Brettingham the elder. Brettingham was almost immediately superseded by James Paine, who was himself
replaced as architect by Robert Adam in 1760.
(See p.188.)

ECH Mid Georgian 70

CL x, 240; xxxiv, 892, 928; cxxii, 720; cxxxi, 1098; clxiii,
194, 262, 322; clxxv, 1610; clxxxi, 30.96

Killerton

BROADCLYST, DEVON

Built in 1778–9 for Sir Thomas Acland, by John
Johnson (1732–1814), with various later additions. In the park there is a Romanesque chapel of
1840–1 by C. R. Cockerell (1788–1863).

Killerton's chief glory is the marvellous grounds
laid out in the 1770s by the Scotsman John Veitch:
the house, to quote one recent writer, 'does not
compete with its surroundings'. Johnson's main
block – undistinguished from the outset, and

deprived of architectural unity by a host of
later additions and alterations – now houses the
Paulise de Bush collection of 18th- to 20th-century
costume.

CL cxxiii, 1132; cxxvi, 173

King John's Hunting Lodge

AXBRIDGE, SOMERSET

A three-storey timber-framed merchant's house of
*c.*1500.

'The title of King John's House', wrote Francis
Gross in 1777, 'is an appellation common to many
ancient structures in which that king had no
concern; King John and the Devil being the
founders, to whom the vulgar impute most of the
ancient buildings, mounds or entrenchments, for
which they cannot assign any other constructor,
with this distinction, that to the king are given
most of the mansions, castles, and other buildings,
whilst the Devil is supposed to have amused
himself chiefly in earthen works.'

The King's Head

AYLESBURY, BUCKINGHAMSHIRE

An old coaching inn with a cobbled stable yard.
Fragments of 15th-century glass survive in the
large window which lights the bar, once the hall of
a medieval house – parts of the building date back
to 1450.

Kingston Lacy

WIMBORNE MINSTER, DORSET

Built 1663–5 for Sir Ralph Bankes by Sir Roger
Pratt; remodelled in 1791 by R. W. F. Brettingham (*c.*1750–1820); recased and remodelled
1835–9 by Sir Charles Barry.

Kingston Lacy may prompt regrets that Barry's
19th-century work effectively destroyed one of
the great Caroline country houses, designed by
Pratt after Bankes's main seat, Corfe Castle, had
been slighted during the Commonwealth. But
Barry's Italianate palace has a power and grace of
its own. The architect of the Houses of Parliament
was commissioned by William John Bankes, who,

accused of an indiscretion with a guardsman, fled
to Italy in 1841, from whence he continued to
oversee the furnishing and decoration of the house
that he never saw completed.

CL vii, 496; xv, 558; cxvii, 99; clxxix, 1016, 1123, 1576,
1674

Knightshayes Court

BOLHAM, DEVON

Begun in 1869 for Sir John Heathcoat-Amory, a
lace manufacturer; designed by William Burges;
interiors completed by John Diblee Crace. (See
p.241.)

CL cxxviii, 664; clxi, 1604; clxxvii, 160, 218, 314; clxxxiv,
10.80

Knole

SEVENOAKS, KENT

Originally built for Archbishop Thomas Bourchier in the mid-15th century; substantially remodelled in 1603–8 for Thomas Sackville, 1st Earl
of Dorset. (See p.94.)

CL xxxi, 772, 796, 826, 862; lxvii, 579; lxxi, 238; xcvii, 72;
xcviii, 460; ci, 660; cxxxviii, 1252; clxi, 1495, 1620; clxxxi,
32.64

Lacock Abbey

LACOCK, WILTSHIRE

Founded in 1232 by Ela, Countess of Salisbury, as
a nunnery for Augustinian canonesses; converted
into a private house after the Dissolution of the
Monasteries by William Sharington. The Gothick
great hall and gateway, 1754–5, are by Sanderson
Miller for John Ivory Talbot; further alterations
were made to the south front *c.*1828–30 by
William Henry Fox Talbot, one of the pioneers of
modern photography.

There can be few other country houses which
retain work of such high quality from widely
different historical periods. Although Sharington
dismantled the abbey church, he retained most of
the ground floor of the cloistral court, building on
the upper storeys. As a result, Lacock still boasts
some fine medieval architecture, and some of the
best Renaissance carving of its date in Britain,
executed by John Chapman, a mason in the
King's Works. Miller's Gothick entrance hall in
no way echoes the true Gothic of the cloister, but
as an expression of mid-18th-century medievalism
it is hard to beat.

CL xiii, 176; liii, 280, 314, 352; lxxiii, 278; xcvi, 192; cxxiii,
950; cxxiv, 997; cxlix, 1465

Lamb House

RYE, EAST SUSSEX

A modest brick-fronted town house built in 1724, Lamb House has seen more than its share of famous characters. Two years after it was built, James Lamb, the mayor of Rye, entertained George I here for three days, after the King's ship had been driven ashore on its way from Hanover. In 1900 Henry James bought the house, and most of the English literary establishment made their way here, including H. G. Wells, Rudyard Kipling and Max Beerbohm. After James' death in 1916, Lamb House was occupied by A. C. and E. F. Benson: Rye became the inspiration behind the latter's *Mapp and Lucia* novels.

CL cxvii, 396

Lanhydrock

BODMIN, CORNWALL

Built 1630–42 for the Robartes family of Truro; rebuilt, following a disastrous fire in 1881, by Richard Coad who was an ex-pupil of George Gilbert Scott.

Almost all that survives of 17th-century Lanhydrock is the gatehouse and the 116-ft long gallery, with its superb barrel-vaulted ceiling containing twenty-four main panels depicting incidents from the Old Testament – from the Creation to the Burial of Isaac. The plasterwork, almost certainly completed by 1642, has been attributed to the Abbots of Frithelstock near Bideford, whose work appears in many country houses in Devon and Cornwall. The late-Victorian building has a solid appeal of its own:

Lanhydrock, Cornwall: the early 17th-century long gallery that survived the fire of 1881. (*NTPL/John Bethell*)

its neo-Jacobean interiors may not be exactly elegant, but they are a splendid expression of comfort and prosperity.

CL xiv, 890; cxlvii, 542; clxi, 868; clxiii, 382, 458; clxxix, 1280

Lawrence House

LAUNCESTON, CORNWALL

A modest town house built in 1753 for a wealthy local lawyer, Humphrey Lawrence; now leased to Launceston Town Council as a museum and civic centre.

Lindisfarne Castle

HOLY ISLAND, NORTHUMBERLAND

Built in the 1540s; restored 1902–12 by Edwin Lutyens for Edward Hudson, founder and proprietor of the magazine *Country Life*. (See p.262.)

CL xxxiii, 830

Little Moreton Hall

CONGLETON, CHESHIRE

Begun in the mid-15th century for Sir Richard de Moreton; extended by the Moreton family over the next 150 years. (See p.76.)

CL xv, 594; xxxix, 302; lxvi, 754, 798; lxxvi, 187; cxvii, 984; clxvii, 369; clxxxiv, 44.48

Lower Brockhampton

BRINGSTY, HEREFORD & WORCESTER

A moated, timber-framed manor house built perhaps as early as 1400 for John Domulton, a descendant of the Brockhampton family which settled here in the 12th century; unusually, a late medieval timber-framed gatehouse straddles the moat.

CL clxxxiv, 1.46

Lyme Park

DISLEY, CHESHIRE

An Elizabethan house remodelled *c.*1725–35 for Peter Legh by Giacomo Leoni. A tower was added on the south front and rooms on the east front were remodelled in 1814–17 for Thomas Legh by Lewis Wyatt (1777–1853).

Leoni's solution to the problem of 'modernising' an Elizabethan courtyard house was to turn the courtyard into an arcaded *cortile*. On the south front his giant portico, raised on a rusticated ground storey and topped with lead statues of Venus, Neptune and Pan, may owe something to Colen Campbell's Wanstead House, although it owes a great deal more to Palladio. Leoni's translation (and revision) of Palladio's *Quattro Libri dell'Architettura* appeared in 1716–20.

CL xvi, 906; xviii, 234; xcvi, 684; c, 210; clvi, 1724, 1858, 1930, 1998

Lytes Cary Manor

CHARLTON MACKRELL, SOMERSET

A small stone manor house, consisting of a chapel (now attached to the house but perhaps originally free-standing) built in 1343; an early 16th-century great hall, reached through a two-storey porch with a fine oriel on the upper floor; and a set of lodgings dated 1533, including a ground-floor parlour with a great chamber above. The ceiling of the great chamber, decorated with plasterwork ribs forming a pattern of stars and diapers, is an unusually early example of its type.

Lytes Carey was rescued from neglect and decay early this century by Sir Walter Jenner, who installed much of the present oak furniture and fittings, many dating from the late 17th and early 18th centuries.

CL cii, 128, 178, 228; cvii, 100; clxxii, 634

Lyveden New Bield

OUNDLE, NORTHAMPTONSHIRE

Begun in 1594 for Sir Thomas Tresham as a lodge to his new manor house at Lyveden; the design may have been provided by Robert Stickelles, Clerk of Works at Richmond Palace. The building was probably incomplete at the time of Tresham's death in September 1605, a few months before his son was imprisoned for his involvement in the Gunpowder Plot.

Thomas Tresham chose an awkward time to adopt the Roman Catholic faith. His conversion took place in 1580, just as anti-Catholic persecution was reaching its peak. Edmund Campion, for example, was executed the next year. True to the spirit of his age, which delighted in symbols, devices and conceits, Tresham sought to express his faith in his building. Lyveden New Bield is designed in the shape of a cross, and is covered with emblems of the passion and mystical references to salvation and the Godhead.

Maister House

HULL, HUMBERSIDE

A Palladian house built in 1743 for Henry Maister by Joseph Page (d.1775). Originally trained as a bricklayer and plasterer, Page has been described as 'probably the first recognisable architect in Hull'. The house that he built for Maister is a fine essay in mid-18th-century Palladianism, with statuary by John Cheere and an ironwork balustrade by Robert Bakewell.

Melford Hall

LONG MELFORD, SUFFOLK

A U-shaped red-brick house built in the mid-16th century for Sir William Cordell, a lawyer; additions, including library and staircase, 1813, by Thomas Hopper for Sir William Parker.

Although Melford has undergone a number of changes since Cordell's time, the most radical of which was the removal of a gatehouse range which originally made the U into an enclosed court, the exterior still retains much of its Elizabethan flavour. And while Hopper's ornate classical Regency library is hardly in keeping with that exterior, the Greek couches and armchairs adorned with owls have a charm of their own.

CL x, 496; lxxxii, 116, 142, 394

Mompesson House, Wiltshire: the staircase. (*NTPL/Angelo Hornak*)

Mompesson House

SALISBURY, WILTSHIRE

An attractive William and Mary house of seven bays, with dormers in a hipped roof, which stands in the cathedral close. It was built in 1701 for the local MP Charles Mompesson. The fine plasterwork in several of the interiors, especially the staircase hall, was commissioned from an unidentified craftsman by Mompesson's brother-in-law and heir, Charles Longueville.

CL xxxiv, 194; lxxiii, 279; cxxiv, 1520; clxi, 842

Monk's House

RODMELL, NR LEWES, EAST SUSSEX

An unassuming, weather-boarded village house bought by Leonard and Virginia Woolf in 1919, and Leonard's home until his death in 1969. Assembled Bloomsburyana include painted furniture by Vanessa Bell and Duncan Grant, landscapes and portraits by Vanessa Bell, and a Chinese shawl given to Virginia Woolf by Ottoline Morrell.

CL clxxiii, 240

Montacute House

MONTACUTE, SOMERSET

Built in the late 1590s, for the wealthy lawyer Edward Phelips; probably by William Arnold. (See p.87.)

CL iii, 464, 496; xv, 810; xxxvii, 820, 870; xxxix, 304; lxi, 992; lxv, 566; lxx, 621; xcix, 23; c, 164; cxviii, 850, 960, 1020; clxx, 1854

Morville Hall

BRIDGNORTH, SHROPSHIRE

An Elizabethan house altered in the 18th century. (Admission by appointment only.)

CL cxii, 464, 532

Moseley Old Hall

WOLVERHAMPTON, STAFFORDSHIRE

Built in 1600 for Henry Pitt, a merchant. Beneath its Victorian redbrick casing, Moseley is a pleasant Elizabethan house – not perhaps of any great architectural merit, but famous for the last three centuries as one of the places in which Charles II sheltered while on the run after the Battle of Worcester in 1651. The secret place where Charles hid when Moseley was searched by Parliamentarian soldiers can still be seen.

CL xciii, 1050

Mottisfont Abbey, Hampshire: a *trompe l'oeil* mural of a smoking plasterwork urn by Rex Whistler in the drawing room. (*NTPL/Jeremy Whitaker*)

Mottisfont Abbey

ROMSEY, HAMPSHIRE

Actually a priory, converted into a dwelling after the Dissolution by William Sandys, Henry VIII's Lord Chamberlain; extensively altered in the 1740s by Sir Richard Mill. Mottisfont's most notable interior is the drawing room, decorated in 1938–9 with Rex Whistler's *trompe-l'oeil* murals imitating Gothic plasterwork.

CL l, 652; cxv, 1310, 1398; cxxii, 288; clxvii, 822

Moulton Hall

MOULTON, NORTH YORKSHIRE

A stone house of 1650, with Dutch gables and a carved staircase. (Admission by appointment only.)

CL lxxix, 250

Mount Stewart House, County Down: the octagonal Ionic hall. (*NTPL/John Bethell*)

Mount Stewart House

NEWTOWNARDS, CO. DOWN

The main block, with a giant portico fronting a balustraded entrance court, was built for the 3rd Marquess of Londonderry in the mid-1830s to the designs of the Irish architect William Vitruvius Morrison (1794–1838), son of Richard Morrison. The early 19th-century west wing is by George Dance the younger (1741–1825), and the Temple of the Winds, a banqueting house on a hill to the south of the main building, 1782–5, by James Stuart.

The interiors of Mount Stewart range from Morrison's splendid but rather monumental octagonal Ionic hall and drawing room to Dance's more sophisticated work, especially his music room and the beautiful domed staircase hall.

CL lxxviii, 357, 380; cxlv, 1261; clxi, 934; clxvii, 646, 754; clxxxiv, 20.180

Newark Park

WOTTON-UNDER-EDGE, GLOUCESTERSHIRE

A compact four-storey lodge built *c.*1550 by an unknown mason for the courtier Sir Nicholas Poyntz; extended in the late 17th century. James Wyatt remodelled the south and west fronts in a Gothic style *c.*1810 for Lewis Clutterbuck; a service wing was added in 1897.

Perched in a marvellous position overlooking the western escarpment of the Cotswolds, Newark Park is a delightful mixture of styles. It originally functioned both as a hunting lodge – it was once surrounded by a deer park – and as a retreat to which Poyntz could escape from the day-to-day cares of his main household at Iron Acton, ten miles away. The building still boasts a number of Tudor features, including a fine Renaissance doorcase on the east front. Two hundred and fifty years later, Wyatt exploited to the full the picturesque potential of the site, adding battlements to create a Romantic castle in the air; yet forming, between the Tudor range and the 17th-century wing, a beautiful neo-classical hall. After a long period of neglect, Newark Park is being restored by the Trust's tenant, Mr Robert Parsons.

CL clxxviii, 943

Nostell Priory

NOSTELL, WEST YORKSHIRE

The original plan (1730?) by the gentleman-architect Colonel James Moyser for Sir Rowland Winn, 4th Bt; executed with alterations, 1735–50, by James Paine. The library, tapestry room, saloon and top hall were decorated in 1766–76 by Robert Adam.

As at Kedleston Hall, Derbyshire (see p.188), Adam was brought in to Nostell to complete the work of another architect (and, as at Kedleston, it was James Paine that he replaced). The resulting interiors, enhanced by some remarkable furniture supplied by Thomas Chippendale, are among his best. Unfortunately, he was allowed to build only one – the family pavilion to the north-east – of the four large wings that he proposed, two with Ionic porticoes flanking the entrance front and two with semicircular central bays overlooking the garden.

ECH Early Georgian 187

CL xxi, 594; xxxvi, 582, 684; cxi, 1248, 1492, 1572, 1652; cxii, 1028; cxxvi, 254

Nunnington Hall

NUNNINGTON, NORTH YORKSHIRE

The earliest surviving parts of Nunnington were built for Robert Huickes, physician to Henry VIII, Edward VI and Elizabeth I. Badly damaged during the Civil War by a Parliamentary garrison, the house was extensively remodelled by Lord Preston after he inherited the estate in 1685. His designer is not known, but the gabled south front and the oak hall – the grandest room in the house, with an elaborate chimneypiece and a classical screen – suggest that he was no provincial mason.

CL lxiii, 148; clxxi, 1678

Oak Cottages

STYAL, CHESHIRE

A group of early 19th-century houses built by the cotton industrialist Samuel Greg for the workers at his Quarry Bank Mill. Each two-up, two-down cottage had its own privy and a vegetable plot.

Oakhurst Cottage

HAMBLEDON, SURREY

A pretty timber-framed cottage dating from the 16th century, and now furnished as a mid-19th-century labourer's cottage. Oakhurst looks as if it has strayed from a Helen Allingham watercolour – with some justification, since Allingham did indeed paint the cottage at the turn of the century. (Admission by appointment only.)

The Old Manor

NORBURY, DERBYSHIRE

Behind and to the north-east of the Caroline Norbury Manor is an upper hall house of *c*.1250, enlarged by Sir Henry Fitzherbert at the beginning of the 14th century. The hall contains a king-post roof, which may have been installed in the 17th century. (Admission by appointment only.)

CL cl, 618; clxxxiv, 18.152

The Old Post Office

TINTAGEL, CORNWALL

Actually a small 14th-century manor house, with a centrally placed hall rising the full height of the building. It gets its name from just after the introduction of the penny post in 1844 when it was used as a post office. A rare survival in Tintagel, which was heavily developed in the 19th century for tourists coming in search of King Arthur.

Old Soar Manor

PLAXTOL, KENT

The solar block attached to a redbrick early Georgian farmhouse is all that remains of the manor house built *c.*1290, which stood here until the 18th century. The 28-ft solar over a barrel-vaulted undercroft opens into two projecting chambers, a chapel and a garderobe.

Ormesby Hall

ORMESBY, CLEVELAND

Built before 1743 by an unknown architect for Dorothy Pennyman; interiors 1772 for Sir James Pennyman, attributed to John Carr of York.

This three-storey Palladian block is attached to a service wing formed out of an earlier house dating from *c.*1600. Carr may have been responsible for the stable block, as well as for the Adamesque ceilings in the drawing room and dining room. 'Wicked Sir James' ran through a fortune in eight years and then had to hand Ormesby over to the bailiffs.

CL cxxv, 410

Packwood House, Warwickshire: the great hall, restored by Baron Ash in the 1920s.
(*NTPL/Jeremy Whitaker*)

Osterley Park

ISLEWORTH, MIDDLESEX

Before 1576, for Sir Thomas Gresham; re-modelled, probably in 1756–9 by William Chambers for Francis Child, and in 1763–80 by Robert Adam for Francis's brother Robert. (See p.195.)

CL lii, 727; lx, 782, 818, 858, 907, 938, 972; lxxxv, 579; lxxxvi, 8; xcix, 440; cxlvii, 1164, 1258; clxxxii, 44.214

Owletts

COBHAM, KENT

A two-storeyed redbrick house built *c.*1683 for a wealthy farmer, Bonham Hayes. The best surviving original feature of the interior is the staircase hall, with its elaborate late-Caroline plasterwork roundels of flowers and fruit. The architect Herbert Baker (1862–1946) was born here.

CL xciv, 1168

Oxburgh Hall

OXBOROUGH, NORFOLK

A moated redbrick courtyard house built for Sir Edmund Bedingfeld sometime after 1476; altered and extended in each subsequent century.

Oxburgh still retains the spirit of the late Middle Ages, not least on account of its chief glory, a splendid three-storey embattled and turreted gatehouse, said to have been the lodgings of Henry VII and his Queen, Elizabeth of York, when they stayed here in August 1497. Extensive 19th-century alterations have added to Oxburgh's charm, rather than spoiling it. John Chessell Buckler (1793–1894) and John Diblee Crace both worked at the house, and their confident High Victorian interiors are every bit as satisfying as Edmund Bedingfeld's gatehouse.

CL i, 548; xiii, 470; lxvi, 194, 224; cxvi, 1843; clxvii, 1480

Packwood House

LAPWORTH, WARWICKSHIRE

Although Packwood's structure is basically Elizabethan (with some fine outbuildings of *c.*1670), in tone and character the house really belongs to the period between the wars, when Baron Ash (a Christian name rather than a title) stripped away various Georgian and Victorian accretions and introduced materials from other buildings – 'as an antidote to the decay and demolition of so many old houses all over the country,' he said. 'I am rescuing whatever I can from other places and preserving it here.'

CL xi, 16; lvi, 218, 250; lviii, 570; lxiii, 643; xc, 61; cxxvi, 532; clxxxiii, 42.108

Paycocke's

COGGESHALL, ESSEX

An early 16th-century timber-framed town house, built by the wealthy wool merchant John Paycocke on the occasion of his son Thomas's marriage to Margaret Harrold. The long street façade has five oriels on the upper floor; below, a beam running its full length is carved with a variety of curious figures, including a dragon and a small person apparently diving into a lily.

CL liii, 920; cxl, 897

Peckover House

WISBECH, CAMBRIDGESHIRE

A brick town house built in 1722, and bought by the Quaker banker Jonathan Peckover in 1777. Panelled interiors, with elaborate rococo and neo-classical plasterwork and carving, were added sometime in the mid-18th century.

CL clxvii, 248

Penrhyn Castle

BANGOR, GWYNEDD

Built in 1819–1835 by Thomas Hopper, for the slate magnate George Dawkins-Pennant. (See p.234.)

ECH Late Georgian 181

CL ii, 377; xiii, 674; cx, 1365; cxviii, 80, 140, 192; clxxviii, 1346; clxxxi, 44.108, 45.74

Petworth House

PETWORTH, WEST SUSSEX

Rebuilt by an unknown architect in 1688 for Charles Seymour, 6th Duke of Somerset, incorporating parts of an earlier house. It was remodelled after a fire in 1714, and further altered in 1756–63 by Matthew Brettingham the elder; in 1774–9 by Matthew Brettingham the younger; and in 1869–72 by Anthony Salvin. (See p.156.)

ECH Baroque 47

CL xxii, 826; xxxix, 306; lviii, 818, 862, 899, 928, 966; lix, 247; ci, 422; cxi, 1236; cxv, 352; cxx, 368; cxxxi, 650; cliii, 1640, 1870; cliv, 626; clxviii, 798, 1030; clxxv, 1698; park, cliv, 620; restoration of sculptures, clxxxiii, 10.160

Philipps House

DINTON, WILTSHIRE

A neo-classical house built in 1814–17 for William Wyndham, by Sir Jeffry Wyatville (1766–1840). The building is a two-storey block, with rows of sash-windows and a parapet concealing a hipped roof. A pedimented portico rises the full height of the south front. Philipps House is let to, and maintained by, the YWCA, and is used as an art centre. (Admission by appointment only.)

CL xciv, 1080

Plas Newydd

LLANFAIRPWLL, ANGLESEY, GWYNEDD

A 16th-century house remodelled between the 1790s and the 1820s by James Wyatt and his assistant, the builder-architect Joseph Potter of Lichfield (*c.*1756–1842).

Although Plas Newydd belongs architecturally to the beginning of the 19th century, cheerfully mixing neo-classical and picturesque Gothic, its heart is in the 1930s, when the 6th Marquess of Anglesey refurbished the house. He employed Rex Whistler to create the vast dining room mural of an Italian town 'bristling with spires, domes and columns'. Whistler himself appears as a gardener, sweeping up leaves.

CL xcix, 342; cxviii, 1198, 1252; cxxxii, 1588; clix, 880, 1686; clx, 18, 722; clxi, 736; clxii, 286

Polesden Lacey, Surrey: the drawing room with Mrs Ronald Greville's portrait above the cabinet. (*NTPL/John Bethell*)

Plas-yn-Rhiw

PWLLHELI, GWYNEDD

A small Tudor house extended in 1634, and again in the mid-18th and early 19th centuries; bought in 1938 and restored by the daughters of a Nottingham architect, Eileen, Lorna and Honora Keating.

Polesden Lacey

DORKING, SURREY

Built in 1821–3 by Thomas Cubitt (1788–1855) for the stationer Joseph Bonsor; remodelled between 1902 and 1906 by Sir Ambrose Poynter for Sir Clinton Dawkins, and again by Mewes & Davis (architects of the Ritz Hotel in London) for Mrs Ronald Greville, whose husband bought the house in 1906.

After its fairly unassuming exterior, which still retains something of the air of a Regency villa, the Edwardian opulence of Polesden Lacey's interiors takes one's breath away. The note of baroque theatricality is struck immediately one walks into the entrance hall, to be faced with Edward Pierce's richly carved oak reredos made in 1685 for Wren's St Matthew's Church, Cheapside in London. Mrs Greville, effectively the creator of Polesden, was an ambitious and dedicated society hostess, carefully cultivating crowned heads and politicians from Edward VII to Ribbentrop. Her home was above all a perfect expression of the last golden age of the country house, a centre for exclusive social gatherings which blended gossip, politics and adultery in more or less equal measure.

CL ciii, 478, 526; cxxxvii, 813, 1410; cxli, 1362; clxix, 376, 442

Powis Castle

WELSHPOOL, POWYS

A medieval stronghold, bought in 1587 by Sir Edward Herbert; several interiors perhaps by William Winde; others by G. F. Bodley (1827–1907) in a Jacobethan style, 1902–4.

Spectacularly placed on a site looking out across the River Severn to the Shropshire hills, Powis is primarily famous for its baroque terraced gardens. However, it contains some fine Caroline and baroque work, notably a marvellously theatrical grand staircase with a ceiling adapted from Veronese's *Apotheosis of Venice* by Antonio Verrio, and walls painted by Verrio's pupil Gerald Lanscroon (d.1737). Elsewhere, Bodley's Jacobethan ceilings seem rather fussy in comparison with the only genuine 16th-century ceiling to survive, that of the long gallery, dated 1593.

CL ix, 16; xxiii, 666; xli, 108, 132; lxxvii, 647; lxxix, 564, 598, 624, 652; cvii, 368; cxi, 1238; cxii, 1635; cxxvi, 533; cxliii, 1382; clxviii, 935; clxxxi, 28.106, 34.79; clxxxiv, 44.72

Priest's House

MUCHELNEY, SOMERSET

A small thatched stone cottage, built *c*.1308 by the Benedictine monks of Muchelney Abbey to house the parish priest. Much altered, but still containing a number of original features, including a Gothic doorway and a four-light, transomed, early 16th-century window to the hall. The hall fireplace stands, rather oddly, against the screens passage. (Admission by appointment only.)

Priest's House

EASTON-ON-THE-HILL, NORTHAMPTONSHIRE

A late medieval, two-storeyed stone building. Originally intended for celibate clergy, it was presumably used by married priests after the Reformation, until it was superseded by the Georgian rectory nearby. The upper floor houses a small local history museum.

Powis Castle, Powys: the baroque grand staircase of the 1670s. (*NTPL/Jeremy Whitaker*)

Princes Risborough Manor House

PRINCES RISBOROUGH, BUCKINGHAMSHIRE

A charming and dignified late 17th-century town house, L-shaped with a pedimented central doorway and dormers. It was once owned by Sir Peter Lely (1618–80), court painter to Charles II. (Admission by appointment only.)

Quebec House

WESTERHAM, KENT

A square, gabled, 17th-century house built from a mixture of brick and Kentish ragstone; the birthplace in 1727 of General James Wolfe. Mementoes include the quilted dressing-gown in which Wolfe's body was brought back to England from Quebec.

CL xlii, 252; lix, 301

Rainham Hall

RAINHAM, ESSEX

Built in 1729 for the merchant and ship-owner John Harle, the house has redbrick façades, stone dressings and dormers in a hipped roof, with an unusual carved wooden Corinthian porch and contemporary interiors.

CL xlvii, 760

Rufford Old Hall

RUFFORD, LANCASHIRE

A half-timbered manor house built for Sir Thomas Hesketh *c*.1420; a 19th-century wing connects a Caroline range to the medieval part.

The great hall is the only part of Hesketh's original house to survive relatively intact – but that survival is one of the most striking of all early interiors. There is an elaborately carved hammer-beam roof; a canopy of state at the upper end of the room; and a rare example of an early 16th-century movable screen: a solid frame enclosing two rows of four traceried panels, with an ornate cornice and three tall finials.

CL lxvi, 528, 570; lxxvi, 188; cviii, 773; cxxiv, 269

St Michael's Mount

MARAZION, CORNWALL

The castle date from the 14th century, with many subsequent additions, including a Victorian wing, 1873–8, by Piers St Aubyn (1815–98).

St Michael's Mount, just off the Cornish coast, has been a Christian holy place since the 5th century, when St Michael is said to have appeared to some local fishermen. In 1070 the island was granted by Robert, Count of Mortain, to the monks of Mont St Michel in Normandy, and during the Middle Ages it functioned as both a religious retreat and a military garrison. In 1647 the Parliamentarian Colonel John St Aubyn was nominated Captain of the Mount, the last military governor to maintain a force there. He bought the Mount in 1659, and over the next two centuries his family converted the fort and the church buildings into a family home.

CL ii, 42; lvi, 672, 714; cxiii, 1593; cxvi, 640

Saltram

PLYMPTON, DEVON

The Tudor house was extensively remodelled for the Parker family by an unidentified architect in the 1740s. Robert Adam created a new saloon and library for John Parker in 1768–72, and converted the library to a dining room in 1779–82. John Foulston made some further alterations in 1818–20. (See p.201.)

ECH Mid Georgian 125
CL lix, 124, 160; cxvii, 985; cxxviii, 1429; cxxxix, 1386, 1480; cxli, 998, 1064, 1160; cxlii, 594

Shaw's Corner

AYOT ST LAWRENCE, HERTFORDSHIRE

An architecturally unremarkable Edwardian villa, the home of George Bernard Shaw from 1906 until his death in 1950. The house is preserved much as it was in his lifetime; mementoes include Shaw's pens and typewriter, and photographs of Gandhi, Lenin and Stalin.

Shugborough

MILFORD, STAFFORDSHIRE

Originally a compact, two-storeyed brick house built for William Anson in 1695. Flanking wings, each with a domed semicircular bow, were added by 1748 by Thomas Wright (1711–86). The house was enlarged *c.*1768 by James Stuart, who also designed a number of buildings in the park. It was extensively remodelled and again enlarged in 1790–8 and 1803–6 by Samuel Wyatt (1737–1807). The west front was remodelled in 1920 by Alun Munby (1870–1938).

Shugborough is very much the creation of Samuel Wyatt. He pulled the whole house together by enlarging Wright's low, spreading wings (thus bringing them into line with the tall main block) and adding to the entrance front a massive, flat-roofed, octostyle Ionic portico aligned with the parapets of the wings, thus creating a strong horizontal emphasis across the whole façade. (He also encased the house in slate, although most of this was replaced with stucco in 1920.) The garden front, which was extended by the addition of a narrow central projecting bay to house the saloon, is less happy.

ECH Mid Georgian 79

CL cxv, 510, 590, 676, 1126, 1220; cxxxix, 964; cl, 546

Sissinghurst Castle

SISSINGHURST, KENT

The remains of a great redbrick mansion put up by Sir Richard Baker in the mid-16th century. The most substantial of the surviving fragments of Baker's house is a romantic four-storey prospect tower with two octagonal turrets – a perfect vantage point from which to view the gardens laid out by Vita Sackville-West and Harold Nicolson in the years following their purchase of the property in 1930.

CL xcii, 410, 458, 506; cxx, 321; cxxi, 467; cxxii, 56; cxliv, 330

Shugborough, Staffordshire: the west front in 1768, from a painting by Nicholas Dall, now hanging in the verandah passage room. (*NTPL/Erik Pelham*)

Sizergh Castle

KENDAL, CUMBRIA

A pele tower built by the Strickland family *c.*1350; 16th-century additions.

The massive 60-ft tower at the heart of Sizergh is evidence enough of its origins as a defensive stronghold, a sanctuary for local people during the frequent border raids which troubled this part of the country for centuries. But later additions to the building suggest a less fraught, more comfortable lifestyle: one of Sizergh's greatest assets is its wealth of warm and often highly decorated oak panelling, the earliest of which, some linenfold in a passage room, dates from Henry VIII's reign. After the Glorious Revolution, Sir Thomas Strickland and his wife accompanied James II into exile in France; portraits and relics bear witness to the Stricklands' devotion to the Stuart cause.

CL xix, 942; lx, 653; cvi, 1128, 1216; clxxiii, 768

Skenfrith Castle

ABERGAVENNY, GWENT

A small early 13th-century moated fortress built by Hubert de Burgh, Earl of Kent, consisting of a curtain wall with circular towers, and a round keep rising from the centre of the enclosed courtyard. The keep is placed on top of a mound, suggesting that Skenfrith was built on the site of an earlier motte and bailey castle.

CL cxix, 98

Smallhythe Place

TENTERDEN, KENT

A 16th-century timber-framed farmhouse, the home of the actress Ellen Terry from 1899 until her death in 1928. Now a theatrical museum, containing exhibits such as Terry's costumes, Sir

Standen, West Sussex, in a watercolour painted by Arthur Melville in 1896. (*NTPL/Jonathan Gibson*)

Arthur Sullivan's monocle, and a letter to the actress from Oscar Wilde – 'Will you accept the first copy of my first play, a drama on modern Russia [*Vera; or, The Nihilists*, 1880]? Perhaps some day I shall be fortunate enough to write something worthy of your playing.'

CL clxxxiv, 35.78

Snowshill Manor

BROADWAY, GLOUCESTERSHIRE

A hall-house of *c*.1500, remodelled in the late 16th century and again in the early 18th.

Snowshill is perhaps best known for the eclectic and often bizarre collections of objects – from cycles to Samurai armour – which were brought together betwen 1919 and 1951 by its then owner Charles Paget Wade. The house itself is of interest both as a small Tudor manor house and for its Arts and Crafts atmosphere.

CL lxii, 470; clxiii, 1358; clxvii, 1178; clxxxii, 50.56

Speke Hall

LIVERPOOL, MERSEYSIDE

A half-timbered Tudor courtyard house begun for Sir William Norris *c*.1490–1506; extended and altered by his grandson, also called Sir William, in 1524–68; and completed (except for some minor additions) for Edward Norris by 1606.

The predominant architectural message of Speke is the decorative potential of wood. The exterior, with its high proportion of timber to infill, is a riot of geometrical patterning, while many of the Tudor interiors are filled with carved and embellished panelling. It has been suggested that the elaborate wainscot at the upper end of the hall, a development of the medieval canopy of state, was imported from the Low Countries, where the Norrises had trading connections.

CL xiii, 336, 368; li, 16, 48; lxxvi, 189; xciv, 378

Springhill

MONEYMORE, CO. LONDONDERRY

A simple, attractive manor house built at the end of the 17th century for Will Conyngham, a member of a staunchly Protestant family who lived here for 300 years. Long sash-windows, a steeply pitched slate roof and a whitewashed façade give the house a provincial French air. Inside, the mainly 18th- and 19th-century interiors contain Protestant relics, including four flintlocks used to defend Londonderry in the siege of 1688–9, and portraits of William and Mary, given by the King to Sir Albert Conyngham, Commander of the Inniskilling Dragoons.

Standen

EAST GRINSTEAD, WEST SUSSEX

Built in 1891–4 by Philip Webb (1831–1915) for J. S. Beale, a London solicitor.

Webb, an Arts and Crafts architect, once wrote: 'Living art – after all is said – is but a representation of right living' – and right living is what Standen is all about. There is no grandeur, no ostentatious display of wealth – just a rambling, comfortable house in the country which blends together stone and brick, weather-boarding, tile-hanging and pebble-dash, as though it had evolved gently over centuries. Standen is a house to live in.

Vict. CH 381

CL xxvii, 666; cxlvii, 494, 554; clxxiii, 1100

George Stephenson's Birthplace,

WYLAM, NORTHUMBERLAND

A little stone tenement beside the River Tyne, originally for four families. In 1781 George Stephenson, the engineer whose *Rocket* marked the beginning of the railway age, was born here.

Sutton House, Hackney: the 'Armada' window looking out onto the courtyard. (*NTPL/Rupert Truman*)

Stoneacre

OTHAM, KENT

A half-timbered Wealden house dating from *c.*1480; heavily restored and extended by its owner, the art critic Aymer Valance, in the 1920s.

Although Stoneacre retains the central hall and solar block which formed the heart of the original late medieval building, its main interest lies in the 20th-century work carried out by Valance, using timbers, windows and furnishings taken from dilapidated Tudor buildings. The additions and restorations are fascinating, telling a great deal more about recent attitudes towards conservation and the past than about the late Middle Ages.

CL lxvii, 420, 468

Stourhead

STOURTON, WILTSHIRE

1721–4 by Colen Campbell for Henry Hoare, a London banker; the flanking pavilions were added by Sir Richard Colt Hoare in 1792. (See p.179.)

ECH Mid Georgian 234

CL ix, 432; lvii, 592; lxxxiii, 608, 638; ci, 652; cvi, 767; cix, 38; cxii, 2083; cxiv, 1956; cxli, 444

Sudbury Hall

SUDBURY, DERBYSHIRE

Built and decorated for George Vernon between the early 1660s and 1691; the architect is unknown, but was almost certainly Vernon himself. (See p.135.)

ECH Caroline 162

CL xvii, 486; xxxix, 306; lxxvii, 622, 650, 682; cxii, 1175; cxxxvi, 226; cxlix, 1428

Sutton House

HACKNEY, LONDON

An H-shaped redbrick house dating from the early 16th century, with later additions; probably built for the Tudor diplomat, Sir Ralph Sadler.

Tattershall Castle

TATTERSHALL, LINCOLNSHIRE

A tower lodging built in the 1430s and 1440s for Henry VI's Treasurer, Ralph, Lord Cromwell. (See p.41.)

CL xiii, 426; xxxviii, 18, 54; lxiii, 566

Tatton Park

KNUTSFORD, CHESHIRE

Remodelled in a severe neo-classical style for the Egerton family by the Wyatts – Samuel, brother of James; and their nephew Lewis.

The original scheme to alter an earlier house (of which little survives save for Thomas Farnolls Pritchard's rococo dining room) was Samuel Wyatt's, drawn up in 1774. It was not begun until after William Tatton Egerton succeeded to the estate in 1780, then came to a halt in 1791, by which time the first four bays of a proposed eleven-bay garden façade had been completed, various internal changes had been made, and a single-storey family wing and separate stable block had been added. In 1808 work was resumed, this time to Lewis Wyatt's designs, which reduced the original scheme to seven bays and added a giant Corinthian portico. Lewis continued to work at Tatton until *c*.1825. Later additions, including a second storey to the family wing by George Henry Stokes (1827–74), have done little to detract from the classical unity of the original design.

CL xix, 414; cxxxvi, 162, 232, 292; clix, 884

Townend

TROUTBECK, CUMBRIA

A yeoman farmhouse dating mainly from the 17th century, Townend is a good example of the vernacular architecture of the Lake District. Its limewashed walls and slate roof provided a home for generations of the Browne family, well-to-do sheep farmers who lived here for more than 400 years. That the house and its contents – which include an impressive range of heavy oak furniture – were preserved was largely due to the efforts of the last George Browne (1834–1914), an antiquary and woodcarver.

Treasurer's House

MARTOCK, SOMERSET

A priest's house consisting of a two-storey hall, which dates from 1293, an earlier solar block, and a 15th-century domestic range. The building was begun by the Treasurer of Wells Cathedral, who obtained the village church in Martock from the monastery of Mont St Michel in France in the early 13th century.

Treasurer's House

YORK, NORTH YORKSHIRE

Originally the medieval residence of the treasurers of York Minster (from 1100 until the office was abolished by Henry VIII), Treasurer's House is a pleasing mixture of 17th- and 18th-century work. The garden front, with its classical central entrance bay, was built *c*.1630; 17th-century Dutch gables on projecting wings rise over later Venetian windows; and the early-18th-century staircase has been attributed to the joiner-architect William Thornton, who worked at Beningbrough.

The Treasurer's House now contains the furniture collection of Frank Green, who did much to preserve the building after acquiring it in 1897.

CL xix, 234; lii, 114, 144

Trerice

NEWQUAY, CORNWALL

Completed in 1573 for Sir John Arundell, of whom the Cornish historian Richard Carew (his son-in-law) wrote: 'Private respects ever with him gave place to the common good; as for frank, well ordered, and continual hospitality, he outwent all show of competence'.

The setting for this frank, well ordered and continual hospitality is of yellow Growan limestone, now weathered to a silvery grey. Decorative scrolled gables – an extremely early instance of their use in this part of the country, suggesting that the inspiration for them may have come from Arundell's military service in the Low Countries – pull the façade together. A massive mullioned and transomed window of twenty-four lights – 576 panes in all – illuminates the two-storeyed great hall, which has a fine plaster ceiling with strap-work, pendants and the initials JA, KA and MA, for John Arundell, his wife Katherine, and his sister Margaret.

CL xxx, 206; cxiv, 613; cxxix, 844

Tudor Merchant's House

TENBY, DYFED

A narrow, three-storeyed, late 15th-century building of lime and sandstone rubble, standing a few yards from the harbour. The interior is much altered, although the house retains a garderobe tower rising through its full height, and some murals on plaster have survived.

Tudor Yeoman's House

COBHAM, KENT

A 16th-century timber-framed yeoman's house, restored by the architect Herbert Baker and given by him to the Trust in 1931. (Admission by appointment only.)

Ty Mawr

PENMACHNO, GWYNEDD

A little 16th-century farmhouse, famous as the birthplace of Bishop William Morgan (*c*.1541–1604), whose 1588 translation of the Bible into Welsh is still in use today.

Uppark

PETERSFIELD, WEST SUSSEX

Built *c*.1690–4 for the Earl of Tankerville, and attributed to William Talman (1650–1719), Comptroller of the King's Works and arch-rival to Sir Christopher Wren. The interiors were re-decorated for Sir Matthew Fetherstonhaugh in the mid-18th century; further alterations were made in 1813, including the north portico, by Humphry Repton (1752–1815).

Uppark contains a series of beautiful rococo interiors and a magnificent collection of carpets, furniture and works of art, much of it assembled on Fetherstonhaugh's Grand Tour in 1749–51. The house remained largely untouched after Repton's Regency additions – until 30 August 1989, when it was badly damaged by fire. Fortunately the structure of the state rooms, and most of the contents, were saved; and at the time of writing (1991) a careful programme of restoration work is under way. Emma Hamilton is said to have danced naked on the dining room table.

ECH Mid Georgian 29

CL xxvii, 702; lxxxix, 520, 540, 562; cxv, 848; clxxxiii, 47.90; clxxxiv, 3.56

Upton House

BANBURY, WARWICKSHIRE

1695 for Sir Rushout Cullen, and tentatively attributed to either William or Francis (1672–1738) Smith of Warwick; remodelled in 1927–9 for the 2nd Viscount Bearsted by Percy Morley Horder (1870–1944).

Morley Horder's alterations to Upton, made partly to house Lord Bearsted's growing art collection, partly to provide extra bedrooms, and partly to remove the effects of some rather injudicious 18th-century additions which had destroyed the symmetry of the original baroque house, involved a drastic – but on the whole rather interesting – reworking of the interior, as well as the building of substantial wings to either side of the main block.

CL xvi, 378; lxxx, 248, 274

The Vyne

SHERBORNE ST JOHN, HAMPSHIRE

Built some time between 1500 and 1520, for William Sandys, one of Henry VIII's most trusted courtiers.

The house was bought in 1653 by a successful barrister called Chaloner Chute. Almost immediately Chute commissioned a series of alterations, most notably a classical portico by John Webb added to the north front – the earliest example for an English country house. The changes carried out from 1770 by Chaloner's great-grandson John, one of the Committee of Taste responsible for remodelling Horace Walpole's

The Vyne, Hampshire: John Chute's magnificent staircase hall. (*NTPL*)

Strawberry Hill – and described by Walpole as 'my oracle in taste, the standard to whom I submitted my trifles, and the genius that presided over poor Strawberry' – included a remarkably dramatic neo-classical staircase.

CL xiii, 838; xlix, 582, 612; lxxii, 405; cxx, 1047; cxxi, 16; cxxiv, 269; cxxxiv, 214; clxxv, 476

Waddesdon Manor

WADDESDON, BUCKINGHAMSHIRE

1874–89, for Baron Ferdinand de Rothschild, by Gabriel-Hippolyte Destailleur.

Perhaps the most extravagant expression of the short-lived French Revival. Rothschild hired a French architect (Destailleur), a French landscape designer called Lainé, even teams of French horses to help with the construction work. The result is startling – a vast pastiche château in the middle of the Buckinghamshire countryside, packed with Rothschild's superb collections of paintings, furniture and porcelain. Gladstone's daughter Mary, who visited the house in 1885, found it all rather too much: 'Felt much oppressed with the extreme gorgeousness and luxury,' she wrote afterwards, adding: 'there is not a book in the house save twenty improper French novels'.

CL iv, 208; xii, 808; cxxi, 1256, 1277; cxxvi, 66; cxlvii, 1154; clxxx, 1060

Wallington

CAMBO, NORTHUMBERLAND

A William and Mary house remodelled in 1738–46 by Daniel Garrett (d.1753) for Sir Walter Calverley Blackett; central hall designed in 1853–4 by John Dobson of Newcastle (1787–1865) for Sir Walter Calverley Trevelyan.

A protégé of both Lord Burlington and Sir Thomas Robinson, Garrett reroofed the original house (built *c.*1688), refenestrated it, rebuilt part of it and remodelled the whole of the interior, creating, in collaboration with the *stuccadore* Pietro Lafrancini, a series of striking rococo set pieces. Equally striking – if rather a shock in the midst of all this 18th-century work – is Dobson's earnest Ruskinian central living hall, painted with flowers and scenes from Northumbrian history by (among others) William Bell Scott, Lady Trevelyan, and Ruskin himself.

CL xliii, 572, 592; cxxviii, 1216; cxxxiii, 1313; cxlvii, 634, 854, 922, 986; cxlix, 1204; clvi, 767

Washington Old Hall

WASHINGTON, TYNE & WEAR

An early 17th-century house, built to a conventional H-plan with a great hall occupying the centre of the building. Famous as the ancestral seat of George Washington's family, it contains a range of Washington memorabilia.

Wallington, Northumberland: John Dobson's central hall, with painted decoration by William Bell Scott, Lady Trevelyan, and John Ruskin.
(*NTPL/Tymn Lintell*)

West Green House

HARTLEY WINTNEY, HAMPSHIRE

A 17th-century house re-fronted in the early 18th century, and remodelled after *c.*1746 for General Henry Hawley, whose brutality in the aftermath of the Battle of Culloden earned him the name of 'Hangman Hawley'. Built of red brick, with sash-windows and pedimented dormers; its over-large saloon of two storeys takes up almost one quarter of the house. (Admission by appointment only.)

CL lxxx, 540; clxxiv, 686; clxxxiii, 28.110

Westwood Manor

BRADFORD-ON-AVON, WILTSHIRE

Westwood was originally the property of the Priory of St Swithin at Winchester and let out to a succession of tenant farmers. The core of the present house is the work of Thomas Culverhouse, who farmed the estate at lease until *c.*1485, and remodelled or extended an earlier building in 1480. Thomas Horton, a prosperous local cloth-ier, had acquired the lease by 1518 and altered many of the interiors – stained glass in the house shows the Horton rebus, the letters HOR over a barrel, or tun. John Farewell, who occupied Westwood in 1616–42, probably pulled down quite a lot of the medieval work, leaving the compact L-shaped house which stands today. Exceptional early 17th-century plaster decoration includes an overmantel which depicts, among other things, two geese hanging a fox and what seems to be a Red Indian on a totem pole.

CL lx, 244, 282; xciv, 377

West Wycombe Park

WEST WYCOMBE, BUCKINGHAMSHIRE

A Queen Anne house transformed into a classical mansion during the middle years of the 18th century for Sir Francis Dashwood, a founder member of the Dilettanti Society, who also laid out its famous gardens.

Dashwood's designer in the remodelling of West Wycombe was probably John Donowell, an architectural draughtsman who made his living by publishing topographical views. There are several references to Donowell in West Wycombe Park's building accounts during the 1750s and early 1760s, and the plan and elevation of the house in the fifth volume of Colen Campbell's *Vitruvius Britannicus* are attributed to 'J. Donowell, Archt'. However, it is possible that he was carry-ing out the schemes of other professional architects and of Dashwood himself. The south front with its double colonnade, for example, may well have been the work of the Italian Giovanni Servandoni (1695–1766). Donowell was sacked in 1764, when a friend of Dashwood wrote: 'I believe the man is honest and does to the best of his abilities, but these I am afraid from the experience I have had of him are not very extensive.' Nicholas Revett, co-author with James Stuart of *The Antiquities of Athens*, designed the Ionic west portico, completed by 1771: it is based on the Temple of Bacchus at Teos, which Revett had surveyed.

ECH Early Georgian 234

CL xxxix, 16, 48; lxxiii, 466, 494; clv, 1618, 1682; clxxxiv, 36.112

Wightwick Manor

WHITEWICK BANK, WEST MIDLANDS

Built in 1887, for Samuel Theodore Mander, a local industrialist, by Edward Ould, who also added a new east wing to the house in 1893, perhaps with help from C. E. Kempe. (See p.254.)

Vict. CH 375

CL cxxxiii, 1242, 1316

Wilderhope Manor

EASTHOPE, SHROPSHIRE

A gabled Elizabethan manor house of local grey limestone with tall brick chimneys and a stone-tiled roof, Wilderhope contains splendid plaster-work ceilings – so splendid, in fact, that they were once thought to be the work of Italians rather than of provincial plasterers. The initials of Francis and Ellen Smallman, who built the house *c.*1586, recur frequently in the moulds punctuating the plaster ribs, alternating with conventional motifs such as the Tudor rose and the fleur-de-lis.

Wimpole Hall

ARRINGTON, CAMBRIDGESHIRE

Built in 1640–70 by Sir Thomas Chicheley (*c.*1613–99), for himself; extensively remodelled subsequently.

Wimpole is a complex house with a spectacular architectural pedigree. The original building was almost certainly designed by Sir Thomas himself. (He was a friend of Roger Pratt, Hugh May and Wren). It was extended in 1713–21 by James Gibbs and decorated by Sir James Thornhill. In the mid-18th century Philip Yorke, 1st Earl of Hardwicke, commissioned Henry Flitcroft to re-face the central block and to make various internal alterations. The 3rd Earl called in Sir John Soane, who designed a new drawing room and a bath-house; and in the 1840s Henry Edward Kendall (1776–1875) extended Wimpole for the 4th Earl. In 1938 it was bought by Captain George Bambridge and his wife, the daughter of Rudyard Kipling, who after her husband's death in 1943 demolished much of Kendall's work and restored the rest of the house.

CL xxiii, 234; lxi, 806, 844; lxx, 590; cxiv, 782; cxxxix, 1240; cxlii, 1400, 1466, 1594; clxvi, 658, 758; clxxxv, 12.110

Woolsthorpe Manor

COLSTERWORTH, LINCOLNSHIRE

A typical early 17th-century yeoman's farmhouse, built sometime after 1623. Famous as the birth-place of Isaac Newton, who was born here on Christmas Day 1642.

Wordsworth House

COCKERMOUTH, CUMBRIA

The modest Georgian house where William Wordsworth was born on 7 April 1770. Seven of the eight rooms are furnished in period and contain items which belonged to the poet in later life, including his bookshelves, his sofa and his long-case clock.

INDEX

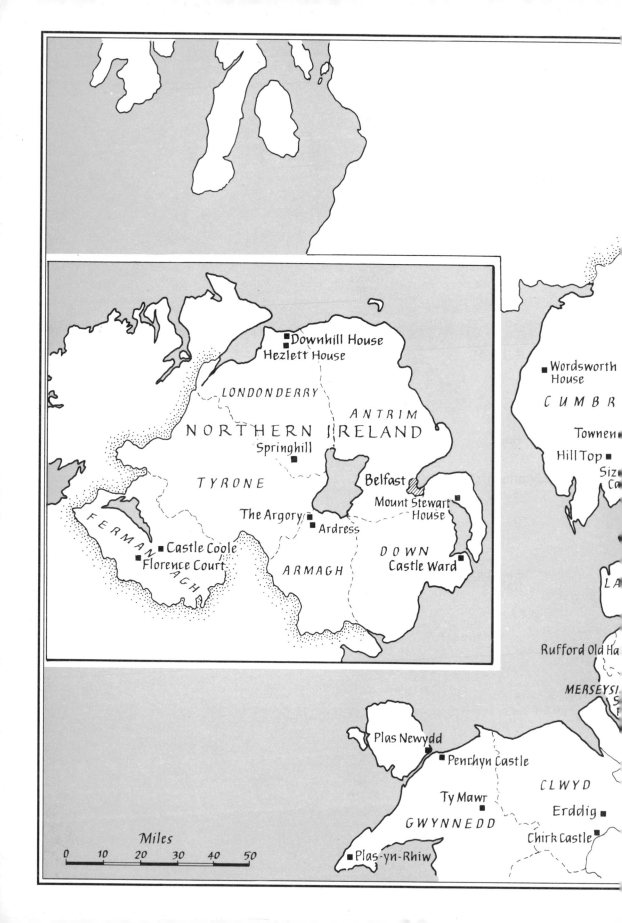

Downhill House
Hezlett House

LONDONDERRY

ANTRIM

NORTHERN IRELAND

Springhill

TYRONE

Belfast

Mount Stewart
House

The Argory

Ardress

FERMANAGH

Castle Coole
Florence Court

ARMAGH

DOWN
Castle Ward

Wordsworth
House

CUMBR

Townen

Hill Top

Size
Ca

LA

Rufford Old Ha

MERSEYSI
S

Plas Newydd

Penrhyn Castle

CLWYD

Ty Mawr

Erddig

GWYNNEDD

Chirk Castle

Plas-yn-Rhiw

Miles

0   10   20   30   40   50